Anti-Oppressive
Social Work Practice

This is dedicated to all the students past, present, and future who continue to inspire us and give meaning to all that we do.

Anti-Oppressive Social Work Practice

Putting Theory Into Action

Karen Morgaine

California State University, Northridge

Moshoula Capous-Desyllas

California State University, Northridge

Los Angeles | London | New Delhi
Singapore | Washington DC

Los Angeles | London | New Delhi
Singapore | Washington DC

FOR INFORMATION:

SAGE Publications, Inc.
2455 Teller Road
Thousand Oaks, California 91320
E-mail: order@sagepub.com

SAGE Publications Ltd.
1 Oliver's Yard
55 City Road
London EC1Y 1SP
United Kingdom

SAGE Publications India Pvt. Ltd.
B 1/I 1 Mohan Cooperative Industrial Area
Mathura Road, New Delhi 110 044
India

SAGE Publications Asia-Pacific Pte. Ltd.
3 Church Street
#10-04 Samsung Hub
Singapore 049483

Acquisitions Editor: Kassie Graves
Editorial Assistant: Elizabeth Luizzi
Production Editor: Olivia Weber-Stenis
Copy Editor: Janet Ford
Typesetter: C&M Digitals (P) Ltd.
Proofreader: Sally Jaskold
Indexer: Molly Hall
Cover Designer: Candice Harman
Marketing Manager: Shari Countryman
Cover Photo: Moshoula Capous-Desyllas

Copyright © 2015 by SAGE Publications, Inc.

Printed in the United States of America

Library of Congress Cataloging-in-Publication Data

Morgaine, Karen.

Anti-oppressive social work practice : putting theory into action / Karen Morgaine, California State University, Northridge, Moshoula Capous-Desyllas, California State University, Northridge.

pages cm
Includes index.

ISBN 978-1-4522-0348-5 (pbk. : alk. paper)

1. Social service—Moral and ethical aspects. 2. Social justice. I. Capous-Desyllas, Moshoula. II. Title.

HV40.M667 2015

174'.936132—dc23   2014007457

This book is printed on acid-free paper.

SUSTAINABLE FORESTRY INITIATIVE
Certified Chain of Custody
Promoting Sustainable Forestry
www.sfiprogram.org
SFI-01268

SFI label applies to text stock

15 16 17 18 19 20 10 9 8 7 6 5 4 3

Brief Contents

Detailed Contents

Preface

*A*nti-Oppressive Social Work Practice: Putting Theory Into Action is an introductory social work practice text that centers on liberation-based and anti-oppressive practice (AOP). As instructors in a social welfare and social justice program, we both taught introductory social work practice courses. Early on, we found that we wanted a text that would combine social welfare history and context, theory and ideology, skills and practice areas, and concrete examples of AOP work that is currently taking place across the United States. Existing AOP resources primarily focus on theory and ideology, yet there are limited examples for students that move beyond concepts to illustrate how to actually engage in AOP on the ground. It is important to highlight how social workers can engage in AOP while maintaining a critically thoughtful and self-reflective lens.

Anti-oppressive practice has strong foundations in Canada (Mullaly, 1997; Baines, 2007); Australia (Ife, 1997); and England (Dominelli, 2009). But, there are very few AOP resources available to social work and social justice students in the United States, which is the gap this text aims to fill. We provide many of the basic elements familiar in generalist practice texts, such as discussions of ethics and values and social work practices and processes from micro through macro. However, the foundation of this text is social justice from an anti-oppressive practice perspective.

OVERALL ORGANIZATION

The text begins with an introduction to our own personal and theoretical context, with examples from our own practice and journey to anti-oppressive work. We start here so that students can proceed with a sense of who we are and what experiences have informed our perspective and approach.

The first three chapters lay the foundation for the rest of the text and cover social justice, values and ethics, and theory. These chapters ground social work practice in meaning and ask students to critically examine their own social positions, identities, and values.

Chapter 4 through Chapter 11 present fields of social work and social justice practice, from micro through macro. Each chapter—individual, families, groups, organizations, communities, policy practice, social movements, and global practice—is situated in historical and ideological contexts and presents a variety of skills and forms of practice. Throughout each chapter, we present strengths and challenges as a way to stimulate ongoing critical analysis.

The final sections of each chapter contain direct practice applications, which are called Stories From the Field. These are personal reflections on AOP and social justice work, primarily contributed by U.S. practitioners and participants, and include both "success stories" and stories of challenges. The authors locate their own social positions, identities, values, and experiences within the context of AOP. These stories are multilayered, varied, and complex. Although they do not provide easy answers, they provide examples of how theories and concepts can be applied in the field. These are culled primarily from throughout the United States so that students can clearly see how AOP can be actualized on the ground.

TEXT FEATURES

Each chapter starts with definitions, concepts, and practice implications and then ends with two to seven stories from the field. This section begins with a short introduction to the concepts addressed in the story. Critical thinking questions then follow each story. Instructors can assign some or all of the application stories. They can be used as in-class small group exercises, or as part of weekly reading assignments.

Additional discussion questions and activities follow the story section in each chapter. The activities vary, and include:

Chapter 1: Application of key social justice and AOP concepts

Chapter 2: Critical thinking questions and writing assignments about social positions, identities, and values and ethics

Chapter 3: A case study with theory application

Chapter 4: Self-reflection questions and experiential drawing activity

Chapter 5: Self-reflection questions and creation of personal genograms, ecomaps, culturegrams, life maps, and additional assessment tools

Chapter 6: A group analysis

Chapter 7: An organizational assessment

Chapter 8: A community mapping exercise

Chapter 9: An organizational policy analysis

Chapter 10: A social movement activity

Chapter 11: An activity on international nongovernmental organizations

At the close of the chapters we provide additional resources, including websites, films, and books. The films may either illuminate concepts presented in the chapter or problematize issues and practices. Instructors can use film clips or entire features or they can assign a film for students to analyze using concepts presented in the chapters. The books listed consist primarily of stories and case examples that supplement and further elaborate on the issues presented in the chapter.

Throughout each chapter we also provide critical thinking questions. We ask students to pause and answer questions or engage in comparative analysis as they read. These questions can be assigned outside of class or used for in-class discussion. We deliberately were judicious in our use of this pedagogical aid so as not to break up the flow of the reading.

Acknowledgments

KAREN

My ongoing journey into teaching social work from an anti-oppressive perspective started years ago, when I began to examine structural oppression, power, and privilege through my work and through my PhD program. I am indebted to many teachers along the way. The individuals and families I worked with for ten years were truly significant in helping to lead me to AOP; I began to reflect on systemic oppressions to a greater extent through my work with them. I thank them and my co-facilitators in domestic violence work—particularly Angi and Janet. In my doctoral program, my primary guides came in the form of my dissertation chair and mentor, Stephanie Wahab; my colleague and coauthor, Moshoula Capous-Desyllas; and the master of social work (MSW), PhD, and undergraduate students I was fortunate to teach over three years at Portland State University.

I am truly grateful for my students at California State University Northridge. They were primary teachers for me and stand out in various ways. A number of students were particularly encouraging in this process, including Jen, Art, Vanessa, Wade, Eddie, Jeff, Nick, Daniel, Shant, Eunice, Deshonay, Natasha, and Megan. I value both their support and their critical approach to social justice work.

Many thanks to all of our wonderful contributors—their stories of anti-oppressive work in action help the theories, concepts, and skills come alive and, hopefully, give support, guidance, and inspiration for aspiring students.

I would like to give a special shout-out to Matthew for his amazing graphics, to Briana for making me laugh a lot, and to Tash for bringing me so much joy along the way, which is truly a gift.

A final debt of gratitude is owed to my coauthor and dearest friend, Moshoula. Your passion, support, and cheerleading have been paramount to my work for years now.

MOSHOULA

There are many people in my life who were essential, directly and indirectly, to the manifestation of this textbook. I am deeply indebted to my respected mentor, dearest friend, and academic inspiration, Stephanie Wahab, who served as my dissertation chair and continues to inform my anti-oppressive theoretical lens. Many thanks to Crystal Tenty, my friend and community partner, for her passion, support, and collaboration on our first social justice-oriented project with sex workers, where we put anti-oppressive theory into action. I want to acknowledge my Distance Option MSW students at Portland State University, who were the first students with whom I engaged in critical dialogue about social justice issues. I am equally grateful to my current and former students at California State University Northridge, who continue to inspire me and from whom I learn every day.

From the moment I embarked on this writing endeavor, the following individuals have been critical to this project. I feel extremely lucky for the creativity and artistic talent of Matthew, whose graphics are featured throughout this textbook. Significant appreciation goes to the students in my fall 2012 social work practice class, whose genograms and eco-maps are featured in this text. I am very grateful to all of our contributors of the stories from the field; most of them are my dearest friends, respected colleagues, and admired social justice workers.

Finally, I am profoundly indebted to Karen, my coauthor, adored friend, and intellectual muse. I cannot imagine embarking on this project with anyone else. Our synergy, laughter, and mutual passion kept me inspired throughout this entire process.

We want to thank our editor at SAGE, Kassie Graves, whose continuous encouragement and unwavering support has been invaluable. She has been a true joy to work with and has made this first book-writing project much easier. In addition, sincere gratitude goes to our developmental editor at SAGE, Becky Smith, who provided excellent feedback on our textbook and whose talent we greatly appreciate. We are extremely thankful to Dean Stella Theodoulou, of the College of Social and Behavioral Sciences, who provided monetary support and course release time so that we could focus on our writing. Her continuous support with academic scholarship has been critical to our ability to pursue this project.

Finally, we would like to thank the following reviewers: Christian Itin, Metropolitan State University of Denver; Jo Dee Gottlieb, Marshall University; Paula Sheridan, Whittier College; and Terrence Allen, North Carolina Central University.

Introduction

Navigating Our Paths and Positions

When I (Karen) started looking for textbooks for the Introduction to Social Work Practice course that I was about to start teaching at my new university, I wanted a generalist practice book that was grounded in a critical, feminist, postcolonial, liberatory, antiracist, and anti-oppressive context. If my intention was to use a book based in U.S. social work, this proved somewhat difficult as the majority of this type of social work writing (in the English language) was being produced in Great Britain, Australia, New Zealand, and Canada. I also wanted there to be examples for students, since one of the critiques of anti-oppressive practice (AOP) has been that it is often difficult to grasp how to actualize AOP concepts "on the ground." After using a book that met some of my requirements for a couple of semesters, it was clear that I needed to write the book I wanted. I enlisted the talents and support of Moshoula, one of my dearest friends and colleagues, and this book was on its way.

Social work in the United States is marked by a long history of polarization between micro practice (typically individual, family, and sometimes group work) and macro practice (typically organizations, communities, policy, and social movement work). This book seeks to illuminate the ways that anti-oppressive social work has the potential to traverse this divide and prioritize "both/and" rather than "either/or." We believe that practice on any level can empower participants while contributing to the dismantling of oppressive structures. Yet, to do this, we must be truly committed to an ongoing critical analysis of our work and the ways in which social work can disempower participants and perpetuate oppressive structures.

KAREN

My path to anti-oppressive and liberatory social work practice was not predetermined or well laid out. To be honest, I would say that when I was doing the majority of my direct practice work, AOP was something I approximated at best. It wasn't until I stepped away from direct practice and moved into the next phase, my doctoral studies and teaching, that I was confronted more clearly with the contradictions and challenges I previously observed in the field.

I started working in the field with a background in psychology. I went to a somewhat nontraditional school for my master's degree, and while I never worked with individuals who were diagnosed with psychosis, I was drawn into reading about radical psychiatry. So I think from early on, I leaned outside the box, if only in my head.

While I was completing my MA, I worked for a short time in a group home setting with adolescent girls. I would have to say that this position and organization was in no way anti-oppressive in approach. I felt I was simply charged with ferrying the young women about—perhaps to normalize their existence, perhaps to bring some happiness to a living situation that likely held little joy for them. I was still finding my way and had yet to develop a sense of who I was in my own work. Looking back, I have a hard time connecting with that time and place. I was acting in accord with a system that rarely encouraged a dynamic and critical approach, and I fell in step with what was expected.

In my primary direct practice work, I held a position for close to ten years in a community mental health setting. I was an individual therapist, family therapist, mental health assessment therapist, and a domestic violence (DV) group facilitator. In the mental health assessment work, I became increasingly wary of the role of diagnosis and the *Diagnostic and Statistical Manual of Mental Disorders* (DSM), which is the standard classification of mental disorders used by mental health professionals. That is not to say that I didn't understand how a common language might facilitate dialogue and perhaps some understanding. But, I did wonder about the usefulness, the accuracy, the potential stigma, and the power that is given to someone in my position. I observed that the function of the diagnosis seemed to be as much for billing purposes as for communication, or understanding, or explanation.

I began, in very small ways, to subvert the DSM's authority. I mostly did so by using the least stigmatizing disorder as an initial diagnosis to get someone in the door; as a result, there were a lot of "adjustment disorders." I didn't believe that after an hour or two I should have the right to label someone with a mental health disorder merely for the purpose of accessing services. I began to question the entire system of diagnosis while at the same time I was charged with diagnosing people on a daily basis—which created a state of dissonance for me.

All during that time, I was part of a team that worked under a contract with the local child protective services (CPS) department. This experience opened my eyes to the ways in which systemic and structural oppression manifest in the individual lives of those in poverty. I worked in a very white community at the time so my major observation was class oppression in the lives of the families and individuals who were referred to our services. Time and time again, it became clear that the majority of the families involved with CPS were struggling in many ways and that their primary child abuse "offense" was poverty.

These families were often bending—sometimes breaking, but also sometimes resisting—under the pressures wrought by having little entry "in." Entry is typically afforded only to those with more privilege, those allowed access, and those who have a greater chance of navigating life's challenges. These women (most of the individuals I worked with were women) typically had limited education and limited job opportunities. They struggled to feed and clothe their children and often had a tenuous (at best) support system. They faced daily choices about which bill they could pay that month and which had to be put off; which school event they might be able to attend if they could get there, how to get childcare for their other children, not have to work; and/or how they could get or keep a job and afford childcare. On top of those challenges, they were then required by CPS to attend a plethora of classes, meetings, and therapy sessions. Failure to meet these expectations often resulted in being labeled as "resistant," "uninterested," "uncaring," or a "bad parent." Further down the line, these "failures" could add up to the loss of their children. For many, there was the additional burden of a drug addiction, a criminal history, and/or a history of trauma.

I also observed that a significant number of caseworkers held some extremely problematic and prejudicial beliefs about the families whose lives they held in their hands. Each week, we went to the CPS office and heard the "cases" that were referred to our program, and often these case reviews were laced with derisive language and attitudes. Over the course of my time at the agency, I emotionally banded together with the two or three other colleagues I worked with as a way to bear the onslaught each week. I fondly remember the debriefing we had every Tuesday over coffee—finding ways to regroup and strategize alternate approaches when necessary.

Over most of my time at the agency, the domestic violence intervention work was the most profound work I did. This was work I was passionate about and made more sense to me. An important part of this work was both the process I went through to do the work and the team I worked with throughout. The initial and primary group included myself and two other women at the agency. One woman was about 10 years my senior, white, in a heterosexual relationship, and had been doing DV work for quite a few years. The other woman was about my age, Latina, lesbian, and although she had not previously done DV work, she had a background working with male sex offenders. The three of us undertook training in a specific DV intervention model over about a year and a half. This training would shape the rest of my work, my outlook on DV, and the way I approached social work and social issues.

The training took us out of state on two occasions, where we were immersed in training sessions with the founder of the model. These sessions were intense in both content and process. Part of the training required us to work through our own experiences regarding dominance and subordination and as a result of this process, we became extremely close. We continued this work on our own, and I remember staying hours after our DV groups, processing our own work and our experiences in the groups. This work, dealing with both men adjudicated with a battering offense and women who had experienced violence, was what sustained me in my direct practice over the years. But, it was not only the work, it was having colleagues to work with who held similar ideological beliefs about DV, seeing it as situated in a patriarchal system of gendered dominance. We allied together to process, vent, and strategize.

My lens became more intersectional as I worked with the model and explored issues of violence with group members. The model was based on gender roles and learning of those roles, and it focused on how gendered violence was a way to maintain an image of dominance. I also explored how other forms of violence were based in the social construction of dominance in regard to race/ethnicity, class, citizenship, and so on.

Additionally, I started observing how the child protection system often revictimized the women who had experienced or were currently experiencing DV; I became increasingly challenged by what I was observing—for example, when dealing with the family decision-making meetings recently introduced in local CPS offices. Perhaps the meetings were started because of a desire to involve families and allow for a greater sense of agency in the process; however, they often became a venue for public shaming. At times, they compromised the women to a greater extent. For example, if you invite everyone to the table and proceed to dictate to the mother that if she "allows" the batterer—who is also present in the family meeting to hear all this—to come into the house, she will likely lose custody of her children, essentially this approach only serves to provide her partner or ex-partner with one more tool in his arsenal.

My colleagues and I started working to shift DV intervention practices in the community. Our position on DV intervention manifested in a variety of ways—in conversations with CPS caseworkers, at community meetings, and in trainings. At times, my colleagues and I were tireless, at other times, just tired. Community batterer's intervention meetings, complicated by a vast array of ideological viewpoints, often deteriorated into power plays and turf wars, often replete with emotional and verbal violence. Sitting in a courtroom as a witness to a parental termination proceeding often became an arena for a judge to interrogate us about the DV program in a dismissive and domineering fashion. While we were buoyed by our commitment to our work and what seemed to be increased awareness about the complexity and pervasiveness of DV, this was sometimes offset by limited change and the enormity of the task at hand.

When I left direct practice I did so primarily due to exhaustion. While I loved doing DV work, I didn't want burnout to compromise my ability to actively engage in the process. Shortly after I left, I entered a PhD program with plans to shift my energies into teaching. As with any new endeavor, this one was fraught with excitement and challenges. Once again, one of the most valuable aspects of this very intense experience was my connection to one of my fellow students, Moshoula, now the coauthor of this text. We allied with one another within weeks of our entry into the program. Looking back, I believe some of the initial points of convergence were related to our shared love of clothing and chocolate rather than to the lofty ideals of a shared consciousness, ideological perspectives, and desire to question commonly held dictums. Nonetheless, we supported one another throughout the program as we attempted to navigate rocky terrain and engage in work that was less status quo and predictable. During this time, my research solidified my interest in social movements and qualitative research, although in retrospect, I wish my work had been more disruptive. Moshoula's work was much more cutting edge and I hold the utmost respect for her commitment and tenacity through the dissertation process.

Landing at the same university as instructors was a serendipitous event. While it is likely that we would have collaborated on this book together regardless of whether we were in the same location, it has been particularly fulfilling to work on this project together in the same place. We provide a sounding board for one another, balancing out each other's strengths and challenges. Our perspectives about social work, social justice work, and anti-oppressive practice are firmly rooted in similar ground, yet we bring our own experiences, social positions, and identities to the work.

My approach to social work is indelibly linked not just to my history in the field, but also to my social location, as I believe is true for all of us. I am white and grew up in very white communities in upstate New York. My family was solidly middle class at a time when there was a more clearly defined "middle class." The people in my family had a variety of educational and professional backgrounds, but shared an expectation of higher education. My family was small and disconnected—growing up, I really only had a connection with my parents and sister, with occasional visits to extended family. I hopped around the country a bit once I graduated high school—fleeing the rural area we moved to when I was 11, never to look back. An urban girl at heart, I loved and lived in New York City, San Francisco, Seattle, and Portland. I lived a heterosexual existence for quite some time though, internally, I identified as bisexual in my youth. Since that time, I have fully embraced a queer identity that is, as far as sexuality goes, exclusively women-centered. My parents came from Catholic backgrounds (Italian and German), but dropped religion when I was relatively young. I tested religious waters a little on my own and now am decisively nonreligious, though I appreciate Eastern spirituality, particularly Buddhist philosophies. I have always been healthy and able-bodied in addition to being relatively privileged in regards to my size and appearance.

I often conceptualize oppression and privilege as two sides of the same coin—and my coin is heavily weighted on the privilege side. Thus, I am compelled to confront privilege and to make that a central part of the work that I endeavor to do, if it is going to have any liberatory function in the world.

MOSHOULA

My journey to anti-oppressive practice and liberatory social work emerged in waves as I moved through and navigated unfamiliar positions of privilege and power in my direct practice work, in various research positions that I held, and later as a doctoral student and educator. Similar to Karen's journey, it wasn't until I moved into the doctoral studies and teaching phase of my life that I began to connect my values and intersecting identities to my experiences in the field, in order to critically reflect on my unique journey.

My story is one of diaspora . . .

My father arrived in the United States illegally and engaged in the underground economy for years. His identity and lived experiences as an undocumented immigrant shaped my family dynamics and my experiences growing up. As non-English speaking immigrants in this country, my parents' approach to life was one of risk-taking, a daily struggle to survive, but also unwavering hope.

and abused (verbally, physically, and sexually). As a case manager, I was trained to work from a cognitive-behavioral approach, in order to change the individual behaviors of these young boys. I also worked in elementary and junior high schools under a gang violence prevention grant. Again, I was working with individual children and youth, but not within the community to create sustainable change in the lives of these children, their families, and neighborhoods.

While my initial experience consisted of working with women, youth, and children, I wanted to gain experience working with previously incarcerated men; I was, quite honestly, scared to work with this population. I always knew my growth occurred in spaces of discomfort and uncertainty. I accepted a position as a clinical therapist working with court mandated, previously incarcerated, "dually-diagnosed" (with mental health issues and drug and alcohol addiction), male veterans of war. I facilitated groups with these adults (primarily men of color) and engaged in therapy with them. This was one of the most powerful experiences in my practice career, on so many levels. I was extremely aware and continuously self-reflective of how I was perceived by the men: a young, heterosexual, able-bodied, educated, woman of color, with a "clean" record, who only used "soft" drugs and alcohol recreationally (in the context of my subculture), and a person who had never suffered the horrors of going to war. I can write pages and pages on this transformative experience, and how my power and privilege (or lack thereof) shifted, based on who I worked with and their own social positions and identities.

Looking back, I regret not having had the language or the experience to work toward changing the racist, classist, hetero-sexist systems that oppressed these men in the first place. I was just then coming into awareness of the effects of the prison-industrial complex on the lives of these men. So my vision was still blurred, and in hopes of creating change through research, soon after starting this work I accepted a research position in the psychiatry department of a prestigious university known for its research and treatment of mental health issues.

As a social work researcher, I worked on an interdisciplinary team alongside psychiatrists and psychologists to monitor the effects of pharmacotherapy on individuals diagnosed with depression. I also explored the effects of maternal depression on children. As I immersed myself in the research study, various ethical dilemmas emerged, including the role of pharmaceutical companies in the research study. The sample population consisted of poor individuals with mental health issues, who got their medication paid for by participating in the research study. In addition, this diagnostic research approach viewed individuals as having a deficit that needed treatment, through pharmaceuticals, instead of addressing larger environmental issues that contributed to their symptoms of depression. Within a few months of involvement in this practice, I quickly realized that I didn't want to continue engaging in this type of research.

My story is one of discovery . . .

My social work practice and research experiences led me to pursue a doctoral degree, with the hopes of engaging in meaningful research that would make a difference and have an impact in the community. I didn't want my research to stay in the privileged space of academia. I began a PhD program with the blessings of my parents, who could not understand why I would want to continue seven more years of schooling. Due to my undergraduate degree, they were still under the impression that I was a "psychologist." Also, they had never encountered social workers in their own country, where social problems were addressed within the family or by the community.

It was in the privileged place of academia where Karen and I began our friendship, based on mutual respect and admiration. Karen always served as an inspiration to me, with her ability to pursue meaningful research while simultaneously teaching and making a difference in the lives of her students. I was always left wondering, how does she do it all, and always so well? While Karen completed her nationally recognized research, and went on to accept a tenure-track faculty position, I struggled a lot with wanting to engage in something meaningful. I wanted to merge my long buried identity as an artist with my newly emerging identity as an activist. I had a burning desire to engage in social justice–oriented research that incorporated the arts.

At this time, I agonized over finding myself in academia (in a world I never imagined for me, given my background and upbringing). I didn't know what to do with my newfound identity as a PhD student, which often brought me confusion and shame. Even uttering to individuals outside of my university life that I was a PhD student, and seeing how differently people then treated me, made me feel like a fraud; I felt like someone who didn't deserve the automatic privilege and power that I was afforded based on my doctoral student status.

After being in the doctoral program for four years without much engagement in the field, I wanted to feel real, authentic, and alive again, so I immersed myself in a community of activists working for the rights, safety, and well-being of individuals working in the sex industry. I engaged in street outreach to homeless women and joined a coalition composed of other service providers working to fill the gaps in services provided to sex workers. I started to work side by side with like-minded social workers, advocates, and activists in the community. My efforts in the community finally felt meaningful, as I worked to dispel stereotypes and stigma against sex workers while also providing marginalized women with access to much needed services.

The changing circumstances in our community in regard to sex workers led to a partnership with a friend, colleague, and fellow activist, Crystal Tenty. These included a change in local prostitution policy, the criminalization of sex workers, and the lack of social services available for sex workers. In addition, we found that the voices of sex workers themselves and their self-identified needs were missing from the community as well as misrepresented within the media. Crystal and I engaged in a community-based photovoice study where we gave women working in various aspects of the sex industry cameras and urged them to photo-document their lived experiences, their needs, and their aspirations. The power of representation was placed in the hands of these women, dismantling privilege and existing power dynamics. A main goal of our study was to (re)present the women's artistic visions and voices as a form of activism through various art exhibits in order to create community awareness and change around issues of importance to sex workers. The details of our social justice-oriented project are discussed in Chapter 3, but here I want to highlight that this was the first time in my life that I was able to merge my identities as a social work researcher, an artist, and an activist and begin to create social change. My journey was liberating.

My story is one of hope and possibility . . .

This photovoice project, also manifesting into my dissertation thesis, was the beginning of my pursuit of using art as a form of activism and social justice. My goal is to place the visual voice and power of representation in the hands of marginalized communities. My experiences solidified my desire to continue to engage in arts-based research that is participatory in spirit and that poses opportunities for creating social change.

I currently hold the privilege of dual citizenship and claim a transnational identity, continuously traveling between my country of origin and my country of residence, with a fluid concept of home and belonging. As a first generation immigrant, I have occupied and navigated spaces in the margins and on the borders, between cultures, languages and identities. This fluid place of constant navigation has allowed me to feel at home in the spaces that I embody, whether they are in academia, in my personal life, or out on the streets. At the same time, they sometimes make me feel like a stranger. To borrow the words of my friend and colleague Gita Mehrotra, maybe some of us are just destined to always be on the borderlands in work and in life.

I recently accepted a tenure-track position in academia. I am constantly reminded of the privileged spaces that I hold as a result of my identities, and struggle daily with the power that I hold through my social locations. I often find that I want to rid myself of my power. Sometimes I don't quite know what to do with it, how to share it, or how to use it to support the empowerment of others. I don't want to burden them with our obligations as social justice workers and agents of social change. I believe that this dilemma is and will be an ongoing tension that I continually learn to navigate, honor, grapple with, and accept in all of its complexity.

This writing endeavor, our anti-oppressive practice textbook, was Karen's initial idea. She came to me with the enthusiasm for and dedication to creating a textbook that would move beyond just providing theoretical and idealistic perspectives. Rather, she wanted to highlight what anti-oppressive work looks like and how it manifests in our profession and within all levels of practice. I am honored to be a part of bringing together the work and voices of amazing scholars, activists, and social workers who are engaging in anti-oppressive social work in the United States.

Our journey together in writing this textbook unfolded our strengths, uncovered our doubts, and situated our voices within the movement toward critical self-awareness, collective consciousness, and action toward change. One of the most sacred and inspiring parts of this project was the collection of diverse voices from the field. In this textbook, we weave our own understanding of anti-oppressive social work practice together with the voices of incredible individuals, groups and organizations who are doing "on the ground" social justice work. This textbook is infused with voices of passion and optimism for a world where all can feel liberated and free from oppression.

In this textbook, and within our own practice, research, and teaching, we approach the social work we do from a place of curiosity and "not-knowing." We understand that practice can be rewarding and simultaneously unsettling. Most of all, we want to inspire hope and a sense of possibility, as well as visions for social change and transformation.

1

Intersections of Social Work and Social Justice

S tudents quite often approach social work with a general idea of "wanting to help," and this chapter asks students to begin to examine what that means both in the context of the profession and the world around them. The varied definitions for social work are compared, including "mainstream" definitions, alternative definitions, and international definitions. The purpose is to move students beyond an often narrow version of social work to a more complex and dynamic understanding of the term and the field.

A key element of this chapter is its examination of various ways to define and conceptualize social justice in the context of these myriad definitions. It presents some of the support for and challenges to bringing social justice into social work practice. Finally, the intersections and challenges of social work practice conceptualized from a social justice perspective are examined in light of anti-oppressive or liberatory practice.

SOCIAL WORK DEFINED

There are many definitions of what social work is, what social workers do, and how social workers should perform their work. What follows are several mainstream and alternative definitions of social work.

The National Association of Social Workers (NASW), the largest member group of social workers in the United States, notes in the preamble to its Code of Ethics:

> The primary mission of the social work profession is to enhance human well-being and help meet the basic human needs of all people, with particular attention to the needs and empowerment of people who are vulnerable, oppressed, and living in poverty. A historic and defining feature of social work is the profession's focus on individual well-being in a social context and the well-being of society. Fundamental to social work is attention to the environmental forces that create, contribute to, and address problems in living. (2008, para. 2)

1

The Council on Social Work Education (CSWE), which governs accreditation for social work education in the United States at both the bachelor level (BSW) and master level (MSW), states that

> the purpose of the social work profession is to promote human and community well-being. Guided by a person and environment construct, a global perspective, respect for human diversity, and knowledge based on scientific inquiry, social work's purpose is actualized through its quest for social and economic justice, the prevention of conditions that limit human rights, the elimination of poverty, and the enhancement of the quality of life for all persons. (CSWE, 2010, p. 1)

Given the influence of both the NASW and the CSWE in the field, it is important for social workers in the United States to understand these two contemporary definitions of social work. You may notice that both of these definitions share a focus on oppressed and poverty-stricken communities, though they also approach these issues with subtle differences in wording.

Although these are standard and well-accepted definitions, social work students and professionals need to critically examine them and examine other definitions outside the mainstream. Both in the United States and globally, the history and context of social work have given rise to these alternative definitions.

The Social Welfare Action Alliance (SWAA) is a national organization of progressive human service workers that lies outside more mainstream organizations, such as the NASW and CSWE. SWAA indicates that their key principles "reflect a concern for social justice, peace, and coalition building with progressive social movements" (Social Welfare Action Alliance, 2014, para. 1). Although the SWAA is considered a more progressive organization, at its 25th anniversary conference in 2011, keynote speaker Michael Reisch (the Daniel Thursz Distinguished Professor of Social Justice at the University of Maryland) stated that it does not always live up to progressive values. NASW, CSWE, and SWAA have all played a role, he says, in

> institutionalizing the implied (if unstated) relationship of the profession to the nation's market-oriented political-economy. Instead of challenging the roots of social problems, we are encouraged to channel clients' needs within existing parameters. Social justice rhetoric masks the social control functions this produces. (Reisch, 2011, p. 7)

It is crucial to note that Reisch points out that even within a more progressive social work organization, such as the SWAA, there is a tendency to prioritize service delivery responses rather than structural problems that could more explicitly support concerns for social justice.

Lena Dominelli, a professor and Head of Social and Community Youth Work at Durham University in England, developed a model of social work that points up the inadequacies of mainstream definitions:

- *Maintenance social work* exemplifies a mainstream, conservative ideology in which social workers neutrally approach the individual or group at hand and attempt to assist through either adaptions or improvements in the environment. The social worker who models this form provides bureaucratically driven service delivery and does not address systemic inequities.
- *Therapeutic social work* is closely related to maintenance social work yet focuses on the individual as the target for the intervention. It addresses emotional and psychological needs and issues with a psychological perspective.
- *Emancipatory social work* is based in a critical analysis of power structures and the societal distribution of resources. This type of social work addresses both individual and policy advocacy work (2009).

A variety of other social work scholars have reinforced the social justice theme. For instance, Iain Ferguson, in his book *Reclaiming social work: Challenging neo-liberalism and promoting social justice*, states that social work includes a

> combination of a value base of respect, empowerment and social justice; the emphasis on a relationship between worker and service user founded on trust and non-judgmental acceptance; a knowledge base which embraces both developmental psychology and also an understanding of social structures and social processes; and a repertoire of methods ranging from individual counseling to advocacy and community work; all these give social work a holistic perspective which makes it unique amongst the helping professions. (Ferguson, 2008, p. 20)

Paulo Freire, in a speech delivered in 1988 at the Social Workers World Conference in Stockholm, Sweden, discussed seven qualities or "virtues" for progressive social workers to develop:

> (1) actions which align with your words; (2) a critical curiosity toward the world and toward those individuals/groups/communities with whom you work; (3) on-going development of competence in your work; (4) tolerance; (5) "impatient patience," (6) an understanding of limits of practice; and (7) an understanding of what is historically possible. (Moch, 2009)

According to the International Federation of Social Workers (IFSW):

The social work profession promotes social change, problem solving in human relationships and the empowerment and liberation of people to enhance well-being. Utilising theories of human behaviour and social systems, social work intervenes at the points where people interact with their environments. Principles of human rights and social justice are fundamental to social work. (2011, para. 2)

How do the above definitions of social work compare and contrast? Do any of them speak more to your idea of social work or challenge your previous concept of what social work is and social workers do? Often students enter into social work education based on their own past experiences with social workers—positive and negative—or with a general sense that they want to join a profession that "helps" people on some level. How do these definitions support or challenge that impulse to "help"?

SOCIAL JUSTICE DEFINED

Social justice is a contested and complex term. While on the surface it may appear straightforward, the term contains multiple layers of meaning. Consider this example from one of the author's personal experiences:

Before teaching a course on social welfare and social justice practice, my work spanned teaching during my doctoral program, research on human rights and domestic violence, and over ten years in the mental health and domestic violence fields. I view my politics as progressive and see my work as focused on oppression and disparities based in social locations. While I researched the intersections between human rights and domestic violence, surprisingly, I never gave that much thought to the term *social justice* and the myriad of meanings that it could evoke.

However, when I started teaching an undergraduate practice course, I began to deliberately situate social work in a social justice framework. It seemed a perfectly natural fit and I did not think social workers or sociologists would contest it as a framework for teaching and learning about social work.

I did have difficulty finding U.S. examples of framing social work as social justice work. The most telling experience was when I suggested that the department change the major name from "social welfare" to "social welfare and social justice." That is when I got "push back" or resistance. The primary concern expressed about this proposed change was that this new name would somehow work to a student's disadvantage once they graduated.

In an impromptu survey, a colleague of mine asked his coworkers in a local mental health agency what they thought of incorporating "social justice" into the name. The answers were almost divided evenly between "that's what we do as social workers," to a more neutral or negative response—with a few mental health workers stating that the term was "too political."

These responses led to a small research project I initiated where I conducted focus groups for social workers in a variety of arenas—mental health, child welfare, domestic violence, aging, and community organization. Interestingly, the contributing social workers all reported that social work should be predicated on the concepts of social justice—although many struggled with defining the term and identifying how to actually engage in social justice-oriented practice (Morgaine, 2014).

The National Association of Social Workers and the Council on Social Work Education—and many practicing social workers, as reflected by this small study—rely on the term *social justice* in their descriptions of social work as a profession. Social justice is also included in the educational requirements for United States social work curricula. So why is *social justice* "too political" or a contested term?

The following sections examine six major definitions and views of social justice: distributive justice, recognition and relational perspectives, the capabilities approach, indigenous and postcolonial views, postmodern views, and religious perspectives.

Distributive Justice Theories

Michael Reisch has written extensively on social work and social justice. In an article outlining the historical trajectory of the meanings and uses of the term *social justice*, he begins with the Old Testament and takes the reader through a whirlwind tour of western philosophical thought pertaining to social justice (Reisch, 2002).

It is important to note that through much of this early historical theorizing, the concept of social justice was applied using the standards of equity that were operating at that time. So, for example, when Plato theorized in *The Republic* about socially just arrangements that were necessary for human well-being and harmony, he maintained his beliefs in the necessity for class distinctions. Therefore, his form of social justice was based on the distribution of goods and rights as befit the social class standing of each individual (Reisch, 2002). Clearly, Plato did not believe in social justice based in equality for all.

Yet, because Plato's philosophy centers on how social justice is distributed to the members of a society (i.e., who is entitled to justice and how it is defined), it is considered a forerunner of the theory known as distributive justice. The question of who should actually benefit from social justice—who should receive the rights, opportunities, and economic benefits in a society—continues to be one of the most contested aspects of the concept. These debates arise because social justice is inextricably tied to concepts of equality and freedom.

Enlightenment Concepts

The development of secular social justice theories is generally considered to have begun during the Enlightenment period in Western Europe and the United States—loosely between the mid-1600s and mid-1700s. This period is characterized by the growth of rationalism, scientific reasoning, and calls for separation of church and state. Marked by both the French Revolution and the American Revolution, questions of freedom and equality were at the forefront of this period. Thomas Hobbes, John Locke, Jean-Jacques Rousseau, Immanuel Kant, Benedict Baruch Spinoza, David Hume, and Mary Wollstonecraft, among many others, wrote on the topic (Zafirovski, 2011).

Although these philosophers focused primarily on the rights of men, there were glimmers of increasing inclusion of oppressed minorities in social justice theorizing. Wollstonecraft, an early British feminist thinker, argued that women should have an education and rights equal to men. Olympe de Gouges wrote about gender equality and slavery and the burgeoning abolitionist movement.

One key concept during this period was "the social contract"—the relationship between individuals and government. For example, Hobbesian theory maintains that for a society to be just, an authoritarian state must maintain control and mete out justice—a necessity driven by the presumed base and antisocial characteristics of humanity (Reisch, 2002). Interestingly, this concept of humankind as needing punitive and strict control continues to be a common thread in social and political theory. For instance, in the contemporary political landscape in the United States, some analysts note that this concept is associated with conservative moral politics and framing (Lakoff, 2002).

In contrast, Locke argued that individuals willingly come together in a society and are morally bound not to harm one another. State powers are based on the consent of those governed and, by this contract, the state is bound to provide security and protection of the individual's rights. Locke's ideas are seen as having contributed significantly to the Declaration of Independence in the United States and to classical liberal thinking (Capeheart & Milovanovic, 2007).

Once again, it is important to view these theories historically, as these tenets of justice and freedom were reserved for white, male property owners. Injustice and justice were weighed on scales that women, people of color, and the landless could not access.

The Marxian Perspective

Karl Marx and Friedrich Engels, on the other hand, did not see human nature as fixed in the way that Hobbes, Locke, and others did. They contextualized the human experience in the political economy. To them, injustice is a result of oppression and inequitable distribution due to imbalances of privilege and power. Through this lens, social justice is approached when rights and resources are distributed based on needs and not simply to those who hold privilege based on their class status or ability to produce.

Marx, Engels, and others embracing this viewpoint ushered in a reformed concept of the social contract of the Enlightenment period. Their idea of the social contract was one of mutual obligations and the rights of individuals (Capeheart & Milovanovic, 2007; Reisch, 2002). It is through this social contract that social justice can develop.

Utilitarianism

Classic utilitarian social justice theory, another approach to distributive justice, was developed by Jeremy Bentham in the late 1700s and further expanded by John Stuart Mill in the late 1800s. In contrast to theories of social justice that were based on a social contract, however, utilitarianism contends that a society is just when the major institutions meet the needs of the majority, measured as net satisfaction. It does not discern among specific paths to satisfaction, it is simply concerned with an overall level of satisfaction versus dissatisfaction. This concept is frequently expressed as "the greatest good for the greatest number." What this presumes is that acts are just and moral if in the end there is more "good" done than harm (Rawls, 1971).

John Rawls, who developed one well-known theory that is a departure from classic utilitarian theory (it is still considered utilitarianism, but shifts from social contract to the concept of fairness), is commonly cited as one of the most important contemporary social justice theorists. In *A Theory of Justice* (1971) Rawls presents his theory of justice as focused on fairness. Instead of viewing social justice as based on a social contract that has already been established, he suggests that social justice itself is the foundation for social arrangements.

In his conceptualization, justice depends on a "veil of ignorance" (Rawls, 1971, p. 12) in which all members of society are ignorant of both their own and others' social standing. Thus, no one person or group is advantaged over others; they are all in a position of equality. If individuals are "rational and mutually disinterested," these social arrangements will be fair (p. 13). It is important to note that Rawls considers the "original position" of being behind a veil of ignorance as hypothetical. It is used to frame the concept of justice as fairness.

According to Rawls, there are two principles of justice:

- All people must have equal access to what he sees as the basic liberties: freedom of conscience or thought; freedom of speech and assembly; political liberty (which is seen as the right to vote and run for office); right to personal property; and freedom from arbitrary arrest.
- Social and economic inequalities should be such that the least advantaged members of society benefit the most. The goal is equality of opportunity, which allows everyone access to positions of power and authority.

These two principles are hierarchical. The first principle must be maintained when applying the second principle (Rawls, 1971).

Egalitarianism and Libertarianism

Two other distributive justice theories of note include strict egalitarianism and libertarianism. A strict egalitarian approach is based on the principle of equal distribution, whereby everyone is given the same level of goods and services. Egalitarianism does not mean that everyone must have the exact same items, but rather presumes items of equal worth. One question that this form of justice raises is how do you measure levels of goods and services to determine equity?

The libertarian approach, demonstrated through libertarian political ideology, is a conservative approach to social justice. It prioritizes individual liberty and property rights and supports very little government intervention into the lives of those governed. Libertarian principles focus on justice based on entitlement to "holdings" (money, property) that are acquired through one's own efforts or through a transfer from someone else who acquired the entitled holdings justly. The free market is seen as the field in which these acquisitions are played out and there is no requirement for the distribution to be equitable (Lamont & Favor, 2008).

Recognition and Relational Perspectives

Some theorists view social justice as a matter of recognizing and accommodating non-mainstream groups, not just redistributing resources. Charles Taylor, a professor emeritus of philosophy at McGill University, and Axel Honneth, a critical theorist in the tradition of the Frankfurt School, have written extensively on the politics of recognition, which centers on the struggles that identity/cultural groups engage in to be recognized in the public sphere (Honneth, 1996; Taylor, 1994). Recognition is seen as directly influencing self-esteem and self-respect, and thus it is a foundational component of social justice. Some examples are recognition of a religious, ethnic, or cultural group's style of dress, such as making accommodations in a school or court setting for a Sikh to wear the kirpan (a ceremonial sword that is never to be removed); recognition of same-sex marriage; and recognition of non-binary gender categories by providing gender neutral restrooms.

Having made significant contributions to social justice theorizing, Nancy Fraser, critical theorist and professor of political and social science, suggests a synthesis between the two perspectives of redistribution and recognition. Fraser believes that over the past few decades, recognition claims have become privileged, particularly given the rise of free-market ideology and the fall of communism, which have pushed redistribution claims to the margins. These recognition claims can be either liberal/progressive or fundamentalist/conservative, such as recognition for rights of Lesbian, Gay, Bisexual, Transgender, Queer, Questioning, and Intersex (LGBTQQI) individuals or support for instituting school prayer.

The disconnect between the recognition and redistribution perspectives has become very polarized. Those in the distributive justice camp often see the recognition camp as having "false consciousness" (Fraser, 2003, p. 8), or a misplaced sense of loyalty to the privileged, and not accurately grounding claims in the reality of extensive global resource and income disparities. In contrast, those in the recognition camp see the distributive justice ideologies as disconnected from politics of diversity and intersectionality and as grounded in an outdated materialist philosophy.

Fraser believes that justice theories require both perspectives. The "emancipatory aspects" of each can be combined to create a more comprehensive theory of social justice. She develops her argument by comparing the two perspectives on several criteria, as shown in Image 1.1.

Fraser argues that we can only fit a group in need of exclusive categorization as either redistribution or recognition when we can clearly classify it as either a class group or a status group. Consider gender-based oppression, which entails both class and status. It cannot easily be remedied by either redistribution or recognition. As a class category, gender is characterized by structural differences between "productive" and "reproductive" labor and the continued economic disparities between males and females. As a status category, gender is characterized by a continued devaluation of traits considered feminine. In this example, for any remedy of injustices both redistribution and recognition need to occur. In addition, the complexity of intersectional identities, such as combined race and gender, is further cause for a "two-pronged" approach (Fraser, 2003, p. 26).

Taylor (1994) and Honneth (1996) have suggested that recognition is merely a matter of the "self-realization" necessary to achieve a "good life" (Fraser, 2003, p. 28). Fraser, however, believes that recognition is an issue of social status and related to justice rather than self-realization. If groups are seen as inferior (or are excluded and so invisible) then they are misrecognized and therefore experience "status subordination." The institutionalized

Image 1.1	Differences Between the Recognition and Redistribution Perspectives on Social Justice	
Criteria	*Recognition Perspective*	*Redistribution Perspective*
Conceptions of injustice	Cultural and rooted in social patterns	Socioeconomic and rooted in economic structures
Remedies for injustice	Cultural or symbolic change to either celebrate difference or deconstruct how difference has been constructed	Economic restructuring to abolish unjust differences
Perceptions of those who experience injustice	Status groups with less respect, privilege, and esteem	Classes or class-like collectivities
Understandings of the differences between and among groups	Either (1) benign, preexisting variations within the constructed hierarchy, or (2) socially constructed variations within the hierarchy	Unjust differences

Source: Adapted from Nancy Fraser, 2003, *Redistribution or Recognition? A Political-Philosophical Exchange,* pp. 13–15, New York: Verso.

patterns that determine cultural value prevent active participation in social life, which is an injustice. To fully participate in social life, members of oppressed groups must experience two conditions: (1) the distribution of material resources must afford participants independence and "voice"; and (2) institutionalized cultural patterns must provide equal respect for all participants and they must have equal opportunity to achieve self-esteem.

Like Fraser, Iris Marion Young (1990) believes that injustice takes myriad forms, beyond only the injustice of disparities in wealth that is at the center of the distributive justice paradigm. Young argues that distributive justice ignores the larger institutional context. Young's concept of justice includes analysis of such institutional structures as the state, the family, civil society, and the workplace. Her conceptualization also includes the rules and norms that guide structures and the language and symbols that are interwoven into institutional and social relations. Young suggests that rights and opportunities are not things, but instead processes that are relational in nature. Domination and oppression can include both distributive concerns related to material goods as well as concerns related to decisionmaking, division of labor, and culture.

The Capabilities Approach

Amartya Sen, who won a Nobel Prize in the economic sciences, contributed to the contemporary dialogue about social justice by developing an approach grounded in individuals' *capabilities* rather than on the distribution of primary goods. Capabilities are what people are able to do and be. They give people the freedom to be able to make choices that will support the pursuit of goals (Sen, 2009). The capabilities approach has been used extensively in international development. From this perspective, groups that assess the health and well-being of citizens compare things, such as health and educational attainment rather than simply the distribution of income and wealth.

Martha Nussbaum, a law and philosophy professor at the University of Chicago, advocates for an evolving and general list of capabilities that can be used throughout the world to provide a framework for assessing social justice (2003). She suggests that the central capabilities listed in Image 1.2 must be guaranteed to all of a country's citizens for that society to be considered "just." Although these capabilities are presented in a list, there is no hierarchy of capabilities; all are equally important. She notes that respect for cultural pluralism, among other safeguards, is built into her list by the dynamic and open-ended nature of the list.

Indigenous and Postcolonial Social Justice

Dominant theories of social justice, such as distributive justice, were developed in western and northern contexts by colonizing nations. In the realm of criminal justice, a restorative justice movement has recently developed to consider the viewpoint of indigenous peoples (Braithwaite & Daly, 1998; Braithwaite & Strang, 2002). However, social justice theorizing has generally paid

Image 1.2	Central Human Capabilities
Life	Being able to live to the end of a human life of normal length; not dying prematurely, or before one's life is so reduced as to be not worth living.
Bodily health	Being able to have good health, including reproductive health; to be adequately nourished; to have adequate shelter.
Bodily integrity	Being able to move freely from place to place; to be secure against violent assault, including sexual assault and domestic violence; having opportunities for sexual satisfaction and for choice in matters of reproduction.
Senses, imagination, and thought	Being able to use the senses to imagine, think, and reason—and to do these things in a truly human way, a way informed and cultivated by an adequate education, including, but by no means limited to, literacy and basic mathematical and scientific training. Being able to use imagination and thought in connection with experiencing and producing works and events of one's own choice, religious, literary, musical, and so forth. Being able to use one's mind in ways protected by guarantees of freedom of expression with respect to both political and artistic speech, and freedom of religious exercise. Being able to have pleasurable experiences and to avoid non-beneficial pain.
Emotions	Being able to have attachments to things and people outside ourselves; to love those who love and care for us, to grieve at their absence; in general to love, to grieve, to experience longing, gratitude, and justified anger. Not having one's emotional development blighted by fear and anxiety. (Supporting this capability means supporting forms of human association that can be shown to be crucial in their development.)
Practical reason	Being able to form a conception of the good and to engage in critical reflection about the planning of one's life. (This entails protection for the liberty of conscience and religious observance.)
Affiliation	Being able to live with and toward others, to recognize and show concern for other human beings, to engage in various forms of social interaction; to be able to imagine the situation of another. (Protecting this capability means protecting institutions that constitute and nourish such forms of affiliation, and also protecting the freedom of assembly and political speech.) Having the social bases of self-respect and non-humiliation; being able to be treated as a dignified being whose worth is equal to that of others. This entails provisions of nondiscrimination on the basis of race, sex, sexual orientation, ethnicity, caste, religion, national origin.
Relations with other species	Being able to live with concern for and in relation to animals, plants, and the world of nature.

(Continued)

Image 1.2 (Continued)	
Play	Being able to laugh, to play, to enjoy recreational activities.
Control over one's environment	Being able to participate effectively in political choices that govern one's life; having the right of political participation, protections of free speech and association. Being able to hold property (both land and material goods), and having property rights on an equal basis with others; having the right to seek employment on an equal basis with others; having the freedom from unwarranted search and seizure. In work, being able to work as a human being, exercising practical reason, and entering into meaningful relationships of mutual recognition with other workers.

Source: Adapted by permission of the publisher from *Creating Capabilities: The Human Development Approach* by Martha C. Nussbaum, pp. 33–34, Cambridge, Mass.: Harvard University Press, Copyright © 2011 by the President and Fellows of Harvard College.

less attention to indigenous and postcolonial notions of social justice. Also, social work has been particularly focused on Rawlsian distributive justice theory (Banerjee, 2005; Morris, 2002).

It is important for social workers to be aware of postcolonial theory and to integrate this into concepts of social justice. Gayatri Chakravorty Spivak, a philosopher and professor at Columbia University, asked the classic question, "Can the subaltern speak?" (1988). The term *subaltern* signifies the Other—the voiceless, dispossessed, unrecognized, colonized peoples. In questioning whether the subaltern can truly speak, Spivak draws attention to the impact of colonization on knowledge and discourse. Using their power and privilege, colonizers define knowledge and create language, laws, interpretations, and norms. For subalterns to speak, and to speak in resistance to the dominant, they must use the language of the dominant discourse, which then erases their voice. Spivak and other postcolonial theorists contend that social justice requires a relationship between the dominant and the subordinate that allows voices to be heard from the ground up. The dominant must be willing to unlearn domination and embrace their duty to others (Capeheart & Milovanvic, 2007).

Postmodern Social Justice

Like postcolonial theorists who assert that social justice must be grounded in relationship and percolate from the bottom up, postmodern theorists prioritize "local" knowledge. Loretta Capeheart and Dragan Milovanvic (2007) identify four primary characteristics of a postmodern theory of social justice:

- Postmodernists question the concept of justice that is based on a foundational notion of what is just (i.e., the notion of a natural state of humankind promulgated by Hobbes) and believe the concepts of justice are unstable and dynamic, therefore problematic.

- Interpretations of social justice by those insiders, such as legal scholars and judges, are suspect. Critiques from outside the system are more trustworthy.
- Directly related to this point is the postmodern critique of "positive jurisprudence" (p. 125) where legal practitioners develop a normative framework as a base for judgments.
- Social justice is active justice, as opposed to the passive (and static) modern concept of justice. Justice should be enacted through a sense of duty and responsibility to others.

For example, prominent postmodern theorist Jean-Francois Lyotard articulated the need for social justice to be situated in "petit narratives" rather than supposedly objective "grand narratives." He stressed the need to understand smaller, diverse, local experiences.

In examining Lyotard's contributions to social justice theory, Capeheart and Milovanvic highlight his focus on petit narratives. Any contracts born out of this knowledge of local experiences need to be temporary and open to continual reassessment by the local communities. Community members may come to agreement through consensus, yet that consensus is ever changing. Lyotard also stresses the need to push limits and work on the margins of the rules to continually shift the boundaries and rules of the game.

In a similar vein, Richard Rorty, a pragmatic postmodernist, relies on understanding through people's everyday practices. He also promotes a ground up approach that is based on "experimenting, tinkering, and doing" (Capeheart & Milovanvic, 2007, p. 131). Rorty gives more credence to judges than Capeheart and Milovanvic do, particularly visionary judges who will push for justice through groundbreaking rulings, such as *Brown v. Board of Education* (1954). Rorty also acknowledges that judges may rule in bad faith, attempting to be seen as acting in accordance with the rule of law, and deliver repressive rulings like *Plessy v. Ferguson* (1896) (Capeheart & Milovanvic, 2007).

Religion and Social Justice

It is important to note that social justice principles have been integrated within many religious doctrines. No definition of social justice would be complete without acknowledging the influence of various religious traditions. As with secular concepts of social justice, religious concepts must be placed in historical context. It is also important to recognize that world religions are multifaceted and have a variety of interpretations. Religious understandings and practices of social justice can range from progressive to conservative, just as secular social justice can. Additionally, as with secular theories, religious ideals of social justice are not without tensions and contradictions. For example, many organized religions condemn LGBTQQI individuals, which then places their practices in question—social justice *for whom*?

Within a Christian belief system, differences in translations, interpretations, and denominations significantly influence the meanings of social justice. However, one commonality is the concept of serving others as a service to God. Christian concepts of social justice are also based in the beliefs of the common good and the rights and responsibilities of individuals

(Poe, 2007). Beyond the more typical forms of distributive justice, Christianity focuses on "restoration of relational harmony" (Poe, 2007, p. 466).

Among Christian religions, Catholicism has a more established history of practicing social justice than many of the other denominations. Examples include such organizations as the Catholic Worker Movement in the United States (Poe, 2007) and liberation theological practices in South and Central America.

The three cornerstones of social justice in the traditional Islamic belief system are freedom of conscience, human equality, and mutual responsibility in society (Khadduir, 2001). However, Islam presumes that wealth will not be equally distributed because human abilities are not equally bestowed. For example, while men and women are equal in spiritual and religious aspects, there are differences based in physical endowments, customs, and responsibilities. Thus, men receive twice the inheritance as women because they are seen as the head of the family, and men are the "overseers of women" because of their place in society versus women's place in the home.

Judaism, particularly as practiced by secular and reform Jews in the United States, is often viewed as a humanitarian and social justice religion. *Tzedakeh* (loosely translated as "charity") is derived from "prophetic" Judaism and is broadly conceptualized as a form of social justice in which those in poverty are entitled to receive a portion of wealth from those who are more fortunate. This sense of obligation extends beyond those of Jewish faith to all of humankind (Legge, 1995).

Buddhism is often seen as so deeply centered on the self and self-awareness that it does not lend itself to developed theories about social justice. However, it has been suggested that through an understanding of the bodhisattva ideal of selflessness and active engagement, a Buddhist philosophy of social justice can be developed (Cho, 2000). Through this ideal, "*her* poverty becomes *my* poverty; *his* tragedy, *my* tragedy" (Cho, 2000, para. 34). Other evidence that Buddhists may be engaged with social issues and injustices include this statement by the Buddha (Jones, 2010):

> He who has understanding and great wisdom does not think of harming himself or another, nor of harming both alike. He rather thinks of his own welfare, of that of others, of that of both, and of the welfare of the whole world. In that way, one shows understanding and great wisdom.

The Intersections of Social Justice and Social Work

Social justice, while a complex and contested term, is the foundation of social work and has been the focus of much scholarship and dialogue, particularly in the last 10 to 15 years. Social justice has been a part of social work since the early beginnings in the Progressive Era, when it was cited by foremothers like Jane Addams and Grace Abbott (Reisch, 2007). Prominent contemporary voices in social work suggest that examining personal and professional meanings of social justice continues to be critical for social workers, given both the foundational role that social justice plays and the need for developing a common language regarding social justice (Reisch, 2002; Reisch, 2007; Van Soest, 2007). Additionally, although social justice is often seen as solely a macro issue rather than a micro issue in social work, contemporary theorists argue that social justice must be integrated into clinical social work practice (Swenson, 1998). National organizations, such as the National Association of Social Workers and the Council on Social Work Education, highlight social justice in their ethics and policy statements (CSWE, 2010; NASW, 2008).

For example, in CSWE's recently updated Educational Policy and Accreditation Standards, one core competency for social work education specifically addresses social justice:

Educational Policy 2.1.5—Advance human rights and social and economic justice—

Each person, regardless of position in society, has basic human rights, such as freedom, safety, privacy, an adequate standard of living, health care, and education. Social workers recognize the global interconnections of oppression and are knowledgeable about theories of justice and strategies to promote human and civil rights. Social work incorporates social justice practices in organizations, institutions, and society to ensure that these basic human rights are distributed equitably and without prejudice. Social workers are to

- understand the forms and mechanisms of oppression and discrimination;
- advocate for human rights and social and economic justice; and
- engage in practices that advance social and economic justice.

Although a number of scholars have suggested ways in which social work can use the organizing principle of social justice in both a micro context (Mullaly, 1997; Swenson, 1998; Wakefield; 1988) and macro context (Beck & Eichler, 2000; Gould, 2000; Haynes & White, 1999; Van Soest, 1994), they still define social justice in a myriad of ways (Reisch, 2002). If the NASW identifies promotion of social justice as a primary role for social workers (NASW, 2008) and CSWE requires all social work programs to teach students about the promotion of social justice (CSWE, 2010) and the term itself is conceptually obscure, how can social workers and social work educators best embrace this foundational aspect of social work? That is the question we now address.

THEORETICAL FRAMEWORK/ FOUNDATION FOR SOCIAL JUSTICE WORK

It is not enough for social workers to believe in social justice and equality; rather, it's important to understand oppression and the dynamics that reproduce it (Dominelli, 2002; Mullaly, 2010). Social justice is a critical process and needs to be a crucial objective in social work in order for a practice to be both ethical and effective. We must understand forces of oppression, privilege, power, and liberation. Privilege needs to be acknowledged and disrupted in order to create possibilities for structural changes and to work toward achieving liberation.

The process of attaining social justice should be "democratic and participatory, inclusive and affirming of human agency and human capacities for working collaboratively to create change" (Adams, Bell, & Griffin, 2007, p. 2). This process involves understanding the implications of individuals' categories of difference, including multiple identities and social group memberships, socially constructed categories of race, class, ethnicity, gender identity/expression, sexual orientation, ability status, age, religion, nationality, citizenship, and other categories of difference. It is imperative that we understand systems of discrimination based on categories of difference and the agency of individuals and groups. We need to consider how these categories of difference create the realities of institutional structures, thus shaping people's daily lived experiences (Hill Collins, 2000). As we examine the meaning of social differences, oppression, and privilege, we need to be aware of how changing societal conditions bring to the surface new contradictions and emerging forms of oppression and how they give rise to new forces for change. The sections that follow delineate these elements of difference.

Defining Individual Social Identities

Identity refers to the distinguishing features or characteristics that identify an individual. Some of these characteristics are embodied, hidden, or inherited. For example, identity characteristics can be physical (e.g., gender, race); invisible (e.g., sexual orientation, religion); psychological (personality); social (e.g., class status) or embodied social roles (e.g., student, parent, employee) (Mullaly, 2010). Identity has been defined as being about "belonging, about what you have in common with some people and what differentiates you from others. At its most basic it gives you a sense of personal location…" (Weeks, 1990, p. 98). There is a difference between personal identity and social identity: personal identity is the way in which one views himself or herself, whereas social identity is the way in which society views him or her (Mullaly, 2010). Identities are formed through interactions with others in a variety of contexts and different aspects of lived experience. They are constructed in relation to others and to the cultures in which individuals are embedded (Bakhtin, 1981; Bell, 2007). By constructed, we mean that as a society, we create and assign social meanings that we attribute to distinct categories of people, creating assumptions of inferiority or superiority, related to privilege and disadvantage. Many factors play a role in the formation of our identities, and thus we each have multiple identities. These various identities intersect and overlap with one another, granting us privilege in some areas and disadvantage in others (Mullaly, 2010).

Trying to conceptualize individual and group identity is further complicated by the ways in which identities are co-constructed and assigned meanings within oppressive systems and structures in our society (Bell, 2007, p.8). The value attached to various social identities is socially determined by the dominant group. Stereotypes about certain social identity groups perpetuate disadvantage, while the dominant group maintains certain privileges associated with their own social identity categories.

Defining Social Identity Groups

Social identity groups consist of people who share a range of physical, cultural, and social characteristics within social identity categories. Society assigns people to groups based on political, social, and historical dynamics that change across time and culture. Social identity categories include socially constructed categories, such as race, ethnicity, class, religion, ability status, age, gender, and sexual orientation. Thus, members of a social group have a certain similarity because of their shared experiences or ways of life that lead them to associate more with one another than with those not identified as being part of the group.

However, group identities are not homogenous, and all members of a particular social group will not necessarily define themselves in exactly the same way. In addition, someone's self-defined group identity may be central; for someone else, it may be at the background of someone's lived reality, emerging at the forefront under different circumstances, contexts, and geographical locations.

Group identities are also historical and contextual. Consider the category Latino. Latinos in the United States are an extremely diverse group comprising people of many different countries of origin, speaking various languages, and from divergent racial, ethnic, and socioeconomic groups, who arrived in the United States under widely different conditions (immigration, colonialization, or slavery), over different time periods (Anzaldua, 1987; Hurtado, Gurin, & Peng, 1994; Oboler, 1995). The label Latino/a may include a Spanish-speaking, upper-class white man from Cuba as well as a Mayan speaking Indian woman from Mexico or Guatemala. The dominant society lumps these individuals together in a group labeled Hispanic to which certain stereotypes are applied. Thus, on one level in a U.S. historical context, they could be said to share a common group experience of oppression. Indeed, this shared experience is often the basis for political organizing across different groups self-named as Latino/a. On another level, their experiences are so divergent as to have little in common at all except when compared to the experiences of non-Latino/as (Bell, 2010, p. 9).

Accordingly, Young (2010) states that a social group is an expression of social relations and is defined, not primarily by a set of shared attributes, but by a sense of identity. For example, what defines Black Americans as a social group is not primarily their skin color. Indeed, some people whose skin color is fairly light identify themselves as black. Many individuals consciously self-identify into social categories, and these individuals may self-identify as Black Americans because they identify with the status of Black Americans and the common history produced by that social status (Young, 2010).

It is crucial to acknowledge the vast diversity inherent in people's different positions within categories of race, class, age, gender, and sexuality, among others. Everyone's identities are fluid and changing over their life course; individuals have unique personalities and complex expressions of their identities which allows everyone to embody various social roles and characteristics in their lifetime.

Understanding individual social identities and social identity groups helps us to conceptualize how people are privileged and oppressed on the basis of social group status:

> If an individual is oppressed, it is by virtue of being a member of a group or category of people that is systematically reduced, molded, immobilized. Thus, to recognize a person as oppressed one has to see that individual as belonging to a group of a certain sort. (Frye, 1983, p. 8)

One conceptual framework for understanding social justice highlights that social identity groups occupy unequal social locations or positions relative to one another (Adams, Blumenfeld, Castañeda, Hackman, Peters, & Zúñiga, 2010).

One group's privileges are directly related to another group's disadvantages. Thus, it is crucial to examine not only oppression, but privilege, and how one's privileged social identities manifest and are upheld in order to maintain and perpetuate oppression. Based on this premise, Adams and his colleagues present four related concepts:

1. Social group identities (such as racial and gender identities) have been used historically to justify and perpetuate the advantages of privileged groups relative to the disadvantages of marginalized groups;

2. These social identities, together with their relative inequality, have been socially constructed within specific historical conditions, although these social constructions are often rationalized as being derived from the "facts of nature" or sustained by unquestionable religious beliefs;

3. The pervasive historical legacies of inequality require a theory of oppression to account for the complex levels and types of privilege and disadvantage that play out at various levels of human society;

4. A theory of oppression also calls for frameworks that envision opportunities for empowerment and explain the success of past and present social movements. (2010, pp.1–2)

Defining Oppression

Social justice scholars define oppression in various ways. Their overlapping definitions provide key concepts for understanding the term.

Oppression is often described as a system that maintains advantage and disadvantage based on stereotyped social group memberships. When these stereotypes of disadvantaged groups are negative, oppression often arises. Stereotypes can be defined as generalizations about the attributes of a specific group that disregard individual diversity.

Oppression manifests on several levels:

- Individual level: destructive attitudes and behaviors of individual persons. For example, a white woman may clutch her purse when she walks by a black man on the street.
- Institutional level: harmful policies, practices, and norms within various institutions, such as family, education, health care, legal system, government, businesses, and religious organizations. For example, some schools in wealthier neighborhoods receive more money than schools in poorer neighborhoods.
- Social/cultural level: promotion of certain values, beliefs, and customs that serve the interests of advantaged social groups and provide justification for social oppression. Examples include the belief that a nuclear family is the only type of family or the higher value placed on such physical traits as thinness, white skin, blond hair, and blue eyes.

Iris Marion Young (1990) discusses oppression as a structural concept with five faces or manifestations of oppression in people's lives. The five faces are exploitation, marginalization, powerlessness, cultural imperialism, and violence.

Donna Baines provides a definition of oppression. She states:

Oppression takes place when a person acts or a policy is enacted unjustly against an individual (or group) because of their affiliation to a specific group. This includes depriving people of a way to make a fair living, to participate in all aspects of social life or to experience basic freedoms and human rights. It also includes imposing belief systems, values, laws and ways of life on other groups through peaceful or violent means. Oppression can be external [as in the examples above], or internal, when groups start to believe and act as if the dominant belief system, values and life way are the best and exclusive reality. Internal oppression often involves self-hate, self-censorship, shame and individual and cultural realities. (Baines, 2007, p. 2)

Similarly, Mullaly defines oppression as occurring when individuals are denied access to opportunities for self-development or survival; excluded from participating in society; assigned an inferior status based on their social group membership or identity; or lack rights that members of a privileged group take for granted (Mullaly, 2010). Adams, Bell, and Griffin define oppression in the following way: "The term *oppression* encapsulates the fusion of institutional and systematic discrimination, personal bias, bigotry, and social prejudice in a complex web of relationships and structures that shade most aspects of life in our society" (2007, p. 3).

Consequently, defining features of oppression include the following:

- Pervasive: social inequality is woven throughout social institutions, as well as embedded within individual consciousness

- Restrictive: oppression represents structural and material limitations that significantly shape individual opportunities and one's sense of possibility
- Hierarchical: oppression signifies a hierarchical relationship in which privileged groups have unearned advantages from the disempowerment of disadvantaged groups
- Complex: power and privilege are relative, because individuals hold multiple, complex, and crosscutting social group memberships that grant relative privilege or disadvantage in different ways, depending on different contexts
- Internalized: oppression also resides in the human psyche and oppressive beliefs are internalized

It is crucial to note that there is no hierarchy of oppressed groups. In other words, one social identity category isn't more oppressed than another. A hierarchy of oppression disregards the ways in which systems of oppression interact and reproduce one another.

Furthermore, Mullally (2010) adds relational aspects to this view of oppression as dynamic, complex, and multi-dimensional. Similarly, Dominelli (2002) believes oppression is socially constructed through people's actions with and behaviors toward others at the interpersonal, cultural, and structural level.

Therefore, oppressive relations do not have predetermined outcomes. Resistance to oppression and action for change can be pursued both by individuals and through groups.

Defining Privilege

The concept of privilege refers to the unearned, unasked for, often invisible benefits and advantages not available to members of disadvantaged social groups. Privilege exists when "one group has something of value that is denied to others simply because of the groups they belong to rather than because of anything they've done or failed to do" (Adams et al., 2010, p. 16).

In general, privilege provides individuals with a certain level of acceptance, power, inclusion, and comfort to navigate the world with ease and without question. Privilege grants credibility, respect, and access. It can also determine who is acknowledged, valued, accounted for, and prioritized in our society. Existing in a privileged social identity category awards the precedence of resources and opportunities over individuals belonging to disadvantaged social identity groups. Privilege also results in the unequal distribution of resources, perpetuating cycles of oppression.

A prolific writer on privilege, particularly racial and gender privilege, Peggy Macintosh discusses two types of privilege:

- Unearned entitlements are things of value that all people should have, such as feeling safe in a public space, being valued for who they are as a person, and being acknowledged for the skills they embody. But, when an unearned entitlement is limited to certain social identity groups, such as whites, males, able-bodied individuals, middle and upper classes, heterosexuals, citizens of the Global North (The Global North refers to the 57 countries with high human development that have a Human Development Index above .8 as reported in the United Nations Development Programme Report of 2005) then it becomes a form of privilege called "unearned advantage" (Johnson, 2006, p. 23).

- Conferred dominance refers to one group having power over another (Macintosh, 2000, as cited in Johnson, 2006, p. 23). An example is the common pattern of men controlling conversations with women, grounded in the cultural assumption that men are supposed to dominate women (Johnson, 2006). A white woman in this circumstance experiences oppression based on her gender. However, if she was having a conversation with a woman of color, she would be in a position of privilege based on her racial social identity and the surrounding cultural stereotypes about people of color.

Image 1.3 is a visual depiction of the origins of oppression and the relationship between various identity categories and privilege. Nearest the center of the tree roots are those identity

Image 1.3   Roots of Privilege

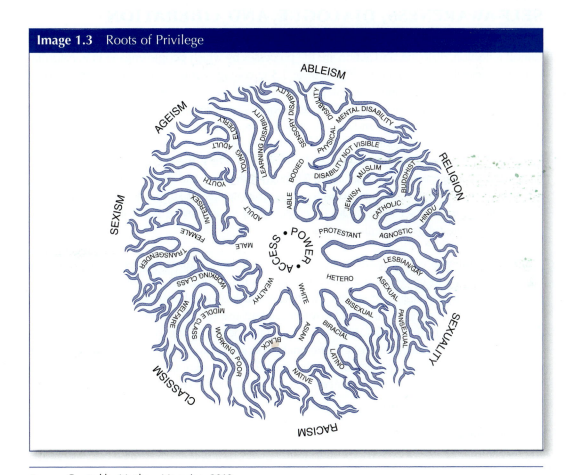

Source: Created by Matthew Morgaine, 2013.

categories and groups that hold privilege, power, and access to resources. These include, but are not limited to, ethnicity/race (white), gender and sex (male), socioeconomic status (ruling wealthy), ability status (able-bodied), spirituality and religion (Protestants and Catholics), age (adult), and sexual orientation (heterosexual). The social identity groups that branch off from the roots of privilege are considered disadvantaged social identity categories, and they hold less power and access to resources.

> Consider your own social identities, and then circle your identities in Image 1.3 in order to locate yourself on this diagram. Feel free to add any social identity category that may not be listed on the roots. Carefully examine where you have located yourself based on your identities. Consider your proximity from the center. What does this location mean for you?

SELF-AWARENESS, DIALOGUE, AND LIBERATION

Critical reflection, dialogue, and action are the processes by which people engage in transformation and societal change (Freire, 1970). Image 1.3 encourages you to begin reflecting on your own intersecting identities and how you personally experience privilege, power, and oppression in society. However, changing oppression also requires "de-centering" our own perspectives to provide space for those voices and experiences that are different from our own (Reisch, 2011). We must also engage in critical dialogue about how oppression, privilege, and power exist based on certain social identity groups and the ways in which these concepts manifest at the individual, cultural, and institutional level. Through individual and group dialogue, reflection, and critical consciousness, we can begin to envision strategies for sustainable social change.

According to Michael Reisch (2011), engaging in social justice work entails that social workers have the following skills and knowledge:

- The ability to envision a socially just society and the actions needed to attain it;
- The ability to understand and work with conflict, dialogue, and community;
- The ability to engage in critical thinking about individual and community issues;
- The ability to apply critical self-awareness and use of self in one's practice;
- The ability to develop strategies that integrate the social and political dimensions of the environment with one's personal experiences; and
- The ability to engage in praxis—the iterative and ongoing integration of ideas and action through experience, learning, and knowledge generation across domains. (p. 17)

Reisch (2011) also points out that because of the unique location of social workers within the institutional fabric of society, we must learn to use a variety of strategies to navigate the structures and systems in which social injustice occurs. These strategies and techniques can include: dialogue, tempered radicalism, the creative use of conflict, coalition building, honoring different standpoints, de-centering dominant viewpoints, and negotiating boundaries with those in authority (p. 19).

As we collaboratively seek these paths for creating social change, those who are oppressed can begin to move toward empowerment and liberation. Liberation can be conceptualized as the process of self-determination, agency, and action. Liberation involves a more subtle transformation as well: "Liberation is not only defined as the attainment of a state of awareness and understanding that transcends cultural belief systems, mindsets, and contexts, but it is a state of wisdom and freedom in being, thought, behavior, affect and relations" (Hanna, Talley, & Guindon, 2000, p. 430). Thus, liberation involves a commitment to not only challenging the roots of oppression and injustice and acting collaboratively, but also empowering all people to realize their full potential while building social solidarity and community capacity for collaborative action.

Bobbie Harro (2008) illustrates the cyclical process for achieving *intrapersonal* (within a person), *interpersonal* (between individuals) and *systemic* (within our systems and structures) liberation.

- Change often begins within individuals (intrapersonal change). They "wake up" when a critical incident creates cognitive dissonance (i.e., something they believed no longer makes sense to them). This critical incident changes what people believe about themselves and those around them. This initiates their own empowerment, they gain inspiration, disrupt the collusion of privilege and internalized oppression, and develop tools for reaching out to others. Reaching out to others can include speaking out against and naming injustices.
- Through our interactions with others (interpersonal change), we raise consciousness, build coalitions, serve as allies, and build community. Through these collective and collaborative efforts with others, we change how we value individuals and see the world, thus questioning assumptions, rules, roles, and systemic structures. As we begin to build community, that community coalesces, and then we can transform our anger and energy into action for social change. Direct, collective action against injustice can take the form of organizing, action planning, lobbying, and fund raising.
- Consequently, we then aim to create change in social policy, cultural assumptions, structures, definitions and rules (systemic change). The values of a diverse and united community begin to shape the system. We take on roles as leaders, collaborators, and teachers and learners through shared power and collective participation. A key to sustained liberatory change is maintaining our efforts so that we spread hope and inspiration and awaken awareness of the possibility for transformation.

Harro's model emphasizes authenticity, critical self-awareness, compassion for others, commitment, and collaboration in order to maintain our liberatory efforts. The cycle of liberation also advocates that we celebrate our efforts and successes.

ANTI-OPPRESSIVE AND LIBERATION-BASED PRACTICE

The models of self-awareness and liberation put forward by Reisch, Harro, and others are useful for social workers who are committed to social justice. They inform anti-oppressive practice (AOP), which has emerged as a social justice-based, anti-discriminatory approach to social work in the United Kingdom, Canada, Australia, New Zealand, and other European countries (Sakamoto & Pitner, 2005). However, the United States is behind in adopting an anti-oppressive approach within the social work profession. While many emerging social workers are embracing anti-oppressive practice in theory and ideology, and grappling with its limitations, there also continues to be a resistance within the profession and in academia.

AOP is informed by radical, progressive, anti-racist, anti-discriminatory, critical, feminist, postmodern and structural social work theory (Campbell, 2003; Dominelli, 2002; Payne, 2005). It promotes equity, inclusion, transformation, and social justice. Typically, social work in the United States has a micro or individual focus. However, anti-oppressive practice incorporates a macro lens, as it highlights the multiple manifestations of oppression and discrimination, and aims to address structural power dynamics in order to create equity for all social groups.

Lena Dominelli, a leading social work theorist, defines anti-oppressive practice as

> a form of social work practice which addresses social divisions and structural inequalities in the work that is done with people whether they be users ("clients") or workers. AOP aims to provide more appropriate and sensitive services by responding to people's needs regardless of their social status. AOP embodies a person centered philosophy; an egalitarian value system concerned with reducing the deleterious effects of structural inequalities upon people's lives; a methodology focusing on both process and outcome; and a way of structuring relationships between individuals that aims to empower users by reducing the negative effects of social hierarchies on their interaction and the work they do together. (Dominelli, 1996, p. 170)

AOP requires that social workers acknowledge the sociopolitical context of the lived experiences of their participants. In other words, social workers should aim to provide direct assistance to individuals affected by oppression, while engaging in change to transform oppressive systems.

In AOP, all levels of social work practice are understood as being interconnected and interdependent (Dominelli, 2002). However, the ultimate goal of anti-oppressive social work practice is to change the structure and procedures of service delivery systems through macro transformations, such as organizational changes, laws, and policies. It is key to note that the burden of change should not be placed on the social worker; but rather, responsibility to transform society also lies in the state (Dalrymple & Burke, 1995). There are five key concepts of anti-oppressive practice (Dalrymple & Burke, 2006; Danso, 2007):

- *Engaging in Critical Self-reflection.* Writings on anti-oppressive social work refer to "critical self reflection," "critical consciousness," "reflexivity," and "critical self-analysis," all of which refer to social workers examining their own values in relation to others' (Dalrymple & Burke, 1995, p. 92; Dominelli, 2002, p. 184). It involves reflecting on the privileges associated with one's intersecting identities and social locations. In social work practice, this entails social workers continuously challenging themselves and maintaining an awareness of difference and power dynamics in the social worker/ participant relationship (Sakamoto & Pitner, 2005). Through this process, social workers are less likely to impose their biases and assumptions on the participants (Sakamoto & Pitner, 2005). Self-awareness also allows for truly starting where the participant "is," instead of starting where the social work might think they "should be" (Sakamoto & Pitner, 2005, p. 443).

- *Assessing Participants' Experience of Oppression.* Critical assessment of participants' intersecting identities and social locations can provide insight into forms of oppression that the participants are experiencing (Danso, 2009). Creating a space for listening and understanding participants' experiences of oppression can take the blame off of the individual participant, shifting the focus from individual failure to structural issues and inequalities that have played a role in the participant's life. An AOP assessment process also allows for a critical examination of prevailing ideologies that shape agency policies and allocation of resources in order to identify if organizational policies are unjust or discriminatory.

- *Empowering Participants.* Empowerment in a practice context means providing participants with the tools and skills to address cultural, structural, and personal barriers that prevent them from gaining control of their lives (Payne, 2005). Empowerment is premised on a recognition and analysis of power, mutual support through consciousness raising, and collective efforts to challenge and change stereotypes (Finn & Jacobson, 2008). Methods for implementing empowerment in the practice setting include education, opportunities for participation and capacity building so that individuals can take action to improve their own life situations (Gutierrez & Lewis, 1999). Addressing obstacles and barriers at the institutional level might include developing alternative services and organizations (Mullaly, 2007), engaging with progressive movements, analyzing critical social policy, and revitalizing the public sector (Danso, 2009).

- *Working in Partnership.* With an AOP approach, it is crucial that the participants are informed about the approaches taken by the social worker and act as collaborators in the change process. Open and clear communication and dialogue are essential. The nature and scope of the social worker's and participants' roles should be transparent (Danso, 2009; Healy, 2005). To engage in meaningful dialogue, all participants must be considered equals (Freire, 1970); the social worker and participant must learn from each other and teach one another (Mullaly, 2010). The aim is to avoid reproducing the same types of social relations that have oppressed the participant in the first place. This equal partnership is referred as accompaniment: a commitment to collaboration and dialogue, attention to the interplay of power, and a mutual and equal exchange of teaching and learning (Finn & Jacobson, 2008).

- *Maintaining Minimal Intervention.* AOP also calls for minimal intervention or intrusion in the participant's life (Healy, 2005). This approach to practice has been informed by the frequent role that social workers engage in as representatives of the state. Over time, they have been subject to a constant pressure to assume a more coercive and interventionist role in policing individuals and families that are considered "deviant" (Langan & Lee, 1989), specifically single parents. This triangular relationship between the state, social workers and participants has led to some well-publicized social tragedies, such as children being left with a parent or placed in a foster home that proved dangerous to them. Social workers are all too often blamed for the tragedy, for either failing to intervene or being overzealous in their interventions. Thus, social workers are rethinking their relationship with the state, and in turn, in what manner and how much they should intervene in people's lives (Dalrymple & Burke, 2006). By the very nature of their role within organizations, social workers often (albeit unconsciously) contribute to the control and surveillance of the people they are seeking to assist (Healy, 2005).

While AOP has many strengths and offers many possibilities for social justice–oriented practice, there are also limitations that need to be considered. Some of the critiques of anti-oppressive practice include issues of power and powerlessness (Tew, 2006). The range and complexity of power relations that may be enacted in a social situation are not always identified in AOP. Concern with a structural analysis of power relations leaves limited room for recognizing that power relations at local levels may be different (Healey, 2005). The lack of clarity around the concept of power might lead to unclear and sometimes contradictory uses of the terms *empowerment* and *emancipation* in social work practice (Danso, 2009).

The "paradox of empowerment" is that the very act of trying to empower someone presumes a degree of power over that person (Bay-Cheng, Lewis, Stewart, & Malley, 2006). This paradox calls into question issues of privilege and disadvantage within the social worker/participant relationship. It raises questions like who has the insight and ability to empower, who needs to be empowered, and what does the state of being empowered even look like? Some argue that participants who are "empowered" by their social workers have unwillingly lost ground in their goals for autonomy and control over their own environment and existence (Simon, 1990). Over-emphasis on victims of power puts the social worker in the role of having to rescue the passive subjects of social oppression, through intervening on their behalf (Danso, 2009). From this lens, the social relations between social worker and participant can appear to be paternalistic (Dominelli, 2002). The "teacher-student" trap (Danso, 2009) raises the question of whether or not AOP can ever achieve equal power relationships (Dalrymple & Burke, 2006). Social work is structured as a helping profession so that social workers are imparting knowledge and resources to the participant. The concern is that AOP can never truly be anti-oppressive since the traditional training that social workers receive predisposes them to these dynamics and differentials (Sakamoto & Pitner, 2005).

In addition, participants lack a voice in the development of AOP theory and approach. Wilson & Beresford (2000) argue that anti-oppressive practice reflects the agenda and interests of academics in positions of power and privilege. Therefore, this argument contends that these academics have appropriated the voices and experiences of participants and marginalized groups (Wilson & Beresford, 2000; Pollack, 2004). Others have critiqued AOP as being too theoretical and not as accessible as some other approaches. Limitations include the lack of practice examples or "on the ground" work, especially in the United States. While its macro-level focus highlights the need to address structural issues, the limited explicit focus on micro-level implementation might lead social workers to neglect individual psychological and personal factors that may increase risk in some contexts (Danso, 2009). Others have also discussed the limited "prescriptive" approaches available for addressing immediate issues that arise within families and affect individuals (Payne, 2005; Sakamoto & Pitner, 2005). In addition, some social workers may feel guilt or blame that they aren't doing enough to change the social structures that perpetuate inequality (Sakamoto & Pitner, 2005). The social justice vision of AOP may seem overwhelming, overly ideological or too ambitious of a task to even attempt, thus discouraging social workers already burdened by increasing workloads.

AOP has also been criticized as another example of western hegemony. Although aboriginal and indigenous peoples have notions of social justice that mirror AOP, for the most part anti-oppressive practice is presented in the literature as a western and nonaboriginal concept. Thus, AOP may be considered just another form of "white" knowledge that colonizes or co-opts indigenous concepts. Alternatively, one might argue that anti-oppressive practice works in harmony with indigenous ways of thinking about social justice.

What does anti-oppressive practice mean to you? Do you see any other limitations of AOP?

STORIES FROM THE FIELD: SOCIAL JUSTICE

1. The Orientalism Express and Urban Trap Lines, by Chuck Fraser   p. 29

   Chuck Fraser writes two poems related to social justice issues. The first poem examines crucial social justice issues related to poverty, oppression, and the power that small groups of privileged elites wield in the lives of the majority. The second poem reflects on the impact of colonization on indigenous and First Nations populations (the First Nations are the various Aboriginal peoples in Canada who are neither Inuit nor Métis) and how this plays out in the lives of individuals in poverty struggling to survive in an urban landscape.

2. Where I Come From / My Journey of Survival and The Prisonification of Indian Women, by Stormy Ogden McCloud   p. 33

   In this poem and story, Stormy Ogden McCloud provides a context for her roots and background, thus informing us of the intersecting forms of oppression she has faced in her life. She describes the challenges she endured in prison as a result of her intersecting identities of race and gender. As an American Indian woman in the prison system, Stormy illustrates her journey of survival and resistance. Through both a micro and macro lens, she identifies how oppression and violence operate in the prison industrial complex, as well as throughout the history of oppression faced by Native people in North America.

3. Victim or Activist: Seeking Personal Change From a Different Perspective, by Charles Ray Cochran   p. 38

   In this story, Charles Ray Cochran, an undergraduate sociology student at the time of this writing, recounts the influence that a Licensed Clinical Social Worker (LCSW) had during a transitional period in his life. Charles shares how his identity as a gay man created tension in his personal and professional life, while simultaneously opening up the space for re-framing his personal struggles in a broader sociopolitical context. This interaction with his LCSW was pivotal to his growth and transformation as an emerging social worker.

4. Leveraging Privilege, by Choya Renata   p. 40

   This story describes the concept of leveraging privilege. Choya Renata provides various examples of how she uses her privilege to address structural oppression and institutional barriers in the lives of her participants. Through her work in the field of domestic violence, she provides strategies for navigating unjust, bureaucratic systems in a way that challenges stereotypes and assumptions about marginalized people.

5. Bringing Our Whole Selves: Storytelling as an Organizing Strategy, by Nitika Raj   p. 41

   This story describes the work of Resource Generation, an organization that works with youth who have wealth and class privilege. Nitika Raj discusses her work with these youth who engage in leveraging their resources and privilege for social change. She locates herself in the work she does by describing her own journey and how this informed her passion for working toward economic and racial justice. Through the development of a new racial justice program that organizes people of color with wealth, intersections of both privilege and oppression are brought to the forefront. Storytelling is used as an organizing tool to examine multiple experiences and identities, engage in individual transformation and take action toward collective, structural change.

1

THE ORIENTALISM EXPRESS

CHUCK FRASER

Subalterns huddle in streets
Like cattle on neo-con ranches
Sharing survival information
Homeless, hungry, and afraid
Self medicating
With alcohol and drugs
How else could one survive
And withstand the nightmares
Of the past and the ones coming
Social policies by stealth
Designed to eradicate them
From this good Earth...
For where else could they go?
Highland clearances, genocides,
Holocausts, ethnic cleansing,
I fear the Nazis are back!
Gramsci's warnings fell upon deaf years
Fascism is back in fashion
New global royalty rewrote the rules
Social murder committed around the world
Subalterns must wear the yellow letter "P"
In plain sight, above their hearts
It's easier to round them up
To take them somewhere safe...
Ice Caps melting, global warming,
Things are not as they seem
No need to panic!
Continue watching corporate media

We will edit and produce the "truth"
Anything else is fake
Churches encourage sheep to pray for
Bureaucrats, politicians and technocrats
Subalterns the yellow canaries
Trillions spent on bail-outs, star wars,
And earthly invasions for oil
Public surveillance increased
Once protected civil liberties taken
In order to protect us (from ourselves)
Foucault's warnings fell by the wayside
Like yesterdays political manifestos and poems
The volcanos of colonialism/elitism
Demand human sacrifices
The fires of hate and discrimination
Await the next good citizen
The one with the yellow "P"
Above the heart
Indicating that in fact
They have one,
Unlike those who crafted
This new social contract
To rid the world of the poor (first)
Be sure to read between the lions, and
Listen for messages of liberation
Between the sounds of jingling jewels
Many species have/are disappearing
From Earth, barely a word said
Is it that much of a stretch
Concerning the notion I've raised?
Neo-Liberals polish global jewellery
With corporate constitutions and
Trade deals designed to benefit the rich
At the expense of the poor

As it has always been
Some day at a higher court
An angel will ask a corporate CEO
About the global atrocities committed
In the name of profit and greed.
The CEO would reply: I was just following orders
From the global royalty, I never thought it
Would ever get that bad
The angel would reply:
It got that bad, when the first citizen
Died on your good streets
Paved with the headstones of the "others."

Urban Trap Lines

Urban trapper
Starts early
Picking up beverage cans
From garbage cans (urban traps)
Heads to the super market parking lot
Standing proud
Like his ancestors looking over the prairie
At the buffalo (before they were made extinct)
He sees four lone carts
Worth a quarter a piece
He rounds them up and collects the coins
Eight garbage cans to check
Fallen change to find
And more from kind hearted folks
Who like to 'street tithe' the poor
It's good for their souls…
Car Wash for lost Loonies
Left on the coin-box (big trap)
Takeout windows from fast-food places
Large cigarette butts to pick

Miles to travel before this Son is done

At the end of a long day

The wise urban trapper

Like the ones of old

Who brought furs to the trading post

Brings his bottles/cans to the depot

And collects their worth

He starts the long walk home

It was a good day

He made $35.78

Scrounged a pouch of tobacco,

For his pipe, the one grandfather gave him

Before he died while out checking traps

On their traditional land, before the clear-cut logging days

And residential schools

Its better this way he thought

I still have my freedom

One day I will go back to the land

And live the old way

Maybe the animals will have returned.

1. What are some of the social justice issues raised in the two poems?

2. Think about the roots of privilege and oppression illustrated in the chapter—what are some of the social categories the poems describe?

3. In the section on Indigenous and Postcolonial Social Justice, Spivak's question about the subaltern is presented. How is Chuck Fraser using the concept of the subaltern in his poem?

2

WHERE I COME FROM / MY JOURNEY OF SURVIVAL

STORMY OGDEN MCCLOUD

Where I come from:

> I come from those tears
> That my mom shed as she hid in the fields
> Her belly round with life
> As my dad chased after her
> With angry words and fist
> Because he was drunk
>
> I come from that anger
> That my dad held in his heart
> Because he was left behind
> To be raised by a white family
> Because his mother passed on
> Giving him life
>
> I come from the pain
> Of these two people
> That had the cards stacked against them
> From the beginning
> She was a white woman
> And he an Indian man
>
> I come from that bitter-sweet love
> Of these two people
> That brought a half-breed child
> Into this world

Where I come from:

> I come from that sweet burning
> As the first swallow of whiskey

Slides down my throat
Taking me along with it for 18 years

I come from that shame and fear
As I sit in a bath full of blood and cold water
Trying to wash away the pain
From my torn and beaten 12 year old body
After being raped by 4 classmates

I come from that special place
That I return to time and again
As the ones that say they love me
Hit, kick, shoot, and rape me
One more time

I come from that blood
That runs down my fingers
As I slide that razor blade
Across my wrist
One more time

Where I come from:

I come from too many bars
And back seats of cars
Too many lovers that had no names
And always
Not enough whiskey

I come from
I will never forget you my Sisters
As I leave them behind
At those prison gates

I come from
The mission system, the reservation system, boarding schools
Mental institutions, jails, prisons

Extermination, assimilation, relocation, self-determination

All meaning

GENOCIDE

Where I come from:

HEY! I'm Indian too

I just do not know what tribe

I think my great-grandmother was Cherokee

Can you teach me how to be Indian?

Can you give my an Indian name

Can you take me to a sweat lodge?

Hey! You think you can get me some of those casino monies?

Where I come from:

I come from the water

That travels over the rocks

That my Aunties listen to

Because they teach her the songs

That will heal our people

I come from that hot acorn soup and dried seaweed

That our women made

To feed the people

I come from the sounds

Of the elderberry clapper sticks

That our men play

As the women dance upon the lands

I come from

That pebble that Raven

Carried in his beak

Dropping it on the lands

That were given to my people

The Prisonification of Indian Women

In the warmth of my fantasy
I awake to the cold gray walls
Of my reality

These words echoed in my mind as the Judge read the sentence, "Ms. Ogden, you are to be sentenced for a period of 5 years to be served at the California Rehabilitation Center located in Norco." My reality is becoming devastatingly more common among the women of the United States. Women are the fastest growing segment of the prison population especially in California, which now has the distinction of having the most women prisoners in the nation. Historically, the most brutal methods of social control are directed at a society's most oppressed groups. And the most brutal form of social control in the United States is the state and federal prison system. The ones that are most likely to be sent to jail and prison are poor women and women of color. In North America a very high proportion of these people are American Indians.

The number of American Indian prisoners, especially the women, is nearly impossible to obtain. The major reason is the prison classification system, which in the majority of prisons classifies prisoners as White, Black, Hispanic, or Other.

> Located outside the door to my room was a small white 8x5 card that listed my last name, Ogden, my state number, W-20170, and my classification, Other. Every morning as I left for my job assignment, I would cross out Other and write AI. Then each afternoon when I returned for count there would be a new card with Other written on it. This went on for a few days when finally the CO approached me, "Next time, Ogden, it will be a write-up and a loss of good time." That next morning, before going to work, I found a permanent laundry marker, tore the card off the wall, and wrote on the wall, American Indian.

Women in prison are fighting to maintain a sense of self within a system that isolates and degrades, a system that is designed to punish. But, for the American Indian woman, we must also fight for our identity.

I write this as a California Indian woman, a tribal woman of Yokuts and Pomo ancestry. I also write as an ex-prisoner of the state of California and a survivor of colonization by the European powers. The history of colonization is a tragic one from the time of European contact to the present day.

Almost every aspect of life of Indian people has been subjected to the unrestricted jurisdiction of the United States. The history of relations between Indian nations and the United States has been marked by oppressive laws and policies designed to undermine the sovereignty of Indian nations and to weaken their culture. These laws were geared toward the total annihilation and then assimilation of Indian people into the mainstream dominant society. Native people have been imprisoned in many different forms, such as, Military forts, Missions, Reservations, Boarding schools, and now the State and Federal prisons. These can only be instruments of racism and a form of social control.

The criminalization and imprisonment of Native people can be interpreted as yet another attempt to control Indian lands and the ongoing attempt to deny Indian sovereignty, as we see by the alarming number of Native people that are being locked up on their own ancestral homelands. No Native person can ever forget that his or her homeland was taken and that they live in poverty on the margin of society, desperately fighting to hold on to their traditional ways of life. Keeping this in mind, it can be said that the Prison Industrial Complex was built right through the lives and the ancestral lands of the Indigenous people of this continent.

1. Stormy relates a story about her identity and the erasure of her identity in the prison system—how is the experience connected to personal and social identity as defined in the chapter?

2. How does Stormy resist individual, cultural, and institutional oppression while she is in prison?

3. In what ways have American Indians/Native Americans/First Nations Peoples experienced the five faces of oppression according to Iris Marion Young (1990): (1) exploitation; (2) marginalization; (3) powerlessness; (4) cultural imperialism; and (5) violence?

4. Are there ways that you have experienced an erasure of one or more of your identities?

3

VICTIM OR ACTIVIST: SEEKING PERSONAL CHANGE FROM A DIFFERENT PERSPECTIVE

CHARLES RAY COCHRAN

I recall one particular session with a social worker in New York during a trying time. I was struggling to end a relationship of seven years, having difficulty with my career—sensing my options were dwindling and feeling a loss of interest—and I was also probably leaving New York. In other words, I had all three of the most stressful things that can happen to an individual happening simultaneously.

I did not know how to move into the next phase of my life. And I was stuck searching for personal failures to all that was happening because, well, I believed that's what responsible people do: There was either something I did not possess or something I had done that brought me to this crisis point. I was a poor planner? Not ambitious enough? Impatient? Weak? Mentally ill? All of these life changes were most certainly a product of my own structural deficiencies and I spent months in a narcissistic spiral of self-investigation.

In my career, as a theater actor and director, the individuals in the theater company were almost exclusively heterosexual and there were definitely tensions. I had grown up with parents who did not approve of my sexual orientation and, so, this triggered a great deal of anxiety for me in the workplace as well. I was not in the closet with any of workmates, but the work I was doing, creative work, was deeply personal and revealed my gay positionality and I really felt that my personal inhibitions kept me from full expression. And because of my sexual orientation and the way that I expressed my gender, the opportunities for employment were few. (Contrary to the popular belief, heterosexism is very strong in the creative fields.)

At one point my therapist, Genna, a licensed clinical social worker, asked me if I really believed that my desire to leave my current work was based on a personal failing. I stated that I believed it was. She then responded by reframing my struggle within a broader, sociopolitical context. She was adamant that I engage in my environment from a different lens—if only briefly and for purely selfish reasons—so that I could better see and understand that some of the career struggles I was facing were rooted in a broader struggle for acceptance, creatively and otherwise, of LGBT individuals and their stories.

The first feeling that I recalled was relief and then a strange kind of elation. Was it possible that I was not at fault and my desire to leave was really about self-preservation? I'm embarrassed to even admit this now, because it speaks to such self-centered focus, but when I left the session that day, I really began to mourn the lost time: Unencumbered and misdirected self-investigation only feeds on itself, but the work that she had insisted I do was far more complex, less about pathology and *far more difficult*.

On some level it's easier to change ourselves; it's more difficult to change the taken-for-granted worlds we inhabit. I was being asked to engage my environment and to struggle with it and to see it for what it was—to stop believing that I was the maker of all that was wrong—a narcissistic position to be sure. By doing so, I was empowered to make decisions about where I wanted to be: I could either reimagine myself in my work and no longer victimized because I would be working for social change, or I could move on. It was truly powerful.

And now that I'm becoming a social worker, I think about that story quite often. I think about our responsibility to really empower people by linking them back to their lives from a very different lens: to see their lives contextualized within their culture and within the sociopolitical structures that oppress—and they can be subtle ones, to be sure. It's my belief that the mythologies of "individualism" in our culture are so institutionalized and so embedded, that we are not only required to *understand* the macro, meso and micro processes of our work and work for change on all levels; we are also required to inspire the client populations we serve in a manner that educates them about those same structural oppressions that work down on them.

1. What forms of privilege and/or oppression are at play in this experience?

2. How does Charles shift his perspective from personal blame to acknowledging the role of social and structural oppression?

3. How do the social worker's actions reflect an anti-oppressive perspective?

4

LEVERAGING PRIVILEGE

CHOYA RENATA

The nature of privilege is such that, when we have privilege and we do nothing with it, its default position is to reinforce existing systems of power, privilege and oppression. Doing nothing, being silent, is not a neutral position; it is a position from which our unexamined privilege fundamentally supports dominant culture, supports the status quo. In order for our privilege to mean something else, we must leverage it. What does leveraging privilege mean? It means a great, almost physical effort to lend privilege to the work and efforts of people who haven't got it. In a literal sense, it may mean sharing information we've had access to because of privilege; modeling systems navigation; holding the doors of eligibility open as wide as possible; appealing destructive decisions; sharing, with permission, someone's story when others don't believe them or hear them; reminding people they're not messed up, it's the system that is a mess, and it's that way for a reason—to perpetuate itself as a dominant power structure.

Sometimes a thing we can do is help a social work participant speak in the language of systems, even though that language may be made of bullshit. For example, when a survivor of domestic violence is applying for a restraining order, you can tell her, "Here is what must be true, so you will need to frame your experience in this way in order for the powers that be to understand your story." In doing this, we must be careful not to say or imply that it's is a better way for her to speak. It's often less true; but it is a way for her to get what she needs, despite systemic barriers.

Another way to understand this is: If a housing program denies a woman on the basis that she has a drug-related criminal record, create an appeal. Did she go to treatment? Collect records, letters from professionals, a letter from her explaining how things were then and how they differ now, and a letter from you. Paint a picture of a human being. Until you help mediate her experience into a form that the powers that be can perceive, she is just another in the monolithic group that makes up "criminals" or "drug users," and individuals working in the housing program may be trained to fear that stereotype. But you know she's a human being, and one deserving of basic human rights. Help the powers that be to see her as a human being, even when that means conforming a little to their weirdly centrist cultural norms. This is how you leverage privilege.

1. How does Choya leverage her own privilege in her work with survivors of intimate personal violence?

2. How might you leverage your privilege at your agency with the people you work with?

5

BRINGING OUR WHOLE SELVES: STORYTELLING AS AN ORGANIZING STRATEGY

NITIKA RAJ

Since 1994, Resource Generation (RG) has been organizing young people (ages 18-35) with wealth and class privilege to become transformative leaders. We envision a world in which all communities are powerful, healthy and living in alignment with the planet—a world that is racially and economically just, in which wealth, land and power are collectively shared. We have a national staff of seven and organize through chapters in various cities run by local member leaders. The broader RG community includes people of all ages and class backgrounds who support the role that young people with wealth play in social change.

At RG, we have a tradition of closing out our annual conference with a powerful circle. One hundred people hold hands, and we start by telling the person next to us, "My liberation depends on your liberation." It continues until each person has spoken, and each person has received the gift of being spoken to.

My story is your story.

My Journey as an Organizer

Our journeys begin before we are born. When India gained independence from British colonization in 1947, the stage was set for generations to come. My parents were born in the early 1950s, in a newly free and impoverished country. Their resilience and struggle is part of my heritage. Their educations and arranged marriage and migration to Kuwait are part of my spirit. Their rapid class mobility through professional jobs and then starting a business are part of my story and inheritance.

I grew up mostly in Kuwait and relocated to India briefly during the Gulf war of 1990. I always knew that I would go abroad for college, a class pattern for an entire generation of my peers. I graduated college in the U.S. as a computer science major, but I spent those years exploring sexism, sexual harassment and violence against women. I came into my own as a survivor of child sexual abuse, and I started graduate school in social work.

After 7 years, the vicarious trauma and internal organizational challenges in social work left me burned out. I realized that survivors knew what they needed and wanted, but often didn't have the financial access, immigration status, or social and family support to make their own choices. My healing had been possible because of my access to resources. I became fiercely politicized to work for economic and racial justice.

I only believe in one kind of justice—the kind where all people have equal access, equal opportunities, and the resources to implement empowered choices within a balanced context of individual and community well-being. I believe in the kind of justice where all people have a genuinely equal chance of thriving.

My personal, political, and professional journeys cannot be separated. As I became more class conscious, I was also coming into my queerness, getting married, getting divorced, and finally becoming financially independent of my family—all in the year I graduated with a MSW. A period of intense chaos and struggle allowed the kind of collapse from which phoenixes rise. I absorbed these experiences and started manifesting extreme illness and pain. After a life-changing diagnosis, I continued with my path of working for social change, healing from trauma, and writing to tell the story.

I share this story because the learnings and praxis are ongoing. I see my role at RG as building the right kind of container, within which multitudes of stories can be held, and collectively we can figure out the right actions forward. On a daily basis, as I organize other young people of color with wealth, I hear more stories of struggle, survival, trauma, abuse, addiction, spirituality, disability, chronic illness, healing, and consciousness. I see how our stories are intertwined and also different. We cannot generalize our experiences, so it is important to share them in their wholeness in order for others to find resonance and dissonance. To organize is to get a group aligned on an issue by asking critical questions, building our shared knowledge, and taking collective action. Making visible is the necessary first step to much social change work.

The Intersection of Economic and Racial Justice

The history of the unequal distribution of wealth in the U.S. is a history of racism. It is impossible to separate the two—race was constructed for the economic gain of white people at the expense of people of color. It's a history that continually needs to be named: a history of genocide, enslavement, internment, xenophobia, and ongoing racial violence. It's also a history of government policies that institutionalized racism like the Homestead Act, redlining, and the GI Bill. And all of this violence has always had a purpose: the accumulation of land, wealth and power.

–Elspeth Gilmore (2012), *Why Resource Generation Is Committed to Racial Justice*

Racial justice has been implicit within RG's long history of work for economic justice. However, we reached a point where it needed to become much more explicit to strengthen our impact. It is a common occurrence to mistake organizing people of color (or racially diversifying a base) for racial justice work. But, we see a large part of RG as the behind-the-scenes and internal work that makes it possible for people of color to stay engaged, and not be driven away by institutional racism.

Since RG's history has been rooted in the experiences of white inheritors, we have had to intentionally examine the unique ways in which communities of color have been barred from and also able to accumulate wealth. The challenge we pose to white wealthy members is to give away unearned wealth and to examine how structural racism has benefitted them. The challenge for wealthy folks of color is to examine how wealth accumulation has divided us from communities of color, to examine horizontal oppression, and to move toward solidarity with all people of color.

Class privilege may have buffered some of the effects of racism in our lives, but it does not protect us from it. Our communities do need to build assets to get out of poverty and thrive, but how do we do this in a way that does not exploit people or the planet?

My job at RG is organizing young people of color who have wealth. As a woman of color leading this newly created program, I often found myself fielding questions about all things relating to people of color and racial justice. Frustrated and overwhelmed, I began to push back. That reaction led to the creation of a Racial Justice Staff Committee that included me, a white program staff member who was also a national organizer, and the white executive director of RG. We then created another racial justice committee for our annual conference to lead structural changes that centered on multi-racial experience rather than a white majority center. Although people of color from various class backgrounds have always been part of the fabric and leadership of Resource Generation, this next phase required greater internal work.

Money Stories: A Powerful Organizing Tool

RG's core organizing strategy is storytelling. Through telling stories, we can reclaim our whole selves at an individual level and also see the full picture at a macro level. Without telling and hearing these stories, our strategies cannot be as effective as they need to be.

One of the challenges of organizing a wealthy class-privileged community is dealing with the guilt that can come with privilege. As we invite people to bring their whole selves, we do so lovingly with the belief that facing our privilege allows us to heal from internalized oppression and take action from an empowered place.

Every RG space includes what we call "money stories." This is the story of how a person or their family came to accumulate wealth. Because class and money are such taboo topics in our society, talking about them can generate both fear and a great opening. In local chapters, members get plugged into praxis groups, which come from the concept named by Paulo Freire: an iterative cycle of theory and practice which continue to build on each other. Small groups of 5-7 people meet monthly for about 6 months to discuss issues of class and money. This structure allows for deeper relationships within which challenging topics can be discussed honestly, and members can receive peer support, feedback, and accountability in moving forward on desired goals. Struggles and goals range from having a challenging discussion with a family member, to making a social change giving plan.

Human beings have the capacity to hold a multitude of seemingly contradictory experiences, without identifying a single, essential "truth." By sharing the fullness of our stories, we invite people into the complexity of our experiences without having to put race or class or any one identity at the forefront. This experience allows for connection and relationship-building across differences, which is critical for building a mass base that can act for social change. It also allows us to realize the gaps in information or family history that we would like to fill, and many people use the opportunity to begin a journey of asking questions that continues long after they age out of RG's programming.

Yes, people age out at 35 (or 40 if they are involved in family philanthropy)! They become alums and continue to do all they did with RG's support—ask questions, make decisions about wealth redistribution and socially responsible investing, organize their peers and families, campaign for progressive taxes on the rich, organize within philanthropic institutions, and work in cross-class and multi-racial partnerships to advocate for justice.

Poetry rests at another intersection of social justice work—the ability to name things that can otherwise only be felt. I leave you with this poem written during weekly writing time at Resource Generation, one of my favorite staff practices.

choices

dis/ability

ability

able

i am able to do something

i am not able to do something

class privilege is an ability

able-bodied

body is able to do something

body is not able to do something

if i am able to do something

it takes a lot of things, people, privileges to make that happen

it helps if you're white

it helps if you have money

it helps if you speak English

it helps if you are not Muslim, Sikh, Arab or Middle Eastern

or Black

or Latino

or indigenous

or any shade of Not White

or can't be made White like Italians Jews the Irish

it helps if your body doesn't hurt when you move, or breathe

it helps if you have paid time off on a day when you feel cloudy

it helps if you can afford therapy

or retail therapy

it helps if you have choices

it helps if you have a community of people to ask for help

or can pay for

support with childcare

or shopping for groceries

or medication

or meditation

or yoga

or warm clothes

it helps if you have an education

it helps if you have a family who can provide for you

it actually really helps to have a lot of money

it helps if you have tax benefits

from being married

or being wealthy

or being in control of making tax policies

it helps so much

to have help

wealthy people can use money to get help

isolate

we are living/viewing life from the vantage point of a castle

or a penthouse in manhattan

people with disabilities are more connected with our need for help, for each other

people with disabilities AND wealth have some difficult choices to make

use money? to access care

or interdependence?

i don't know what the right answers are

because there could be so many

and all available choices could be exercised

and still not feel right or be right for someone, or a people, or a time and place

perhaps we need to be asking different questions.

1. What are some of the intersecting identities that Nitika discloses in her personal account and poetry?

2. What are some of the intersecting identities that you hold and how do they offer positions of privilege or represent marginalized identities?

3. What are some of the tools that RG uses to examine multiple identities in order to both leverage privilege and dismantle oppression?

DISCUSSION QUESTIONS

1. Describe the common themes that emerge throughout these stories of social justice.

2. How do these stories speak to the challenges of doing social justice work?

3. How do you envision incorporating social justice work in your own practice taking into account issues of privilege and oppression based on your intersecting identities?

ACTIVITIES

1. Taking into consideration the different theoretical approaches to social justice discussed in this chapter (distributive, recognition, capabilities, indigenous and postcolonial, post-modern, and religious), create a table comparing the strengths and limitations of each approach and the ways in which they intersect with each other as well as diverge from one another.

2. Using Nussbaum's list of ten central human capabilities, examine how each one is applicable to you and to an individual or group you work with in a field placement capacity. What are the micro, mezzo, and macro factors that might be necessary to fulfill each capability?

ADDITIONAL RESOURCES

Websites

Radical Social Work News (US) http://www.rankandfiler.net/

Social Work Action Alliance (US) http://www.socialwelfareactionalliance.org/index.html

Social Work Action Network (GB) http://www.socialworkfuture.org/

Films

American history X (1998). T. Kaye

Ask not (2009). J. Symons

Banished (2008). M. Williams

Bastard out of Carolina (1996). A. Huston

Crash (2004). P. Haggis

Rabbit-proof fence (2002). P. Noyce

Surviving Katrina (2006). J. Dent

The believer (2001). H. Bean

The Black power mixtape 1967–1975 (2011). G. H. Olsson

The house I live in (2012). E. Jarecki

Tulia, Texas (2008). C. Herrman & K. Whalen

Twilight Los Angeles (2000). M. Levin

When the levees broke: A requiem in four acts (2006). D. Asevedo, J. Asevedo, & S. S. Alexander

Books

Alexander, M. (2012). *The new Jim Crow: Mass incarceration in the age of colorblindness*. New York: The New Press.

Baldwin, J. (1993). *The fire next time*. New York: Vintage Books.

Freire, P. (2000). *Pedagogy of the oppressed*. New York: Bloomsbury.

hooks, b. (2000). *Where we stand: Class matters*. New York: Routledge Press.

Kivel, P. (2011). *Uprooting racism: How white people can work for social justice*. Gabriola Island, BC, Canada: New Society Publishers.

Moraga, C., & Anzuldua, G. (2002). *This bridge called my back: Writings by radical women of color*. Bloomington, IN: Third Woman Press.

Segrest, M. (1994). *Memoir of a race traitor*. Cambridge, MA: South End Press.

Sibley, J. H. (2011). *Being and homelessness: Notes from an underground artist*. Greenwich, CT: Wordsworth Greenwich Press.

Smith, A. (2005). *Conquest: Sexual violence and American Indian genocide*. Cambridge, MA: South End Press.

Tea, M. (2004). *Without a net: The female experience of growing up working class*. Berkeley, CA: Seal Press.

West, C. (2001). *Race matters*. Boston: Beacon Press.

Zinn, H. (2003). A people's history of the United States: 1492 to present. New York: Harper Collins.

2

Social Work
Values and Ethics

V alues and ethics often go hand in hand, and perhaps for good reason. Our values are intimately connected to who we are, how we view ourselves and others, and the actions we take in the world. Ethics typically stem from our value base—for example, what we value drives how we discern "right" from "wrong," and how we make decisions.

While there is a significant body of philosophical and theoretical work on ethics and ethical standards in general, as well as how they relate to social work, there tends to be a lesser focus on values. One reason for this may be that ethics are more tangible or easily defined, yet values are the foundation for decision making.

VALUES IN SOCIAL WORK

Throughout your education and career in social work, you will likely hear that social work is a uniquely "value laden" endeavor. While this has a ring of truth to it, it can be said that all we do in our lives stems from what we value and believe. What may be unique to social change work is that we are working with not only our own set of values, but with the values of individuals, groups, and communities that we come into contact with and those values often take center stage—whether we are aware of this or not. Not only will these values be diverse and dynamic, they may also create conflict or tension.

Imagine you are attending a community meeting as a youth advocate and the discussion is focused on a proposal for a new youth center. The community members present a variety of different positions and concerns—1) how much supervision will the youth have, 2) how late will the center stay open, 3) what impact will the increased traffic have on the surrounding community, 4) will this impact crime in the area—either positively or negatively, 5) how will the center be funded, among others. You, on the other hand, have a commitment to hearing from the youth about their ideas and concerns and they are noticeably absent from the discussion. Additionally, you are concerned about the proposed location, as it is in a relatively affluent neighborhood and the youth that you work with more directly live in a surrounding neighborhood. Given the historical tensions between youth in the adjoining neighborhoods, you believe that the proposed location may discourage some of the youth from utilizing the center.

> What are some of the values prompting the community member concerns and your concerns? How are these values interconnected or at odds with one another?

Knowing what we value as individuals, groups, and communities is essential for collaboration and social change work. Clarification exercises specific to values are commonly used for this purpose. The exercises are used by therapists, educators, life coaches, organizational consultants, and community organizers. These exercises can take a number of forms, from checking off and reflecting on a list of values; answering questions related to a scenario that may reveal underlying values; or examining past accomplishments and future goals. We don't typically examine our values, even though they contribute significantly to who we are and how we make choices throughout our lives.

> As a group or individually, create a comprehensive list of potential values that a person involved in social justice work might hold, whether they are your own values or not. Then, on your own, check off those that you most identify with. Here you can be creative—you can simply choose all the values that speak to you; you could rank the values from most important to least important; or you could group them in some fashion—core values, secondary values, and so on. Once you have sorted through the list, examine where you learned those values. For many people, family, school, peers, and religious or spiritual beliefs are significant factors in their development of a value system; yet, media, the political environment, and cultural and social factors also influence us. If you share your results with the group, you will notice that students identify with different values and assign priorities differently.
>   Reflecting on the two exercises above, identify some of the ways in which our values and the values of the people we work with may strengthen and challenge the working relationship.

[handwritten note in right margin: Potential assignment]

Historical Social Work Values

Looking back at the history of social work it is possible to identify how certain values have influenced the field and how values have shifted in prominence over time. If we consider the origins of social work in the United States in the late 1800s to the early 1900s and use the Charity Organization Societies and the Settlement House Movement as our foundation, we discover a number of differing values and viewpoints that have molded the profession.

Charity Organization Societies

Charity Organization Societies (COS) developed in the United States in 1877, close to ten years after the first COS in Britain was organized in 1869. Historians have suggested that the COS developed to address the burgeoning poverty in urban areas which was becoming more populated due to industrialization and immigration/migration patterns. Prior to this time, charity and social service support were more likely the province of churches. Arising from concerns that direct aid would lead to the "pauperization" of the recipients, Charity Organization Societies decided that to stem the tide of poverty, it was necessary to regulate aid and to determine who was "worthy" of such aid.

COS services were based on providing "friendly visitors" to families in need. These friendly visitors would teach families how to be thrifty and work hard, while, through their own example, also encouraging "moral uplift." COS prioritized objectivity and professional training of the staff providing services and were influenced by theories of social Darwinism (Hansan, n.d. a).

In her book, *Friendly Visiting among the Poor,* Mary Richmond gives this example of the role of a friendly visitor:

> There is a deep satisfaction in protecting such families from the careless, patronizing charity of the thoughtless almsgiver, whose unsteady hand would give them a feast to-day and a famine to-morrow. There is deep satisfaction in coöperating with such families to conquer difficulties. There is a deeper satisfaction, however, in turning a sham home into a real one; in teaching the slatternly, irresponsible mother the pleasure of a cleanly, well-ordered home; in helping a man who has lost his sense of responsibility toward wife and children to regain it. Even at the risk of drawing a too gloomy picture, I dwell in this chapter, therefore, upon the husband and father who is either lazy or drunken or both. (1907, para. 3)

An 1899 article examining the economic aspects of Charity Organization Societies highlighted three core purposes (Prevey, 1899):

- Cooperation: a way to create a centralized system of charity so as to avoid duplication of services.
- Adequate knowledge: an information gathering process in which the friendly visitors would assess family circumstances as a way to "detect frauds and determine what kind of aid is needed" (Prevey, 1899, p. 2). This assessment process was necessary because "often the thing which the poor think they need would be harmful to them, while a kindly investigation will reveal some other way in which they can be permanently helped" (Prevey, 1899, p. 2).
- Personal service: the core of the friendly visitor philosophy, described as:

> The thing which distinguishes charity organization is simply the substitution of a helpful form of visiting from a harmful one. The common fault with ordinary

visiting by the well-to-do among the poor is that they go as almsgivers. The poor are discouraged from making the best of things because it diminishes their chances of obtaining alms. The friendly visitors of the charity organization society are not allowed to give alms. They go not only to give good advice and to instruct, but to carry something of the higher life to those whose advantages are less. . . . The contact of rich and poor, not in the position of the patron and dependent, but as friends, is of mutual benefit. It tends to remove ill feeling between the classes, encourages and uplifts the poor and broadens the sympathies of the rich. (Prevey, 1899, p. 3)

In the first chapter, "General Suggestions for Friendly Visitors," of the 1883 *Handbook for Friendly Visitors Among the Poor* the majority of the 21 initial suggestions focus on the role of the visitor to provide "uplift" and hope while teaching the poor to be thrifty. While a couple of the suggestions do mention informing the poor of their rights (as tenants for example), the primary message is to be thrifty, make do, and become more moral as a way of coping and enhancing your life in poverty. For example, suggestion number 19 states:

The poorest poor are those who *have no wholesome contact with society or with each other.* They are those who have fallen into a sordid, isolated, and indifferent life, which is more animal than human. Your first aim should be to strengthen their family ties, "to turn the hearts of the fathers to the children," of husband to wife. Seek to awaken and cherish their home affections, to cultivate courtesy of speech and manner, and to prompt the little mutual sacrifices which make life gracious; and encourage every effort to make home a pleasant and attractive place. (Charity Organization Society of the City of New York, 1883, p. 5)

> While these excerpts give insight into the COS philosophy regarding causes and solutions for poverty, they also shine a light on values that underpin the philosophy of the Charity Organization Society movement—what values do you see inherent in these writings?

Settlement House Movement

The Settlement House Movement (SHM) in the United States was directly influenced by the first settlement house, Toynbee Hall that was established in East London in 1884. Initially, the vision of the "settlers" was to engage in research about poverty and aid to those in poverty (through moral uplift) by settling in impoverished neighborhoods. After U.S. social workers visited Toynbee Hall, a number of settlement houses were developed in the United States, including the Neighborhood Guild in 1886 on the Lower East Side of New York City founded by Stanton A. Coit, and Hull House on the West Side of Chicago founded in 1889 by Jane Addams and Ellen Gates Starr.

While their initial philosophy of providing support to needy families through positive role modeling was similar to the COS philosophy, the philosophy and methods of the SHM shifted as a result of observing the actual living conditions in the urban "slums." The settlement house workers (or "residents") in the United States, often led by women, focused significant efforts on research, which ultimately led to advocacy and social reform work (Hansan, n.d. b).

Jane Addams, in her essay "The Subjective Necessity for Social Settlement," writes:

> The Settlement then, is an experimental effort to aid in the solution of the social and industrial problems which are engendered by the modern conditions of life in a great city. It insists that these problems are not confined to any one portion of a city. It is an attempt to relieve, at the same time, the over-accumulation at one end of society and the destitution at the other; but it assumes that this over-accumulation and destitution is most sorely felt in the things that pertain to social and educational privileges. From its very nature it can stand for no political or social propaganda. It must, in a sense, give the warm welcome of an inn to all such propaganda, if perchance one of them be found an angel. The only thing to be dreaded in the Settlement is that it lose its flexibility, its power of quick adaptation, its readiness to change its methods as its environment may demand. It must be open to conviction and must have a deep and abiding sense of tolerance. It must be hospitable and ready for experiment. It should demand from its residents a scientific patience in the accumulation of facts and the steady holding of their sympathies as one of the best instruments for that accumulation. It must be grounded in a philosophy whose foundation is on the solidarity of the human race, a philosophy which will not waver when the race happens to be represented by a drunken woman or an idiot boy. Its residents must be emptied of all conceit of opinion and all self-assertion, and ready to arouse and interpret the public opinion of their neighborhood. They must be content to live quietly side by side with their neighbors, until they grow into a sense of relationship and mutual interests. Their neighbors are held apart by differences of race and language which the residents can more easily overcome. They are bound to see the needs of their neighborhood as a whole, to furnish data for legislation, and to use their influence to secure it. In short, residents are pledged to devote themselves to the duties of good citizenship and to the arousing of the social energies which too largely lie dormant in every neighborhood given over to industrialism.

Like the writings of the Charity Organization Societies, Addams's essay hints both at theories about poverty and at values of the Settlement House Movement and the workers who chose to live as residents in the settlement houses. What are some of the values you can identify in the Addams essay? How do they compare and contrast with those of the COS writings?

They are bound to regard the entire life of their city as organic, to make an effort to unify it, and to protest against its over-differentiation. (1892, pp. 126–127)

Contemporary Social Work Values

Social workers are expected to become familiar with values of the profession defined by the National Association of Social Work (NASW) and the Council on Social Work Education (CSWE). These values were initially based in the historical social work values, but have continued to evolve. Other contemporary social work groups have further extended professional values.

The NASW highlights social work values in the preamble of its *Code of Ethics*:

> The mission of the social work profession is rooted in a set of core values. These core values, embraced by social workers throughout the profession's history are the foundation of social work's unique purpose and perspective:
> - Service
> - Social justice
> - Dignity and worth of the person
> - Importance of human relationships
> - Integrity
> - Competence
>
> This constellation of core values reflects what is unique to the social work profession. Core values, and the principles that flow from them, must be balanced within the context and complexity of the human experience. (NASW, 2008, para. 7)

In the 2008 version of CSWE's *Educational Policy and Accreditation Standards,* social work values are listed as:

> Service, social justice, the dignity and worth of the person, the importance of human relationships, integrity, competence, human rights, and scientific inquiry are among the core values of social work. These values underpin the explicit and implicit curriculum and frame the profession's commitment to respect for all people and the quest for social and economic justice. (p. 2)

CSWE notes that the first six values listed are based in NASW values; human rights and scientific inquiry are core values added by CSWE.

The International Federation of Social Workers (IFSW) indicates that social work "values are based on the respect for the equality, worth, and dignity of all people" (2012, para. 3). Clearly there are significant overlaps in the values that are highlighted in values statements by NASW, CSWE, and the IFSW.

Reviewing additional values statements by other social work organizations has the potential to provide a more expansive ground to consider anti-oppressive social work values. For example, the National Association of Black Social Workers (NABSW), established in 1968, has prioritized advocacy work to "address social issues and concerns of the Black community" (NABSW, 2012a, para. 1). The mission of NABSW indicates that their vision is guided by the principles of the Nguzo Saba, which are unity, self-determination, collective work and responsibility, cooperative economics, purpose, creativity, and faith, and the seven cardinal virtues of Ma'at, which are right, truth, justice, order, reciprocity, balance, and harmony (NABSW, 2012b, para.2). (The Nguzo Saba are the seven principles found in the celebration of Kwanzaa. Ma'at is a philosophical and spiritual system that is a component of Egyptian cosmology.)

The Radical Social Work Group (RSWG), a New York City–based group that started meeting in 2008, lists the following values:

- Anti-racist, anti-oppressive social work practice that challenges the institutions of which social work is a part.
- Being accountable to the people we work for, to each other, ourselves and the planet. Being allies.
- We struggle to go beyond being "anti" to working toward the creation of something.
- Basing our work on the common values of human rights and social justice.
- Moving beyond our fears and being independent of the institutions that use social work and social workers as a means of control.
- Creating a world view that doesn't box people in.
- Creating a space free of coercion; respecting one another's self-determination: politics, identity and choices.
- Creating a practice that really respects human beings as human beings.
- Honoring culture, ethnicity, race, class, gender, sexual orientation, "crazy"/ "not crazy."
- We are committed to a true democracy (and what that might mean or look like); transparency.
- We understand that there's a fight to be had within social work schools to transform the field and combat conservatism.

We will not reduce human beings to "cases" to be "managed," manipulated or coerced, or ourselves to mere "workers." (n.d., para. 5)

How do these various statements of values intersect or contrast with one another? How do they compare to the values you identified in the COS and SHM writings and with the values you identified for yourself?

Progressive and Anti-Oppressive Values

In 2008, the Commonweal Institute, a progressive think tank, published "Modern Progressive Values: Realizing America's Potential," which outlined three sets of values culled from a variety of sources. Their work was based on George Lakoff's call for progressives to develop a set of shared values to counter the tendency for the political left to build their platform on issues rather than values (Gillette, 2008).

While these values can have varied meanings to people based on their individual life histories, cultures, locations, and political ideologies, the institute identifies progressive values as falling into the following three categories:

- Freedom/Security which relates to the balance between individual rights and individual protections (typically vis-à-vis the government)
- Community/The Commons which refers to how groups interact and share resources with one another
- Truth/Justice which is concerned with rules that "mediate between individuals and groups" (Gillette, 2008, p. 13).

Social work has typically leaned more toward liberal ideology with its focus on social justice and rights, although each set of values can be framed in either a liberal or conservative framework.

Consider the value of freedom. From a liberal perspective, it tends to refer to freedom of choice and speech and self-determination. These stem from the idea that individuals have civil liberties and that the government has a role in providing and protecting these rights as long as others are not deprived of their own individual rights in the process. From a conservative perspective, however, it can also mean freedom from government taxation, which allows people to be free to make money without government interference. It also suggests freedom from governmental regulations in the corporate sector. This position is a dilemma from the liberal perspective, because an unfettered market is perceived to cause significant deprivation to individuals and communities through environmental degradation, increased economic disparities, and rewards to the small percentage of elites in society.

> Think about how each term in the values pairs can have a variety of meanings depending on individual beliefs and ideological perspectives.

To summarize, AOP social workers and theorists typically highlight values of equality, social justice, self-reflexivity, self-determination, diversity, power sharing, inclusion, consciousness-raising, alliance building, social change, and activism (Dalrymple & Burke, 1995; Dominelli, 2002a; Larson, 2008).

Additional values that are crucial to a dynamic and critical anti-oppressive practice are humility and "not knowing." Since emancipatory practice highlights the importance of examining power and privilege, and working toward dismantling oppressive structures, it is imperative that social workers who approach their work from this framework are able to appreciate the value of questioning and of not being the "expert."

> One way to counteract the tendency to represent ourselves as "the experts" is to honestly evaluate the actions of our organizations, our profession, and ourselves—do they truly actualize the values we promote? How do we define these values and how would the individuals and communities we work with define them?

Critical Reflectivity on Values

Much of the critique of AOP (Wilson & Beresford, 2000), and social work in general, suggests that situating the profession in values, such as social justice and equality, without on going critical reflection, can become merely rhetorical and perpetuate injustices that those values purport to address. To combat this tendency, Mary Ellen Kondrat (1999) developed a model for "practitioner self-awareness" that is well suited to anti-oppressive and emancipatory social work practice.

Kondrat's model of critical reflectivity identifies three types of questions—questions about "the world," "my world," and "correspondences and contradictions"—that can prompt a more complex examination of micro and macro issues related to values and beliefs. Image 2.1 lists these questions.

Image 2.1   Questions for Practitioner Self-Awareness

Questions about "the world"

- What are the structures of my society, in particular, those structures related to power, inequality, and marginalization?
- On what basis are these structures rationalized by members of society?
- What social behaviors, values, or assumptions hold such structures in place?
- What is my location in relation to each of these structures? What do I know about how people in my location are supposed to act with regard to others in the same location (location in relation to the social categories class, race, power, gender or other) or toward those in other social groups?
- Who benefits from such structural arrangements and who loses? How do I benefit or lose?
- In what ways do my assumptions and activities contribute to the maintenance or transformation of such social structures?

- What have I discovered (what can I discover) about the extended structural consequences of my social actions and that of others?

Questions about "my world"

- What do I believe about myself, my place in the world, and about the place of people like or different from me?
- What assumptions do I make and what values do I hold about my social world and its structures, including structures of systematic domination and inequality?
- What is my understanding about how to act in relation to someone who belongs to a different class, race, status, and so forth? And from what sources have I learned these social lessons?
- Which of these structural arrangements have I internalized? How do I rationalize them? How do my actions reflect or repudiate these beliefs and values?

Questions about the ways I understand "my world" and "the world"

- In what ways are my values, beliefs, attitudes, assumptions, and self-understandings reflections of economic, social, educational, or other systems?
- To what extent do I accept (or accept uncritically) the values, beliefs, assumptions, and prescriptions I have received as a result of my socialization into particular communities?
- To what extent do I accept the structures of my society as unproblematic, especially structures related to power and privilege? To what extent am I able or willing to raise questions about them?
- Are there inconsistencies or distortions between my received beliefs/assumptions and the concrete conditions of individual and group life? How do I account for these contradictions?
- In what ways are my perspectives, beliefs, values, and assumptions related to my self-interest and perceived needs?
- Are there contradictions between my avowed intentions or values and the structural outcomes of my activities?

Source: Kondrat, M. E. (1999). Who is the "self" in self-aware: Professional self-awareness from a critical theory perspective. *Social Services Review*, 73(4), 451–477. Reprinted by permission of University of Chicago Press.

Building on your earlier values assessment, use Kondrat's series of questions in Image 2.1 to more fully examine your values and beliefs. Focus on how these values and beliefs reflect social location, power and privilege, and experiences of marginalization.

ETHICS THEORY IN SOCIAL WORK

At its core, the study of ethics prompts us to discern between right and wrong or good and bad.

> Stop here for a moment and ask yourself if any challenges immediately come to mind when you imagine making these distinctions. Perhaps you immediately thought about the subjective nature of "goodness" or "badness" (or "right" or "wrong"). How do we make these determinations? Who decides what is right and wrong? Is there a universal "goodness"? Is something always good or bad or does it depend on the context in which that event or action is occurring? What influences do history, culture, and/or religion have on our sense of goodness and morality?

Ethics, or moral philosophy, has roots in Northern/Western philosophy. In various regions of the global South/East, there is no direct equivalent to the term *ethics,* although there are clear concepts of morality and right and wrong. For instance, in the global South/East and for some indigenous communities, ethics are situated in the morality and character of the individual—a good person—whereas in global North/West, ethics are typically situated in the actions of the individual.

Ethics can be viewed through a variety of lenses: principle-based; character- and relationship-based, which includes virtue-based ethics and the ethics of care; and narrative and case-based ethics, which utilizes stories and narrative accounts to make ethical decisions. Until recently, principle-based ethics have taken center stage in social work.

Principle-Based Ethics

The focus of principle-based ethics is to identify universal ethical principles. Frederic Reamer, who has made significant contributions to the examination of ethics in social work from a Northern/Western perspective, considers metaethics and normative ethics to be the two branches of ethical inquiry within this tradition (Reamer, 1993). Another way of conceptualizing these two components is to imagine that metaethics is the roots on which normative ethics branch, as shown in Image 2.2. Normative ethics grow out of the metaethical roots while applied ethics are based on both metaethics and normative ethics.

Metaethics

Metaethics requires that we examine the core ethical concepts, such as right and wrong, fairness, justice, and duty. What do we actually mean by the terms we apply to ethics and ethical decision-making? We may often take certain terms for granted until these types of questions are posed. For example, if we agree that as human beings we are ethically bound to treat others fairly, metaethical inquiry asks, what is meant by "fairness" and how do we validate the meaning of fairness?

Image 2.2 visually depicts the two schools of metaethics—cognitivism and noncognitivism—and the two different perspectives of each school of thought—intuitionism and naturalism and emotivism and prescriptivism. Those who take a cognitivist approach believe that we

Image 2.2 Relationship Between Metaethics and Normative Ethics

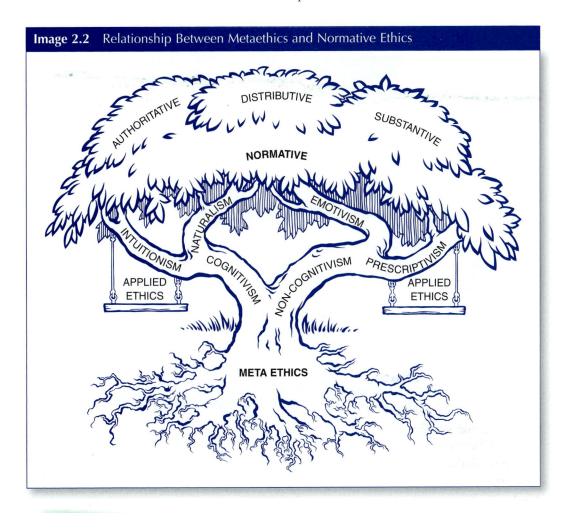

can determine whether our statements regarding ethical concepts are actually true or false. Moral judgments can be deemed as containing an objective truth. Cognitivism can be further delineated into the belief that the claims of truth or falsehood are based on intuition and cannot be empirically determined (intuitionism) and the belief that these claims can be empirically validated through scientific inquiry (naturalism) (Reamer, 1993).

In contrast, noncognitivists believe that statements regarding ethical concepts are merely grounded in individual beliefs and have no inherent truth-value. Claims about ethical concepts, such as fairness, duty, goodness, and so on, cannot be verified as either true or false—ultimately moral knowledge is an impossibility. According to emotivists, these claims are simply a reflection of the individual's feeling at the present moment; "emotion" is the root of a moral claim, which drives moral declarations. According to prescriptivists, a moral belief expressed is simply an individual's response to a directive; statements like "do not kill" are prescriptivist declarations (Garner & Rosen, 1967; Reamer, 1993).

Normative Ethics

Normative ethics are concerned with determining standards of morality which we can use to regulate ethical conduct. Unlike metaethics, normative ethics is concerned with the actual application of ethics—think of it as ethics in action. In social work, practitioners are often confronted with ethical dilemmas that require them to determine the right course of action. Ideally, normative ethics should be grounded in the core questions that metaethics pose.

Social work organizations in many countries have created ethical codes (similar to many other professions) to assist with these decisions. The NASW Code of Ethics is one example of normative ethics—a set of guidelines that direct social workers in the United States in ethical decision making.

Normative ethics wrestles with three different questions:

- The authoritative question—why should we consider ethical obligations, particularly given these obligations to others may conflict with our interest?
- The distributive question—whose interests should we consider and how should goods and resources be distributed among individuals?
- The substantive question—what actions and resources should we deem good and worthwhile and why? (Reamer, 1993)

Let's take a closer look at these questions, starting with the authoritative question. Why should we be ethical in our practice? Reamer (1993) argues that there are a number of factors at play when social workers determine the manner in which to intervene:

- Technical considerations (e.g., what is often called "practice wisdom") that are influenced by training, theoretical frameworks, and individual beliefs about beneficial forms of intervention.
- Empirical considerations that are based on research evidence regarding efficacy of forms of intervention.
- Ethical considerations that are ultimately the primary justification for social work interventions.

The second question, the distributive question, takes us back to many issues that were brought up in Chapter 1 regarding social justice, particularly distributive justice. Who are we obligated to and how do we distribute resources? Do our obligations extend to all human beings, or only to those in our family, community, state, or country? Do they extend to animals and the environment? Are we ethically obligated to others simply because of our professional expectations or are we drawn to a social change profession because of our individual ethical beliefs?

Often the answer comes down to the issue of need, which then brings up a metaethical question—how do we define need? Who are we obligated to assist and how? For early social workers, both in the COS and SHM, religious ideals about helping the needy were founda-tional to their work, although they also had a desire to teach "foreigners" and assimilate those seen as lacking in a particular set of values and behaviors.

An important social work dilemma regarding self-determination and harm can be contex-tualized within the question of who we are obligated to assist. Self-determination—which appears in the NASW Code of Ethics on a number of occasions—requires that social workers "respect the inherent dignity and worth of the person" (NASW, 2008, para. 21). It is an exam-ple of a positive obligation. Related to the concept of positive liberty, which is the freedom to make one's own decisions and to have the resources to do so, positive obligations require acknowledgment of an individual's free will. Negative obligations, based on the concept of negative liberty, relate to an individual's freedom from coercion (Reamer, 1993). Social work-ers are confronted with both a positive obligation to "respect and promote the right of clients to self-determination" and a negative obligation which states that "social workers may limit clients' right to self-determination when, in the social workers' professional judgment, clients' actions or potential actions pose a serious, foreseeable and imminent risk to themselves or others" (NASW, 2008, para. 28). Typically, in high-risk situations, the negative obligation to protect someone trumps the positive obligation to support self-determination.

It is often in the more nuanced situations that the ethical or "right" pathway becomes more difficult to ascertain. Unfortunately, it is also these more nuanced areas that sometimes go unquestioned. Rights of children, individuals who are or have been incarcerated, who have a developmental disability, and/or who have been diagnosed with a mental illness can bring us face to face with questions of self-determination versus risk. One way that this gets played out is through paternalistic, "for your own good" thinking. Reamer (1993) identifies three ways that paternalism takes place in social work:

- Interference with a participant's actions or intentions
- Withholding of information
- Dissemination of misinformation

> What are some examples of these forms of paternalism?

How resources are distributed is a primary question that social workers contend with in their work. Resource allocation can be determined a variety of ways, including through con-sideration of equality, need, compensation, and/or contribution. Equality can be determined by equality of outcome, which suggests that eligible participants should all receive equal shares of the service or good (i.e., mental health services, cash assistance, housing subsidies). Equality of process implies that eligible participants all have equal opportunity to receive services (i.e., "first come, first served"). This interpretation of equality can also be used in a lottery system where participants all have an equal chance of receiving services (Reamer, 1993).

Services are also distributed based on need, which in normative ethics is driven by some predetermined mechanism, such as a means tested program that measures need using a standard like the official poverty line. Compensation typically takes into account need, yet is often based on historical events, such as victim's assistance or veteran's benefits programs. However, in the case of affirmative action programs, compensation considers historical disparities based on group membership, particularly race/ethnicity. Distribution based on contribution is typically either a fee-for-service or funds that are distributed based on previous contributions, such as social security insurance payments (Reamer, 1993).

Now we can consider the substantive question. What actions are "good," or ethical? For social workers, the decision often comes down to negotiating two ethical principles that are in conflict. The conflict between self-determination and harm to self or others is one example—how do we determine the action to take if we value each ethical principle? One way to decide is to distinguish between prima facie duty, which is duty that we ought to perform as if all things are equal, and actual duty, which is the decision made when confronted with conflicting obligations (Reamer, 1993). Two corresponding philosophical approaches address these issues:

- Deontology, or duty-based ethics, is connected to the work of 18th-century philosopher Immanuel Kant. Deontologists suggest that there are certain actions that are inherently right or good. For example, a deontological approach states that it is inherently wrong to lie to a participant.
- Teleology, or action-based ethics, is connected to the works of 19th-century ethicists Jeremy Bentham and John Stuart Mill (Banks and Nøhr, 2011). Teleologists suggest that goodness lies in the consequences of certain actions. For example, a teleological approach states that if the consequence of lying to a participant promotes greater good, then taking that action is the ethically right action to take.

Teleologists either follow an egoist approach, which states that it is good to maximize our individual benefit, or a utilitarian approach, which is based in the Bentham and Mill philosophies regarding the greatest good for the greatest number (as discussed in Chapter 1). Clearly an egoist approach is antithetical to social work, and social workers often take a utilitarian approach. Utilitarianism is not without its own flaws, however, as the greatest good for the greatest number can often discount historically oppressed groups and privilege the majority (Reamer, 1993).

Virtue-Based Ethics

A number of ethicists promote a move away from a strict deontological or teleological approach to ethics in social work (and other professions) and a return to virtue-based ethics as a way to determine the "goodness" of an action (Clark, 2006; McBeath & Webb, 2002; see also Banks, 1997/2001 and Hugman & Smith, 1995).

Virtue ethics focuses on the character of the individual rather than on universal norms and intended outcomes. Virtue-based theories, in the global North and West, stem from Aristotle's philosophy of the development of personal virtues. He considered personal virtues the driving factor in our ethical decision making. Aristotle identified two types of personal virtues (McBeath & Webb, 2002):

- Intellectual virtues, such as wisdom, prudence, and understanding, which are obtained through education and instruction
- Moral virtues, such as liberality and temperance, which were acquired through the modeling of others and the development of good habits

Contemporary social work theorists have returned to concepts of virtue-based ethics because of their concerns about automatic, duty-based responses to ethical directives. They believe that thoughtful judgment produces more appropriate responses and that a virtue-based ethics is a more dynamic, flexible, responsive foundation for ethical decision-making (McBeath & Webb, 2002). A person's virtues are developed through training, dialogue, and application of judgment and perception to ethical dilemmas and case studies.

Ethics of Care

In her 1982 book, *In a Different Voice*, Carol Gilligan contends that women demonstrate a different morality than men due to their greater interest in relationships (as cited in Orme, 2002). Prioritizing relationships in ethical actions is based on the belief that people are inter-dependent. Moral reasoning that prioritizes relationships rather than duty or outcomes, such as the ethics of care, thus challenges the deontological and teleological moral philosophies, which some see as being overly rational and masculinist. Proponents of applying an ethics of care to social work suggest that its main benefits are to increase dialogue regarding ethical issues and to allow for a multiplicity of voices to be heard (Orme, 2002). More to the point, the moral issues which preoccupy us most and which touch us most deeply derive not from problems of justice in the economy and polity, but precisely from the quality of our relations with others in the "spheres of kinship, love, friendship and sex" (Seyla Benhabib, as cited in Orme, p. 807).

The discourse of "care" is not without its challenges. One of the most frequent critiques of Gilligan's work is that her theory seems to make the concept of "care" the exclusive province of women. While it is possible to point to the expectations placed on women to be caring and caretakers, this is acknowledged by most as a socially constructed role, not as an inherent characteristic of women. Additional critiques include the potential for caring to be overly "maternalistic" and prone to infantilize those who require care. They caution that care should not take on a controlling, surveillance role in which there are expectations of gratitude and dependency (Orme, 2002).

Mekada J. Graham (2007) provides an important commentary on the ethics of care through a black feminist lens which utilizes standpoint and intersectional theories (see Hill Collins, 2000; hooks, 2000) that place black women at the center of analysis and acknowledges the importance of race, gender, culture, and history. The African-centered perspective that Graham cites envisions ethics as an outgrowth of individual personhood, which develops in interdependent relationships with others. She also refers to Ma'at, a philosophical and spiritual system that is a component of Egyptian cosmology. Ma'at envisions an ethics of care that incorporates the balance between care for oneself and care for others—"I think therefore we are" (Graham, 2007, p. 204).

Communitarian Ethics

Similar to the ethics of care, communitarian ethics are situated in relationships. Significant to communitarian ethics is the good of the larger community. However, communitarian ethics differ from the "greatest good" philosophy in that a communitarian focuses on the entire community, not just the majority; whereas in contrast, utilitarian ethics leave out the minority. Communitarian ethics are grounded in indigenous worldviews and values. Therefore, collectivity and collective rights, respect for the land, and family ties that extend beyond blood to the country and to spiritual life are the values that influence ethics and ethical decision-making (Green & Baldry, 2008). Bénézet Bujo, an African moral theologian, offers an informed critique on communitarian ethics (Maina, 2008). Although Bujo prioritizes community over individualism, individual self-determination and agency are still present. According to Bujo, neither individual nor community comes first; each "presupposes the other" (as cited in Maina, p. 196). The ideal communitarian ethical perspective in this case believes that every individual in the community contributes to the well-being of the community while the community supports all individuals in the community. Additionally, there is interdependence among humans, animals, and the environment. In this system there are no "ready-made" moral decisions as there is continuing dialogue (palaver) that is ever changing and open to improvement. Despite Bujo's prominence in the theory of communitarian ethics, he has been criticized for not paying enough attention to Western influence (particularly in African urban areas); failing to attend to the vast diversity in African culture (i.e., presuming one static African philosophy); and not mentioning how the palaver can truly be a communal process when historically women have been excluded.

Ethics in International and Cross-Cultural Social Work

Whether social workers are practicing in individual direct practice, group/community work, policy advocacy, or in international work, the impacts of immigration/migration and globalization touch all levels of social change work. Thus, social workers are confronted with making ethical decisions that cross-cultural boundaries and must contend with the question of universality of ethics. A simplistic approach suggests that social workers are bound to the ethical code in the country in which they are practicing. However, for many social workers debates and subsequent tensions develop when practice occurs in a culturally multifaceted arena which, particularly in urban settings, can be a daily occurrence.

In 2004, the International Federation of Social Work (IFSW) created a set of international social work ethics in collaboration with the International Association of Schools of Social Work (IASSW). The creation of these global social work standards was an attempt to give practical expression to the aim of IASSW as some saw the formulation of international guidelines for social work education and training to be the core business of IASSW (Sewpaul & Jones, 2004, p. 503). These standards are an attempt to:

- protect the consumers, clients, or service users of social work services;
- take account of the impact of globalisation on social work curricula and social work practice;
- facilitate articulation across universities on a global level;
- facilitate the movement of social workers from one country to another;
- draw a distinction between social workers and non–social workers;
- benchmark national standards against international standards;
- facilitate partnerships and international student and staff exchange programs;
- enable IASSW and IFSW, in developing such guidelines, to play a facilitative role in helping those faculties, centres, departments or schools of social work that lack the resources to meet such guidelines.

A number of cautions and caveats were included in this document regarding the creation of global standards, primarily on issues related to countries' resources to meet educational standards and confirmation that neither the IASSW nor the IFSW intended to play a role in monitoring, controlling, or accrediting any schools of social work (Sewpaul & Jones, 2004). At the same time, the document suggested that the standards were intended to be broad enough to allow for context-specific application and specific enough to provide salient guidelines.

Kam-Shing Yip (2004) has critiqued this document, noting that application of universal standards might encourage professional imperialism and dominance, particularly by English speaking countries. Yip suggests that the "universal components" of the document are based on westernized ideologies of "individualism, democracy, and Christianity" (p. 604). In contrast, countries in Africa, Asia, and the Middle East may have different interpretations of such values as oppression, social justice, human rights, equality, and social change. For example, in a domestic violence case, Yip suggests that a westernized approach would stress individual rights of the abused woman, yet in the Chinese culture, responsibilities toward others are often stressed. For example, a social work intervention with the abused woman might be more successful if she were reminded that she has a responsibility toward her child (to provide safety) than if she were told that she had the right to assert and protect herself. Summarizing the overall concerns with universalizing standards in the IFSW and IASSW document, Yip states:

> The affirming of rights but ignoring responsibility, the advocating of equality but neglecting social norms and social order, the asserting of the individual but disregarding collectivity . . . seems to belittle the fundamental cultural differences between Asian and Eurocentric countries. . . . Thus, the diversity of culture advocated by this document tends to regard non-Eurocentric cultures only as minority cultures as in western multicultural societies. That means that these minority cultures should still be submissive to the Eurocentric American culture. (p. 605)

In light of modern and postmodern theories, and in Jean-Francois Lyotard's definition of a metanarrative, the IASSW document can be seen as a "privileged discourse against which all other discourses are situated, characterized and evaluated" (cited in Williams & Sewpaul, 2004, p. 559). Another important postmodern critique notes that the document was not able to accurately represent the complex, divergent thinking of all parties consulted; the IASSW and IFSW representatives on the committee that created the document hailed from only eleven different countries (Sewpaul & Jones, 2004, pp. 509–510). So, who is represented in the document? Additionally, one language was used to write the document, which then becomes a platform for translation. A postmodern critique would suggest that this is another way in which power and hegemony become institutionalized within the document.

These arguments about the IASSW document revolve around the relative value placed on cultural relativism, the view that all rules, codes of conduct, and morality are attached to specific cultures and that what may be considered unethical in one context may be considered acceptable in another. This is in contrast to the universality view that there are certain rules, codes of conduct, and moral dictates that cross all cultural, social, and historical contexts. Image 2.3 is useful when conceptualizing the role of universalism and relativism in ethical decision making. To take a strict universalist stance (at the left end of the continuum) is to believe that cultural context is irrelevant to ethical decision making At the other end of the continuum is a rigid relativist position, which suggests that culture and context determine all ethical decision making. In the center of the continuum are the "moderate mid-range positions" which attend to culture and context to varying degrees (Healy, 2007).

To offer an often used example to clarify, we can look at the issue of violence against women, specifically in the form of physical assault in the home. A strictly relativist position would state that if certain cultural, religious, social norms support male dominance to a degree that a husband is "honor-bound" to physically assault his wife in order to maintain a stable household, then that cultural norm should be respected. A strictly universalist position would state that physical assault is always unethical and no matter what the cultural dictates, universal guidelines would prevail. One moderate mid-range position could take

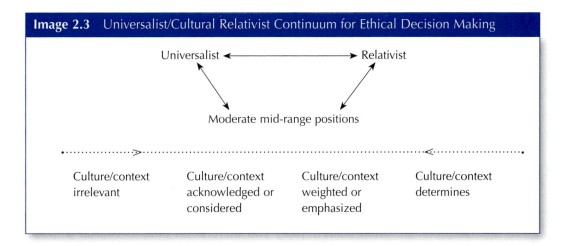

Image 2.3   Universalist/Cultural Relativist Continuum for Ethical Decision Making

Source: Healy, 2007, p. 16.

us back to Yip's example. Instead of presuming a universal "right," respecting a cultural norm of responsibility would still produce safety for the wife and child.

Another way to take the moderate mid-range position might be to delineate between "primary" and "secondary" values (Hugman, 2010). Based on "ethical pluralism" (see Hinman, 2003; Kekes, 1993), primary values are seen as those that can apply across contexts and are pursued in themselves while secondary values are seen as situationally specific and are often a vehicle through which primary values are pursued. For instance, human rights, social justice, virtue, relationship, harmony, and responsibility, among others, are primary values, while self-determination, confidentiality, and specific terms used in codes of ethics, among others, are secondary values (Hugman, 2010). While this conceptualization may not address all ethical challenges and tensions, it focuses on the application of primary values alongside contextually dependent secondary values.

The dialogue regarding universality of human rights and ethical standards continually brings us back to the question of how to identify, understand, and respect diverse cultures in a dynamic, global world. "Culture" is a complex term that is "articulated at several levels" (Gray & Allegritti, 2003, p. 313), through language, customs, communications, social institutions, art and literature, and so on. Culture varies across and within identities and continually changes in response to social, historical, and political events. In addition, within a "cultural group" there are ongoing internal dialogues, varied narratives, and dissenting voices that may or may not be acknowledged (Benhabib, 2002). Also, culture is often used as a stand-in for nation, implying that in nation-states there is one homogenous culture, yet this is a problematic notion which privileges dominant/powerful groups and marginalizes minority groups (Gray & Allegritti, 2003). Given the contested, political, and dynamic nature of cultures, the challenge of articulating a set of universal social work ethics continues.

- To what extent are they compatible with anti-oppressive ethics and can therefore be used with some purpose?
- To what extent do they appear to be in conflict with anti-oppressive ethics, and need to be resisted, either by insider strategies, or by whistle-blowing or by collective and political means?
- To what extent are conflicting interests and principles involved? (Clifford and Burke, 2009, p. 193)

In the proceses of consultation and dialogue and evaluating evidence and perspectives, accessing a variety of voices and perspectives is crucial. While this does not suggest an uncritical acceptance of all perspectives and "evidence," it is important to acknowledge a variety of positions when engaging in a critical decision-making process. This includes examining both dominant and muted voices, and an inclusion of interdisciplinary perspectives. This process requires active questioning: Why are some perspectives dominant? Is it because those perspectives are genuinely reflective of "best practices," which are socially just and equitable, or are those perspectives dominant due to power and privilege differentials in research, position, or "voice"? An additional concern during these phases of the process is the time required to adequately engage in dialogue and research given the pressures and constraints in the social welfare system in general.

In reviewing relevant ethics, Clifford and Burke (2009) suggest that a broad anti-oppressive framework calls for both awareness of personal values and beliefs and a pluralist approach, which requires that practitioners refrain from imposing their value system on others. They question the prioritizing approach, in which higher-order concepts would trump those lower on the list (see Lowenberg & Dologoff, 1996); yet, they also suggest that this hierarchical screen could provide some guidance if utilized within an anti-oppressive framework.

At the decision-making juncture and in the best-case scenario, practitioners are reminded that the previous steps support a decision that will be a result of meaningful dialogue and reflection. However, in real life, agreement across affected parties may not have been reached.

What we hope is clear at this juncture in the book is that we are not offering formulaic answers and approaches. One of the hallmarks of anti-oppressive practice is an emphasis on reflective analysis, which includes analysis of self, others, and institutions through a lens of context, history, and power. In addition, values and ethics are not static and require continual evaluation if we are going to engage in a practice that aims to be emancipatory. Thus, it is important for practitioners to find the time and space to evaluate and reevaluate their values and beliefs throughout their work. Those who criticize social work's move toward greater efficiency and managerialism (such as Mullaly, 2001) help us remember to take time to reflect. If we do not, we will fall prey to a robotic application of norms, standards, and guidelines that may not serve, or may even damage, the very people we are intending to serve and ally with in our work. Ethical guidelines can be an important tool for practitioners, yet there is also value in critique and evaluation so that anti-oppressive practice does not become an empty promise.

STORIES FROM THE FIELD: VALUES AND ETHICS

1

MIDNIGHT INTELLIGENCE: DREAMING UP CRITICAL APPROACHES TO SOCIAL WORK

JESSIE WORKMAN AND MEG PANICHELLI

We met each other in the summer of 2010 when Meg moved to Santa Fe, NM, from Philadelphia. In Philly, she had been working with women who traded sex for money and used drugs. Jessie worked and continues to work at a nonprofit organization providing emergency shelter and other resources to formerly incarcerated youth and young people experiencing homelessness. We connected and started taking sunset walks, following sleepy train tracks into the desert and talking about the work that we do. Our conversations would start and it felt like they should never stop. So many nights, we sat on Jessie's steps, a little cold, the stars above us, smoking cigarettes, speaking quickly and passionately about the oppression and struggles youth and drug users were experiencing institutionally, systemically, personally and with their families. We talked about intersections of racism, sexism, homophobia and transphobia; and about how we approached our work as white queers. We reflected on our struggles, conflicts, identities, supposed radical ideas and how quickly these ideologies needed to transform to meet the needs of the folks we were working with.

We both believe that our attempt to spark, create and produce knowledge outside of the academy is important. So we share this piece with you. It is an excerpt of a remote interview we did with each other in an attempt to emulate some of the conversations we have shared in the last year. It is meant to capture our grappling with the work that we do and the ways in which we approach that work. We are re-envisioning what is possible, building on the beliefs we hold to be true and breaking open the old notions that no longer serve us.

> Question: If you were to look back over your life thus far, what would you identify as your most important life skills? How did you attain these skills (who, if anyone, taught you? how? when?)

Meg: I really appreciate this question, Jessie, especially right now as I'm trying to be super conscious about self-reflexivity as it relates to research and "Ph.D." school. When I'm reflecting now on my different positions of privilege and power, I think about the social locations I occupy currently and I often forget to go back through my own history. The question also made me think a lot about how these different skills are coming into my life right now as a first generation college student and in my first year of a Ph.D. program. I realize that the skills a person (myself) needs to survive are flexible and changing at multiple times and in different spaces. Maybe that is kind of obvious. Anyway, I've thought about five skills that I've seen as fluent throughout my life:

- Stay positive
- Believe you can overcome anything

- Communicate
- Build solid relationships
- Be self-reflexive

The first two skills I was first taught when I played basketball. I started playing in third grade and after that spent most nights after school and days during the summer playing. My goal was always to get a college scholarship and I needed to do whatever I could to achieve this. My dad was my coach and we spent a lot of time processing after games. One of the keys to following my "dreams" was to stay positive. That comes up a lot now, but I also know I can't be positive all of the time and I don't want to be. As for the 2nd skill, I think it is based on some sort of class privilege. When I was in 5th grade I had a basketball coach tell me he didn't want to put me in the game because he wanted to win. I left at the end of the game crying and woke up the next day ready to prove him wrong. The next time he saw me play I was playing with 6th grade boys and doing really well. Communication and building solid relationships go together for me. All of the friendships and romantic relationships that have failed have happened because I wasn't stating my needs and was just trying to understand the rules by which all people involved were playing the game. I also have felt like there are different communication standards for masculine and feminine identified people. Also, when I think about sex and sexuality and teaching people about this stuff it all comes down to learning how to communicate and starting that from a young age. I didn't start at a young age and now it's a struggle I feel constantly challenged to work and process through.

The last skill of self-reflexivity takes the form of working on my internalized oppression, racism, sexism, transphobia and ableism. It really rose to the surface when I started teaching young kids of color at a public school and more when working with folks using drugs and working in the sex trade. My goal is to constantly work toward being an ally to folks experiencing oppression differently than myself and so this "skill" is always being worked on.

Jessie: One of my important life skills (which happens to be a deficit too) is the ability to keep my emotions and reactions controlled and under the surface. I imagine that I learned this skill from observing and being in close proximity to my stoic father. This skill serves to protect me and allow me to be in many different environments and situations without reacting immediately. It also allows me to stay calm and hold a space for people when they are having a rough time.

The ability to adapt to my surroundings is a skill that goes along with the first one. Have you ever heard the phrase "God bless the flexible because they are not easily bent out of shape"? I live by that one. I can eat anything, sleep damn near anywhere and through damn near anything; I am hard to rile. I credit my mother for that one, she raised me to be able to adapt and she is that way too. Also, just by the fact of experiencing a relative amount of trauma and chaos growing up, I learned how to roll with it, all of it, the punches and the good times too.

Another skill is perseverance. Somehow I have learned that I can keep trying. I believe this is my single most important life skill. I have witnessed great change in myself and in my life in the last few years and the key has been not giving up, no matter what—picking myself up off the floor and putting one foot in front of the other and trying again. I have strong faith in the overall goodness of the world, despite where we are at as a whole right now; that faith serves as a driving force helping me to keep trying. Again I also must credit my mother, she showed me by her own example what it means to keep moving forward and growing upwards no matter what.

In his soft sad morning voice he explains to me that on his mind is the conversation that he had with his five-year-old sister last night. She told him she was hungry. He walked her through the kitchen over the phone and listened to her describe the hotel room shelves, mini fridge, floor—all empty. No food for his sister. Hungry.

"When I was there the little ones were never hungry. Jessie, I gotta get back there so I can get a job."

The real truth is in the words he doesn't speak. The boy is nearly broken by the weight of responsibility he is being forced to shoulder and the sadness has carved space for itself on his face. Inside him it is overflowing, but there's no more room for it and he doesn't cry. Instead his face is ripe with grief, almost bursting, his lips are quivering and his eyes are full and deep like still waters. His mother is working and away all day. His mother's boyfriend does drugs while the kids do everything they can to get full on empty.

There is nothing I can do for him. I witness his silence after conversations with hungry younger siblings, witness him withdraw into himself as he pushes feet forward toward the juvenile jail he must report to all day everyday despite his lack of current charges. Despite the fact that all he ever did was what he had to in order to take care of his family.

I witness myself withdraw into myself when wracked with the reality that I can do next to nothing for the young people I spend my days with. I can witness. I can speak what I know to be the truth about human nature, about what is right, about resilience and resistance. Faith and fight. Strength and change. And I can be an ear and a shoulder, strive to be an anchor.

Sometimes with a van full of teenagers and the sun setting I drive too fast, turn up the music on full blast and we go for a cruise. In the music we find solace and understanding. When I pull back into the parking lot they are mostly sleeping and all relaxed. We slowly put arms and legs together and walk back into the shelter that they sometimes call home.

We have shared our own stories to show how we acquire and share knowledge when doing social justice and anti-oppressive social work. We believe the most important piece here for us is to truly center, value and acknowledge the folks we work with and have worked with as the experts of their own lives. They know how to survive by sharing skills and have been doing it for far longer than academics have recognized that outsiders can have valuable knowledge too.

1. If you were to look back over your life thus far, what would you identify as your most important life skills? How did you attain these skills (who, if anyone, taught you? how? when?)?

2. If you were to name life skills that seem to be most important to the folks you work with, what would those skills be? How are they taught, learned, shared, passed along, prioritized? How does your presence affect that skill sharing?

3. How do you see your personal identities influencing your interactions with your clients? Does being who you are bring you closer to the knowledge being shared? Do you ever share that information with clients? What impact does that have?

4. How do the pieces and intersections of your identity impact how you think social work and social change work should be done? How does it impact how you interact with the population you are working with?

2

NAVIGATING PERSONAL AND PROFESSIONAL ETHICAL ISSUES AND BOUNDARIES IN SOCIAL JUSTICE LAWYERING

GABRIEL ARKLES, ANYA MUKARJI-CONNOLLY, AND OWEN DANIEL-MCCARTER

In the following paragraphs, Gabriel, Owen, and Anya engage in a dialogue about how their values help them navigate privilege and oppression dynamics with clients, with colleagues, and within the broader social justice movement.

Gabriel: The way that I would handle the boundary between the personal and the professional is that I would sometimes explicitly name my race and class privilege, but not always. I would also usually come out to my clients as trans, in the hope that it would allow them to feel a bit safer.

Some clients took a lot of leadership there. I remember one homeless black trans woman I met with on Riker's. She was in jail for shoplifting and told me how angry she was when she saw wealthy white gay men wandering around Chelsea with their nice things looking down on her. She asked me why I got to be on the visitor's side of the table while she was on the prisoner's side of the table. I said I thought she had already named some of the reasons like my race and my wealth. We talked about it some more before moving into her legal issues. I appreciated that she addressed directly what could have been the elephant in the room. To me, it seemed like the rest of our conversation was more frank and trusting than other client interviews I had done in that jail that day.

I would often talk about politics and visions for change with my clients, but I would sometimes hold back when my views were different from theirs. At the time I thought I was being responsible because they might feel pressured to agree with me given the power dynamics in our relationship. In retrospect I think that was wrong. I think I was creating more of a power dynamic by withholding my views. I was protecting myself from being challenged—no one could disagree with me if I didn't tell them what I thought.

Owen: Gabriel, I could not agree more! I try to explain my identity when it feels appropriate and in line with our core values at the Transformative Justice Law Project (TJLP). I actually find that sometimes we don't do the best work at TJLP of explaining our core values to our clients, which can add to the power dynamics you were referencing.

Oftentimes, I find that my experience as a transgender person is hugely different from my clients' experiences and my thinking about the larger systemic problems with the criminal legal system can also be quite different from theirs (and theirs are quite different from each other). So that can really change the way that I think about prison abolition, transformative justice, and gender self-determination.

It can certainly be a challenge to have these conversations while maintaining necessary boundaries. We really find that transparency can be the best and most affirming way to go, especially explaining why we have to maintain distance instead of mystifying the need for distance.

3

ODE TO MY TEARS

MINH DANG

like a kiss on the nape of my neck
a touch of my lover's hand on my hip
you slip from the corner
crevice of my eye
caress my cheeks and say
I love you

you fall
every day like Autumn leaves
float down
fog up my glasses
sprinkle on my face
you sing me songs
like morning sermons
chant prayers that hum like lullabies

you whisper in my ear *you'll be okay*
and rock me back to sleep
drip drops land on curves of my lips
your tang like honey and lime
I lick your beads and swallow you
absorb you
like air to fill my lungs

I follow your streams to
open valleys
where noon time showers

carve canyons inside my chest

your flow enfolds

my body

replenishes

the ground

I walk on

and remind me

I am still

alive

Seven years ago, I wrote this poem to celebrate the tears of grief. At the time, I was in the process of cutting ties with my abusive birth family. I was also taking an undergraduate college poetry class, in which I was asked to write a poem that celebrated something personal to me that was not a human being. Given that I was in the early stages of acknowledging my parents' abuse, I could not fathom praising much of anything. My days were centered on managing the overwhelming pain I was feeling. I came to learn that my tears would be a normal and expected part of my life. This poem was written to acknowledge the healing and relief that tears of grief actually bring.

My healing journey and personal struggle for justice began as a senior at UC Berkeley. I was a seasoned student leader and an activist fighting for racial, economic, and social justice. I was also a young woman suffering from 20 years of incest, neglect, physical and emotional abuse, and a decade of sex trafficking by my parents. My social justice work became an escape from my trauma and my feelings of helplessness, shame, and fear. However, I began to see that displacing my emotions was affecting my physical and mental health and limiting my capacity to address the social injustices I cared deeply about. I began to break the chains of my parents' abuse by working nearly full time at UC Berkeley's Public Service Center.

By establishing financial independence from my parents, I was able meet my basic needs and secure my physical safety away from them. With this newfound sense of safety, I told a trusted friend about the abuse I was suffering and he introduced me to a trauma-informed therapist and a peer support group, Adult Survivors of Childhood Abuse. Within a few months, I resigned from my student leadership positions and turned my focus away from social justice toward my own personal justice. Healing and liberation became the focus of my life. In addition to attending over fifteen hours a week of therapy and support groups, I organized my friendships, daily activities, and my work life to help me cope with my pervasive trauma symptoms.

Because self-care and personal narratives were already valued in my line of work, I shared my traumatic history and my healing process with colleagues at the Public Service Center. Not only did they support my healing, my colleagues encouraged me to share my process of self-care and healing with the students who were my clients at the center. My colleagues appeared awakened by, or at least reminded of, the reality that even college students at UC Berkeley could suffer from grave injustice and violence; and they valued my insights into how we could support students in their personal lives while supporting them in their community involvement and leadership development.

After a few years at the Public Service Center, I grew into the role of director of the Bonner Leaders Program. This is a national program that develops student leaders through community-based service. My participation in the Bonner Community, along with my personal healing journey, taught me the most important lesson I have learned about social justice work: Seeking justice in the world is intimately tied to seeking justice in my own life. For me, justice in my own life meant ending my parents' abuse or seeking refuge, healing the wounds of trauma and living a healthy and whole life. My vision of social justice was similar: that communities seeking justice would eradicate oppression, heal the wounds of violence, and create conditions to flourish and thrive. Thus, healing at all levels is an essential component of justice.

Through the culture of social justice circles, I have participated in promoted self-care and healing, more often than not, effective practices were not in place or did not occur. It was apparent to me that many students, like myself, were sacrificing their own physical and mental health while supporting important social causes. While we verbally supported taking actions to maintain personal well-being, we were in fact acting as if personal health and community healing are mutually exclusive, if not incompatible. I, too, lamented leaving my student activist commitments and psychologically whipped myself for being selfish. I thought of myself as someone who was no longer contributing to social justice actions and only committed to personal healing.

My perspective was indirectly challenged by one of my colleagues, who expressed his respect for my commitment to social justice. Though he was older than I, he shared that he looked to me for direction and vision in our Center's work. When I asked him what social justice commitments he was referring to, he pointed to various aspects of my work as a service-learning professional. It was through this conversation, that I finally realized how my social justice commitment had not disappeared. It merely took a new form. My colleague helped me validate that even though I no longer channeled my energy to grassroots organizing, my social justice work through my profession was "legit."

Legitimizing professional social justice work also opened my mind to other new perspectives. I realized that I had not "given up" social justice work to pursue personal justice, but rather that I was enhancing my social justice work through my personal justice journey. As I mentioned, my personal justice journey was partially instigated by awareness of my declining effectiveness as a student activist and leader. I began to see that in order to truly understand the social injustices of the people I was serving, I needed to make sure that my own issues were not clouding my empathy, my decision-making processes, or my ideas of appropriate action steps. Processing my trauma also allowed me to be more present, open, and creative when talking with community members. Instead of using social justice work as an escape from my feelings, my labors in personal healing allowed me to use my feelings as the fuel for my social justice work.

As I continued to heal my own wounds, I continued to replenish my commitment to social justice. My feelings began to buoy me instead of bring me down. As a result, I decided to make it my life's purpose and philosophy to join personal and community healing in all that I do.

In my role as Bonner Program Director, I worked with students to enact change in San Francisco Bay Area communities while also working with them to enact change in their personal lives. Through storytelling, self-reflection, and deep dialogue, I encouraged students to rethink—that is, think again—about how we talk about and engage in diversity work, civic engagement, and service-learning. I asked them to join me in coupling their personal healing with community healing. In the classroom and in informal spaces, this meant welcoming all of our emotions, including our tears of grief.

The students I worked with, and all of us, are facing a world that is filled with many hurts and a system of oppression that has pervaded our everyday ways of relating with one another. Carrying this pain and taking on a responsibility of transforming the systems that create this pain, is a heavy load. I invited my students to lay down their loads, and to share their experiences of hurt, harm, and injustice that mirror the pain of those in the communities they served.

The foundation for sharing stories of pain and injustice was built on an annual overnight retreat designed for each incoming class of student leaders. Together with my students, we created "safe space" guidelines that would allow them to feel comfortable to share about their lives. I asked each of them to follow my lead and to share "life maps" and life stories. By sharing broad strokes and a few details about my own experiences of hurt and pain in my birth family, I set the tone for vulnerability and demonstrated the possibilities for open disclosure. Time and time again, students would share deep and personal experiences that they previously held quietly to themselves. They shared about abuse, discrimination, loss, and insecurities. They shed and they shared many tears. They also exchanged comforting gestures, touch, and loving facial expressions.

In reflecting on the experience, students expressed relief in being heard and empathy in hearing others. They also expressed a heightened commitment to fight for social justice to create a world where people do not need to experience undue hurt and harm.

After the retreats, I thanked each person individually for their contribution and openness, followed up regarding any additional emotional support they needed, and invited students to continue to share their stories throughout the duration of the program. Many of them did and many continued to disclose their traumatic histories and support one another with difficult experiences. I referred students to available resources for healing and continued to share with them how my personal healing motivated, enhanced, and sustained my social justice work. I invited them to share the ways in which they too were motivated by personal history and asked them to take a deeper look at why they were serving. I asked, what personal experience ties you to the fight for social justice? I reminded them of how my fight for justice for others without fighting for my own personal justice was not a successful path and imparted a hope that they avoid the pitfalls that I encountered.

Through this process, I learned that students yearned for this attention to their own lives and yet like me, felt selfish and guilty. However, I also learned that by sharing our wounds, we begin to open ourselves up to moving beyond devastation and disappointment toward hope and joy. We also begin to lay down our weapons. If we do not grieve our hurts and our losses, we will try to seek revenge and make someone else hurt the way that we do. We will try to control and change the outer world, because we feel helpless to our inner world. Rather than face the dark places of our inner world (which we often believe we must face alone), we face the darkness in other people. It is often said that the darkness in others that we most loathe is the darkness we fear in ourselves. Let us all face the darkness together, and seek beauty and joy in communion.

The philosophy of joining personal and community healing drove me to pursue a degree in Social Work and is essential in my practice as an up-and-coming social worker. With my classmates, colleagues, and with my clients, I seek to address the human need for emotional liberation and connection. On my path, I have learned that when we speak the truth about who we are, what we feel, and what we want, we begin to shape a new world. My hope for social work practice is to encourage deeper understanding of the connection between service provider and service recipient. The communities we serve are not outside of us; we are those communities. If we do not serve ourselves, we are not serving our communities.

As a young woman of color, child of Vietnamese refugees, and a survivor of child abuse and sexual exploitation, I represent many of the communities that social workers serve. Yet, though I lived in the projects for eight years, I also drove forty minutes to good suburban public schools and attended UC Berkeley. The privilege of my education and citizenship status allowed me access to countless social, political, and financial resources. Thus, as I and many social workers straddle the world of both service provider and service recipient, we have a unique position to promote the mutual pursuit of personal healing and community healing.

In order to build community of healing with one another, we must share deeply of ourselves and connect through our personal experiences. How can we do this honestly if we are worn down, and unsatisfied with the state of our own lives? In my experience, addressing my need for personal healing has made me a more effective activist and practitioner. It is through my body and my soul that I contribute to the fight for liberation. And as Walt Whitman writes, "I celebrate myself, and sing myself, and what I assume you shall assume, for every atom belonging to me as good belongs to you." I share with you the atoms of my soul, my story, as they equally belong to you. I hope that this story inspires you to tell yours, to invite the stories of people unheard, and to rejoice in your tears, as they will always remind you of your humanity.

1. How does the author's transformation inform her perspectives and decisions in life?

2. Minh recounts how her own personal healing has been an important element in her social justice work and in her decision to engage in anti-oppressive social work practice. She states, "I began to see that in order to truly understand the social injustices of the people I was serving, I needed to make sure that my own issues were not clouding my empathy, my decision-making processes, or my ideas of appropriate action steps"; in what ways have you begun to examine your own "issues"?

3. How might your own history and family dynamics influence your values and your work in the field?

4. Are there ways in which this history may raise ethical challenges for you?

4

GIVING AND ASKING FOR PERMISSION

HEIDI GROVE AND JUSTON COOPER (JC)

Heidi Grove and JC are cofounders of the grassroots start up nonprofit organization, The Youth Connection (TYC). They work with disconnected youth (also referred to as "at risk" youth) in the greater Colorado region. Below, they engage in dialogue about their work with youth and how they approach their work from an anti-oppressive lens.

JC: In our work with our clients, who are young people facing oppression, we are committed to sharing power. How we get *power with* a client is through permission. Once a young person gives you permission to work with them, the playing field is leveled; that permission equalizes the power.

When we engage young people we always introduce ourselves to the young people first. We also don't use titles so that it doesn't intimidate them to know what our positions are. I think an important thing we do really well is to allow the youth to take ownership of what will happen. We also make sure that we are just as transparent with them as they are with us. We are mandated reporters, we have an obligation to their safety and ours, so we have established those rules, but we've already established the relationship and the equalization of the power.

Heidi: I completely agree. When we coach young people we ask, "What do you think you should do?" They give us three options. We break it down with them about what's legal and those kinds of things. We also tell them from the very beginning that if they ever feel unsafe, to come find us.

A prime example is a young man who was distant and disassociated during his first time here. We had set our criteria with him from the very beginning when we said: "Hey, we are staff, we are here to support you and build a relationship." There was one day he actually showed up banging on our door at two o'clock in the afternoon. We go downstairs and he literally empties his pockets and hands us all the weapons that you can even imagine seeing. And says, "I feel I am going to hurt somebody and the voices in my head are telling me that I am going to hurt somebody and that's not right and I am handing these to you and I think I need to go somewhere to be safe."

JC: So he gave us permission to put him on a psychiatric hold. And how often does that happen? It is really rare, but it was possible because we'd built a relationship from power *with* him. He felt safe with us. In a traditional scenario like this one, the professional would have called the cops and said that the young person had no choice. The young man would have been taken away in handcuffs embarrassed in front of his peers. But based on the relationship of power *with,* he came to us and he requested to put himself on hold.

We had transparency and collaboration. We had collaborative relationships with the officers who showed up and their approach was different. It wasn't as aggressive and they understood, and they knew that we knew who they were. The young person also knew that we had a good relationship with the officers.

Heidi: We even told the young person from the very beginning that we should call the cops in this situation, and we explained what was going to happen. We informed him that we have to put handcuffs on first for safety reasons, not just for him, but for the police, for the transport, and for all of the staff. We explained to him that the handcuffs were a legal requirement for situations like this one, not because he had done anything wrong. The cops completely worked with us and they did exactly what we told him and the staff that they were going to do, so we didn't have a single incident with him. He freely put his hands behind his back, looked both of us and he said, "I love you guys. I will see you guys in a couple of weeks."

1. How do the authors of this story articulate the idea of "giving and asking for permission"?

2. What values and ethics do you see at play in this incident?

3. Can you think of a situation in a practicum or internship or work setting that was either a demonstration of *power with* or a situation that could have benefited from this approach?

5

FINDING LOVE, FACING FEAR, AND FINDING A LIFE'S WORK

CHARLES RAY COCHRAN

Recently a friend of mine had a period of anxiety in which he believed he had seroconverted, which is the medical term for the development of HIV antibodies. He was experiencing some health problems and contacted his physician. The doctor ordered a series of lab tests, suggesting that they "rule out HIV." This physician's request only fed my friend's anxiety: he had already been concerned about AIDS.

We exchanged text messages while my friend was waiting for a blood draw. He was close to tears. It seemed to me, based on those exchanges, that he absolutely believed he had seroconverted and he spent some time running through his possible reaction to the news of his seroconversion. This friend is not someone who seemed especially prone to high-risk behaviors. I sent him a text asking if he had engaged in any high-risk behaviors that would lead him to believe he may have exposed himself to the virus. His response: "No."

No? But, I certainly understood. I had been working with HIV/AIDS populations and I had received HIV/AIDS education. In addition, as a gay man, I had experienced many years of my own personal fear and anxiety around seroconversion.

Being young and gay in the 1980s and 1990s, HIV and AIDs and the persistent threat of contracting the virus had become a dark monster that embodied a lot of my deep fears about control, illness, alienation, stigma and, ultimately, death. It was about the worst happening. I would never have admitted it at the time—and there are those, now, who would have difficulty with my assessment—but it came to represent the ultimate punishment for a life lived as a "sexual deviant." It was also, in a more complex manner, the embodiment of the subterranean and shadowy aspects of living outside the socially constructed "ideal" at the intersection of sexual identity and procreation and family. And while stigma and alienation still exist for those living with the disease, it is better now than it was. This was, after all, long before same-sex marriage and LGBT sexual identity and its integration into everyday life; it was the dark period of the Moral Majority and Ronald Reagan.

In my younger years I had my sexual experimentations, but I was not particularly sexually adventurous. I generally did not go to bars, bathhouses or clubs and my sexual partners were mostly men that I was actually dating. There were the occasional drunken encounters, but I don't recall ever putting myself at high risk for transmission. And I had very few sexual partners in comparison to many of the young gay men I knew. But, regardless of my actual low-risk or no-risk sexual behaviors, I frequently experienced AIDS panic. I began to notice a monolithic, irrational, horrific fear of AIDS that would show up at times. It would present when I was happy and all was going well; it would also present when my life was chaotic. And it was generally unrelated to my actual sexual behaviors at the time.

In the first six months of a relationship with a man I would live with for eight years, I recall an evening spent in tears and explaining to him that he was dating someone who probably had AIDS. Was he sure he could handle it? I had him so convinced that I was ill, that he began to cry as well. There was absolutely nothing wrong with me and now when I think of that evening, I am embarrassed. For whatever reason, I had a deep fear that persistently swallowed me up and paralyzed me in an ego-driven death grip.

This fear continued for many years and it actually informed dating decisions. When HIV/AIDS still meant that one would more than likely die from complications, I dated one man who informed me after we had been intimate for the first time that he was HIV positive. I ended our relationship immediately and cut off all contact. I think of him often now and would give a great deal to speak with him one last time. I dated another who was so irritated by my irrational fears that he took me to my first ACT-UP meeting in 1989. He knew that I needed to use my anxiety more productively. I continued to go to those meetings even though I stopped seeing him. And this dating pattern continued even though drug therapies made outcomes less certain: on two other occasions, long after the cocktail therapies began to save lives, I dated men who were HIV positive and I still withdrew when they disclosed their positive status to me. Disingenuously, I told them that I could not date someone who was HIV positive because I was too concerned about falling in love with someone who could die from the disease. In truth, I was mostly concerned about transmission.

And then I met Peter, who was diagnosed HIV positive in 1998. We began dating in 2004 and it would take him a few months to reveal the full picture of his health to me. He disclosed his HIV status early in our dating; some time later, he gently revealed that he had AIDS; then, several weeks after that, he told me that in 1998 his HIV/AIDS diagnosis had been revealed when he was diagnosed with a combination of pneumonia and non-Hodgkin lymphoma. He had been told to get his affairs in order. And, yet, here he was—back from the brink. "I'm okay, now. I'm in remission," he tried to reassure me.

I did have my 4 a.m. panic attacks. I woke up in the middle of the night a few times in tears and stared at him as he slept. But, for some inexplicable reason I did not run away. I liked him almost immediately. And I felt a deep kinship and familiarity—I knew we shared a great deal in common. As a result, I just wanted to be with him as much as possible. I began to spend more and more time at his home, spending many nights with him. Before his illnesses, Peter had been a graphic artist by trade, and I became especially familiar with a collage he had created inside the door to his medicine cabinet in the bathroom. It was mostly beefcake: Pictures of handsome, shirtless men in magazine ads, as well as a photo of a particular favorite of Peter's, Ryan Reynolds lounging on a couch. Typical gay fantasy, I thought.

Also included in the medicine cabinet collage was a film criticism on the Lord of the Rings trilogy and the protagonist, Frodo, in particular. The clipping focused on Frodo's story as Quest and anti-Quest. Frodo is just a little guy going on about his business when, suddenly, he is tapped to fight these enormously dark powers. Frodo's journey is fraught with tension and confusion: he is not born with unique agency, nor is he a superhero inherent magical abilities; he agonizes over his path, is certainly given what he needs, but only as he goes on the trek. On his journey, Frodo learns to become a hero.

Peter also had many photos on his refrigerator, less collage and more slapdash. Mostly these were photos of friends and loved ones over the years, but one photo stood out: it was a snapshot of a skeletal Peter in faded jeans many sizes too big for him, weighing less than one hundred pounds, and surrounded by all his friends. It was a photo taken at his farewell party.

The juxtaposition of the photo of a skeletal Peter along with the beefcake and the Lord of the Rings clipping, had an impact on me: I began to see that the photos of the bronzed young men were not just about erotic images to feed a fantasy, but were also, perhaps, about health and vitality and the quest. Peter was on his own hero's journey. I cannot explain why, but the medicine cabinet collage and the reference to Frodo were like anthropological angels walking me deeper into my love for him. And as I loved him more and more, my irrational fears dissipated.

Peter and I just celebrated our eighth anniversary. He is extremely healthy and vital. I no longer have that irrational health panic; I do struggle, however, with the practicalities and realities of being in a mixed-status relationship. Mostly, these are not irrational fears. Mostly. These are the real concerns about the subtleties and complexities of a mixed-status relationship. I have more information and practical knowledge about what it means to live with HIV/AIDS as I've become more intimate with Peter's day-to-day health concerns and emotional struggles. But most importantly, Peter's health is not emotionally quarantined in our relationship: while he is certainly the one who carries the burden of the illness, we are both living with HIV/AIDS now.

This realization became relevant when I was attending information sessions for Social Work graduate programs in Southern California. I noticed a pattern when the fieldwork was explained. Most of the programs emphasized that we would be sent to agencies to work with populations that might bring personal discomfort. Did we struggle with witnessing violence and its aftermath? We might be sent to a shelter for survivors of domestic partner abuse. How did we feel about that? In one session they even stated that, in our first year, they would purposely send us to work with a population that might "bring up our fears." As I listened, I thought about my AIDS panic and knew that this was some form of confirmation: for me, the path to becoming a social worker and the population I wish to serve was related to my fears, my relationship with Peter, and the waning panic as I acquired deeper life experiential knowledge and understanding of the disease. I now wish to serve the population that I feared the most.

My focus now is on assisting those with HIV/AIDS who are aging with the disease and facing unique struggles. These are battles that no one else has ever faced. No one knows, yet, what it means to be aging or elderly with HIV/AIDS, while also being a sexual minority status and living with the emotional stresses of profound and catastrophic mass-bereavement as many watched their friends and lovers die. Like my partner, Peter, these are men and women on an uncharted, hero's journey. And I feel a kind of love that is difficult to describe.

1. In what ways does Charles locate himself in a historical and political era of fear and repression and in what ways does this influence his emotions?

2. How does Charles undergo growth and transformation as his perspective shifts?

3. How does Charles's positionality inform his fear and anxiety about HIV/AIDS and influence his personal and romantic relationships?

4. Think about your own experiences in life. What populations make you feel uncomfortable or fearful, and how do you navigate your emotions?

DISCUSSION QUESTIONS

1. What feelings and thoughts came up for you in response to these stories?

2. How did the varied positionalities of the authors intersect with their values?

3. What sorts of ethical dilemmas emerge from the stories and how did they navigate these challenges?

ACTIVITIES

1. Explore your values

   With regard to your personal values

   a. What values are most important to you?

   b. Where did these values come from? Parents? Life experiences? Peers? Mentors?

   c. How have these values influenced your life in other ways? Give examples.

   d. What attitudes, beliefs, or knowledge do you use to explain the world and human behavior? What do you believe are the causes of individual and/or societal problems?

   e. What is your perspective about change?

   f. How have the lenses of privilege and of oppression influenced your life?

   With regard to the social work profession

   a. How do you want to make a difference as a social worker?

   b. What values and biases do you bring to your attitudes regarding social work?

   c. In what ways do your intersecting identities (class, race, age, gender, and so on) influence your perceptions of social problems and solutions?

2. While we do not advocate a "cookie cutter" approach to ethical issues or challenges, we believe that critical examination of the varied responses that you and your peers have to potential value tensions and ethical dilemmas can be instructive as a way to open up dialogue. Consider the following scenarios and how you might respond to them.

   a. A social worker becomes engaged to a person who, until two months ago, was a service user at the agency that employs the social worker

b. A social worker overclaims a mileage allowance in order to fund a group for participants

c. A social worker refuses to work with same-sex couples because of religious beliefs

d. A social worker invites participants to pray

e. A social worker appears on local television with participants to publicize their plight

f. A social worker is working as a dancer in a lap dancing club on their own time

ADDITIONAL RESOURCES

Websites

IFSW Statement of Ethical Principles: http://ifsw.org/policies/statement-of-ethical-principles/

NASW Code of Ethics: https://www.socialworkers.org/pubs/code/code.asp

National Codes of Ethics from IFSW member organizations: http://ifsw.org/resources/publications/national-codes-of-ethics/

Films

American violet (2008). T. Disney

Argo (2012). B. Affleck

Blood diamond (2006). E. Zwick

Brubaker (1980). S. Rosenberg

Do the right thing (1989). S. Lee

Erin Brockovich (2000). S. Soderbergh

Girl, interrupted (1999). J. Mangold

Hotel Rwanda (2004). T. George

How to die in Oregon (2011).P. Richardson

In whose honor (1997). J. Rosenstein

Maria full of grace (2004).J. Marston

Silverlake life: The view from here (1993). T. Joslin & P. Friedman

Thank you for smoking (2005). J. Reitman

The corporation (2003). J. Abbott & M. Achbar

The insider (1999). M. Mann

Wall Street (1987). O. Stone

Books

Belkin, L. (1993). *First do no harm*. New York: Ballantine Books.

Jordan, H. (2008). *Mudbound*. Chapel Hill, NC: Algonquin Books.

Picoult, J. (1996). *Mercy*. New York: Pocket Books.

Roy, A. (1997). *The god of small things*. New York: Harper Collins.

Yalom, I. (1996). *Lying on the couch*. New York: Harper Collins.

3

Theoretical Perspectives on Social Work

As we navigate our world, we try to make sense of the various experiences in our day-to-day life. In order to understand and explain our actions, interactions, and the events we witness, we use theory everyday to create and engage. We carry with us personal and cultural theories that we apply to our life and the way we interpret the events in our life. Oftentimes, we don't even realize that we use theories in our everyday personal lives. We may consciously or subconsciously "test" these theories, to determine whether we continue to use them to inform our behaviors, or not use them and instead shift our ways of thinking and acting.

These kinds of theories are personally or culturally constructed (informal theory). This chapter is more concerned with theories that are scientifically constructed within academia (formal theory). An academic or formal theory can be defined as an "organized statement of ideas about the world" (Payne, 2005b, p. 5) or as a set of statements or principles developed to explain a phenomenon, especially one that has been repeatedly tested or is widely accepted. A theory can also be a concept that is not yet verified, but if true, explains certain facts or phenomena.

> Consider your own positionality, history, and experiences in life. What theories do you remember learning as you were growing up? What are some of the theories that you created or maintained to help you interpret experiences, make sense of circumstances, and understand various situations in life? What are some theories that you've learned in life (from family, culture, tradition) that don't reflect the ways in which you view the world?

THE IMPORTANCE OF THEORY IN SOCIAL WORK

All social work practice is informed by formal and informal theories of what social work is; how to execute social work; and how to understand the world of the client, service user, or participant (Payne, 2005b). Theories seek to describe what is going on; they seek to explain certain behavior or phenomena; they seek to predict specific events; and they seek to control and manage events or changes (Mullaly, 2007). Social work theories also help us to understand the contextual nature of behavior. These different contexts can include biological, physiological, psychological, sociocultural, spiritual, economic, political, and historical contexts.

Theories can offer guidelines for therapeutic and social interventions. These types of theories on how to perform or execute social work are called practice theories. For example, based on our view of social work as social justice–oriented work, the focus of this textbook is anti-oppressive theory. Theories that highlight the participant's world have a focus on the problems and social realities that social workers encounter in their practice. Theories also shape the way we view participants and how we conduct assessments, interventions, and research. In selecting what theories to use in practice, social workers contribute to how the social work profession is constructed. What social workers do in the field defines what social work becomes (Payne, 2005b).

THE CONSTRUCTION OF SOCIAL WORK THEORIES

All theory is socially constructed, meaning that it develops and exists in a society already shaped by other ideas and assumptions of what is considered acceptable behavior. People acting on their interpretations and their knowledge of the world around them create theories that explain what they see, and the theories in turn influence what people see and how they interpret it. The social construction of theory is an ongoing, dynamic process. Thus, our perspectives and understanding of human behavior are continuously changing.

Theory is shaped by the values, meanings, and assumptions that individuals hold about the world. Consequently, the theories used in social work represent different social and political views about how welfare should be provided and the changes that need to be made (individually or socially).

Malcolm Payne, who wrote a textbook on social work theory (2005b), suggests that social work theories reflect three different views of how social welfare should be provided. The following approaches are further described in Image 3.1.

- *Reflexive-therapeutic views:* This approach to social work practice attempts to work on changing the participants without taking into account the social and structural inequalities that exist and need to be changed. The relationship between the social worker's world view and the participant's world view is mutually influential and constantly in flux due to dialogue. The idea is for social workers to assist participants to gain power over their feelings and take control of their own lives. Once personal power is achieved, individuals, groups, and communities can overcome suffering and disadvantage.
- *Individualist-reformist views:* Through this perspective, social workers are preserving social order and providing support to those who need it so that the participants can

maintain stability, fulfill their potential, and live within the current system. Like reflexive-therapeutic views, this approach seeks to change the participant existing within the system without taking into account the need to change the system itself.

- *Socialist-collectivist views:* From this perspective, social workers aim to empower individuals, groups, and communities to engage in co-learning, dialogue, and collaborative action toward changing their realities and transforming the systems that perpetuate oppression. The assumption is that individuals cannot be fully empowered unless society is transformed, and so the existing social order is questioned. The central value behind this view of social work is the pursuit of social justice.

Payne (2005b) points up the differences between those perspectives that seek to change individuals and those that seek to transform society. He argues that reflexive-therapeutic views and individualist-reformist views seek to maintain social order, thereby preserving the interests of the elite, not those who are most oppressed. In contrast, supporters of socialist-collectivist views advocate for changing societies and social structures. Opponents of socialist-collectivist views believe that these goals are too idealistic and unrealistic in implementation. They also

Image 3.1 Ways of Viewing the Goals and Methods of Social Work Practice			
	Reflexive-Therapeutic Views	*Individualist-Reformist Views*	*Socialist-Collectivist Views*
Also known as	Therapeutic helping (Dominelli, 2002b)	Maintenance approach (Dominelli, 2002b)	Emancipatory approach (Dominelli, 2002b), transformational approach (Pease & Fook, 1999)
Focus	To assist individuals, groups, and communities to achieve growth and self-fulfillment using a therapeutic approach	To meet individuals' needs and improve services while also ensuring efficiency of service delivery	To seek cooperation and solidarity among those most marginalized and oppressed in society so that they can gain power over their own lives
Theories within this view (Mullaly, 2010)	Psychodynamic theories, behavioral theories, client-centered theories, psycho-social theories, clinical theories, family therapies, casework	General systems theory, ecosystems (ecological) theory, life model theories, problem-solving strengths, perspective theories	Feminist theory, Marxist theory, radical theories, structural theories, antiracist theories, anti-oppressive theories, critical postmodern theories, postcolonial theories, indigenous (decolonizing) theories, narrative therapies, just therapy

Source: Adapted from Payne, 2005b.

assert that stakeholders who finance and support social service agencies prefer to maintain the social order and create a better fit between society and individuals. Therefore, they do not seek or embrace major changes (Payne, 2005b).

Those who hold reflexive-therapeutic views and individualist-reformist views often believe that through their work with individuals, small changes can occur that provide a stepping stone for larger social changes. However, Kivel (2006) believes that a social worker's focus on social service design and delivery is a disadvantage to long-term social change. Social service agencies may become preoccupied with maintaining established wealth and existing poverty through the system of "helping" others instead of developing ways to create community power for change. Thus, many socialist-collectivist social workers advocate for placing our energy into mobilizing communities to battle against exclusion, marginalization, criminalization, and violence, while "simultaneously engaging in a long-term struggle for redistribution of wealth and power" (Kivel, 2006, p. 23).

> Take a moment to reflect on the three perspectives and approaches to social work practice presented by Payne (2005). What are the contributions of each perspective to the social work profession? How do you view social work practice? Which view of social work most aligns with your own values and worldview?

THEORETICAL FRAMEWORKS FOR SOCIAL WORK PRACTICE

The theories that inform social work include both traditional theories and critical or progressive theories. First, we examine the most common, traditional, mainstream social work theories, the ones that are predominant in the field today. Progressive theories are highlighted at the end of the section; this second group of theories is central to the anti-oppressive approach to social justice work.

Traditional Social Work Theories

Conventional, mainstream social work theories primarily focus on individual change, addressing "individuals in need," with a limited focus on social change. Conventional social work theories do not recognize communal responsibility for constructing the social world (Pozzuto, Angell, & Dezendorf, 2005) nor do they question the organization of society. The active role that people play in constructing society and its structures is hidden by the assumed "naturalness" of social structures that remain unquestioned. Accordingly, through solely focusing on individual change, the current social order is maintained and unchallenged.

General Systems Theory

General systems theory was developed during the 1940s and 1950s in the fields of management and psychology (Payne, 2002). In the 1970s, drawing on the physical sciences, Ludwig von Bertalanffy suggested that all of the social sciences could be integrated by using systems as a unit of analysis (De Hoyos, 1989). Dr. von Bertalanffy's interest in how systems maintain homeostasis (balance and order) influenced the work of other theorists who offered a comprehensive account of social work from a systems perspective (see Goldstein, 1973; Pincus & Minaham, 1973).

Social systems theory had its major impact on social work in the 1970s. Social workers were trying to move away from a psychiatric focus toward greater inclusion of environmental factors. Three different types of systems were identified: informal systems (family, friends, neighborhoods); formal systems (church, clubs, associations, trade unions); and social systems (schools, employers, state structures). Systems theory as it is applied to social work focuses on the interactions and interdependence between people and these systems.

The major concern of systems theory is explaining change, and the goal is maintaining balance within each system. The underlying assumption is that human systems (from the micro to the macro) are intricately connected and must be viewed holistically—(i.e., how these systems interact together to integrate into a whole). Another concern is that human social systems are analogous to biological systems in certain respects. For example, social systems attempt to protect their survival though adaptation and self-preservation. Social systems are also interrelated and interdependent. Thus, people and their environments are involved in a process of continual adaptation to one another.

Systems theorists argue that one of the purposes of social work is to link people with resource systems and promote the effective working of these systems (Payne, 2002). From this perspective, the focus is on how these systems maintain themselves, influence other systems, and work together to function as a whole.

One conceptual model for social work practice identifies four systems central to the change process:

- The *change agent system* includes the social worker, the social service agency, and the formal and informal resources they command.
- The *client system* includes the individual people, groups, families, and communities who seek help and engage with the change agent system.
- The *target system* involves the individual person, people, or group whom the change agent system and client system is trying to change to achieve client system's change efforts.
- The *action system* is all of the people with whom the change agent system works to achieve the change efforts (Pincus & Minaham, 1973, p. 63)

The focus here is on the connections of families and groups, their resources, and their effective functioning. Systems perspectives see social work as preserving a more effective social order rather than promoting radical change (Payne, 2002).

Ecological (Ecosystems) Theory

Since the 1980s, ecological theory, also known as ecosystems theory, has expanded the focus of social work practice by emphasizing the interaction between people and their environment, formalizing the important notion of environmental intervention. Whereas systems theory is primarily concerned with explaining change, ecological/ecosystems theory is primarily concerned with explaining humans in interaction (De Hoyos, 1989).

An ecological approach focuses on the way human beings and their environment accommodate each other. This interaction is dynamic. Harmony between individuals and their environment is achieved through mutual interaction, negotiation, and compromise (De Hoyos, 1989).

Urie Bronfenbrenner's work in ecosystems theory considers how people adapt to their environments and cope with problems (1979). The focus is on the settings in which people play out various roles and the interactions among these aspects that might impact people's functioning. Bronfenbrenner (1979) proposed five layers of experience that have an impact on individuals (see Image 3.2):

- *Microsystem:* all the roles and relationships that a person has in their immediate environment. In this layer, attention is focused on family, school, neighborhood, church, workplace, and other places that have an immediate and persistent impact on the individual.
- *Mesosystem:* the interactions among two or more micro system environments, such as family and workplace, or school and family. An example of a mesosystem experience is when someone brings home the tension generated at work.
- *Exosystem:* all of the external social settings where things happen that tangentially affect the individual, such as school boards or businesses. An example of an experience at this level is policy decisions about a school closure and its effect on the community.
- *Macrosystem:* all the larger cultural and social factors that affect the other levels of a person's environment hence the person's development. An example is social attitudes about gay marriage, resulting in discrimination against individuals.
- *Chronosystem:* patterns of change over the life course. An example of this is a divorce, birth, or a death in the family that changes the family dynamics.

Ecosystems theory helps social workers to see how one individual is nested within different layers of his or her environment, while examining how these interconnected social systems influence one another.

Despite the fact that most schools of social work train practitioners to use systems theory and ecological/ecosystems theory, these theories have a number of limitations when they are applied in the practice setting:

- Viewing reality as a system of information exchanges omits social contexts as well as the complex and important dynamics that exist in participants' lives.
- The biological aspects of participants' lives are given limited attention.

Image 3.2

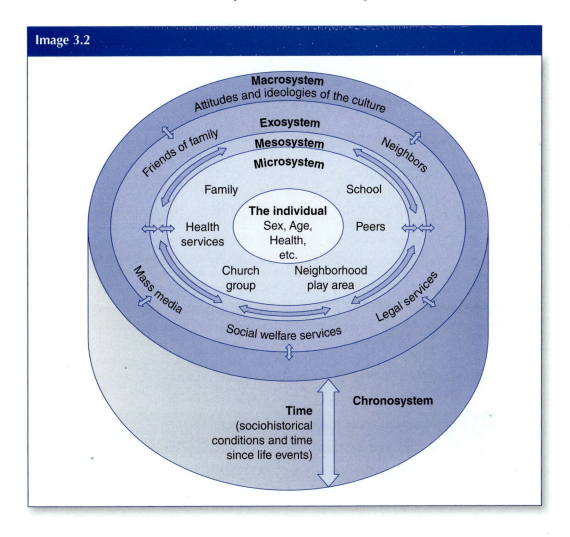

- If every part of the system has equal weight (as systems and ecosystems theorists seem to imply), elements of little importance may be overemphasized (Whitchurch & Constantine, 1993).
- Concentrating on current functioning, and overlooking past functioning, threatens to limit the analysis of a person's environment. For example, the focus on the "here-and-now situation and possibilities for intervention" contributes to a neglect of history (Finn & Jacobson, 2008).
- The levels and types of interventions required in particular circumstances are not clearly specified (Payne, 2005). Two social workers applying the theory to the same participant could choose completely different realms on which to focus; therefore the theory appears to lack validity & reliability.

- Because these theories accept dominant values and consensus assumptions, they do not work toward changing the unjust structures that perpetuate oppression (Dominelli & McLeod, 1989).
- These theories ignore differences in power, privilege, and oppression and assuming equality reinforces political inequality.
- These theories are too problem-oriented and ignore positive areas of functioning in participants' lives.

Person-in-Environment (PIE) Perspective

Systems and ecological theory inform the "person-in-environment" (PIE) perspective that emerged in the late 1980s. The goal of creating PIE was to have an assessment tool that all social workers could use, regardless of agency setting, to describe, classify, and code problems presented by participants (Karls & Wandrei, 1992). PIE aims to provide a common language for social workers to use in order to describe participant's problems and plans for effective interventions. Image 3.3 shows the four distinct factors of PIE that can be used to assess a participant's problems.

PIE offers a uniform system for describing, classifying, and coding the participant's presenting problems. However, similar to general systems and ecosystems perspectives, the focus is on the participant's problems rather than strengths. Focusing on a participant's problems can emphasize deficits rather than abilities and motivation for change. The result is that we come to see the deficit as defining the person (Payne, 2011).

Image 3.3	Factors of the Person-in-Environment (PIE) Perspective Used in Assessing Participants' Social Role Functioning	
PIE Factor	*Type of Problem*	*Format of Assessment Document*
1	Performance of activities of daily living required by culture or community for the individual's age or stage of life	Description of participant's problem, assessment of its severity, length of time it has existed, physical and psychological strength of participant
2	Environment influences, including problems in the social institutions that exist to help the participant	Description of environmental factors, environmental problems identified in assessment, and estimate of their severity and duration
3	Mental disorders	Identification of axes within the *Diagnostic and Statistical Manual of Mental Disorders* (DSM)
4	Physical health conditions	Narrative of presenting physical health or medical issues

Source: Adapted from Karls and Wandrei, 1992, pp. 82–83.

What might be some of the limitations to focusing solely on a participant's problems? What are some of the implications of a problem-focused approach to social work practice?

Strengths Perspective

In the 1990s, a strengths-based approach emerged in response to the problem-focused approaches that then dominated social work practice. The paradigm began to shift toward seeing individuals, families, and communities in light of their capacities, talents, competencies, possibilities, visions, values, and hopes. Resilience—the notion that people survive and thrive despite risk factors for various types of problems—was highlighted (Early & GlenMaye, 2000). A strengths-based approach to social work practice views people as having a range of experiences, characteristics, and roles that contribute to who that person is (Saleebey, 1997). A strengths perspective recognizes human capacity, agency, and self-determination.

From this perspective, social workers acknowledge an individual or family system's capacity to survive, regenerate, and grow out of crises and challenges in life. Social workers who practice from a strengths-based perspective value the human potential to learn, change, adapt, and identify what they want in life. The center of change is the participant. Social workers practicing from a strengths approach encourage participants to define and ascribe meaning to their own situations as "experts" in their own lives (Early & GlenMaye, 2000). Social workers create a space for participants to tell their own stories and then to retell those stories in a way that highlights their own expertise (Chapin & Cox, 2001). Individual uniqueness and self-determination are strongly acknowledged.

Another major focus of strengths-based social work is the collaboration and partnership between social worker and participant. The participant's vision for how they want to lead their life informs the goals and activities selected in order to meet those goals. Oftentimes, families are also invited to participate in the intervention process (Early & GlenMaye, 2000). The social worker hears the participant's or family's story about how they have survived thus far, what they want, and how they think things are going for them in different aspects of their lives. The social worker illuminates the strengths that exist and helps the participant(s) create a vision of what life would look like when they no longer "have" the problem (de Shazer, 1991).

The strengths perspective is seen as an enhanced lens through which to view the person and environment connection (Finn & Jacobson, 2008). It also shifts the way in which social workers practice by giving the participant a voice and influence over the decisions that affect his or her life. The relationship between the social worker and participant is based on collaboration, dialogue, and understanding. So, instead of asking "what's wrong?" the social worker poses "what's possible?" (Saleebey, 1997). The social worker spends less time identifying problems and looking for causes and more time trying to identify resources that the participant already has to solve problems.

However, government mandates and funding issues often require social workers to collect extensive background information on the participants (Rogers, 2010). Thus, the strengths approach is often supplemented by more probing of participant's problems for bureaucratic reasons. Also, different social workers define the meaning of strengths differently. In addition, as a micro-oriented theory, it falls short of actually making any structural changes to existing oppressive social structures. In that regard, this approach tends to avoid focusing on the struggles and experiences of those most marginalized in society. There is also the assumption that all environments have resources, which is not the case for everyone, particularly marginalized communities.

Critical and Progressive Social Work Theories

Unlike the traditional social work theories, critical and progressive theories seek to transform the current social order. These change-based theories are critical of existing social arrangements that are unjust and perpetuate oppression. Based on the notion that current social institutions are incapable of meeting human needs, progressive social work theories seek to foster emancipatory practice for individual and societal transformation.

Empowerment Theories

Theories of empowerment build on people's strengths, resiliency, and resources (Robbins, Chatterjee, & Canda, 2006). In comparison to traditional theories and approaches, they are more concerned with helping people to realize their highest strengths and engage in actions that promote social justice and change (Gutierrez & Ortega, 1991). To achieve this, they identify and address any personal and political barriers and dynamics that maintain discrimination and oppression. Empowerment theories seek to articulate the linkages between the personal and the political, building on the traditions of self-help, mutual support, and collective action (Finn & Jacobson, 2008).

An empowerment approach involves educating people about unequal and unjust social and structural conditions and analyzing power relations with those who are oppressed. Useful techniques include consciousness raising and collective efforts to challenge oppressive social conditions (Gutierrez & Lewis, 1999). On a personal level, social workers also make a commitment to assist with actions that increase individual and community power. In individual practice, efforts are focused on strengthening an individual's power within the system, as well as facilitating social participation and resource utilization (Song, 2011). The individual and collective voices of those who are oppressed must all be heard.

Similar to strengths-based perspectives, an empowerment approach supports client participation in all aspects of the decision-making process affecting their lives. Empowerment theories also seek egalitarian working relationships between the social worker and participant.

The effects of powerlessness, and the attainment of empowerment, occur on three different levels (Gutierrez & Lewis, 1999). For example:

- *Individual level:* a person feels positive about their self-esteem, self-efficacy and mastery, is able to set goals and take action to achieve these goals, while viewing oneself with a "goodness-of-fit" with the environment.
- *Interpersonal level:* a person feels assertive about interpersonal interactions, is able to form partnerships with people and gains respect and honor from others.
- *Socio-Political level:* a person has knowledge about his/her own right, holds positive attitudes toward the possibility of changing the environment by taking collective action and is willing to take action to pursue social justice. (Song, 2011, p. 1018)

It isn't enough for social workers to just focus on an individual sense of personal power, providing skills or working toward social change (Gutierrez & Lewis, 1999); empowerment needs to take place on all three levels.

While empowerment perspectives have gained credibility and recognition within the social work profession, some critics point out that social workers are most likely to embrace the language of empowerment rather than the actual practice (Finn & Jacobson, 2008). Other scholars highlight the main dilemma of empowerment: empowering others without executing people's empowerment for them (Adams, 1996). In addition, some of the key assumptions, goals, and practices of empowerment can actually perpetuate hierarchical power relations between social workers and participants (Solas, 1996). Empowerment may give the illusion of equality while still maintaining the authoritarian relationship of professional-client, because the professional may be viewed as the one with the power to give to participants. In fact, the very act of defining someone as "disempowered" can be disempowering (Fook, 2002).

In addition, some people do not easily fit into groupings of either "powerful" or "powerless," sometimes simultaneously embodying both as a result of their identities and social memberships. Furthermore, two people might have the exact same experience or circumstance, but one may feel empowered and the other person may feel disempowered. What is empowering for some people may be disempowering for others.

To avoid using empowerment to maintain existing power inequalities, the social worker must have a complex understanding of how power works in relation to different people and various circumstances. The following elements need to be taken into account:

- the contextual and changing nature of power;
- how power operates at different levels, often simultaneously and in contradictory ways;
- how power is experienced by different people; and
- the creative, as well as controlling, possibilities that power entails (Fook, 2002, page 103).

When we use an empowerment model, we need to ask such important questions as "empowerment for what?" and "empowerment for whom?" (Fook, 2002, p. 48). We also need to maintain a social justice perspective that addresses oppression first and foremost (Ward & Mullender, 1991).

> Consider a time when you felt empowered, as well as a time when you felt powerless. Take a few moments to draw these experiences by hand on a blank sheet of paper. Don't worry about how well you draw; focus on how you want to visually represent your experiences. Now, take a moment to reflect on what you drew and the events or incident that took place. Consider the following: How did power manifest in your experiences? What are some of the assumptions you make about power, who has it, where it comes from, what it allows you to do or prevents you from doing.

Feminist Theories

The use of feminist theories in social work contributes to understanding and responding to the oppression of women in society. Feminist social work emerged in the 1960s from activism by women working with other women in their communities, and then linking their personal and local circumstances with public issues (Payne, 2005b).

Various feminist perspectives have emerged to explain women's unequal status in society. Image 3.4 highlights the differences among the following perspectives:

- *Liberal Feminism:* focuses on how sex differences between men and women are translated into gender differences through cultural assumptions, which in turn affect social relations. The goal is promoting gender equality and removing any political, social, legal, or economic obstacles that prevent women from having equal access to resources. Liberal feminists aim to change the socialization process so that children are not raised to believe and accept gender inequalities.
- *Radical Feminism:* focuses on patriarchy, a social system characterized by men's power and privilege, as the root of all oppression. Radical feminists celebrate differences between men and women and aim to form separate structures that are women-centered (Nes & Iadicola, 1989).
- *Socialist and Marxist Feminism:* focuses on the intersections between class and gender oppression. Under capitalism, women are seen as a "reserve army of labor" who are exploited for free labor in the home by carrying out domestic tasks and childcare.
- *Black Feminism:* focuses on privileging the voices of women of color whose voices were often excluded from feminist theorizing (Collins, 2000). Black feminism highlights racism and the connections of black women's experiences to the history of slavery, focusing on historic social and structural oppression. Black women are thought to have a heightened experience of oppression in comparison to white women.

- *Standpoint Feminism:* focuses on granting epistemic privilege (the privilege of knowing) to those who are marginalized. By virtue of what they experience and how they understand it, marginalized individuals may better understand certain aspects of the social structure than those who are privileged (Harding, 2004). Therefore, the perspectives of marginalized groups are more complete and more valuable (Haraway, 1988; Harding, 2004). Some standpoint feminists assert that the dominant groups' view is more superficial. However, feminist standpoint theories do not account for the possible status of some individuals who are part of a dominant group, or whose position continues to shift between the two. Nevertheless, feminist standpoint theories are committed to the emancipation of marginalized or oppressed groups through valuing the socially constructed category of women. They aim to mobilize collective action for change.
- *Postmodern Feminism:* focuses on the construction of social categories of sex and gender through language and discourse that creates social scripts of how women are and should be treated. One of the major contributions is the deconstruction and rejection of socially created categories. Postmodern feminist theories reject the notion that there is an essential nature of women, only one way to be a woman. They also reject the binary categories of man or woman. These feminist theories honor multiple truths, multiple roles, and multiple realities of individuals.
- *Postcolonial and Transnational Feminism:* focuses on the intersections among nationhood, race, gender, sexuality, and economic oppression on a global scale, in the context of globalization and capitalism. Transnational feminists inquire into the social, political, and economic conditions that compose imperialism and the connections of these conditions to colonialism and nationalism. Postcolonial and transnational feminists attend to the role of gender, the state, race, class, and sexuality in the organization of resistance to hegemonies during the process of making and unmaking nations and nation-states.

Despite the differences among these feminist lenses, there is a commonality among them in the ways in which they inform social work practice. Feminist social work theories focus on understanding the lives and experiences of women from their own perspectives and values. They address the political, social, and economic marginalization of women, and the systems of thought and practice that have marginalized them. Feminist theories highlight questions of power and authority, difference, and domination. Feminist social work theories examine concepts of discourse and the ways that language is used to construct power relations (Dominelli, 2002b). In practice, feminist social work highlights the following:

- Relationship (valuing interpersonal connections with others, based on sensitivity, reciprocity, and mutual help)
- Power (moving beyond ingrained relationships of domination and resistance as a way to challenge oppression)

Image 3.4 Feminist Perspectives in Social Work		
Perspective	*Focus of Study*	*In Practice*
Liberal feminism	How sex differences are translated into gender differences through cultural assumptions, which in turn affect social relations	Promoting gender equality by removing political, social, legal, and economic obstacles that prevent women's equal access to resources; promoting child-raising practices that embrace gender equality
Radical feminism	How patriarchy (a social system characterized by men's power and privilege) underlies all oppression	Celebrating differences between men and women; forming separate women-centered social structures
Socialist and Marxist feminism	How class and gender intersect to create oppression; how women are exploited for free labor in the home (domestic tasks and childcare)	Promoting work for women outside of domestic roles and using a class-based and patriarchal lens to examine "who controls the resources?" and "which institutions are keeping those people in control of the resources?"
Black feminism	How the history of slavery and ongoing racism have created social and structural oppression for women of color	Struggling against racial, sexual, heterosexual, and class oppression, with practice based upon the lens that the major systems of oppression are interlocking
Standpoint feminism	How the knowledge of marginalized groups differs from, and improves upon, the knowledge of privileged groups	Valuing the more complete experience and knowledge of marginalized and oppressed individuals; mobilizing collective action for change in the social construction of women's status
Postmodern feminism	How the construction of social categories based on sex and gender have influenced social scripts for how women should be treated	Deconstructing notions about the essential nature of women and binary sex and gender categories; honoring multiple truths, roles, and realities that affect individuals
Postcolonial and transnational feminism	How nationhood, race, gender, sexuality, and economic oppression interact in the context of globalization and capitalism	Organizing resistance to hegemonies of capitalism and imperialism as nations and nation-states evolve

Source: Adapted from Collins, 2000; Harding, 2004; Nes & Iadicola, 1989.

- Language (acknowledging and confronting its power and implications)
- Diversity (accepting that there are multiple truths and multiple realities)
- Voice (valuing the voices and perspectives of those most marginalized)
- Agency (considering individuals as active agents capable of making decisions for themselves in all aspects of their lives)
- Reflexivity (attending to process, not product, and self-questioning practice approaches)
- Interconnectedness (recognizing the interdependent nature of human relationships)
- Collectivity (looking for collective solutions to individual problems)
- Challenge (deconstructing systems of oppression, particularly patriarchal hierarchies, and contesting dominant ideologies)
- Empowerment (increasing opportunities for empowerment through egalitarian process)
- Creativity (seeking non-dominant forms of representation and knowing)
- Commitment to social change (acknowledging the principle that "the personal is political")

Feminist methods of social work practice center around collaboration and group work to achieve critical consciousness of issues that affect women and those persons most marginalized in society. Practice approaches include engaging in dialogue, equalizing power in the social worker-participant relationship, centering women's experiences, and providing spaces for sharing experiences related to intersecting identities to create inspiration for action. From a feminist perspective, social workers are loyal to the participants rather than to agencies or systems; thus, they seek to include participants' voices and participation in the process (Payne, 2005b). In comparison with critical social work practice, feminist practice provides a wider range of explanations of oppression (using an intersectional lens) and prioritizes personal and interpersonal experiences as an expression of oppression and as contributors to social change (Healy, K., 2000).

Liberation Theories and Empowerment Education

Liberation theories focus on eliminating the causes and addressing the effects of social oppression, educating individuals to move from oppression to liberation and then taking collective action to change oppressive cultural and social structures. Empowerment education for critical consciousness, also commonly referred to as liberation theology, emerged as a concept in the 1950s and 1960s through the teachings and writings of Brazilian educator Paulo Freire. Awakening a critical consciousness means educating people to perceive the social, political, and economic contradictions in their life. In essence, oppressed individuals become self-liberators.

One of Freire's central tenets is that education is not neutral; it takes place within the context of people's lives. In class or community settings, adults and young people bring with them their life experiences, current pressures, and future expectations. However, with the proper tools, anyone is capable of looking critically at the world, his or her personal and social reality, and the contradictions that exist everywhere (Freire, 1970).

Within this context Freire (1973) asks:

- Who does education serve and for what purpose?
- Does education socialize individuals to be passive objects of learning who accept the status quo, or does it encourage people to question the critical issues of the day and challenge the systems and power?

According to Freire, the purpose of education should be individual liberation so that learners can be both subjects and actors in their own lives and within society (Wallerstein & Bernstein, 1988). For Freire, all pedagogy is a call to action for change and social justice.

Freire acknowledges that established knowledge comes from those in power; therefore, less powerful individuals are left voiceless. As a remedy, he proposes a dialogue approach, where everyone participates as equal learners who co-create knowledge. The goal of group dialogue is for participants to reveal the causes of their status and location in society, focusing on the influence of the socioeconomic, political, cultural, and historical context of their personal lives (Wallerstein & Bernstein, 1988). This exercise in critical thinking and reflection then moves toward praxis: actions that people can take to become empowered in their lives and within their communities. Freire (1970) conceptualizes praxis as the dynamic of reflective action or active reflection, where words and action are closely intertwined.

Freire believes that those who are underprivileged are preoccupied with survival and often lack an understanding of how power structures work. The oppressed often share the oppressor's viewpoint, blaming themselves for their own powerlessness. Freire (1985) states:

> The oppressed, having internalized the image of the oppressor and adopted his guidelines, are fearful of freedom. Freedom would require them to eject this image and replace it with autonomy and responsibility. Freedom is acquired by conquest, not by gift. It must be pursued constantly and responsibly. Freedom is not an ideal located outside of [us]; nor is it an idea which becomes a myth. It is rather the indispensable condition for the quest for human completion. (p. 31)

Social work practice using liberation theory emphasizes that participants must work to improve the quality of life and justice in communities. A social worker would encourage clients to share and speak from their own experiences, identify a common theme among their own situations, create an analytical perspective from which to understand root causes, and develop solutions and strategies for change. Thus, empowering education teaches more than individual development; it is directed at individual change, community quality of life, and structural changes for social justice.

Radical and Structural Social Work

Radical and structural approaches to social work, influenced by Marxist social theories, were developed between the 1960s and 1980s. These theoretical perspectives are concerned with the broad socioeconomic and political dimensions of society (specifically capitalism) and their impact in creating unequal relations among individuals (Mullaly, 1997). Radical and structural social work rejects the traditional social work practice that accepts existing social policies based on economic liberalism or rationalism (Payne, 2005b). From the radical/structural perspective, society is composed of groups with conflicting interests who compete for resources, power, and the prevalence of their own views of the world. Thus, social problems are the result of "defective rules" that punish and pathologize marginalized groups (Mullaly, 1997, p. 120).

Radical and structural approaches emerged as an alternative to what was seen as social work practice that focused on individuals and their pathologies. Radical and structural social work does not ignore individual problems, instead it shifts the focus to structures (Hick, Peters, Corner, & London, 2012). Personal problems are connected to broader societal conditions, characterized by inequalities of power and lack of access to resources (Moreau, 1979; Mullaly, 1997). This paradigm shift reflected a desire to move away from "blaming" the individual "victim" for their problems (Fook, 2002).

Structural social work suggests that the power hierarchies within and among institutions and structures result in inequality and oppression. From this perspective, the participant is at the receiving end of systemic inequality and exploitation (Finn & Jacobson, 2008). Practice methods aim to break down these power hierarchies and unjust institutions by promoting consciousness of social inequalities, political action, and social change. Using the feminist notion that the personal is political, social workers bring together people to connect with and realize their state of oppression and its connection to unequal social structures (Payne, 2005b). The approach is also similar to Freire's support of dialogue: collectively questioning existing hierarchies and assumptions, and critically analyzing how structures are implicated in one's oppression and identity. The social worker aims to build solidarity and communal action in order to facilitate political action.

To summarize, there are five ways that social workers can implement a radical and structural approach to social work practice (Payne, 2005b; Wood & Tully, 2006):

- deconstructing sociopolitical discourse to reveal the relationship with individual struggles;
- providing participants with insider information;
- connecting people to needed resources;
- helping participants negotiate problematic situations; and
- changing social structures, where realistic.

Structural and radical social work has gained popularity in Canada, Australia, and the United Kingdom. This approach has been praised for its potential to animate political alliances and anti-globalization movements (Weinberg, 2008). However, there are also significant critiques. In particular, in the United States many social workers consider it "too political" and unrealistic for achieving structural change (Finn & Jacobson, 2008). Some have suggested that an overemphasis on structural change ignores the individual needs of participants. Another critique is the idea of participants as "victims" of structural oppression rather than as actors capable of taking action in the process of personal and societal change (Fook, 2000; Ife, 1997). Thus, radical and structural approaches are limited in their exploration of a participant's role as an agent of change at an individual level (Weinberg, 2008). There is also criticism that a radical and structural approach maintains a view of micro and macro practice being separate (Fook, 2002) since; radical, structural social work practice takes place at the macro level. In addition, some critics suggest that a structural view of power is limited because it views all power as only "power over," or a means of structural control, ignoring other forms of power, for example, "power with" or "power from within."

Anti-Discriminatory, Anti-Oppressive, and Antiracist Theories

The theoretical underpinnings of anti-oppressive practice theories were discussed in Chapter 1. This section is a brief overview of the intersection of anti-oppression, anti-discriminatory and antiracist theories and their contribution to social work's theoretical knowledge base.

Anti-discriminatory, anti-oppressive, and antiracist theories emerged in the 1990s, building on social work practice models from radical, structural, feminist, critical, empowerment, and liberatory frameworks. Anti-discriminatory and antiracist theories focused on combating institutionalized discrimination of all groups, since institutions represent the interests of powerful groups (Payne, 2005b). Specifically, anti-oppressive theories are "grounded in the lived experiences, both collective and individual, of intersecting and multiple oppressions" (Moosa-Mitha, 2005, p. 62).

The concept of intersectionality is foundational to the development of anti-oppressive theories. Initially coined by Kimberlé Crenshaw in 1989, *intersectionality* refers to the merging and mingling of multiple markers of difference (Ludvig, 2006), the interplay of oppressions based on multiple identities, and relational and structural marginalization.

Anti-discriminatory, anti-oppressive and antiracist theories all focus on discrimination and oppression within people's experience of social relations. However, each specific theory has its own emphasis:

- Anti-discrimination theories: exclusion based on identity categories and markers of difference;
- Anti-oppressive theories: the concept of *power* (Lister, 2012); privilege and oppression based on intersecting identity categories;
- Antiracist theories: race as a primary structure of oppression that is rooted in colonialism, capitalism, and patriarchy (Yee, 2005). Antiracist approaches challenge the Eurocentric bias of mainstream social work (Dominelli, 1988).

An understanding of power is central to anti-oppressive, anti-discriminatory, antiracist theories. *Power* can be defined as "the capacity, held individually or collectively, to influence either groups or individuals (including oneself) in a given context" (Smith, 2008, p. 23). Power operates in three different modes (Smith, 2008):

- Personal power: individual characteristics of people (for example, gender and age) that might play a role in such situations as intimate partner violence;
- Positional power: social position (for example, power in the workplace or within organizations); and
- Relational power: relationships between individuals' power and that of groups (for example, the changing nature of family relationships).

There are many ways to conceptualize power, and many scholars have explored its meaning and proposed interpretations of its defining features. In one study, for example, the researchers invited women involved in grassroots organizations in Tapalehui, Mexico, to engage in a discussion about women's power, activism, and possibilities for change (Townsend, Zapata, Rowlands, Albereti, & Mercado, 1999). Drawing from these women's experiences, the researchers identified four forms of power:

- Power *over*—when institutions, groups, and individuals practice oppression of others;
- Power *from within*—when people come together and discuss common struggles and hopes;
- Power *with*—when individuals organize to address the conditions and circumstances that affect their lives; and
- Power *to do*—when power is articulated in concrete ways, such as making plans for earning money, designing projects, or acquiring funding.

One useful conceptualization of power asserts that it is something that cannot be owned by one person, group or organization. Rather, power is fluid, multidimensional, and contextual (Smith, 2008). Thus, inequalities of power can also be fluid, affected by changes in individual and group circumstances, and by people's responses to these changes. On the other hand, stable power arrangements can perpetuate discrimination and oppression. Of course, anti-discrimination, antiracist theories place importance on responding to discrimination and oppression, and acknowledging different conceptualizations of power. These theories value "self-definition, giving voice to one's own experiences and knowledge derived from the experiences of marginalization" (Moosa-Mitha, 2005, p. 62).

Because social workers occupy positions of power and influence, discrimination regarding participants is quite possible (Thompson, 1993). Anti-discriminatory practice must include an attempt to eradicate discrimination from our own practice, challenge it in the practice of others, and challenge it in the institutional structures in which we operate.

By the same token, we cannot begin to speak about racism and racial oppression unless we acknowledge institutionalized white privilege and the ways in which people of color have become racialized. By identifying how whiteness perpetuates oppression, one can understand how power and control operate to perpetuate injustice (Yee, 2005). Social work practice from an antiracist lens would place the voices of people of color at the forefront of decision making, service and practice development, community work, and policy development. Thus, social workers aim to understand oppression from oppressed groups themselves.

The goal of anti-discriminatory/anti-oppressive/antiracist social work practice is to achieve equality and social justice for marginalized and oppressed groups. Through this lens, social work practice manifests in the following ways (Yee, 2005):

- understanding of how people's intersecting identities are socially located within oppressive systems;
- challenging the belief that people can only be biologically and culturally defined;
- giving direct assistance to individuals affected by oppression;
- changing the oppressive structure and procedures of service delivery systems through organizational changes, laws, and policies; and
- identifying, naming, and challenging current oppressive systems.

> Consider antiracist theories and their contribution to anti-discriminatory, anti-oppressive approaches. How might an explicit focus on white privilege, advantage, and dominance contribute to understanding oppression and disadvantage? What might be some of the limitations of antiracist theories?

These theories envision that transformation and liberation occurs when "difference is treated as the basis rather than the site of exclusion, for membership in society" (Moosa-Mitha, 2005, p. 63). This requires acknowledging difference and the differential nature of oppression, without losing the sense of collective experiences of oppression.

Eco-Critical Theories

An eco-critical (or eco-social) approach to social work emerged in the 1990s in response to the need to expand ecological and ecosystem theories to focus on environmental justice, sustainability and inclusiveness. The resulting eco-critical social work theories were influenced by theories in other disciplines that spawned environmental movements, environmental sociology, and sustainable development initiatives (Närhi, 2004). Social workers who adopt an eco-critical approach focus on the problems, challenges, and resources affecting the relationship between participants' living environment and welfare. These social workers see participants as potential leaders and encourage their agencies to undertake broad, sustainable community work and to build a sense of belonging (Coates, 2003).

In response to globalization, social worker John Coates (2003) developed an approach that is concerned with sustainable development in all societies, not just those societies that don't have access to resources. Borrowing from systems theory, Coates emphasizes that the earth is a closed system, with limited resources, therefore, our lives and lifestyles should be sustainable. He highlights the need for understanding the interdependence between eco-logical and social issues, local and global connectedness, and accountability. All life forms have value, as they are symbiotic.

Coates (2003) proposes that social work practice from an eco-critical approach should focus on the following:

- developing caring and nurturing communities;
- identifying and developing activities that benefit the common good for people and the environment;
- promoting and enabling active, inclusive partnerships;
- building capacity in individuals, communities, and the bio-region;
- promoting decentralized and localized decision-making and helping it to work toward sustainable solutions;
- promoting community and environmental health;
- promoting environmental justice in conjunction with social justice;
- reducing human and ecological stress; and
- focusing on natural methods of healing and spirituality.

In order for social work to achieve these objectives, the profession must move beyond a preoccupation with personal and social development and begin to see "individual well-being as embedded in community, which is itself embedded in Earth" (Coates, 2003, p. 156). To begin with, the development and well-being of an individual derives from a deep connection to the natural world (Norton, 2012). People and nature are neighbors and participants. Furthermore, larger forces, such as social injustice, social exclusion, and discrepancies in access to human resources must also take into account the environment (Matthies, Närhi, & Ward, 2001). This perspective points up the effects of spatial marginalization and urban segregation (Närhi, 2004).

The eco-critical perspective can accommodate micro, mezzo, and macro level assessment and intervention (Norton, 2012):

- Micro level: an eco-critical assessment might explore a participant's contact with nature as a way to cope. The focus of the social work intervention might be enhanc-ing human-nature connections.
- Mezzo level: a social worker could examine organizations (such as hospitals, prisons, schools, social service agencies, long term care, residential, and psychiatric facilities) and look at whether they offer open courtyards or open spaces as a place for social workers and participants to be exposed to nature. A social worker might also resist corporatism and support community actions that promote sustainability, such as

community gardens, community-supported agriculture, "green economies," growing and buying locally, and recycling.

- Macro level: The awareness of humans as a part of their environment, as well as a part of nature, extends to understanding that those who are most affected by environmental degradation are poor people and people of color. Attention would be paid to giving the oppressed equal access to natural resources in the form of a healthy environment in which to live (Norton, 2012). Social workers would aim to influence and question existing structures and policies and would include environmental issues as part of the change process. Local knowledge, action and decision making are critical in these endeavors, as is the use of local resources for development (Närhi, 2004). Social workers could aid the process through advocacy and policymaking that promotes ecological justice. Social workers could voice their concerns for environmental legislation that addresses the need for clean air and water, alternative energy, and solutions to global climate change (Norton, 2012).

Take a few moments to consider eco-critical approaches to social work. What is our role and responsibility to the environment as social workers?

Social work with participant groups who live in self-contained environments (e.g., nursing homes, juvenile detention centers, mental hospitals) are often alienated from the natural environment. Can you see any benefits in trying to reconnect them with the natural environment?

EVALUATION OF SOCIAL WORK THEORIES

In this chapter, we reflected on the strengths and weaknesses of both traditional and progressive social work theories. But, it is important to go further. Given the inherently ideological and socially constructed essence of theories, it is crucial that all theories are critically examined, questioned, and critiqued.

The questions in Image 3.5 can aid in critically analyzing any social work theory. As we apply them in our social work practice, we must keep in mind that all theories are value-laden and come out of a socio-historical context.

Image 3.5   Standards for Critiquing Social Work Theories

1   What specific aspects of human relationships and social structures (individual, familial, communal, political, cultural, economic, and environmental) does the theory emphasize?

2   What is the historical, political, and professional context for the development of the particular theory?

3 What is the theory's relevance to individuals, families, groups, organizations, institutions, and communities?

4 How consistent is the theory with the values and ethics of social work practice?

5 What assumptions does the theory hold about human beings, the nature of human behavior, the natural environment, and the way the world should operate?

6 How well does this theory reflect the participation of marginalized individuals (from disadvantaged groups) in society?

7 How well does this theory contribute to personal and social transformation?

Source: Adapted from Robbins, Chatterjee, and Canda, 2006; Finn and Jacobson, 2008.

STORIES FROM THE FIELD: THEORETICAL PERSPECTIVES

1 The Violence of "Inaccessibility," and Understanding Mom, by Whitney Stark   p. 119

This story illustrates how to use and apply theory in direct practice. Whitney Stark highlights how we can teach feminist critical theory to our participants. She describes her process of teaching socially conscious video production to disconnected teenagers in a way that serves to educate and empower youth. The opportunity to teach critical theory to youth in high school provided a space for critical dialogue about power, capitalism, racism, sexism, classism, and other forms of oppression. The youth were able to connect structural issues to their individual experiences. Whitney resists the assumptions of her agency supervisor, whose comment implied that poor youth of color could not possibly be capable of learning and understanding complex theory. The assumption that marginalized people are incapable of accessing theory perpetuates violence and oppression against them. Whitney also demonstrates how theory can be used with individuals in case management so that theory can be applied to shift one's perspective of their situation and circumstances.

2 The First Revolution Is Internal, by Daniel Moore   p. 122

This story highlights the voice of an undergraduate social welfare student and his path to understanding anti-oppressive theory and practice. Daniel Moore explores his personal journey of acknowledging his privileged identities and existing oppression at the individual, social, and institutional level. He situates his experiences and his use of the anti-oppressive approach to social work in his work at the organization CAUSE (Central Coast Alliance United for a Sustainable Economy). Daniel highlights the importance of self-reflecting on

(Continued)

(Continued)

our intersecting identities and paying attention to the language we use in our interactions with others.

3 Visions and Voices: Understanding the Needs and Aspirations of Sex Workers Through Photovoice, by Moshoula Capous-Desyllas   p. 125

This story describes the process of using photovoice with sex workers living and working in Portland, Oregon, in order to understand their needs and aspirations. A main goal of this community-based project was to present the women's artistic visions and voices as a form of activism to create community awareness and change around issues of importance to sex workers. Moshoula presents the different theories that informed this project in order to highlight how theory connects to praxis. She discusses her collaboration with her community partner, Crystal Tenty, and how this community-based project served to challenge assumptions about individuals working in the sex work industry, address stereotypes and stigma about sex work, and create social change. Moshoula ends her story by reflecting on the process.

1

THE VIOLENCE OF "INACCESSIBILITY," AND UNDERSTANDING MOM

WHITNEY STARK

When I worked at an alternative high school and in after school programs teaching socially conscious video production, I would always teach critical and feminist media theory. We would talk about concepts like ideology, structural violence, and societal norms to be able to talk about whatever topics the students were interested in making media about.

I would introduce words like *hegemony*, *ideology*, and *homophobia*, etc., on their first day. The best word to have them break down was ide-ology (idea-/-ology), because it sounds sophisticated, but also describes a common concept. It shows that, even with the big words, we aren't doing anything too differently from how they talk about things anyway, just with new tools to name stuff that otherwise would be difficult to discuss. In any case, most of the young people already had the tools to figure out what these new words and concepts meant. But, highlighting these words helped the students understand social critique, something most people do anyway, in different ways and it helped recognize those ways as politically effective.

In my classes we would do a media literacy lesson and talk about things like corporate structures and ownership, sexism in advertisement, racism in representation. Even when someone commented thinking they were just being a smart ass, they were usually offering relevant social critique. One of my favorite moments was in a session on the second day of a program and I was showing an ad for the Puffy fragrance from 2007, where Diddy is shown behind a woman, holding her up against a wall, and I asked them to evaluate it. One young person, under-his-breath-but-loud-enough-for-everyone-to-hear, said "looks like a rape." Of course when I asked "what?" he didn't repeat it and people giggled and looked around. You know, it was the second day. So when I said "exactly," and we took that comment seriously and started looking at the "sexy" ad and others in that way, we had a really good discussion about how rape culture works.

We would also read ideas from anti-oppression, feminist and media/documentary theorists and practitioners whom I had read during my undergraduate studies, especially one of my favorites, Trinh T. Minh-ha. I would let them know that they were doing college level stuff, which I think is important for their confidence. And, in my experience, these discussions always worked. Discussing the concepts of gatekeeper roles, strategy and framework helped these young people read other media closely and make their media intentionally.

I would also always incorporate feminist ideas of situated knowledges and standpoint theory. I developed a lesson plan (see Image 3.6) that took about two minutes to explain. But, it showed how different people, according to their differing, intersecting social locations, have different views, understandings, and experiences of things, and those perspectives were all true and also limited. I used the lesson to help the students recognize the legitimacy of typically under-represented positions as well as to critique hegemonic, false impositions of "objectivity." We would talk about using this way of understanding when thinking about the media they wanted to produce and the media that is mainstream or has already been produced.

Image 3.6 Lesson Plan: Situated Feminisms and Standpoint Theory

As a facilitator, choose an object in the room that is visible to all and where at least one other person (let's call them Ryan) is sitting at a different angle to, resulting in a different vantage than your own. I will be choosing this pink, leopard-print Nike.

My view: Ryan's View (let's pretend the other shoes aren't there):

Now describe the following scenario:

I am making a documentary on this shoe. Now, in my documentary, I would say that this is a pink shoe. On the left side of the shoe there is a large black rubber piece. In the center of the shoes is check mark-like swoosh beginning with it's curve to the left and continuing to the right edge of the shoe.

Now, in Ryan's documentary, they would say that the shoe is pink, it has a large black rubber piece to the right of it, there is a check mark-like swoosh that leads to the left edge of the shoe.... etc.

All of these are truths, neither person is lying, it just depends on the vantage point. And where we come from shapes how we see all sorts of truths, whether it be about our shoes, our selves, our histories, other folks, groups of other folks, what deciding factor makes a group of folks and anything else. What we need to decide then is how we tell a story (or talk about a subject). Will we incorporate other vantage points? Is it fiction if we do not? And if we decide not to, or if we realize that we will never be able to incorporate all vantage points, will we incorporate, in our "documentary" our own social location to be more transparent?

As Trinh T. Minh-ha, documentarian, sociologist, and dreamboat says:
"Every representation of truth involves elements of fiction, and the difference between so-called documentary and fiction in their depiction of reality is a question of degrees of fictitiousness. The more one tries to clarify the line dividing the two, the deeper one gets tangled in the artifice of boundaries."

Source: Created by Whitney Stark, 2012, stark.whitney@gmail.com. Quote by Trinh T. Minh-ha, 1991. *When the Moon Waxes Red: Representation, Gender and Cultural Politics.* New York: Routledge.

After I led my introductory discussion in a summer program, my supervisor, who was in the office and had overheard, told me that the administration was impressed because I could have such a high-level discussion with these kids. They also said I was lucky to have kids in my class who were able to get it and have that kind of discussion. Honestly, that observation was really offensive to me. Assuming that critical thinking is not something that these kids could do is such a prejudice and an oppressive monopolization of tools. When kids take Biology, or English classes or get a job or whatever else, they learn new concepts and tools to work with. It's quite revolting to act as if feminist, radical concepts and theory, connecting structural to personal ideas and experiences, is not something that some people (young people, people of color, poor people, people with disabilities) would be able to "get" or use. This kind of theoretical work comes specifically from, for and as social justice tools. To write these kinds of ideas off as "inaccessible" and so not to even be discussed with certain groups of people is a co-optation and displacement of the radical critiques of how ivory towers are built and maintained. Systematically depriving any person of tools meant for building coalitions and moving toward social justice is wrong. A lot of the time these young folks were able readily to connect personal experience to larger structures, maybe in part because they hadn't gone through so much academic and social training like me or my supervisor. It isn't necessarily a good thing to be able to disassociate yourself from everyone else and assume some sort of false objectivity in order to be "legitimate" or "academic" or "professional."

In one instance my framework of feminist situated theory actually helped an individual with problem. When I was a case manager for homeless youth I had a client with an abusive mother who could also probably be characterized as having certain mental illness or disabilities. My client was trying to understand why their mother treated them the way she did. They felt they couldn't understand themselves and couldn't figure out their own identity without trying to understand this element. I used that standpoint lesson plan to talk about ways of recognizing that maybe their mother operates in the world in a different way than this person would ever be able to understand. I tried to show my client the value of accepting the unsettled ground that you always have to live on, thinking through what tools you could use to help yourself from where you are and what you can understand and control, and recognizing the roles of larger social structures and values in personal interactions—ideas echoed in much feminist ideology. We talked about ideas of chosen family as well. Which, to me, is very queer. And of course it wasn't any sort of final answer, but these concepts were a tool for my client to use in thinking through their situation differently and working out their own needs, goals, and ways of working toward them. These tools gave the client the agency to decide what, how and how much of their mother, or maybe more their mother's abusive relations, they were going to take.

1. How does Whitney's approach to teaching theory to marginalized youth reflect an anti-oppressive practice perspective?

2. What assumptions does Whitney hold about marginalized youth in comparison to her supervisor's assumptions?

3. How does Whitney use theory in case management?

4. Would this approach be useful or challenging in your own direct practice work with participants? Explain.

that we are conscious of the systems of oppression that are laced throughout our society. It requires that we face up to our role in the oppression of others. I do not consider myself homophobic or anti-gay, but that sentiment is woven into our society, into our language. I am responsible for the words that come out of my mouth and it is up to me to think critically about the way language has been used to oppress. It was not the first time I had used the term "gay" in a derogatory way from a place of heterosexual privilege. But, suddenly I was faced with the real human impact of my flippant use of the language. I did end up apologizing to Glenn and was graciously forgiven, but even if Glenn had chosen not to forgive me, I had a responsibility to show that I was aware of my wrongdoing and to begin the process of changing my behavior.

Anti-oppressive practice is not about being superhuman. In fact it's the opposite. It is about embracing humanity and all its diversity, openly and equally. In the process, I will, and have, made huge mistakes, but I feel like I now have a strong foundation from which I can be conscious and aware, critically reflective and actively pursuant toward change. I am fortunate to be at a place in my life where I am surrounded by people who really are approaching justice work from an anti-oppressive framework—from my family, to the organization where I am interning, to the professors at the university I am attending.

A little saying from Lao Tzu:

Watch your thoughts;

They become words.

Watch your words;

They become actions.

Watch your actions;

They become habits.

Watch your habits;

They become your character.

Watch your character;

It becomes your destiny.

1. How does Daniel locate himself and address his privileged identities?

2. How does he define and conceptualize anti-oppressive theory and practice?

3. What stands out for you in his reflection of an internal revolution?

4. How does he negotiate the tensions that he experiences with his use of oppressive language?

3

VISIONS AND VOICES: UNDERSTANDING THE NEEDS AND ASPIRATIONS OF SEX WORKERS THROUGH PHOTOVOICE

MOSHOULA CAPOUS-DESYLLAS

The collaborative photovoice project described here emerged out of circumstances in Portland, Oregon, relating to sex workers: a change in local prostitution policy, the criminalization of sex workers, and the lack of social services available for sex workers. In addition, the voices of sex workers and their self-identified needs were missing from the community and misrepresented within the media. A main goal of this community-based project was to present the women's artistic visions and voices as a form of activism to create community awareness and change.

Community Context

Beginning in 1995, the City of Portland enacted the Prostitution Free Zone (PFZ) ordinance, allowing law enforcement to issue citations meant to exclude individuals suspected of engaging in prostitution from a designated area (along 82nd Ave). For ninety days, anyone arrested for prostitution in this area was not allowed to return without submitting an appeal, even if they had never been charged. The implementation of PFZs resulted in the segregation of public space and the criminalization of behavior without actual legal indictment. Not only were sex workers targeted under this policy, but also women and transgender individuals of color, poor people, and other marginalized folks. These marginalized individuals were profiled and arrested for being on the street.

After the PFZ ordinance expired in 2007, the community responded in an uproar. There was an influx of complaints from neighborhood associations regarding visible street workers in their neighborhoods and a perceived increase in crime. This response contributed to the further stigmatization and marginalization of individuals working in the sex industry in Portland.

During the summer months of 2008, I attended numerous town hall meetings focused on addressing the needs of sex workers and those of the community living around the 82nd Avenue neighborhood. I observed that the voices of law enforcement, business owners, neighborhood associations, and radical feminists were present. However, the diverse voices and perspectives of sex workers themselves were silenced and missing from the community dialogue meetings.

Many discriminatory statements were made, and actions taken against sex workers, by members of the community, law enforcement, neighborhood associations, and anti-prostitution groups. In response to the injustice, various social workers and sex worker advocates (myself included) highlighted the need to address the underlying causes of sex work, including oppression based on race, class, gender, sexual orientation, citizenship status, and so on. We made efforts to explain that improved access to housing, employment, and treatment services would be a better response than criminalization.

Meanwhile, no agencies in Portland existed that provided social services to sex workers to address their specific needs. At the time of this project, the only service available for female sex workers consisted of a mandatory drug and alcohol treatment program available solely to those previously incarcerated and arrested on a drug offense. In an attempt to address the gap in services available to sex workers, the Sex Worker Outreach Coalition (SWOC) was created. SWOC was a network of social service providers in Portland that met monthly to address issues related to the sex industry and to find better ways to create and coordinate services for sex workers. I joined SWOC as an ally and advocate to sex workers, and subsequently met Crystal Tenty, my community partner in this project.

While our efforts as SWOC advocates gave us a powerful place within the community and contributed to the activism surrounding the PFZs, the voices of individuals currently working in the sex industry and their self-identified needs still were missing. Taking into account the community unrest over the termination of the PFZs, the lack of social services available for sex workers, the significance of sex workers' own voices and their need for self-representation, as well as the power of art, Crystal and I decided to collaborate on this project using the arts-based method of photovoice.

The process of photovoice entails giving cameras to individuals who use photography to identify, represent, and enhance their communities. Photovoice utilizes the power of the visual image to communicate life experiences and perceptions, which then has the power to influence social policy. Specifically, this method is used in communities with limited power or status to communicate to influential community advocates where change must occur (Wang & Burris, 1997).

My desire to engage in this project with sex workers followed my initial interest in the feminist debates on sex work. The complexity and politicized nature of sex work challenged me to examine my own ideas about sex work, acquired through media representations and images. As a social worker, prior to engaging in this project, my clinical experience with individuals working in the sex industry was limited to working in a drug and alcohol treatment program that served both dual-diagnosed, previously incarcerated individuals (some of whom had worked in the sex industry) and children of sex workers. I had never engaged in sex work, nor had I ever participated in other aspects of the sex industry. I acknowledged that my reality was very different from the reality of the project participants, but after getting to know the women who participated in the project, I was surprised to see where our lives intersected.

Theoretically and philosophically, I believe that women's experiences of working in the sex industry vary according to age, social location, gender, race, and even personality or mood. I consider it important to avoid moralistic positions when discussing commercial sex work between consenting adults. I believe in a sex workers' rights-based approach which demands citizenship rights, including their right to work with dignity and safety, and without discrimination. Thus, it was important to participate in a project that would provide an opportunity for female sex workers in Portland to express and represent their needs and aspirations in a creative, effective, and meaningful way with the potential for empowerment and community change. Through the use of photovoice, sex workers utilized visual representation (photography) to generate art, collaboratively create knowledge, and raise awareness of their needs.

Theoretical and Practical Framework

This project was informed by feminist theory, Freire's approach to empowerment education and a participatory approach to documentary photography. These theories attempt to look at how social, political, and economic structures influence and shape individual experiences, perspectives, and identities. Placing marginalized voices at the center is a principal component of re-shaping and re-formulating oppressive social structures. Feminist theories focus on power, agency, process, interconnectedness, creativity, multiple truths and realities, and the importance of human relationships. Freire's approach asserts that bringing people together in a group enables them to critically analyze their community and the everyday social and political factors that shape and influence their experiences and daily lives. Collective dialogue raises consciousness, which in turn can lead to action for social change.

This project was also rooted in a participatory approach to documentary photography. In the 1970s, professional photographers started giving cameras to people who had typically been the subjects of their photographs. These ordinary individuals then had a way to use their grassroots voices and images to advocate social change. Through these theoretical lenses the personal is political, and the primary focus is on dialogue, empowerment, and collective action for social change.

Visions and Voices Project

A total of eleven female sex workers were invited to participate in this photovoice project. They were from diverse ethnic and racial backgrounds, as well as ability status. The women were between the ages of 18 to 52 years old, with varied educational experience and social class backgrounds. They were engaged in street work, escorting, exotic dancing and stripping, bondage-domination-sadomasochism (BDSM) work, erotic massage, and erotic nude modeling. Their duration of their sex work experience ranged from seven months to 39 years. Some of the women had children or were in a serious relationship. Their living situations varied (from living on the streets to living in a house with roommates), and for some, changed over time.

Crystal and I gave each participant her own 35mm camera to take a total of 36 photographs of her needs and aspirations. After the women had gone back to their communities to photo document their lives, their rolls of film were developed and individual dialogue sessions were held with each participant to reflect and discuss her images. Afterwards, each woman was invited to two group dialogue sessions where we brought everyone together so that they could share their photographs and experiences with one another. The women decided that they wanted to host community art exhibits displaying their images in order to educate the community about their needs and aspirations.

The photographs taken by the women were represented in various community locations over a period of two years: local cafes, public libraries, three universities, two art galleries, a bookstore, and a social service agency. The traveling exhibit served to inform policy makers, law enforcement, influential community advocates, and the broader public about sex workers' needs and important issues in their lives. The variety of locations provided a traveling forum for sex workers to share their lived experiences, perspectives, and artwork with individuals in the community. The women also had the opportunity to sell their printed images at the art shows and generate income. While this project did not have any immediate or direct effects on local policy decisions, it received a lot of media attention and community support. The art exhibits were featured in two local newspapers and televised on the local news station.

Various themes emerged from their visions and voices:

- diverse experiences of sex work (in other words, there is no universal sex worker experience);
- shared experiences of stigma and stereotyping related to working in the sex industry;

The experience of empowerment through the arts is in accord with other studies that describe engagement with photovoice as an opportunity for women to experience participation and self-determination.

Image 3.8 Shared Experiences of Stigma and Stereotyping (Photovoice Project)

"Sometimes working in this industry you feel fenced-in, because there's a certain stereotype.... The one thing that people love you and like you for, is the one thing people inevitably throw in your face and despise you for. If a guy takes an interest in you, you think it's very complimentary, but then he's like, 'oh, why don't you just go suck up to some guy and get your money the way you do—' or they call you 'big whore,' so you feel fenced-in in that way—there's no way around it or out of it." —Alex

"I don't get anxious about the dates; I get anxious about the police. I get terrified. I don't feel safe until I get into a guy's car because I got kidnapped one time by the police. They took me somewhere—it wasn't even a station—where all these cops, who weren't even on duty, were there. They held me there for two hours, told me I was under arrest, for nothing! I was crying and they had me handcuffed and they were like, 'Don't get your AIDS-diseased tears on our desk!' They were calling me 'fucking bitch' and 'nasty whore.' Then they go, 'Well, we're not going to arrest you 'cause you'll be out the next day doing the same thing.'" —Sarah

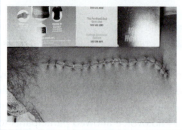

"This one time, I almost got murdered by this man [client] and I thought that I was gonna die. He was saying that he was gonna kill me because I was a whore and his mother was a whore and he was angry...." —Merry Mag

Empowerment through the arts

Jasmine (31 years old), working as a street worker and escort, identified her desire not to be ashamed, took action to achieve her goal, and photographed her accomplishment. Mouse presented a photograph of herself on the top of the roof to symbolize her aspiration to be more spontaneous. See their photos in Image 3.10.

Image 3.9   Use of Art as Activism and as a Form of Resistance (Photovoice Project)

"This little girl playground theme is about the stereotype of sex workers as wounded, hurt, vulnerable, and helpless. I want to call attention to the sexualization of victimhood, to voyeurism, to the objectification of sex workers in discourses about them. I want to encourage people to question their impulse to help, to save, to define what's 'really' going on." — Grahm

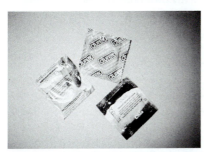

"Three or more condoms can get you arrested for prostitution. I HATE that law. It makes me SSSSICK. Here women are trying to protect themselves and others against AIDS and Hepatitis and other diseases, and they're gonna arrest them for it?!" —Sarah

All but one of the woman presented mixed feelings about sex work in regard to personal power, agency, freedom, and choice. A few women identified the need for existence and photographed events in their lives as a way to prove things happened. Photographing themselves and their surroundings communicated their presence in this world. Some of the women photographed their bodies or the body parts of others to represent their needs and aspirations. The photographed bodies represent sites of struggle, power, strength, independence, choice, and vulnerability.

Participation in this project was an opportunity for self-representation and a way for the women to assert their agency through their visions and voices. Being considered agents capable of investigating their own situations can feel empowering and make this kind of a project more useful to them. It is important to repeat that none of the women in this project saw themselves as victims without choices, even if they had experienced emotional, physical, and sexual violence, poverty, or drug addiction. All of the women emphasized that working in the sex industry was their choice. This lies contrary to radical feminist beliefs that "few women would choose prostitution."

As story tellers, the participants in this project held the power of sharing and self-representation, as well as the freedom to re-invent themselves. The women also used storytelling as a way to create meaning for their images. The stories they shared consisted of their past experiences and provided a perspective on their social locations and circumstances in life.

Reflections on the process

This project gave me the opportunity to hear the rich stories of a marginalized group of women I might not have otherwise connected with. It challenged my own biases, fears, and assumptions.

Image 3.10   Empowerment Through the Arts (Photovoice Project)

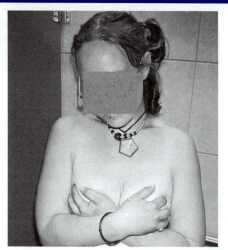

"This is my primal naked self. This is me and I am confronting you with myself; there's no armor, nothing. I want to be able to show myself without shame.... I'm very self-conscious of people seeing me naked … so it's an aspiration to be comfortable with my own body for once."
—Jasmine

"It was the first time I climbed up on top of my house. I want to do that more often in my life. I want to think of spontaneous, seemingly impossible things that I've never done before and just do them. The airplane trail and having me so small in the corner really emphasizes how large I felt the possibilities were at that moment. So, to use the cliché, the sky is the limit. That's really how I felt standing on the apex of the roof right there."   —Mouse

I cherish my unique relationships with each of the participants. At the same time, this project stimulated, inspired and transformed me. I did not know what to expect from the women and assumed their photographs would fit into neat categories of needs and aspirations, either based on type of work, race, class, or age. I did not take into account intersectionality and the complexity of human existence, past and present, and the various forces shaping visions for the future. I had not even considered the different subcultures existing within the sex industry. I assumed that sex workers embodied more or less, one stereotypical "type." I was inspired by the diversity of images, their emotional impact, and the creative ways in which the women depicted themselves and their experiences.

This project gave me a sense of empathy and a deeper feeling of awareness. I gained a greater appreciation for the complexity of these women's lives and some of the inherent contradictions of working in the sex industry. I attribute these contradictions to the multiple and often contested identities of the participants. I also acknowledge that contradictions exist within each and every one of us. There were times when I felt sad about the women's experiences of violence, as well as outrage at the injustices and unfair policies that criminalize those engaged in sex work. We experienced a range of emotions together in the individual dialogue sessions; we cried, we laughed. In the end, I admired how the women stretched their boundaries of personal expression and told powerful stories of strength, empowerment, and resilience. Art allowed us to step both deeper inside and venture outside of ourselves and our experiences. This arts-based project also fostered my relationships with members of the community who shared similar values, interests, and appreciation for art. In addition, collaboration with my community partner provided support, guidance, and personal growth. Our many months of working together, sharing and exchanging ideas, inspired different ways of understanding the photovoice process. We combined our skills and visions to bring together the women, social service providers, and members of the community at different points during the project to create awareness and social change.

1. What tenets of feminist theory are represented in this story?

2. How are the major approaches of each theory mentioned in this story (feminist, liberation, documentary photography, and intersectionality) reflected at each stage of this photovoice project?

3. What is the role of intersectionality theory in understanding the unique, complex, and multi-layered experiences of sex workers?

4. In what ways doe this photovoice project challenge your own assumptions about sex workers?

5. How might you incorporate the photovoice method at your internship or social service organization? What implications does it have for social work practice with individuals, groups, and communities? What potential does photovoice have for implementing policy change?

DISCUSSION QUESTIONS

1. Take a few moments to consider your internship placement or the social work agency where you work. Which theories or theoretical approaches best reflect the approach used at your internship or work? Do you agree with this theoretical approach? Why or why not? If not, which theories or approaches would be a better fit, considering the agency, its location, and the population it serves?

2. Which theories or theoretical approaches most align with your own values? Please explain.

ACTIVITIES

Jasmine is a 25-year-old biracial (Afro-Caribbean and Puerto Rican) cisgendered, heterosexual woman living in Queens, New York. The majority of Jasmine's maternal family live in Jamaica so she is rarely able to travel home to see them. She is very close to one paternal aunt who lives within 15 minutes of her. Jasmine has been living with her boyfriend of six years for the past 3 years; they have two children together, Ana, age 2 and Jenessa, age 4. Jasmine comes from a devoutly Christian family, although she identifies as an Agnostic herself, which has caused a significant amount of family tension.

Jasmine is currently completing her BA in elementary education; she has one more semester to go, but is unsure if she will be able to register for the upcoming semester due to financial difficulties. Jasmine's brother, Adam, has recently come out as gay and is experiencing a great deal of emotional and verbal abuse in the family. Adam is 18 years old and is hoping to be able to move to Queens from Jamaica so he can escape the abuse. Jasmine plans to have Adam stay with her until he is able to find a job and a place of his own, although she lives in a two-bedroom apartment and space will be tight.

Jasmine's boyfriend, Anthony, has been emotionally and verbally abusive toward her for the majority of their relationship. His abuse began as subtle manipulation and isolation; for example, he would often suggest that if she "really loved" him she would not go out with her friends to study after classes. After cancelling on her friends continuously she found that she no longer receives invitations to go out after class. Due to this isolation, her only consistent support person is her aunt Josephina who lives in a nearby neighborhood in Queens and who watches the girls three times a week without pay when Jasmine is at school. Anthony has started to make demeaning comments about Josephina, suggesting that she is not a good influence on the children and that Jasmine needs to find an alternative for childcare. Jasmine knows that they cannot afford to pay a childcare provider, which is contributing to her stress regarding finances and her concerns about being able to complete her degree as planned.

Jasmine has been going to school full time and does not currently have paid employment. She qualifies for some financial aid at school, which covers most of her tuition, and she has taken out moderate loans to cover the rest of the tuition, books, and transportation expenses. Anthony worked full time as a carpenter, but recently his hours have been cut by 25% and they are having trouble paying monthly bills.

One week ago, Anthony began berating Jasmine's family and making offensive comments about Adam's sexuality. Anthony stated, "no way is that fag going to be allowed to stay in my house!" Jasmine, who is fiercely loyal to Adam, told Anthony she was adamant that he stays with them. Anthony pinned Jasmine up against the wall and told her that it was his house and she had no say in the matter. This was the first time that Anthony had physically assaulted Jasmine and she has been scared and anxious ever since. Jasmine has also struggled with anxiety for five years, which manifests in exaggerated startle responses, sleeplessness, nightmares, and racing thoughts.

a. Apply one traditional theory and one progressive theory to the scenario presented here.

b. How does each approach define the problem(s)?

c. How do the different theoretical perspectives approach the prospect of change?

d. What are some of the strengths and limitations of the theories applied?

ADDITIONAL RESOURCES

Websites

http://www.freireproject.org/

http://www.feminist.com/activism/

Films

Blacking up: Hip Hop's remix of race & identity (2010). R. A. Clift

Flag wars (2003). L. G. Bryant & L. Poitras

Frozen river (2008). C. Hunt

Made in L.A. (2007). A. Carracedo & R. Bahar

Books

Anzaldúa, G. (2012). *Borderlands/la frontera: The new mestiza*. San Francisco, CA: Aunt Lute Books.

Anzaldúa, G., & Keating, A. (2012). *This bridge we call home: Radical visions for transformation*. New York: Routledge.

hooks, b. (2000). *Feminism is for everybody: Passionate politics*. Cambridge, MA: South End Press.

hooks, b. (2000). *Feminist theory: From margin to center* (2nd ed.). Cambridge, MA: South End Press.

Satrapi, M. (2007). *The complete Persepolis*. New York: Pantheon Books.

4

Anti-Oppressive Practice With Individuals

The previous chapters provided a conceptual foundation for social work practice as we discussed the intersections of social work and social justice, the values and ethics of social work, and the theoretical foundations that inform practice at the micro, mezzo, and macro level. In the following chapters, we present anti-oppressive practice with individuals, families, groups, organizations, and communities, in addition to policy practice, social movements, and global anti-oppressive social work.

This chapter highlights anti-oppressive practice with individuals. It is organized based on the four phases of anti-oppressive practice: engagement, teaching and learning (also known as assessment), action and accompaniment (also known as intervention), and evaluation. Image 4.1 shows these four stages of practice.

THE LANGUAGE OF PRACTICE

Anti-oppressive work with individuals requires attention to the language that we use in our practice. The words we use to describe the people we work with characterize the nature of the relationship and how we are involved in their lives (Dalrymple & Burke, 2006). Language is also critical for representing the identities of individuals.

Some of the common terms used in social work practice to address the individuals we work with include: *client, patient, service user, consumer, member, customer, participant, ally, collaborator, survivor, recipient, expert by experience, attendee,* and *constituent.* The term *client* is the one most commonly seen throughout the social work literature and in the field, and it is considered by many to be the most internationally recognized term (Dalrymple & Burke, 2006; Payne, 2011). Thompson and Thompson (2008) believe the term *client* connotes "professionalism and a commitment to treating people with respect" (p. 24); *clients* are sometimes referred to as *patients* by social workers who work in the medical field.

However, the term *client* is also criticized because of its implied inequality, as well as its separateness and passivity. The term objectifies the social work relationship: the professional

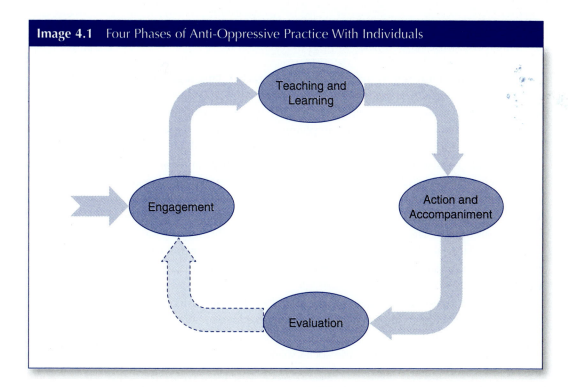

Image 4.1 Four Phases of Anti-Oppressive Practice With Individuals

assumes power and identifies what the passive client needs. This, in turn, "sets up the idea of the 'good' client as one who accepts the professionalism of the social worker to assess their needs and willingly acts on what they were asked to without question" (McLaughlin, 2009, p. 1103). In addition, Finn and Jacobson stress that

> too often, our understanding of "clients" reinforces a notion of the problem being located within the person and thus limiting our cognizance of the social conditions that contribute to and exacerbate individual pain and struggle. The label of helping systems often keeps social workers from seeing the full personhood of those with whom we work. This, in turn, leads us to making assumptions about a person's capacity for participation in the change process, thereby limiting his role from the moment of engagement. (2008, p. 214)

Clients are also referred to as *consumers* or *customers* of purchased services (Payne, 2005b). These terms can be particularly offensive to AOP social workers. For example:

> My feeling about *customer* is that language which derives from economically based market relations and, as such, is alien to the founding principles of the welfare state and social work—that is, the provision of a service which [is] universally

available, and never based on the ability to "buy"—a condition that the word *customer* implies. (Hennessy, 2011, p. 5)

Recently, the term *service user* entered our practice language. Some assert that *service user* suggests a sense of power, in that a user of services has the right to object if the service they receive does not meet their standards for service (Hick, Peters, Corner, & London, 2010). Others criticize the term for implying that one is a passive recipient of services (Dalrymple & Burke, 2006). In a Community Care (2008) (which is an organization made up of service users who participate in on-line discussion groups for the rights and interests of the recipients of social services) discussion about terminology, one commentator noted, "Personally, I see the term *service user* as mildly derogative. Maybe it's the word "user," which has mostly negative connotations. I much prefer the term *client*, which I feel offers a certain amount of dignity to the person involved with the service" (as cited in Hennessey, 2011, p. 6). More to the point, the term *service user* encourages social workers to think of individuals in a single, dependent role and ignore the multiple identities of clients (McLaughlin, 2009).

In contrast, referring to a client as an *expert by experience* encourages us to acknowledge the unique knowledge base rooted in an individual's experience with our services. McLaughlin (2009) points out that this term suggests a more egalitarian relationship of equals than most of the other terms. One person in the social work relationship has expertise accrued through their training and practice, and the other has expertise accrued through their experience.

In truth, each of these terms carries certain historical, social, and cultural weight and implications (Finn & Jacobson, 2008). Each term also suggests the kinds of relationships we have with others. The language of practice often highlights power differences in the relationship. Different labels also conjure up distinctive identities. It is important to consider how the way that we name, label, and refer to people shapes (1) the social work relationship; (2) the activities that shape social work practice; and (3) the perceptions of individual personhood, identities, abilities, and capacities.

In the spirit of anti-oppressive approaches to practice, we are more inclined to use the term *participant* to refer to the people we work with, in order to emphasize the participatory nature of social work practice. We are aware of the ways in which language can reflect power relations and have an impact on the people we work with. Thus, we prefer to use language that acknowledges dialogue, partnership, and the co-creation of knowledge and plans for action toward change. We also encourage using the words that people themselves understand and words that they wish to use to define and address themselves.

> What are some other ways to describe the relationship between those who provide services and those who receive them? Which term most resonates with you for referring to the people you work with in your own social work practice?

AWARENESS OF SELF

Having self-awareness (knowing one's self or having self-knowledge) is critical in order to begin to have a deeper awareness of others. Self-awareness is the ability to perceive aspects of our personality, value system, behaviors, emotions, habits, reactions, motivations, and thought processes. Possessing self-knowledge allows us to see and understand where our thoughts and emotions are taking us. Social workers who practice self-awareness are interested in critically pondering events and circumstances, as well as their feelings and actions, and thinking about where they come from. Thus, they are able to provide an account of their motivations, or the reasons they are acting, feeling, and thinking in certain ways (Hennessey, 2011). Self-awareness also helps social workers understand how others perceive them and their responses in the moment.

Anti-oppressive social work requires us to locate ourselves, along with participants, within a broader social context. We need to consider not just the participants' complexities, but also how our own intersecting identities inform our experiences, thoughts, feelings, and behaviors, as well as our relationships with others. Our values, social differences, and various power dynamics affect and influence our interactions with others, both emotionally and intellectually (Burke & Harrison, 1998; Clifford, 1998). Self-awareness includes the ability to position our identities and individual life experiences, and their accompanying emotions, within a social and structural framework. These four aspects of self-awareness are discussed below.

Practicing Self-Awareness

Practicing awareness of self involves the act of self-reflexivity, or self-reflection. It is critical to gain better insight into ourselves by focusing attention on the details of our personality, behavior, and values:

> It requires going beyond surface content to contemplate meanings, to submerge oneself in thoughtful reverie, to question taken-for-granted assumptions about reality, to consider the significance of situations and circumstances, and to share these thoughts with other through critical dialogue and critical question posing. (Finn & Jacobson, 2008, p. 43)

Self-awareness is a process that takes time and practice.

Understanding Our Feelings and Emotions

Social workers come into close contact with human pain, suffering, and sadness. In the process of engaging sensitively with participants, we must acknowledge our own feelings and work toward understanding our emotional state in a constructive and meaningful way.

An enhanced awareness of self allows us to attain a deeper awareness of the other person and to guide us in our work together. Not only is it important to be attuned to our feelings and those of the participant, but we must also be attuned to the meanings behind those feelings (Clarke, 2006).

The following activities and self-questioning can help in the process of understanding one's feelings and emotions:

- Bringing one's feelings to the level of full awareness and assessing, with the help of personal reflection, mindfulness, and supervision.
- Asking, would my feelings adversely affect the participant if they were known?
- Asking, can I use my emotions in my work in such a way that they become a constructive source for the participant? (Hennessey, 2011, p. 17)

Accessing emotions, processing them, naming them, interpreting them, and navigating them are all critical to this process (Hennessey, 2011).

Oftentimes, the argument is made that being a professional means that we need to separate ourselves from our personal feelings and "manage" or "contain" those feelings so that we can work with our participants in a professional manner. What are your thoughts about this expectation? Under what circumstances could the act of sharing or revealing your feelings and emotions with your participant be creative for social work practice? Under what circumstances could the act of sharing or revealing your feelings and emotions with your participant be disadvantageous or even damaging for social work practice? When is it most useful "to use one's self" as a resource for one's work?

Understanding Our Social Location

It is important to acknowledge and recognize that we bring into our practice our own intersecting identities, cultural orientation, lived experiences, values, and worldview. Examining and remaining conscious of our values and beliefs is imperative. Awareness of our social location is critical if we are to guard against the participant feeling disempowered (Hick et al., 2010).

As social workers, we must acknowledge unjust social relations and the unjustifiable ways that "power over" is structured based on social identity categories. Power differences that exist between the social worker and the participant in regard to gender, ethnicity, race, culture, age, class, ability status, sexual orientation, citizenship status, and other categories of difference must be recognized and addressed. We also need to understand and acknowledge the social, political, and economic structures embedded within our social work practice.

Acknowledging Our Power as Social Workers

As social workers, we hold power and privilege associated with our roles, titles, and education. The use of critical consciousness deepens our awareness of our privilege as well as our experiences of oppression. In our encounters with participants and staff at our agencies, we need to challenge these hierarchical assumptions and the power dynamics inherent in the social worker/participant relationship and seek more egalitarian and collaborative approaches. We need to provide participants with choices, shared assessment, and collaborative feedback on the process.

Being transparent and open about our role and the power we hold as social workers undercuts the inherent power differences. Transparency about the intent of our work with participants is essential. We might share the rationale behind our questions, agency services, possible interventions, and our interpretations of the participant's situation (Moreau, Frosst, Frayne, Hlywa, Leonard, & Rowell, 1993). To avoid a false equality, the nature of the relationship and role expectations should be openly discussed, and power differences should be acknowledged in ways that make sense to the participant while promoting participant self-knowledge and respecting the participant's lived expertise (McWhirter & McWhirter, 2007).

RELATIONSHIP-BASED PRACTICE

Relationship is at the very heart of social work practice. Relationship can be defined as the dynamic interaction of attitudes and emotions, as well as the bond between the social worker and the participant. Social work is carried out within an interconnected system of human relationships, and a positive relationship between the social worker and the participant encourages and facilitates their active involvement and their investment in participation.

These relationships are also formed within the context of an agency or organization, and influenced and shaped by larger socioeconomic, political, structural, and cultural contexts. These contexts hold particular views about poor people, individuals with disabilities, single mothers, marriage and divorce, sexual relationships, gender roles, undocumented persons, drug and alcohol use, and so on. Thus, as previously mentioned, self-awareness is crucial in working with individuals in order to combat the prejudices of other people, organizations, and structures. Often social workers serve as the "face" of the agency, associated with its laws, powers, and procedures (Hennessey, 2011). This is why the very first moments of contact, the first interaction and the initial meeting with the participant are all critical for shaping the relationship. The social worker's self is often the participant's most direct experience of the humanity in social work.

The relationships between social workers and participants are important because they are the starting point for building trust, connection, partnership, and accountability, and for supporting people's self-empowerment. In a study of participants' perspectives, the researchers found that the social worker who is most likely to develop a positive relationship is one who is "respectful, attentive, interested, caring, trustworthy, friendly, genuine, unpretentious, sympathetic, warm, concerned, empathetic, accepting, compassionate, understanding, supportive, reassuring, patient, comforting, and considerate" (Kadushin & Kadushin, 1997, as cited in Lundy, 2011, p. 153). The desire to convey these personality traits and practice skills raises the following question: "How can I use and offer who I am in such a way that my personality or character becomes a resource that is creative and available to my client?" (Hennessey, 2011, p. 20).

The following relationship-based practice skills are critical to creating a meaningful relationship between social workers and participants:

- Commitment and growing ability to know one's self;
- Commitment to try to know and understand the other person—their life's influences, their ways of thinking, feeling and behaving;
- Consciously raising knowledge about one's self and the other person; thinking and reflecting on it;
- Critical awareness in order to relate in deeper ways with the participant; and
- Offering and using the self in the relationship (Hennessey, 2011, p. 20)

In order to build a relationship based on our genuine, honest selves rather than the assumptions and biases that we carry with us, try expressing genuine curiosity and taking a stance of "not-knowing." Shulman (2009) believes that

> as we demonstrate to our clients our humanness, vulnerability, willingness to risk, spontaneity, honesty, and our lack of defensiveness (or defensiveness for which we later apologize), we will be modeling the very behaviors we hope to see in our clients. These qualities contribute to an effective working alliance in which the client has the opportunity to explore issues of concern and receive the necessary support and resources in order to make changes. (as cited in Lundy, 2011, p. 153)

A positive relationship is based on equality and sharing. Strong relationships between social workers and participants are a solid foundation for collaboration. They are consistently associated with positive outcomes and are a strong basis for change and transformation (Kadushin & Kadushin, 1997). The key elements of a strong relationship include the qualities of a social worker as shown in Image 4.2.

ENGAGEMENT

Engagement is considered the first step in our work with participants. However, it can also be considered an on-going process that is essential in all of the phases of practice with individuals. In either case, engagement is shaped by mutual understanding, empathy, compassion,

Image 4.2 Key Social Worker Qualities for Building a Strong Relationship With Participants

Quality	Definition	Manifestation in Practice
Warmth	Interest in and concern about participant without expectations for participant or relationship	Be attentive; use caring facial expressions, open body language, and soothing tone of voice
Unconditional positive regard for participant	Nonjudgmental acceptance regardless of own values and perspectives	Express respect and concern for participant regardless of behavior; acknowledge dignity and worth of participant; provide space for participants to be themselves and express themselves freely
Genuineness and authenticity	Honesty and sincerity in emotions and actions; emphasis on congruence in feelings and behaviors in order to build trust; thoughtful self-disclosure	Be human, down to earth, spontaneous, and ready to share own reactions with participants
Mutuality	Commitment to partnership with participants in order to reduce power differences and enhance participant self-determination	Make decisions by consensus rather than coercion; encourage participant initiative in seeking solutions and solving own problems
Humor	Spontaneous and informal playfulness to lighten a difficult conversation, put matters in a more hopeful perspective, relieve anxiety, help participant with coping, equalize power dynamics, and provide insight	Base humor on similarity of values and attitudes and time humorous comments appropriately; never make fun of participant or use humor at participant's expense
Caring and connectedness	Genuine attitude of empathy, interest, and service, giving priority to participants	Express interest in participant ("caring about"); undertake tasks on behalf of participant ("caring for")

Source: Adapted from Birkenmaier, Berg-Weger, and Dewees, 2011; Cohen, 1989; Kadushin and Kadushin, 1997; Payne, 2011; Shebib, 2003.

sincerity, humility, dedication, and commitment. It involves a dynamic interaction from a place of not knowing and a place of curiosity. It must be undertaken with a commitment to bring one's entire being into the process of discovery. Engagement entails embracing the uncertainties in the relationship with a participant, exploring the complexities, and being open to the possibilities for transformation.

Empathy

Empathy is a way of "hearing" what another person is "saying," both verbally and nonverbally, at the emotional level. It means being in touch with yourself (your feelings and emotions) while at same time engaging with the feelings of the other person (Hennessey, 2011). It entails feeling with the participant (empathy) rather than for them (sympathy) (Kadushin & Kadushin, 1997). Empathy involves the social worker's ability to convey a sense of being present, while understanding the participant's words, emotions, experiences, and layers of meaning (Jong & Berg, 2002). Empathy can take the form of silent listening or verbal questioning (Hennessey, 2011), whichever works better to let participants know that you are listening and understand what they are saying.

Helping participants generate words to describe their feelings can facilitate a person's ability to describe their inner world. For example, consider a social worker who senses great fear in a 43-year-old woman who has just been diagnosed with cancer. The social worker could gently inquire of the woman, "I wonder if you are feeling less sure about the future now that you've learned this news . . . ?" (Hennessey, 2011, p. 84). This question might elicit the participant's unarticulated fears, and perhaps she may be willing to explore them or seek other words that better represent her emotions.

Empathy involves feeling what the participant is going through, reflecting on the situation and presenting circumstances, and communicating that understanding. This process has long been viewed as essential to the development of meaningful relationships between the social worker and participant (Lundy, 2011).

Mutual Empathy

While it is critical for a social worker to demonstrate empathy with their participant, mutual empathy highlights the importance of reciprocity between the social worker and participant. Mutual empathy fosters mutual empowerment, and both contribute to the participant's capacity for growth and to development of the social worker-participant relationship. When there is mutual care for and about each other, both the social worker and participant attain feelings of empowerment, self-worth, and self-esteem (Norton, 2012).

There are five major features of mutually empowering relationships (Enns, 2004):

- *Zest:* the vitality and energy that come from positive interactions;
- *Action:* a more intricate interplay between individuals;
- *Knowledge:* an increase in information and self-awareness through interpersonal communication and interaction;
- *Self-worth:* the feeling of value from having an authentic relationship; and
- *Desire:* the drive for more empowering and meaningful connections.

Tuning-In

The practice of empathy entails the ability to "tune-in" to one's own feelings and biases prior to meeting the participant (Schwartz, 2010). Tuning-in involves getting in touch with one's own personal biases, values, feelings, and concerns regarding the participant, the participant's situation, and the presenting issue. It is also a time to consider the strengths, potential, and possibilities of participants. The social worker reflects on the differences and commonalities between oneself and the participant, preparing to effectively respond to difficult situations and to build a connection (Lundy, 2011). The process of anticipating how an initial meeting may unfold can prepare the social worker to become a more sensitive listener.

To sensitize themselves to potential concerns and feelings that emerge during the encounter with the participant, social workers can draw on personal memories, literature on human behavior, and input from colleagues and supervisors (Shulman, 2009). The goal is to deepen their understanding of the participant's struggles and experiences of oppression. Tuning-in prepares the social worker to enter the world of the participant, while developing and strengthening the working relationship.

Although tuning in is a preparatory step, it is also tentative (Shulman, 2009). Social workers need to be open to the possible emergence of feelings, issues, and responses that are completely different from what one might have anticipated from the tuning-in process. We must be prepared for the complexity of feelings and varied circumstances and allow spaces for feelings of uncertainty.

Observation and Noticing

Observing and noticing our environment and the context of our interactions with participants is an important way of gathering information that helps us acknowledge both the limitations and possibilities for shaping the relationship with our participants (Finn & Jacobson, 2008).

Taking in the physical context of our work—the meeting place, the social work agency setting, and the agency location, including how it is embedded within the community—is one way of noticing. The things we notice and the emotions that emerge give us only a partial sense of the context, which is an important beginning nevertheless.

Taking in the physical and environmental context of our work, we also notice and observe the social context. This aspect of noticing takes place through verbal and nonverbal communication. We also can notice the people who interact with one another within the context of our practice.

Through our observations, questions naturally emerge:

- How do we interpret the mood, tone, and type of the setting?
- What does our surrounding consist of?

- Is the set-up conducive to facilitating open communication?
- What emotions are evoked with our observations of the setting and the site where our social work practice takes place?
- What sorts of patterns of social interactions are evidenced in this setting?
- What new things do we notice that may not have been initially evident or apparent?
- What sorts of challenges or limitations might the environment or setting pose?
- How might our positionality inform what we are observing and noticing around us?

Body Consciousness

One revealing aspect of engagement to observe is the ways in which we use our own body and the messages being communicated to us by the participant's body language. Nonverbal communication is important for creating an attentive, supportive, and respectful atmosphere. When observing the body language of others or when reflecting on our own body language, we need to take into account different cultural norms and not make assumptions or generalizations.

Participants rely on the following nonverbal behaviors of social workers to judge whether they are being heard and respected (Okun, 1992):

- tone of voice that matches the participant's voice;
- eye contact;
- occasional head nodding to show that the social worker is following what the participant is saying;
- varying facial expressions in response to what the participant says;
- smiling at appropriate points to demonstrate warmth and understanding;
- gesturing occasionally;
- sitting close to the participant;
- using a moderate rate of speech; and
- leaning slightly toward the participant to indicate interest and concentration.

What are some other nonverbal behaviors that you might add to this list?

The nonverbal communication of participants, such as smiling, rolling their eyes, looking off into space, heaving a sigh, crossing their legs and arms, changing their tone of voice, or falling silent, are all important ways of communicating their thoughts and emotions (Jong & Berg, 2002). Noticing these nonverbal signs can provide an opportunity to mention them and explore their meaning with participants.

Also, the body communicates even without movement. For example, participants form impressions of social workers from general body build, height, weight, skin, hair, and eye color, as well as style of dress, adornment, and smell. Our bodies reveal other identities, such as race, nationality, ability status, gender, social class, and so on, and assessments are made of one's power, attractiveness, and approachability.

Listening

Listening is critical to our communication with participants. Because the listener is quiet, we tend to think of listening as a passive act; however, listening requires a considerable amount of internal activity (Kadushin & Kadushin, 1997). Listening entails carefully following what is said explicitly, as well as implicitly. It requires being attentive and receptive. Active and attentive listening necessitates listening carefully with compassion and an open mind for different layers of meaning implicit in personal and cultural narratives. Good listeners are committed to listening, physically and mentally prepared to allow others to speak, and willing to withhold interruption (Gambrill, 1997).

A commitment to listening means acknowledging that what other people say is important and suspending our assumptions and judgments about others. Careful listening is also aided by the assumption of "not knowing," because thinking we know something may prevent us from really hearing what is said.

Reflexive Listening

Reflexive listening is a social work tool that promotes a relationship with the participant. It entails listening for and reflecting on the participant's choice of language. Incorporating the participant's words, terms, and phrases into the dialogue is critical so that professional language and jargon do not override and distort the participant's meanings (Clarke, 2006). One effective method for reflexive listening is echoing participants' key words (Jong & Berg, 2002). Key words are often emotionally charged and given special emphasis. Repeating or emphasizing them to participants is a way to go deeper into what they mean and their representation or relevance in the participant's life. Listening to their words shows that you are reaching for meaning and clarifying understanding.

Summarizing and paraphrasing are also important in reflexive listening. In summarizing, the social worker restates the participant's thoughts, actions, or feelings. Paraphrasing involves extrapolating the essence of what the participant said and then restating it. Paraphrasing demonstrates that you really hear the participant and provide them with an invitation to clarify and expand their stories (Jong & Berg, 2002). Accurate paraphrasing and reflections are part of active listening.

Radical Listening

Radical listening goes beyond reflexive listening. It requires inviting and attending to all aspects of a participant's stories in order to understand the meanings they make of their life experiences (Weingarten, 1995). Radical listening recognizes that participants are experts in their own lives (Dewees, 2006).

According to Wood and Tully (2006), radical listening involves three skills:

- *Listening through social consciousness:* being emotionally, mentally and physically responsive to the complexities of the participant's life; taking a genuine interest in and seeking to understand their experiences through their intersecting identities.
- *Attending:* focusing entirely on what the other person is saying, as well as what they are not saying, from their subjective experiences in life.
- *Immersing:* fully entering the space when you are with the participant. Immersion can also be described as entering a mental zone where you fully bring yourself to enter the participant's world and deeply focus on their stories.

Silences

The silence often encountered when engaging with a participant is an important form of communication, even though it may cause concern or discomfort. The difficulty with silence is that it is hard to understand exactly what the participant is "saying" in that moment (Birkenmaier, Berg-Weger, & Dewees, 2011; Shulman, 2009). For example, silence could have any of these meanings and interpretations:

- The participant may be reflecting on the discussion, gathering and organizing their thoughts;
- The participant may be taking a break from the work at hand;
- The participant may be struggling to find a way to express a painful or buried emotion;
- The participant may be confused and sorting out their thoughts, not understanding a question or what is expected from them;
- The participant may be angry with the social worker and showing this emotion through silence;
- The participant may be demonstrating that the social worker was way off base in their response and misunderstood what the participant was expressing;
- The participant may be working to develop trust with the social worker, using silence to provide a sense of dignity and control over their lives and the conversation or using it as a way to avoid rejection;
- The participant may be a quiet person, so perhaps more open-ended questions may assist with creating dialogue; and
- The participant may have achieved closure on the topic.

Since silence can carry a variety of meanings, it's also important for us as social workers to be aware of our (and the participants) internal and external responses—that is, emotions in the moments of silence as well as body language in response. Shulman (2009) indicates that allowing for silence can be a sign of respect and a way to allow the participant time to process. In those moments, the social worker can ask, "You've grown quiet in the last few moments. What are you thinking about?" (Shulman, 2009, pp. 129–130). If the silence is a sign of negativity, it's important to be able to sit with the discomfort of receiving negative feedback from participants and engaging in dialogue about the emotion.

Consider a social situation that you have been in recently, where you or someone else present had difficulty making or engaging in conversation. How did you and others around you react to the silences? What emotions did you experience? What nonverbal communication (body language, eye contact, body posture, and so on) did you notice during those silences? How does this experience relate to working with participants who may have difficulty speaking?

Dialogue

In its most basic sense, dialogue is a mutual exchange of information, thoughts, and ideas between two or more people. However in the social work setting, dialogue is specifically a shared exploration toward greater understanding, connection, or possibility. It is a process of genuine interaction through which people listen to each other deeply enough to be changed by what they learn. Dialogue is about expanding our capacity for attention, awareness, and learning with each other and from each other. The process—democratic discussion among equals—is as important as the content.

Dialogue as a form of democratic, liberatory practice and knowledge creation is informed by the writings and teachings of Paulo Freire. As a Brazilian educator in the 1950s, Freire initiated a successful literacy and political consciousness program for the poor living in shanty towns in Brazil (Wallerstein & Bernstein, 1988). He was concerned about social transformation and hoped to use dialogue to awaken a critical consciousness whereby people perceived the social, political, and economic contradictions in their life, and took personal and collaborative action against the oppressive elements. It is this consciousness that has the power to transform and create change (Taylor, 1993). In his teachings and theory, Freire proposes a dialogue approach where everyone participates as equal learners who cocreate knowledge. He believes that knowledge is always actively manufactured in dialogue (Roberts, 1999).

Social workers position themselves as cofacilitators and collaborators in a dialogic approach to creating and understanding meaning. We engage in a shared exploration of meanings by promoting mutual dialogue instead of a top-down interaction. We aim to foster a social worker-participant relationship where we can learn from and teach one another.

Resistance Reframed

Throughout this section on engagement, we discuss various ways to enhance our experiences with participants in order to build a strong relationship and develop deeper meaning from our interactions. However, many of our participants have experienced individual, social, and structural oppression and discrimination, so they may be less trusting, more suspicious, and not eager to engage with us. Some participants who have experienced systemic injustice or who have encountered individuals who abuse their power over them may have little reason to put their trust in "helpers" and "helping systems" (Finn & Jacobson, 2008, p. 248).

The resistance to open up and engage is often seen as the participant's problem. Some of the labels used to refer to "resistant" participants—*uncooperative, negative, full of attitude, in denial, untrusting, often hostile, disrespectful, defensive, unmotivated, mandated, involuntary*—are all words that social workers use when asked to describe participants who exhibit some form of resistance (Jong & Berg, 2002).

A plethora of social work literature provides strategies for enhancing participant motivation and compliance. However, what is most important is to acknowledge that resistance is part of our work, and doesn't necessarily imply something negative or that the participant has a problem. Some participants may use resistance as a survival strategy: to protect against further oppression or to maintain power over their lives. It is critical that we respect and honor resistance, and reframe it as a form of agency and self-determination.

> Think about your own work or field site. How have you seen resistance? How is resistance talked about? How is it addressed? What are some potential barriers to engagement? What are some of the spaces of possibility that emerge for alternative ways of accomplishing our work?

Cultural Humility

The discourse of cultural competence (also known as ethnic-sensitive or multicultural practice) in traditional approaches to social work creates a demand for social workers to seek knowledge about the cultural characteristics of their participants. This information is usually provided in a "dictionary-type" understanding about various ethnic cultures, such as how to work with Latinos, Asians, African-Americans, Native-Americans, and so on. The notion of cultural competence perpetuates the assumption that social workers need to have a certain type of cultural knowledge about different groups of people in order to work with difference.

However, many critique this approach to practice since it creates stereotyping and "othering" of non-dominant groups. Keep in mind that early scholarly work on ethnic sensitivity and cultural competence consisted of writings by predominately white social workers who needed tools for working with the ethnic and racial "other": "These approaches often rely on a simplistic understanding of 'cultures' as homogenous entities identifiable by common history, language, customs, values, belief systems, and practices" (Finn & Jacobson, 2008, p. 219). In addition, many of these practices and norms reflect the norms and values of the majority group and don't account for any group diversity and difference (Yee, 2005). Oftentimes, intergenerational, historical, and geographical differences between and within ethnic groups are ignored. Last but not least, cultural identities are continually evolving (Dean, 2001).

Many social workers are challenging the assumption that one can achieve "cultural competence." Instead, we urge social workers to approach their work from a place of not knowing about people's cultures, histories, and experiences in life (Dean, 2001). This standpoint replaces cultural competency with "cultural humility" and a commitment to ongoing learning and understanding. The focus is "open exploration and negotiated understandings rather than the acquisition of specific expert knowledge" (Clarke, 2006, p. 252).

Commitment to Uncertainty

The beauty in social work lies in its complexity, unpredictability, and uncertainty. The complexity of social work arises in different ways:

- through the diversity, range, and depth of people's problems;
- because of the different roles required of social workers;
- through different organizational arrangements for providing services;
- because of the variety of multi-professional teams;
- through the tasks associated with working in partnership with participants who receive services; and
- through the range of different disciplines, theories, knowledge and skills which social workers draw their work (Adams, 2009, pp. 236–237).

The complexity and multi-faceted aspects of social work require us to accept not knowing and commit to accepting uncertainty. Taking a position of not knowing entails genuine curiosity, dedication, and open-mindedness to alternative views. A commitment to uncertainty opens spaces for learning, transformation, and possibility. Coming from a place of not knowing also breaks down hierarchy and creates conversational spaces that do not perpetuate the myth of the social worker as the expert (Clarke, 2006). This, in turn, supports the notion of the participant as the "expert" (Dean, 2001). A commitment to uncertainty, indeterminacy, and unpredictability enforces our continual attempts to self-reflect and to consider: what we are doing, how we are doing it, why we are doing it, and with what possible outcomes (Parton, 2009).

TEACHING AND LEARNING, OR ASSESSMENT

The engagement phase of social work practice eventually becomes more of a teaching and learning process, which is also referred to as the assessment stage of our work with participants. Instead of using a traditional model of assessment where social workers act as "experts" through the questioning of participants, or instead of simply following agency procedures, teaching and learning involves a mutual exchange of information, in keeping with anti-oppressive practice. This phase of the interaction is the opportunity for participants to tell their story and to situate themselves and their concerns. Together, social workers and participants co-construct an understanding of the participant's situation as partners in the process of assessment.

As social workers, we are given the privilege of gaining access into participants' intimate thoughts, world views, and life experiences. We are both learners and teachers in this process of gathering information from individuals who are the experts in their own lives. This teaching and learning partnership entails trust, respect, honesty, and shared risk-taking (Allison, 2005).

Communicating basic respect is essential in order to successfully engage participants in a working alliance. Treating the participant with unconditional positive regard means communicating (through verbal and nonverbal behavior) the participant's inherent value as a human being (O'Hare, 2009, p. 130).

Collaboration

Collaboration is a partnership between the social worker and participant. In the teaching and learning phase, collaboration entails gathering "data" or information with the participants involved as equal partners in the process. All aspects of the participant's life and situation are taken into account. This joint exchange of information acknowledges that participants are the experts on their situations and values the uniqueness of each individual.

When we are collaborating with the participant to collect information about their lives, it's also important to consider why we are co-creating the assessment. We need to question our agency's reasons for making assessments, as well as the purpose served by gathering this information (Parker & Bradley, 2010).

Imagine a situation where a collaborative partnership may be difficult. Now, think of one when it might be impossible. Alternatively, when can collaboration be ideal? What gives you hope about a collaborative partnership? What reservations do you have about a collaborative partnership?

Power Dynamics

As both teachers and learners in the assessment process, we need to be aware of and critically reflect on the power dynamics that exist between social workers and participants. By virtue of our positions and the roles we embody as social workers, we hold power to attach labels to others, provide or deny access to resources, impose sanctions, and make recommendations that have significant social, political, and economic implications and consequences in the lives of participants (Finn & Jacobson, 2008). We are also afforded informal power based on our credentials, titles, and access to information. Oftentimes, we also work within social welfare agencies that function as social control organizations. The helping relationship itself takes place within the context of racism, classism, sexism, heterosexism, ageism, ableism, and other forms of oppression. Along with the power that is afforded to us through our role as social workers, we hold power (and oftentimes privilege) through our social locations and intersecting identities.

In our work with participants, it is important for us to explore and identify feelings of power and powerlessness. If someone is a member of a group that has been historically and/or systematically exploited or discriminated against, there is the possibility that he or she may (to varying degrees) internalize these messages and, in the process, feel powerless to change their situation (Lundy, 2011). Feelings of powerlessness may also arise from the participant's position as one seeking assistance from someone else with access to resources when they, themselves, do not have access.

As we identify and acknowledge issues of power, our aim is to reduce power differentials between us and our participants. Many participants "in the system" have experienced services and programs being "done to" or "done for" them. It is critical that we do not perpetuate these unequal power dynamics, but rather, be willing to "do with" participants (Cohen, 1989).

Unequal power dynamics between social worker and participant can be approached through collaboration, the teaching and learning process of assessment, and the recognition of the knowledge and capacities of participants gained through lived experience. Moreau and Frosst (1993) propose that we can decrease power differentials by "maintaining respect for the participant's dignity and autonomy, validating strengths, articulating limits to the professional role, clear contracting, reducing distance, sharing rationale behind interventions, encouraging self-help, and the use of groups and self-disclosure" (p. 126). Participant power can be increased in a variety of practical ways, including the techniques listed in Image 4.3.

Access to Files

It's imperative that we treat the information gathered about participants with care and sensitivity, paying attention to confidentiality and the power that we have as social workers. However, involving participants in collecting and storing information about themselves is

Image 4.3   Techniques for Overcoming Power Differentials
Between Participant and Social Worker

- Use first names
- Employ simple language, avoiding jargon and diagnostic or medical terminology
- Use self-disclosure to demystify your values and identities
- Explain the limits of your role
- Point out participants' strengths and encourage participants to help themselves
- Explain the rationale for interventions
- Ensure that participants see what is written and hear what is being said about them
- Protect participants' confidentiality

Source: Adapted from Lundy, 2011; Moreau and Frosst, 1993

empowering. What we write about participants in case records and agency files should be easily accessible to participants (Dalrymple & Burke, 2006). The act of sharing access to records contributes to the collaborative values of transparency, accountability, trust, power symmetries, and participation. Providing access to files also ensures the accuracy of information gathered about the participant and places the power and control of representation in their hands (Dalrymple & Burke, 2006).

It is important to note that opening up records to the participants can bring up ethical issues, particularly in the cases where records may be used as evidence (for example, in cases of child or elder abuse). However, ethical concerns must be balanced against the practical and ethical value of providing access as a sign that one is working in partnership with participants.

What are some of the benefits to transparency in our work with participants through sharing what is written about them? What are some of the challenges or limitations to this participatory approach of gathering, storing, and providing access to information?

Self-Disclosure

The extent to which social workers should reveal their feelings, share their emotions, and self-disclose aspects of their self to participants remains a controversial issue. Most traditional social workers label this type of involvement as "unprofessional." However, for a social worker seeking to promote social justice in practice, the issue is quite different. Expecting participants to disclose the most personal and profound aspects of themselves, to bare their hearts and souls, while social workers sit back and reveal little about themselves, sets up an inherently unequal, non-collaborative relationship. By presenting and sharing aspects of our self and our experiences with the participant, we move away from being "clinical, detached and distant professionals" (Lundy, 2011, p. 176).

Offering a personal view or sharing a personal experience should always be for the benefit of the participant. As a social worker, sharing your own feelings, ideas, attitudes, perspectives, and experiences with the participant conveys understanding of others' experiences and allows spontaneity. It can indicate that speaking about particular issues is safe within this relationship (O'Hara, 2011). If it can be done without imposing the social worker's judgment, self-disclosure also mitigates the participants' feelings of dependency evoked by taking help. The social worker's self-disclosure may also present new ways of viewing a situation and envisioning possible outcomes (Gambrill, 1997).

> When considering if or when to self-disclose or share your perspective, helpful questions to ask might be "what purpose will this serve?" or "what is the motive behind the self-disclosure?" Consider, then, when might it be appropriate to self-disclose to a participant? In what instances or situations would you be less inclined to self-disclose or share your perspective or view?

Critical Self-Reflection

In the teaching and learning phase of working with participants, continuing critical self-reflection serves as an anchor for collaboratively assessing the participant's situation. There are three approaches to critical reflection in this phase:

- Bringing past experiences to bear on the unique problems presented by the participant;
- Using reflection creatively to develop new ways of perceiving the problem; and
- Creating new opportunities to experiment in reframing the problems, that is, trying to secure a fit between the person's problems and the way of reframing them (Rolfe, Freshwater, & Jasper, 2001, p. 137).

Through critical reflection the participant can also transform information into knowledge. Self-reflection can be used to explore the power dynamics of one's situation, as well as one's behaviors, assumptions, and interactions (McWhirter & McWhirter, 2007).

Questions

As the social worker and participant work together to explore the participant's definition of the presenting issue, they work to identify inner resources (strengths) and other useful resources that exist in their living situation. One way to collaboratively identify needs and resources is by posing relevant, thought provoking questions. Posing critical questions helps the participant tell their story and prioritize what they want to change. This process also generates important information about their situation and can influence them to think about their situation in a different way or from a new perspective (Lundy, 2011)

Social workers must take care to avoid some types of questions (Birkenmaier, Berg-Weger, & Dewees, 2011):

- Leading questions: could shape the participant's response to match what they believe the social worker wants to hear.
- Excessive questions: could place the social worker in control of the dialogue and cause the participant to feel interrogated.
- Multiple questions: could be confusing because the participant will not know which one of two or more questions should be answered.
- Irrelevant questions: could cause confusion because they are not connected to the conversation or dialogue.

Structural Inequality

In our process of teaching and learning from one another, an anti-oppressive approach to practice assesses the participant's situation within a structural context. We make direct links between participant's economic and social position in society and their emotional and physical health. We assist the participant in obtaining a critical understanding of the connection between their personal problem within a social context, in order to move beyond an individualistic understanding of problems and solutions.

Exploring "symptoms" of anxiety, anger, sadness, and depression through this lens acknowledges the oppressive social structures that exist. Social structures are oppressive based on power imbalances, ideological role restrictions, and social labeling (Fook, 1993). With our participants, we can also explore root causes of problems as they are connected to social structures through institutions (such as schools, government, medical services, and policing systems) and oppressive social relations (such as racism, classism, sexism, ageism, ableism, homophobia, and so on).

Fostering the participant's understanding of the links between personal problems and oppression by societal structures ensures that participants have the space to make their own decisions about the causes of oppression in their lives. Redefining problems to illuminate their structural origins also helps participants to deconstruct oppressive discourse and reinterpret experiences from alternative perspectives. This process of deconstruction and reinterpretation entails developing awareness of the ways in which individuals and their families adapt and conform to their social and economic conditions, as well as the ways that they resist and challenge them.

For the practitioner, a dialogical approach (asking questions, sharing information, or voicing an opinion whenever those contributions would add to the analysis of the issue) is useful in exploring structural issues with participants (Olivier, 2010). The key concern is to avoid imposing our own structural assessment onto the participant and discounting her or his understanding of the problem situation. In the context of the participant's lives and within the broader society, we must develop an ongoing commitment to work alongside the participant toward understanding the causes, dynamics, and consequences of oppression, privilege, and power and to act on that awareness (McWhirter & McWhirter, 2007).

Reframing, Re-visioning, and Re-storying

Assessments are not simple fact-finding exercises; rather they represent a co-construction of a narrative or story between social workers and participants (Parker & Bradley, 2010). It's crucial that we encourage the participant's own words about their problems and their life. Accepting their definitions and stories serves to validate their understanding of the problem.

It's equally critical that we join participants in exploring the range of possibilities for change (Lundy, 2004). As social workers, we can listen for stories and narratives in order to understand how our participants understand their problems and the ways in which they organize, interpret, and communicate to others the meaning of their lived experiences (Clarke, 2006).

Instead of collecting information about the problems in participants' lives so that we can make an "expert assessment" and prescribe a "scientific or evidence-based practice solution," we should encourage the participant to tell the story, or provide a narrative of the problem. The goal is to reframe the situation and create a new perspective on how to manage or overcome it (Parton, 2009).

Reframing, re-visioning, and re-storying involve helping the participant see life in new ways. Social workers can ask helpful questions in co-constructing new stories or frames of reference that make solution building possible. This form of sharing invites the participant to experiment with different possibilities that they may not have previously considered.

Storytelling introduces new possibilities and proposes innovative actions to address problems in life. The types of stories that participants tell about themselves need to be unpacked and re-storied within the collaborative relationship to reveal oppressive storylines, hidden strengths, and hidden areas of resistance (Baines, 2007). Participants' narratives allow them to feel a sense of control, personal agency, and power to move on. Sharing stories is also a way to externalize a problem or to place self-experience within a broader sociocultural and sociopolitical framework (Clarke, 2006). Stories and narratives honor the voices of oppressed individuals who, based on their social group memberships, previously lacked social voice (Agger, 1998). Narratives and stories are especially effective with individuals whose cognitive style is highly receptive to imagery and fantasy (Comas-Diaz, 2007).

Similar to storytelling and narrative, testimony is a special type of narrative that emerged in Chile in response to political repression and terrorism. Testimony chronicles one's traumatic experiences and their effect on the individual and family (Aron, 1992; Comas-Diaz,

2008). Testimony has been described as "bearing witness" and a "verbal journey to the past." It validates personal experience as a basis for truth and knowledge. It also has the potential to transform painful experiences of oppression into consciousness and action (Cienfuegos & Monelli, 1983; Comas-Diaz, 2008).

Individual Strengths

Concurrent with identifying and working with participant's strengths, cooperative exploration of the participant's situation is crucial in the teaching and learning process. Collaboratively identifying individual strengths focuses on positive aspects of the participant's lives, with the intention of increasing motivation, capacity, and potential for making informed life choices. Acknowledging participants' strengths honors the power of the self to heal and the need for an alliance with hope that life might really be otherwise (Saleebey, 1996). As social workers, we can identify and communicate strengths, while nurturing talents, skills, capacities, and choices. This process also includes consideration of previous efforts already made to resolve difficulties in life and trying to address presenting issues, including earlier failures, frustrations, and disappointments (Poulin, 2000). This creates awareness of the participant's prior barriers while providing additional information about the participant's strengths and resources.

ACTION AND ACCOMPANIMENT, OR INTERVENTION

The next phase of our shared work with the participant is often referred to as the intervention phase. However, in the spirit of a collaborative and participatory approach to social work practice, we follow in the footsteps of other social workers who emphasize action and accompaniment instead of intervention (Comas-Diaz, 2007; Finn & Jacobson, 2008).

The term *intervention* carries with it the suggestion of the expert social worker acting or intervening on a passive subject (Finn & Jacobson, 2008). The word *intervene* can also imply interfering in the lives of others. An anti-oppressive approach to practice involves minimal intervention in our participants' lives (Dalrymple & Burke, 2006) and nonintrusive collaboration.

Instead of intervening, we encourage social workers to accept an invitation from participants to accompany them as they take action toward change. Wilson and Whitmore (1995) call for a commitment to solidarity, equality in the relationship, and a focus on the process. This process of taking action and accompanying our participants challenges the top-down approach of traditional social work practice.

Accompaniment entails walking alongside our participants and allowing ourselves to be led by them from a perspective of not-knowing and curiosity. Accompanying someone, instead of intervening, also acknowledges individual agency, self-determination, and the capacity for action of all who are involved in the process.

When taking action, social workers and participants need to lead and follow one another, their roles fluid and interchangeable (Lee, 2001). The social worker builds bridges to the participant's unique experiences and can guide the development of consciousness. It is important to always keep in mind that action takes place within a certain sociopolitical, economic, and historical context. Thus, it is critical to also attend to the circumstances surrounding the actions we take with our participants. Action can manifest in various ways for the participant as well as the social worker. For example:

- ***Planning collaboratively.*** When working collaboratively with our participants to create a plan for action, we need to honor agency and self-determination. Agency refers to the capacity of individuals to act independently and to make their own free choices. It refers to the capability of people to have an impact on their lives and within their social environment. With a sense of agency, participants realize that they have more power to negotiate their positions and impact and influence the world around them (Adams, Dominelli, & Payne, 2009). Self-determination is the recognition of participants' rights and their need to make their own choices and decisions as the experts in their own lives. As social workers accompanying participants, we need to respect and trust the ways in which people make their own choices, even if they may be different from our own. Self-confidence and satisfaction emerge, not when social workers take over for participants rather when participants exercise responsibility, agency, and live as best as they can with the results of their choices (Jong & Berg, 2002).

- ***Fostering participatory decision making.*** Collaboration is fostered by participant participation in all aspects of the decision-making process (Poulin, 2000). Through dialogue, the social worker and the participant can work together to develop a shared vision of what the participant can work toward, in order to create concrete goals. The process begins with the participant's vision of how things should be different. From then on, social workers must make a committed effort to attend to the four core values of participatory decision making: full participation and investment in the process; mutual understanding and respect; inclusive solutions; and shared responsibility and accountability (Kaner, Lind, Toldi, Fisk, & Berger, 2007).

- ***Supporting and creating alliances.*** Throughout the process of accompaniment, social workers can engage in conversations that support participants in deconstructing, resisting, challenging, and reconstructing the structures of society that affect them (Fook, 2002). Social workers can collaborate with participants toward building alliances and coalitions (Moreau et al., 1993). We can refer participants to similar groups, networks and community organizations related to their situation. Bringing people together serves to validate and acknowledge collective experience. By coming together with others, participants can situate the circumstances of their lives within a broader social context. The result is less self-blame, isolation, and alienation, and more stimulation for social change.

- *Activating resources.* A partnership in action is based on the assumption that the social worker and participant are both resources. Resources also include the social support networks of participants. The participant should have a voice in defining the resources and in determining how they will be utilized (Poulin, 2000). As allies and advocates, social workers are responsible for giving the participant information about their rights and entitlements (Moreau et al., 1993). A social worker might share information about agency structure and appeals processes, encourage letter writing as a way to voice concerns, accompany participants to meetings, explore alternative options for taking action, and at times, subvert and challenge oppressive agency policy and structure. When the participant has an immediate need for resources, we must provide resources for survival like food, shelter, clothing, and emotional support. However, we must understand that our participants are entitled to these basic human rights. When adequate resources are not available, social workers can either advocate for change in formal resources, policies, or programs that aren't meeting the participant's needs, or they can create resources where none have been developed.

Social workers play various roles in taking action with participants for change and these roles define their engaged activities. Some of the roles that social workers embody in order to facilitate participants' empowerment and change are shown in Image 4.4.

Image 4.4	Social Work Roles in the Action and Accompaniment (Intervention) Phase of Practice With Individuals	
Role	Key Activities	Anti-Oppressive Rationale
Advocate	Stepping forward and speaking on behalf of our participants and their rights and speaking out against injustices and oppressive policies, practices, and social arrangements	Anti-oppressive practice requires that we use our position of power and privilege to stand up for participants who are experiencing exclusion, marginalization, and powerlessness
Broker	Being familiar with community services, and continually learning about new resources, knowing generally about eligibility requirements, cultivating resources, making referrals, and knowing about any possible barriers to accessing services	In their professional role, social workers have access to certain resources and are responsible for using their power and privilege and directly linking participants to the pertinent resources
Collaborator	Joining our participant and working together as partners	A collective approach to taking action helps to equalize existing power differences and promotes joint responsibility and accountability for actions

Role	Key Activities	Anti-Oppressive Rationale
Enabler	Conveying hope, reducing resistance and ambivalence, and identifying and supporting personal strengths and social assets	Participants need to identify, respect, and make effective use of their own knowledge, lived experiences, skills, and expertise
Facilitator	Bringing people together, encouraging dialogue, building trust, addressing power, promoting participation, and motivating change-oriented action	Teamwork and collective group work is an important part of anti-oppressive practice for building solidarity and taking collective action for change
Learner	Learning nonjudgmentally about and from participants, with commitment, constant openness, and critical curiosity	Participants are the experts in their own lives and they carry with them rich lived experiences and know what is best for them
Mediator	Helping to reconcile differences between people by honoring different viewpoints, finding commonalities and compromise, building alliances and solidarity, and reaching mutually satisfying agreements	Dialogue is necessary to the process because it creates understanding informed by respect and value and thereby aids in resolving conflict
Teacher	Bringing our lived experiences, knowledge, and skills to bear and sharing them with participants	Participants have the capacity to learn and apply new skills in order to enhance their lives and circumstances

Source: Adapted from Hepworth, Rooney, Rooney, Strom-Gottfried, & Larsen, 2010.

EVALUATION

Within the context of anti-oppressive work with individuals, we define evaluation as a systematic collection of information about the process, activities, and outcomes of the work between a social worker and the participant. Agencies, programs, and policies also need to be evaluated, but here we focus on assessing our work specifically with participants. It is important to understand and know how effective our efforts are and what adjustments may be needed. We can ask questions, such as "Where are we in our work together, how is it going, what is left to do?" (Lee, 2001, p. 206).

Evaluation from an anti-oppressive approach should always incorporate the views of everyone involved in the process. It can involve formal or informal feedback from the participant and social worker, using collaborative efforts to identify perceptions of the process and identify outcomes of their work together.

The results of evaluation may be passed along to funders, administrators, agency boards, and social workers who are interested in the quality of services received. In reviewing our work with participants and reflecting on the outcomes, we can continuously work to improve the quality of services and enhance accountability to our participants.

Evaluation takes place throughout our relationship with participants, at all stages of our interaction. Ongoing evaluation gives us an idea about our progress with the participant. It also ensures accountability for the social worker and participant and provides motivation for continued and sustainable change. There are two major types of evaluations:

1. Formative or process evaluation: this is carried out at regular intervals (or different points in time) in our work with the participant. The information can be used as continuous feedback to inform and reshape the process (Dalrymple & Burke, 2006; Parsons, 1998). The focus is on what is happening in the interaction or intervention.

2. Summative or outcome evaluation: this is concerned with the outcomes, effectiveness, and impact of the interaction or intervention.

You can better understand the interaction of these two types of evaluation by comparing it to monitoring a journey. Process evaluation is about continuously checking where we are going to make sure we are on the path that we want. At the end of the journey, we provide an outcome evaluation of whether we reached the final destination, where we wanted to be.

From the empowerment perspective, there are three levels from which to assess and evaluate our work with participants—micro, mezzo, and macro (see Image 4.5). These evaluations can be implemented in a variety of ways. Oftentimes they are in the form of questionnaires, structured or semi-structured interviews, surveys, or small and large group discussions. However, creative methods, such as the following approaches, have the potential for offering new insights (Burke, 1998, p. 53; Garaway, 1995; Sutherland, 1995).

- Pictures drawn by individuals or groups
- Photos taken by individuals or groups
- Problem stories using real events that are evaluated by a group
- Creative expression of the process, such as drama, role playing, songs, dances, sculpturing (e.g., engaging in a collective presentation in which people use themselves to present a situation or theme in silence, without movement)
- Diaries or collages
- Group meetings, workshops, or focus groups
- Murals and timelines
- Web charts (to trace the root causes and implications of a specific phenomenon)

Depending on the participant(s) and the situation, visual and dramatic forms of data collection for evaluation may uncover important information that might not otherwise surface (Burke, 1998).

Image 4.5	Levels of Evaluation From the Empowerment Perspective	
Level	Focus	Measures of Participants' Success
Micro	Participants' perception of their ability to make choices	Self-efficacy, self-awareness, self-acceptance, self-esteem, understanding of rights, critical thinking
Mezzo	Participants' ability to influence others	Knowledge and skills, assertiveness; ability to set limits on giving, asking for help, solving problems, practicing new skills, accessing resources
Macro	Participants' involvement in groups or activities that could improve the status of the larger community	Participation in mutual aid groups and neighborhood groups, political action or participation, contributions

Source: Adapted from Parsons, 1995, *Empowerment-Based Social Work Practice: A Study of Process and Outcomes.* Paper presented at the Annual Program Meeting for the Council on Social Work Education, San Diego, CA.

It is important to note that oftentimes, participants are left out of the evaluation process. From the traditional point of view, participatory approaches to evaluation are viewed as a revolutionary activity, as it implicitly questions the power relations and politics of evaluation (Phillips, Palfrey, & Thomas, 1994). We believe that evaluation must include the voice of the participant. A collective process is one way to enhance responsibility and keep people honest (Cousins & Whitmore, 1998).

The Shaping Lives project was set up in 1996 to bring together lessons from participants on anti-oppressive practice. Findings from four development projects provided insight into participant's needs regarding evaluation of services. Participants felt that while it was important to evaluate services in terms of their outcomes, the subjective perspectives of individual participants should be included. Furthermore, participants didn't want to just monitor and evaluate service delivery, they wanted to be involved in defining the outcomes and working toward achieving them (Dalrymple & Burke, 2006).

One method of ensuring that evaluation is meaningful and relevant for participants is participatory evaluation, which recognizes and prioritizes the wisdom and knowledge of the participant. It enables participants to own the evaluation process rather than be 'subjected' to it, ensuring that all parts of the evaluation process are relevant to the participants rather than elements being imposed on them (Graham & Harris, 2005). The principles of participatory evaluation are listed in Image 4.6.

It should be noted that two key issues have been raised with regards to including participants in the evaluation process. One is the need to acknowledge the participant's definitions of the outcomes (Shaping Our Lives National User Network, 2003). The other concern is the question of whose agendas, issues, concerns, and interests the evaluation is seeking to advance (Beresford, 2005; Dalrymple & Burke, 2006).

STORIES FROM THE FIELD: ANTI-OPPRESSIVE PRACTICE WITH INDIVIDUALS

1 Rooting Our Practice in Justice: Language as a Tool of Transformation, by Heather Horizon Greene   p. 168

This story examines how we use language in our healing practice and the impact that language can and does have in either supporting or hindering the practice of social justice. Heather Horizon Greene discusses how she integrates anti-oppressive language into her clinical work. She urges us to consider our use of language in the clinical setting and how we can use language as a tool of intention and justice rather than oppression.

2 Who the Fuck Are You? Working Toward Accountability, by Whitney Stark   p. 171

This story from the field describes Whitney Stark's process of learning to work toward transparency and accountability in her complicated role of being a social worker and holding privileged identities. Through her experiences as a case manager, she explains why being transparent and holding oneself accountable is critical for social justice and anti-oppressive work. (add a space after period and before Whitney) Whitney illustrates the power of wearing one's self in the work that we do, while critiquing professionalism and what a professional dress code represents as it relates to power and oppression.

3 Use of Self-Disclosure: Being Personable and Not Personal, by Heidi Grove and Juston Cooper   p. 175

This story is informed by the work that Heidi Grove and Juston Cooper engage in with disconnected youth at their agency, The Youth Connection. They provide an example of how to self-disclose in a way that takes into account the purpose behind the self-disclosure. Heidi and JC work from a metaphoric principle; to learn how to be personable and not personal. Their dialogue reveals the need to continually self-reflect on what they share with their participants.

4 Getting All Fired Up: The Voice of a Participant, by Samantha Rogers   p. 177

This story features the voice of Samantha Rogers, a woman of color who served for over 17 years in prison. She shares her story of surviving the prison industrial complex, inviting readers to listen to what inspired her transformation and change from within.

5 Rachel's Story: A Collaboration of Not Knowing, by Carly Goldberg   p. 178

This story illustrates the power of using narrative and storytelling practice to capture the voice of a participant, Rachel, a refugee who came to Carly Goldberg for services. Rather than documenting the refugee's story in a traditional way through standard clinical case notes, Carly wrote in a creative way that provided the space for individual and collective liberation. Her method of documenting, retelling, re-storying, and sharing this narrative challenges social work's dominant forms of representing experiences, particularly in its storytelling format.

This story represents the power of self-reflexivity. Meg Panichelli reflects on her experiences of engaging in anti-oppressive social work with street workers while locating herself in the work that she does. Meg highlights how she navigates spaces of discomfort, intense emotions, and the tensions of having the privilege to access intimate stories about the lives of her participants.

This story details the experiences of a social worker's journey of teaching and learning. Carly Goldberg worked in HIV prevention at an urban AIDS social service organization and illustrates her strategy for engaging in HIV and AIDS education with the story of one participant who experienced multiple barriers and was unable to read. This story suggests a concrete way for us to provide access to resources for our participants in a creative and empowering manner.

1

ROOTING OUR PRACTICE IN JUSTICE: LANGUAGE AS A TOOL OF TRANSFORMATION

HEATHER HORIZON GREENE

Though my name for this work has evolved over the years, I've been a practitioner of anti-oppressive social work for over 11 years. These days, I most love the idea of calling it justice-centered social work, choosing justice as the core of my work.

Language was actually the entry point for me into this work. While working at my BSW [bachelor's of social work] internship, I listened uncomfortably as a co-intern, and future social worker, made rude, offensive and homophobic jokes about a gay staff member in our agency. Listening to the student's cruel statements, I was offended and saddened, and yet struggled to say out loud, as I hope I would today, "that makes me uncomfortable; please stop." Though there were many lessons for me as I continued to process the experience, it was the beginning of a journey that has continually pushed me to look at how we use language in our healing practice and at the impact language can and does have in the practice of justice.

Language is a tool of our craft. How we talk (with our peers and colleagues) and write (in our progress notes) about folks, in addition to how we talk with participants, can powerfully transform and strengthen the overall intention of our work. Language is one tool, one way, to help us bring our practice into alignment with our values. Paying careful attention to our use of language is one of many ways we can, in fact, root our practice in an awareness of justice.

While exchanging emails recently with a colleague, I had an opportunity to think a bit more about what my practice of justice-centered language looks like today. Part of our correspondence is reprinted here with permission.

My colleague's inquiry: What has been your experience of integrating anti-oppressive language into your clinical work? Particularly with paperwork and things that other people will read and see? I find myself daunted to put such things forward when I think about having to explain or being criticized by others. Which isn't to say I always back down about it, but I do tend to censor myself more than I like.

My response: A few thoughts. There are certainly some therapy modalities that are [more anti-oppressive]. Some of those are narrative approach, strengths perspective, empowerment work, consciousness raising, feminist theory, client-centered practice, and even more evidence-based practices like DBT (Dialectical Behavior Therapy). Those practices have a more natural commitment to power sharing and each person (therapist and client) brings their own unique offering and starting place rather than the value-based hierarchy of some of the more traditional psychotherapy models. (And therefore they bring a more natural professional discourse that is more aligned with anti-oppressive work.) Even if we have a "radical" framework, I can think of a number of times when I have thought someone would understand or relate to the language of anti-oppression, though it turned out to be a barrier. I think we see that in a lot of empowerment work, where folks don't often think about their life experience in terms of oppression—though sometimes that is how we (have learned to) understand it. So, I think of these justice-rooted theories and knowledge bases as informing how I practice and how I understand change—and acknowledge the importance of that—but I also have a commitment to "meeting folks where they are" and honoring their self-wisdom and intuitive expertise in their own healing process.

With paperwork, I think there are very practical and natural ways to talk about folks in ways that are person-centered; acknowledge people's strengths and resilience (and identities); are narrative-based, which reflects a commitment to deep listening (which is also radical and anti-oppressive); and validate and normalize rather than pathologize, people's lived experiences. To me this can read as intentional and mindful rather than radical and I think when you're able to bring presence and intentionality to charting, folks who read the charts will often notice the positive. It's more "sparkly" because it is more in alignment with treating people with integrity and often more in alignment with our values in general; it's actually nice to model that value for other practitioners. I think too when we get to the assessment piece of our notes, that is where we get to most use our voice naturally.

I can understand that this way of taking notes might feel daunting, and would also be curious to know more about that for you. I think I would recommend starting with a small commitment. Can you commit to using someone's name more often rather than using the word patient or client? See how that feels. And I also want to offer that it's possible that this more intentional use of language would not be polarizing or criticized, although it's possible that it would be. I would like to suggest, however, that you can develop and balance the skill of writing intentionally about people while capturing the situations in ways that meet insurance or diagnostic criteria, yet are healing and not pathologizing.

I guess I would also be curious to know where you feel you are censoring yourself. There's probably a lot of good information there about your own edges, the (rightly identified!) problems with the system, the environment you're working in and the folks (colleagues) you're working with.

So a quick summary:

- use person-centered language;
- include/acknowledge people's strengths, resilience and identities;
- listen deeply and try to capture some of what you hear;
- validate and normalize people's experience;
- try not to pathologize people (I have to really work on this, since I work in such a pathologizing environment, and this is really the professional culture);
- be intentional and mindful in your writing; and
- use your voice to honor your own boundaries and starting place.

This conversation feels quite relevant and timely for me, so I wanted to offer it here in the hopes of encouraging us to think about our language use and how we can use language as a tool and listen, situate and shift, but sometimes you just can't. It is a really weird system that sets up this need to control resources. I am hoping that radical anti-oppression, feminist thinking and harm reduction is teaching us that transforming possibilities takes place in part through situating ourselves, being accountable, and recognizing people as their own experts.

Breaking the standards and practices of these weird professionalizations can often open up a different kind of interaction that doesn't maintain the same stale and stagnant, old structures. Revealing more about yourself can allow space for better harm reduction, more openness, and more freedom to shift strategies. I am not saying that you should disclose everything about yourself just for the hell of it or that your relationship in this setting is not particular, but transparency and accountability help to change the power dynamics. If people know a bit who you are, and if they know that you acknowledge that who you are informs what you think and suggest, they can make better informed decisions about what help they want from you and how they want to use it. I am not there to try and tell these people how to live their lives. I am there to help them do whatever it is they want and need to do. Why else would I be at that job?

1. What does Whitney say about the significance of accountability and transparency in working with individuals? How is this helpful for anti-oppressive work?

2. How does Whitney address gender oppression at her organization and what are the reasons for the agency's resistance?

3. How does she practice accountability through self-representation?

4. What are her critiques of "professional attire"? Do you agree or disagree with her perspective and approach?

5. How do you represent yourself as a social worker at your internship or agency placement?

3

USE OF SELF-DISCLOSURE:
BEING PERSONABLE AND NOT PERSONAL

HEIDI GROVE AND JUSTON COOPER (JC)

Heidi: Our question is always, if you are going to do self-disclosure, what's the purpose behind it? Is it for the young person, the participant, to gain some insight? Or is it for you, the social worker? If it's for you, then it's not appropriate.

JC: Absolutely. And that's hard to measure, but we work on it and we are aware. We do self-disclosure, but we self-disclose on a kind of metaphoric principle: being personable and not personal. As a staff in training, we've done a lot of self-growth work, from the professional and academic to the personal and spiritual. So our self-disclosure is from a personable approach, not a personal approach, which allows us to have a barrier. But, I do think social work students or people coming into this work are taught about conventional psychological concepts around linking: how you are not supposed to link with a client, how you are not supposed to self-disclose to a client. I think a more integrative approach is more appropriate for understanding how to disclose and what to disclose.

Heidi: And for what purpose? I can give you an example. We are dealing with a young man who just came back to Colorado. He was in federal prison at the age of eighteen because he was smuggling drugs over the Mexican border. He and I were talking and he was really struggling with the concept of having a federal felony. And the reason he stayed in federal prison for as long as he did was because he didn't snitch. He was going on and on and on that "snitches are bitches, they deserve to be in ditches." He kept saying it over and over again. So I pulled him aside and said "let's go for a walk." So we were walking and talking about the concept of "snitches are bitches and they should be in ditches" and I look at him and I say, "Let me tell you a story, the story of a fifteen-year-old girl who got herself in pretty deep and had the DEA knocking on her door. The gang threatened to kill her family." I asked the guy, "Did she deserve to die? Because she had to make a choice?" And he said "no, no, that's not cool, like you are dragging in your family, that's not right." And he paused and said, "that was you, Heidi, wasn't it?" And I replied, "Yes it was." And he responded with, "Wow . . . " I said, "Do I deserve to be in a ditch?" He was like, "naaaah." He said, "You did what you had to do to take care of yourself, I understand that." He never used that phrase since.

So when we say self-disclosure, it's got to have a purpose. In this case it wasn't me saying, "Hey I am cool because I did this." It was like, "Hey look at the consequences of your choices in the words that you are using."

5

RACHEL'S STORY: A COLLABORATION OF NOT KNOWING

CARLY GOLDBERG

In the 10 years of my clinical experience with refugee and immigrant women, my approach to practice has shifted. After I worked with a woman named Rachel, something inside me changed. I transformed my thinking around the need to introduce anti-oppressive, intersectional, global, critical race, feminist, and theory as a concept into social work practice.

My initial meeting with Rachel left me absolutely speechless, as if I had never had one ounce of knowledge in the field. I felt a deep lack of perspective and standpoint and discourse to fully understand Rachel and her multiple, distinct, and intersectional identities. When I realized in that moment that I did not have a way to understand her, I decided to write up a narrative. If I had written up a case study from a traditional clinical standpoint, my case notes would have read: "Rachel the 30 year old, HIV positive woman who came from West Africa just three months before we met . . . " But, I felt that in order to mirror what I was writing about I needed to write it in a creative, narrative way. My method of documenting, retelling and sharing this story is in itself a form of anti-oppressive practice, as it challenges dominant forms of representing experiences, particularly in its storytelling format.

Here is Rachel's story:

She was dark, very dark. Petite and drowning in remnants of African garb layered with donated clothing from decades past. Her face served as the backdrop to a story that deafeningly reverberates around the globe. An African woman infected with HIV. With her narrow back pressed up against the dimly lit office wall, covered in flyers about local HIV/AIDS resources and pamphlets promoting safer sex practices, she was lost. Her eyes, though—they stood out, all on their own. In the first few minutes of our meeting her eyes alone told me her story. The terror, the loss, the isolation, the trauma.

The second Liberian civil war displaced not only Rachel's body, but her mind and spirit too. Via a refugee camp in Ghana, Rachel arrived in New York just three months prior to our initial meeting. She came with her two children, ages four and eight, her decreasing CD4 count, susceptibility to opportunistic infections, and her all-too-vivid memories of murder and rape. I, a white, privileged, American-born, ethnically Jewish and faithfully Buddhist, licensed and master's-trained social worker, was to acquaint her with safer sex practices and tell her how she should reduce the spread of HIV infection.

Her eyes drifted off and her gaze became noticeably fixed on her not so distant past—the tears gently rolled down her face. Stumbling for words like a fish out of water gasping for air, I choked. I choked on my discomfort, my lack of experience in working with refugee survivors of genocide and civil unrest, choked on my mother tongue, and choked on the knowledge and experience that I have come to rely on in my social work practice. To proceed and meet the agency requirements for our initial meeting and complete a psychosocial assessment I feared may have resulted in a further trauma given her precarious mental status.

I was paralyzed by indecision. I did not know if I should meet Rachel where she was, as that was a very scary, difficult, and unfamiliar place for not only me but for her as well, or to continue on with the assessment, risking further injury to her. I am sure that in that moment, my desperate attempt to search for the right words sounded just as convoluted to her as it sounded to me, if not more so. Clinically, the only thing I felt that I could do in that instance was to reassure her that she had shown great courage and strength by coming to meet with me and that she was not alone. However, the "not knowing," my uncertainty in that moment, seemed like a curse and not at all the gift I would later recognize it to be.

Rachel to me is a prime example of women in their distinctive multiplicities and voices. Rachel shared her story and herself by way of her whispers, tears, yelling, laughter, and more often than not, traumatized silence. Working with Rachel forced me outside of my personal and professional comfort zone and challenged me to put my clinical practice and theoretical underpinnings to the test.

That morning I accompanied Rachel mostly in silence to visits to the obstetrician to discuss the risk of perinatal HIV transmission to her unborn child and to the gynecologist to diagnose HPV and possible cervical cancer. Finally the silence broke. While laying on the examination table with a specula protruding from her vagina, left for what seemed an eternity for the resident to call her attending physician, tears of discomfort and utter fear flowed down her face. She quietly spoke, telling me about the herbs from Africa and the hanger she used in a desperate attempt to abort her fetus. Then she became silent. We together were able to sit exposed with one another.

At the end of what was an excruciatingly long morning, she and I went to Quizno's to get lunch before she returned to a demanding job standing on her feet all day working in a clothing factory. As we walked down the street, I tripped. She laughed. It was the first time I had ever seen her smile. As we approached the restaurant I explained to her what type of food they have at this American restaurant. To my surprise the steak hoagie and 32-ounce pink lemonade was a big hit. As we went our separate ways late that morning, just being slightly more comfortable in our "not knowing" proved to be the beginning of one of my most important social work relationships. I was able through her narrative and storytelling to reflect on my own story and together we began to sit with each other's differences, uniqueness, and consciousness, thereby creating a deeper, richer dialogue and space in which to work.

1. How does this creative manner of documenting a participant's story align with an anti-oppressive approach to practice?

2. How do the two women's stories and identities intersect in their interactions together?

3. How does Carly navigate her fears, tensions, uncertainties, and "not knowing"?

4. How might you envision the creative process of re-storying with the participants at your agency?

6

DRIVE SLOW IN THE SNOW

MEG PANICHELLI

It was snowing and I was afraid to drive home.

Afraid, not just because the roads were icy, but because

I simultaneously wanted to throw up, fall asleep, crawl into my not yet lovers' arms, and

shoot up to take away the disgusting combination of guilt, neediness, fear causing me to be nauseous. What just happened?

Who can I tell this to?

What if I flashback and pass out when I drive home? It's 1am. I have to be in the car pool at 8am tomorrow. Is my roommate crush still awake?

My MSW class will think weird things, question my credibility and safety and decisions. The Institutional Review Board (IRB) committee specifically wanted to know how I would manage my safety.

It was February, or maybe March. At this point I can't remember exactly, but it is a moment that is worth limitless reflection. It was my first research experience. As part of my MSW internship I conducted an individual needs assessment by doing a number of qualitative interviews with participants of the program I worked for. Prior to the needs assessment, I spent a lot of time with a feminist sociologist who helped me manage my internal conflicts about doing research. At this point, I was in the final quarter of my MSW program and had not been introduced to the world of AOP social work research or practice. I was trying to figure out how to do it by combining what I was learning in my community-based social work class, using feminist qualitative research methods, using intersectionality as a lens for the work, and trusting what I felt in my heart was the "right way" to do anti-oppressive work in the world.

My interviews were with women who injected drugs and traded sex for money on the street. These were folks with whom I'd been building a relationship for years, through my daily nonprofit work at the needle exchange. But, in these interviews, something different happened. They really let me into their intimate worlds, and they didn't have to. And it was confusing.

I really appreciated the time they were giving me to interview them about their experiences working on the street. My intention with the project was to use the findings to create trainings for providers across the city who worked with women who exchanged sex for money, drugs or something they needed. I wanted to talk to welfare agencies and legal services and health clinics and hospital staff and case managers and mental health clinics. I had big ideas. Still, the process of this research felt complicated for me—as a white person, a provider, a queer, a student with a desire to get a PhD, as a non–drug user, with a stable living situation, as someone who lived in a different neighborhood, and ultimately as someone with the power to decide what to do with the findings.

Throughout my work in this community, with daily outreach and contact, there were many ways that I felt an insider. Still in this work I never really asked the folks very personal questions. I often learned very personal information, but it came up organically. Anyway, I got to the point where it was time to conduct interviews and I built up the nerve to start asking people if they wanted to participate. The first 3 (out of 6) people I tried calling had their phones shut off. I was both relieved and disappointed. A week later I got a call from two of these folks who were in need of supplies. While on the phone I asked if they wanted to get interviewed and said if they did I would give them $50. They both were excited and honored. They both said, "wow, it's really cool that you want to hear our stories. No one ever wants to know about our lives." I was kind of shocked, because I knew that in many places sex workers and drug users are over-researched and I was trying to be cautious of the distrust of researchers and academics this research can create.

These folks were special to me, and I really wanted to make them feel that way. It felt like such a privilege to interview people about their daily lives. I recognize that the media often make sex work sexy and appealing, but the women in my study didn't find their daily lives sexy or appealing. I don't say this to paint them as victims, but to recognize the varied experiences of sex workers. Every day, each of us in our quest to survive normalizes experiences that others may find "fascinating." Yes, my position as a researcher was totally complicated. Essentially researchers colonize people's lives. We take their daily experiences, study them and institutionalize these experiences under the guise of knowledge production. There is a lot of responsibility there and a lot of need for accountability. We have a real obligation to do important, effective and community-based work with this knowledge. I spent a lot of time reflecting and feeling guilty, confused, passionate and excited about all of this.

For these interviews, I wanted to cause as little disruption to the participants' lives, so I said that I would meet them wherever they wanted. Each of them wanted to meet in the places that they were staying, their intimate spaces. Rooms where they sleep, where they throw their dirty underwear on the floor, where they make instant coffee and tea using the hotplate on the floor, where they keep ashtrays with cigarettes, where they shoot up safely, where they listen to music and have dance parties in between dates, and in rooms that may be someone else's intimate space in three weeks.

One particular night stands out for me. Two participants asked if they could be interviewed at the same time. They lived together and were aunt and niece. They shared a room in the front of the house together. As a novice researcher I felt a bit awkward about how all of this would go down. But, if this was what would work for them I figured I would try it. So I asked that, while one was being interviewed, the other one just do their own thing as best she could. The three hours I spent in that particular room doing those two interviews were heavy. They were heavy atmospherically with smoke, emotionally with feelings and experiences. I think the energy, mixed in with the smoke, feelings and heat, weighed on us all.

Throughout the interview the aunt would look out the window and comment, "it's snowing, it's still snowing, it's really coming down . . . " And it was, and I wanted to hurry the interviews and get home. In total I had done three interviews that night, each lasting over an hour. No one told me that would be a draining idea. I also hate driving in the snow and I didn't want to get caught spending the night in that room. I had to be at school early the next morning and I knew rush hour would be a mess of snow, slush and ice. Aside from that, the feelings in my body motivated me get out of there, ASAP.

It's interesting as a researcher, a teacher, and a facilitator, to think about how we make our feelings and experiences transparent. While the two women were very clearly sharing deep, intense stories, I tried to not react in any sort of judgmental way. I expressed empathy, concern, emotion in the moments that it seemed that these ladies wanted me too (and which felt sincere). But, what I couldn't talk about was how the stories of sexual abuse and rape were triggering, how I was thankful my own participation in the industry often meant seeing clients who were lawyers and that we were always warm when we fucked, or how sick I feel when I watch needles go into people's bodies. The combination of these feelings made me check out. Thankfully, I was tape recording the conversation and could listen to it and transcribe it later onto the white computer screen, removed from the heaviness of that room.

At that same moment and even now almost 2 years later, I am overcome with guilt writing these words on the page, striving to stay aware of the loads of privilege that allowed me to leave that room and drive home safely that night. How the next morning I gave my roommate crush chocolate and how later that night we were fucking in my bed. How I got to get out of there and do what I wanted. Do whatever it took to never end up in that place.

My research goals have always in part been to dispel portraits of sex workers as victims. I worry that this story probably paints the two women I interviewed as victimized, unfortunate, poor, without access, etc., etc. Although that is not my intention, and the majority of my thesis lauded the strengths of these women and this community, right now I want to recognize that all of us in the research process have feelings, reactions, and experiences that are triggers. Some of us have the resources, privilege and power to access support without fear of stigma, criminalization, and other dire consequences. I do.

I am still left with the question of how this critical reflexive component that is central to AOP or Feminist research and practice, can be used to make change. I fantasize about the answer to this question often. I want to say that this form of reflection on the work acknowledges institutional oppression and the way that internalized oppression has shaped the thoughts that enter and leave our brains. So for me, it's important to acknowledge that lives are complicated, that people are surviving, that I as researcher and service provider benefit from my participants' marginalization, that my struggles and triggers are not separate, that my struggles are inextricable from those of the folks I've worked with, that I am often aware of how and when I check out. Acknowledging these realities demonstrates that "I/we" are never objective or neutral in the work we do and that reflexivity is a critical component to engaging in Feminist social work practice and research.

I hope in the future to challenge my students, colleagues and friends to engage in this conversation. I want to complicate the work that they do and to express the range of emotions, thoughts, feelings, challenges and barriers that arise in the work so they can do better work. Because, really, what is anti-oppressive/feminist social work? I think we are trying to figure it out.

1. What feelings and responses came up for you after reading this personal reflection?

2. How does Meg's life intersect with the lives of the participants?

3. How does this form of reflection "acknowledge institutional oppression and the way that internalized oppression has shaped the thoughts that enter and leave our brains"?

4. How does Meg navigate the tensions, discomforts, and intense emotions connected to her work with sex workers?

7

ABC'S OF HIV PREVENTION:
LITERACY AS A PATHWAY TO HIV EDUCATION

CARLY GOLDBERG

When I accepted a position as a social worker specializing in HIV prevention at an urban AIDS services organization, I could not have imagined that the activism encompassed by my clinical work would include advocacy for literacy. But, I eventually realized that the most profound pathway toward freedom—prevention of communicable diseases, the ability to navigate our complicated medical system, and communication with intimate partners—all begins with a foundation of literacy.

This was evident upon meeting one client who was involved in the HIV prevention program at my agency. He was in his 50s or 60s and learning to read for the first time. He probably had developmental disabilities and was diagnosed as having HIV and being at risk of re-infection. This man was scared and not sure about what to make of his experience of living with HIV and his encounter with me. A lot of his fears seemed to also be connected to not having access to information about his own health and well-being.

Once I learned that he could not read and write in English, I went to the children's hospital in Philadelphia and obtained a series of children's books that contained images and words. This was the start of our teaching and learning journey together. Together, we created sessions that would help him understand why we were together, but also teach him how to read the HIV prevention materials. The thing he valued the most was learning how to read.

I recognized that this skill was critical for him; he was so focused and eager to learn. But, although he was very determined, he was also self-conscious and had a lot of insecurity in his inability to read. Due to his social location, he had been denied this basic human right. However, I wasn't going to deny him that right to literacy and just feed him the information. I wasn't going to impose the material on him either. I wanted him to feel empowered in accessing the information himself. So I introduced to him the idea of learning about HIV prevention and education through pamphlets acquired at the local children's hospital and worksheets especially designed for him. He felt cared for and supported and I felt honored to share this process with him.

It's interesting to note that the AIDS service organization that I worked for challenged my efforts with this client. They asked me, "Why are you using children's books?" I would say, "How could we not honor where he is?" It's thinking outside of the constructed boxes that allows for profound change.

This was anti-oppressive work because it involved sharing the privilege of being able to read and giving another person access to it. I believe that anti-oppressive social work is about working within the constraints of the system and the agency. We have to deal with structural oppression and find creative ways to work around oppressive systems, whether they are intentionally oppressive or not. It's important to understand that not everyone is the same and people cannot really be treated equally. One needs to think outside the box and find creative ways to provide access to resources for our clients.

1. How does Carly increase her participant's access to resources?

2. What creative ideas do you have for providing resources to the participants at your agency?

DISCUSSION QUESTIONS

1. Take a few moments to consider your internship placement or the social work agency where you work. What phase(s) of anti-oppressive practice are you currently engaged in? Considering this phase and the various concepts presented within that phase, in what ways are you practicing from an anti-oppressive lens?

2. Regarding your internship placement or the social work agency where you work, which phase of anti-oppressive practice may be difficult for you to implement and why? Which phases may be easier for you to implement and why?

ACTIVITIES

1. As a way of building self-awareness, answer these questions:

   a. Personal: Who Are You? What are some of your personal strengths and weaknesses? What are your core beliefs about life? What are your fears and dreams?

   b. Social: Who Are You in Public? Who are you when you are with people? What kind of impression do you try to make? What kinds of people do you like to hang out with?

   c. Relationships: Who Are You In Romantic Relationships? What are your primary beliefs about love? What do you want in a relationship? What are your deal-breakers? Are there patterns in your relationships?

2. Describe a context in which you may be asked to work with a participant to address issues which might prevent you from conveying genuine empathy. What is it about these participant issues that may be challenging for you?

3. As a means of exploring your thoughts and feelings about power and powerlessness, draw an image depicting these feelings. This creative drawing activity is not about creating "good art," it is about using images to represent and express your experiences of power and powerlessness in a nonverbal way. On a blank piece of paper, draw a line down the center of the page. On one side of the page, draw a situation that made you feel powerful. On the other side of the page, draw a picture that represents a time when you felt powerless. The purpose of this creative exercise is to begin to use alternative forms of representation in order to shift our perspectives and understanding of power and to begin to see things from a new lens.

Once you are finished with your drawing, turn to a partner and share the following:

    a. What images did you use to represent your experiences of feeling power and powerlessness?

    b. Why did you select these images and what meaning do they have for you?

    c. What was this experience like for you?

    d. What did you discover from doing this exercise that you did not know before?

4. Self-disclosure can be uncomfortable. Identify a situation when you felt uncomfortable because someone was disclosing something personal about themselves.

    a. What was the reason for your discomfort?

    b. How did you respond to the self-disclosure?

    c. In reflecting back on this experience, what did you learn about self-disclosure that you can apply to your work with participants?

ADDITIONAL RESOURCES

Websites

Shaping Our Lives: A National Network of Service Users and Disabled People (Great Britain) http://www.shapingourlives.org.uk/

Films

Big mamma (2000). T. Seretean

One drop rule (2001). J. Banks

The undocumented (2013). M. Williams

Two spirits (2009). L. Nibley

Books

Danticat, E. (1998). *Breath, eyes, memory*. New York: Vintage.

Eugenides, J. (2007). *Middlesex*. New York: Picador.

Fitch, J. (2001). *White oleander*. New York: Little, Brown.

Take a few moments to reflect on the concept of family. What is your definition of family? Has your definition of family changed over time? If so, how has it changed? Who are the members of your family? How has your family composition changed over time (for example, separation of parents, new partnerships, death, births, extended family entering or leaving)?

FAMILIES IN CONTEXT

Every family has at least two members. Thus, we need to acknowledge at least two individual family member's personal struggles, intersecting identities, needs, and strengths. We need to recognize how each individual takes on certain roles and communication patterns and relational tasks within the family.

It is also important to engage with and tune-in to the family as a whole. The obvious factor is family dynamics and the relationships among members. It is also critical to acknowledge the richness of family history and the influence of multiple generations of family members. This history, or the lack of historical context in some cases, influences and shapes each participant's perception of their family and their role within it.

Anti-oppressive work with families requires social workers to recognize and understand not only these internal family forces, but also the external forces that deeply affect family well-being. External social, economic, political, and environmental factors play a significant role in the well-being of families. Regardless of their composition, socioeconomic status, racial and cultural identification, or stage of development, families are influenced and shaped by their social and physical environment (Hodges, Burwell, & Ortega, 1998). Cultural stereotypes, discrimination, environmental injustice, racism, poverty, violence, and other forms of oppression all negatively affect families. The struggle to survive during social and economic crises can have an impact on relationships, physical and mental health status, and self-worth (Lundy, 2004).

In their work with families, AOP social workers generally focus on these four areas of difficulties related to a family's basic needs and rights:

- *Communication:* How do family members communicate with each other? How do they discuss differences and express anger, affection, joy, and sadness? How are decisions made?
- *Links to and place in society:* How are family members connected to other people, institutions, and material resources? What are their social and economic positions in society, their social class, ethnic background, and experiences of discrimination?
- *Rules:* What are the expectations of behavior, or the rules, within a family? Who makes them? Who enforces them? What happens when a member acts outside of the expectations? Which rules enforce inequality within the family?
- *Self-worth:* How do family members think about themselves? (Virginia Satir as cited in Lundy, 2004, pp. 117–118)

Building on these four areas, we can use a social justice lens to examine issues of power, privilege, and oppression at the individual, social/cultural, and institutional levels.

VISUAL REPRESENTATION OF FAMILY RELATIONSHIPS AND STRUGGLES

To learn more about a family, we certainly engage in dialogue with individual family members and the family as a whole. However, a variety of visual methods have been developed to represent participants' selves, family relationships, family structure and dynamics, social support networks, circumstances, major life events, and other presenting issues within a family. Some of these visual tools are described in the following sections.

These tools are often used during the "assessment," or teaching and learning phase to assist family members in communicating and sharing information with social workers about their lives. Gathering information collaboratively can nurture the family's relationships. Doing these visual representations also gives the participant and the family an active role in the assessment. These participatory activities encourage the development of a participant's and a family's motivations to work with the social worker to create change. Also, being actively involved in creating these visuals may enable participants and their families to feel like they are actually "doing something," thus restoring confidence in their ability to take a degree of control over their own lives (Parker & Bradley, 2010). These activities can also evoke powerful emotions within those completing them, leading to discussion about important issues that social workers may not have recognized nor had the opportunity to explore if the participant or family hadn't undertaken the activity.

Genograms

A genogram, like a family tree, is a visual display of the family and its structure at a particular point in time (Parker & Bradley, 2010). Genograms tend to be more specific and detailed than family trees, often displaying two or more generations of a family. Genograms include information about the sex or gender, race, ethnicity, and mental health issues of family members. Genograms can include not only biologically and legally related family members, but also anyone who has been important in the individual's life, including friends, lovers, partners, and pets.

Genograms are used in many different ways: to engage and assess individuals and families, to reframe and detoxify family issues, to highlight life transitions, to unblock a dysfunctional family system, to clarify family patterns, to connect individuals and families to their history, and to help participants revisualize their future (McGoldrick, Gerson, Petry, & Gil, 2008). Genograms can also be used to emphasize existing and potential resources and strengths of family members. Thus, a genogram is a tool that contributes to the concept of looking at the person in the context of their environment. Genograms are also used to gather and organize information about repetition across generations. They can be drawn to focus on specific traits, characteristics, and behaviors that wind through generations of the participant's family. They can map intergenerational family patterns, relationships, and life transitions. For example, genograms often trace immigration patterns, health issues (such as cancer or diabetes), births, deaths, partnerships, longevity of marital relationships, family separations, geographical mobility, citizenships status, job type, and drug use or alcoholism.

The history that is described in a genogram is unique for each individual or family, and there is no "right" or "wrong" way to create one. Encouraging the participant and their family to use their creativity through this medium of representation can be powerful and healing, opening up spaces for shifting perspectives and envisioning new possibilities.

A set of standard symbols is used to communicate social data in genograms (see Image 5.1). Males are usually depicted through squares and females are depicted through circles. In the center of each circle and square, the following information is recorded: birth date, age, occupation, and name of person. Death in the family is represented with an "x" through the circle or square. A couple is connected by a straight line. Separation is noted with one slash across the line, two slashes in the case of divorce. Children are placed below their parents according to age (with the oldest first). Dates for births, marriages, separations, and deaths can be added.

Image 5.2 is an example of a genogram using the basic symbols. (It is based on the story of Jasmine presented in Story 3 of Chapter 3.)

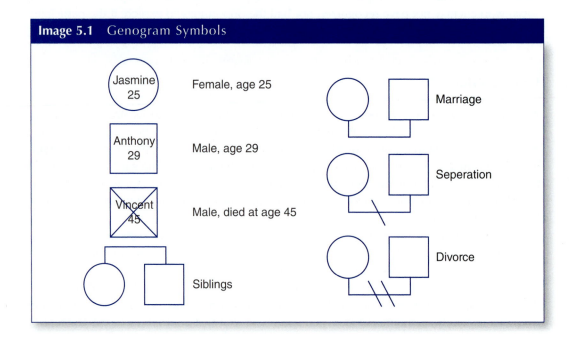

Image 5.1   Genogram Symbols

Image 5.2

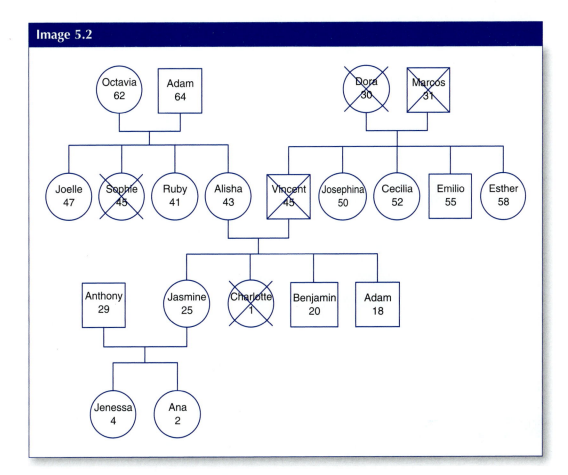

Social workers can encourage participants and family members to go beyond just using the basic symbols, however, and use various creative means to represent their family lineage. A few examples of this type of genogram are featured in Image 5.3.

When working with young children or families, social workers can encourage the creation of family play genograms. Family members choose from an array of miniature people, animals, and other small objects to represent the family. Children, youth, and adults often find this miniaturized world an engaging way to express their inner experience: the thoughts, emotions, and fantasies about themselves and their family members (McGoldrick et al., 2008). This exercise can bring out interesting information about family members' views of one another and their history and relationships, as well as emotions about those who are deceased. A discussion about the symbols used by the creator of the family play genogram activates their creativity, fantasy, and imagination.

In family play genograms, the figures can even be moved around to set up scenarios, such as coveted future relationships with family members. This activity allows for forming

Image 5.3   Creative Genograms

By Liliana Jimenez

By Christie Barboza

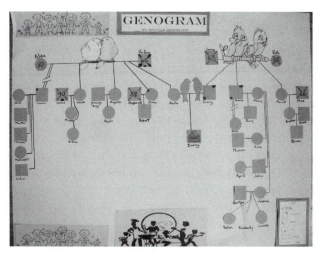

By Irving Mendleson

Image 5.4 Children's Family Play Genograms

By Stella Reinheimer, age 5

By Demetri Reinheimer, age 3

new narratives and for re-storying one's history. Family members have greater flexibility in imagining possibilities for change, while acknowledging that the content of their history exists, but may or may not inform their present circumstances (McGoldrick et al., 2008).

Using family play has the potential to enliven the encounter with our participants, incorporating humor, play, and new insights about family patterns and significant life events. The examples in Image 5.4 were created by a 5-year-old girl and a 3-year-old boy using toys that they each selected to represent their family members.

Ecomaps

An ecomap (ecological map) is visual tool used to situate and document individual and family relationships within a social context. Ecomaps identify the family members and wider social networks, community resources, agencies, and institutions that the individual or family has contact with. This visual tool explores how an individual or family is connected, delineating energy flow, resource flow, and the nature of relationships. Ecomaps can help an individual or family see their isolation or lack of support network or, on the other hand, all of the supports that are available to them.

The symbols of the genogram are used in an eco-map to depict the immediate family members. The nature of the relationship between family members and their various systems is depicted through lines and arrows. Some of the systems act as inputs, some as outputs, and in some cases individuals and systems have a two-way interaction. Some of these interactions require more energy, and they are often depicted as stressful relationships. The standard lines and arrows that are used to communicate interactional and relational data in ecomaps are shown in Image 5.5. An example of an ecomap is shown in Image 5.6.

Social workers can encourage participants and family members to go beyond the basic symbols to represent family and social networks. Participants can use various creative means to represent their connections and can also combine the genogram and ecomap. Image 5.7 presents two examples of this type of more creative ecomap.

Image 5.5 Ecomap Symbols

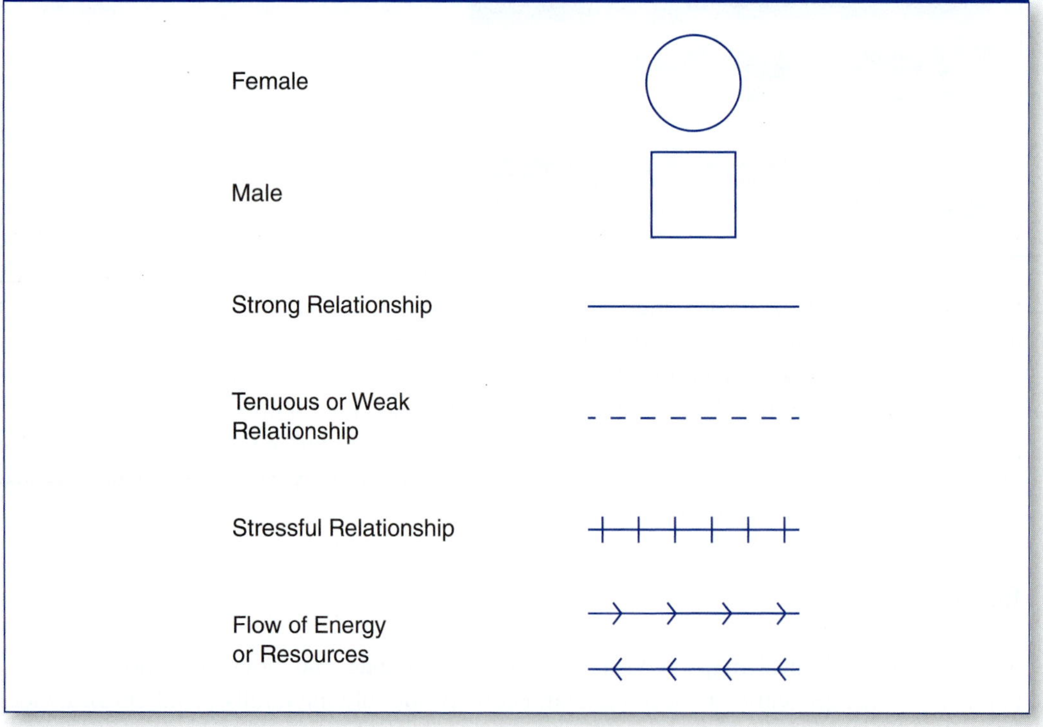

Female

Male

Strong Relationship

Tenuous or Weak Relationship

Stressful Relationship

Flow of Energy or Resources

Image 5.6 Example of an Ecomap

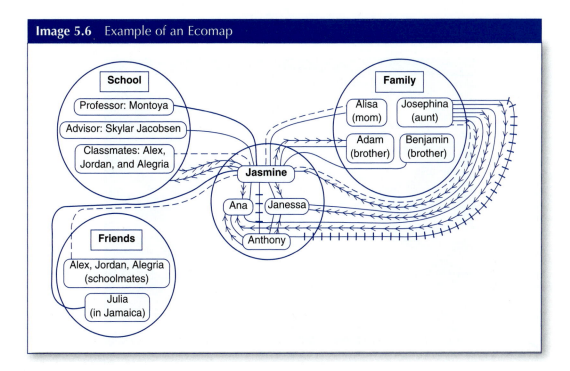

Social Network Maps

Like the ecomap, a social network map collects information about the person's social network (the interconnected systems wherein participants and families interact), the support provided, and the nature of the relationships (Tracy & Whittaker, 1990). While the ecomap illustrates relationships outside of the family unit, it does not represent the function of these relationships; however, the social network map does. It provides aids in assessing social support in the lives of participants and their families. Generally, the social network map gathers information on members of the person's network in seven areas:

- those living in the household;
- other family members and relatives;
- friends;
- colleagues from work or school;
- people from recreational, social & religious groups/organizations;
- neighbors;
- community members; and
- other social agencies (Lundy, 2011, p. 161).

See Image 5.8 for an example of a social network map.

Image 5.7   Creative Ecomaps

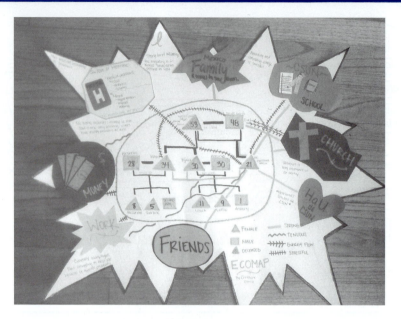

By Christiane Garcia

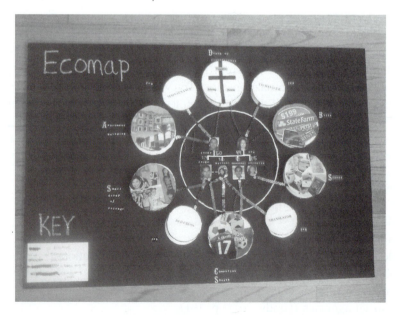

By Marisol Huerta

Image 5.8 Example of a Social Network Map

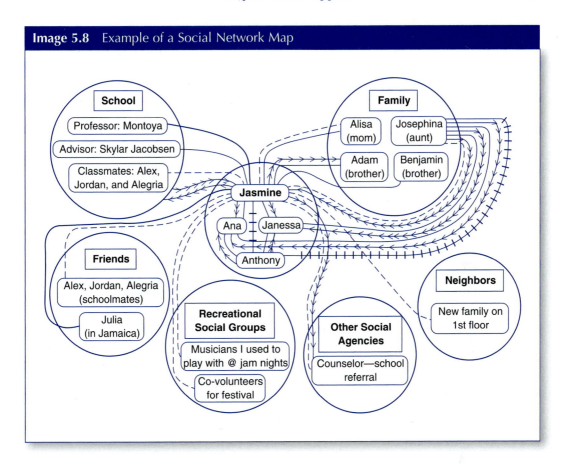

The complexities revealed in a participant's social network map are not always easy to decipher. The following questions can be used for translating the information presented in social network maps into the participant's and family members' goals:

- Who is/could be in the network?
- What are the strengths and resources of the social network (generally and specifically)?
- Are there gaps in areas of needed support? What are they?
- Is there a balanced exchange of support? Reciprocity? Is anyone overburdened? What changes could promote balance/reciprocity?
- Which network members are particularly responsive, effective, and dependable? Are there enough individuals meeting these criteria?
- Which network members are critical/demanding in a stress-producing, unproductive way?
- What are the barriers to using social support services? (Strom-Gottfried, 1999, p. 135)

Image 5.9 Example of a Culturagram

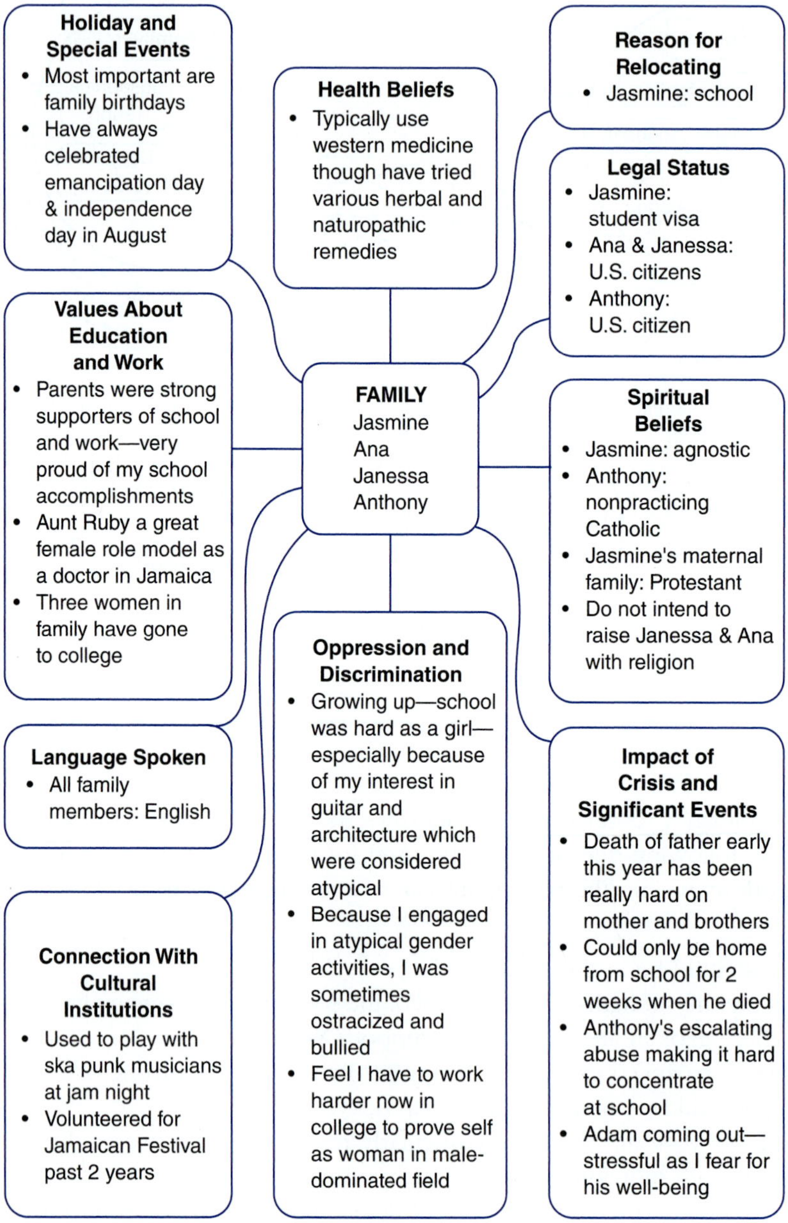

Holiday and Special Events
- Most important are family birthdays
- Have always celebrated emancipation day & independence day in August

Health Beliefs
- Typically use western medicine though have tried various herbal and naturopathic remedies

Reason for Relocating
- Jasmine: school

Legal Status
- Jasmine: student visa
- Ana & Janessa: U.S. citizens
- Anthony: U.S. citizen

Values About Education and Work
- Parents were strong supporters of school and work—very proud of my school accomplishments
- Aunt Ruby a great female role model as a doctor in Jamaica
- Three women in family have gone to college

FAMILY
Jasmine
Ana
Janessa
Anthony

Spiritual Beliefs
- Jasmine: agnostic
- Anthony: nonpracticing Catholic
- Jasmine's maternal family: Protestant
- Do not intend to raise Janessa & Ana with religion

Language Spoken
- All family members: English

Oppression and Discrimination
- Growing up—school was hard as a girl—especially because of my interest in guitar and architecture which were considered atypical
- Because I engaged in atypical gender activities, I was sometimes ostracized and bullied
- Feel I have to work harder now in college to prove self as woman in male-dominated field

Connection With Cultural Institutions
- Used to play with ska punk musicians at jam night
- Volunteered for Jamaican Festival past 2 years

Impact of Crisis and Significant Events
- Death of father early this year has been really hard on mother and brothers
- Could only be home from school for 2 weeks when he died
- Anthony's escalating abuse making it hard to concentrate at school
- Adam coming out—stressful as I fear for his well-being

Culturagrams

A culturagram combines elements of the genogram and the ecomap, but instead of focusing on relationships between people and systems, it visually depicts various aspects of someone's culture and interactions. A culturagram is a graphical representation showing the various aspects of a social culture and its effects on individual family members (see Image 5.9, which continues the story of Jasmine presented in Story 3 of Chapter 3). These interactions are portrayed in the same manner as in the ecomap. The cultural elements that could influence the individual or family include the following:

- Reasons for immigration;
- Time in the country;
- Legal or undocumented status;
- Age of family members at the time of immigration;
- Language spoken at home and in the community;
- Connection with cultural institutions;
- Health beliefs;
- Spiritual beliefs and practices;
- Holidays and special events;
- Impact of crisis and significant events;
- Values held about family, education, and work; and
- Economic transactions (remittances to country of origin). (Parker & Bradley, 2010, pp. 53–54)

Lifeline Maps

A lifeline map (also referred to as a Life Road Map or a Life-Flow Diagram) is used with participants to chronologically record major life events. Lifeline maps can either be depicted on a horizontal line (Lundy, 2011) or vertically (Hennessey, 2011). Lifeline maps include major events that occur in someone's life and the route the person has taken to get to where they are today. Creating a lifeline map provides the participant and family members with a visual depiction of changes over time, as well as significant life events. Charting these key moments offers an opportunity to see life patterns and times of change, to identify the influences that have shaped who they are and the decisions they've made in life, to discuss coping strategies, and to record progress.

A lifeline map starts with the person's date of birth and covers important moments and events in life up until the current moment. Ages or dates of major events can be included as reference points. Image 5.10 is a simple example. Some lifeline maps document the same major events and list the corresponding emotions. Incorporating emotions into a lifeline map depicts both the social and emotional influences that shape an individual. This activity provides the participant with the opportunity to track the course of their life, their corresponding emotions, and major life events.

Image 5.10 Example of a Lifeline Map

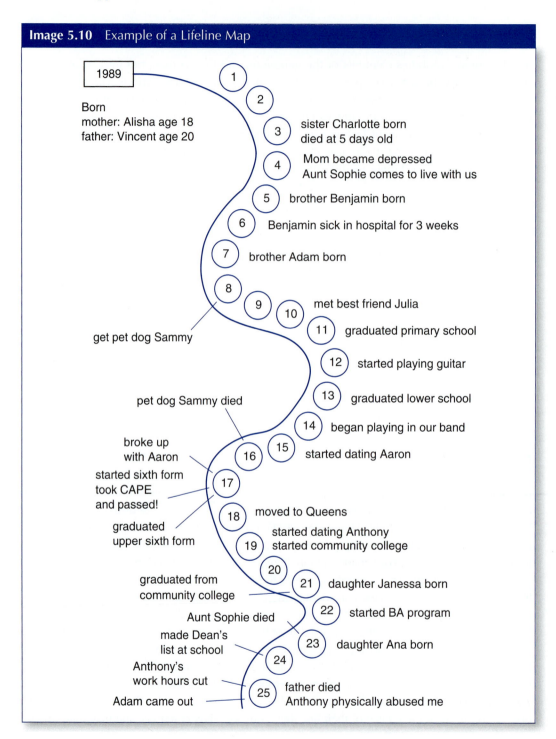

1989

Born
mother: Alisha age 18
father: Vincent age 20

1

2

3 sister Charlotte born
died at 5 days old

4 Mom became depressed
Aunt Sophie comes to live with us

5 brother Benjamin born

6 Benjamin sick in hospital for 3 weeks

7 brother Adam born

8

9

10 met best friend Julia

get pet dog Sammy

11 graduated primary school

12 started playing guitar

pet dog Sammy died

13 graduated lower school

14 began playing in our band

broke up
with Aaron

15

16 started dating Aaron

started sixth form
took CAPE
and passed!

17

18 moved to Queens

graduated
upper sixth form

19 started dating Anthony
started community college

20

graduated from
community college

21 daughter Janessa born

22 started BA program

Aunt Sophie died

made Dean's
list at school

23 daughter Ana born

24

Anthony's
work hours cut

25 father died
Anthony physically abused me

Adam came out

Flow Diagrams

A flow diagram serves the same purpose as a lifeline map, but it charts movement (see Image 5.11). Participants are asked to complete a box for every place where they have lived and moved to, including dates and length of time spent at each place (Parker & Bradley, 2010). A flow diagram can be helpful for depicting family composition at various stages in life, assisting the participants to reflect on family or individual transitions.

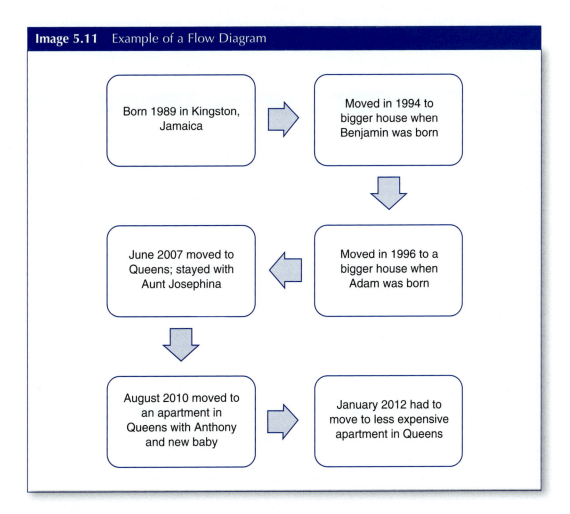

Image 5.11   Example of a Flow Diagram

Born 1989 in Kingston, Jamaica

Moved in 1994 to bigger house when Benjamin was born

June 2007 moved to Queens; stayed with Aunt Josephina

Moved in 1996 to a bigger house when Adam was born

August 2010 moved to an apartment in Queens with Anthony and new baby

January 2012 had to move to less expensive apartment in Queens

Road Maps

Similarly, a life road map is a pictorial representation of the major events and occurrences in the life of the participant or family. Initially, life road maps were developed for use with children in care settings, but they are currently used with adults and older people as well (Parker & Bradley, 2010). A road map can validate the perceptions of the participant, who decides on the events to include, and can demonstrate respect for their active participation in displaying their experiences.

The road map activity begins with the participant or family members drawing a "road" with a number of bends and turns, then writing brief comments about events in their life at each twist and turn in the road (Parker & Bradley, 2010). As the events are written on the road, the social worker has the opportunity to learn more about how the participant or various family members construct their world, how they perceive it working (or not) and how they themselves interact with it. Image 5.12 is an example of a road map.

Image 5.12   Example of a Life Road Map

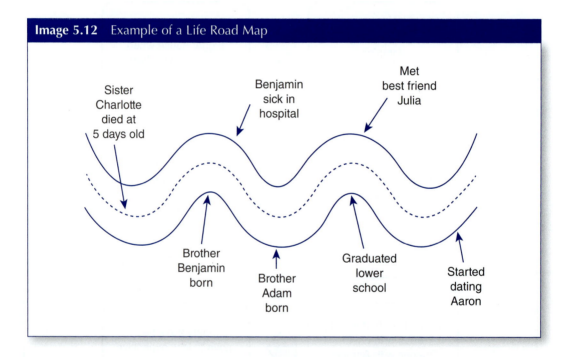

Consider the various and diverse ways that a social worker, participants, and their families can visually engage in and collaboratively depict information about the family's history, family dynamics, environmental influences, current circumstances, experiences, and goals in life. What are the contributions of each of these visual methods for learning and sharing? What are some of the challenges or limitations of each of these visual methods for learning and sharing? How might you change or add to each creative method presented here?

BASIC PRINCIPLES IN WORKING WITH FAMILIES

Similar to our work with individuals, there are key principles that guide our anti-oppressive work with families. They include addressing issues of power within the context of family, acknowledging structural barriers that contribute to family challenges, highlighting family strengths, and working toward family empowerment. These principles are discussed in detail in the following sections.

Addressing Issues of Power

Different family members exert different amounts and forms of power in relation to one another, based on their roles and identities. Issues of power as they relate to each family member's social locations are also important to examine within the family. But, many social workers face challenges in raising the issue of power and privilege among family members. Oftentimes social workers struggle with addressing issues of power between family members while maintaining the investment and accountability of those family members who hold power and privilege, but do not want to give it up.

There are three basic strategies for raising issues of power within families (Parker, 2004):

- *Structuring the sessions for consciousness-raising:* may include intentionally asking questions that reveal the distribution of privilege and power in family relationships with one another. For example, a social worker might ask how much money each person in the family makes, something that is usually not done in traditional social work approaches. Introducing the concept of money as a form of power brings issues of power and privilege into the conversation. It also provides an opportunity to explore decision making, responsibilities, and structure with the family.
- *Boldly naming power issues:* should be attempted by a social worker only once a strong relationship has been built with the family. The social worker overtly identifies any "power-over" behaviors or problematic power issues observed when working with a family.
- *Indirectly raising power issues:* can be achieved through listening to families and gently asking probing questions in order to move toward an explanation of the connections between presenting issues and power.

Acknowledging Structural Barriers

Traditional ways of engaging with families focus on deficit, with participant families often labeled as pathological, disorganized, or dysfunctional (Hodges, Burwell, & Ortega, 1998). When family members internalize these pathologies, they feel even more powerless over their environment. Mainstream methods of "intervention" with families are informed by the belief that if the family system changes, then all significant problems can be addressed and resolved.

This assumption is challenged by AOP social workers. Accounting for structural issues related to poverty, unemployment, inadequate housing, environmental issues, crime, violence, and a lack of accessible services and available resources is important to marginalized families (Volser, 1990). Social workers should make connections between families and existing social, political, economic, and environmental structures. It is critical to look beyond the family dynamics in order to understand and address the structural conditions that impact family well-being.

Highlighting Strengths of Families

Family strengths are sources of resilience within unequal social structures and should be discussed with participants. These are the basic principles for strengths-based approaches to working with families:

- Listen to their story;
- Acknowledge their pain;
- Look for and highlight their strengths;
- Ask questions about survival, supports, positive moments in their lives;
- Ask questions about interests, dreams, goals, aspirations, and family pride;
- Link strengths to family member's goals and dreams;
- Link family resources to achieve goals and dreams;
- Find opportunities for family members to be teachers; and
- Acknowledge that they are experts in their own lives (Benard, 2006, p. 214)

In our work with families, we enter into a relationship with all of the family members who are looking for resources in order to support their change, growth, and positive development. We must keep in mind that strengths come in an incredibly wide variety of forms and interpretations.

Working Toward Family Empowerment

Empowerment approaches to working with families build on the strengths-based perspective, which accepts families in all their forms and structures, but move beyond it. AOP social workers help families gain access to their power. Families and family members already have personal and collective power; we assist in removing the oppressive barriers that prevent families from accessing their own power (Wise, 2005).

Here are seven principles for working with families from an empowerment approach (Wise, 2005):

- *Build on strengths and resources, and diminish oppressive factors.* The greatest untapped resource for strengthening families is the knowledge, wisdom, and lived experiences of each family and its members. These strengths need to be identified by the family itself. The social worker can facilitate the process through dialogue and various visual methods (such as the genogram, ecomap, and so on). After the family reviews existing and potential resources, family members can begin to mobilize formal and informal resources. The social worker can assist with strategizing ways to reduce oppressive factors in their life. Oppressive factors include poverty, violence, addictions, prejudice, and so on. The social worker and the family respond to oppression at personal, interpersonal, and social/community levels. For example, family members must face their oppressors within the family, holding other members accountable for their behavior.
- *Promote multicultural respect.* Within each family, there are individual differences associated with each family member's various identities. They might include race, socioeconomic status, ethnicity, age, gender, spiritual beliefs, sexual orientation, citizenship status, language, ability, and developmental stage. Thus, practice with families requires attention to intersectionality and multicultural awareness. Family stories of survival and coping, as well as narratives of ancestors and the family history of transitions, crises, rituals and celebrations help to bring family members' multiple identities to the forefront. The social worker assists the family in examining how privilege and oppression operate on and within their family based on intersecting identities. The family works together to identify stereotypes and confront barriers associated with their diverse intersecting identities.
- *Recognize needs at three levels of empowerment.* Families know what they need at the personal, interpersonal, and community level in order to better respond to the events and challenges that they face. Social workers help families identify and create solutions that are directly linked to the concerns they express. We provide on-going support to families by providing information about what is happening, increasing their skills for coping with the situation, and providing support from others who have faced similar experiences.
- *Provide the resources so families can empower themselves.* By identifying and mobilizing resources, we help facilitate action by the family's members. Social workers seek to maintain balance in helping by promoting participation and collaboration (accompanying the process) and not doing the actual work for the family.
- *Help families realize that support is needed from each other, from other families, and from the community.* Oftentimes, the most empowering efforts are those that reconnect one family member to another or connect families with other families in similar situations. These other families can demonstrate the possibility of surviving their

experiences and can share information and coping skills. They can also serve as a source of inspiration and solidarity building to create community change where needed. In general, working to create supports for families within the community contributes to sustainable change, growth, and support. Extended family networks, kinship networks, and religious institutions can also be sources of support for families.

- *Establish and maintain a "power with" relationship.* Social workers come to the practice setting with various types of power: power from their expertise, power from their interpersonal skills, and power related to the resources they can access through their role. Families come to the practice setting with the same types of power as well. It is crucial to share power and partnership with families. "Power with" entails mutually teaching and learning, and maintaining a collaborative and participatory approach to identify challenges, mobilize resources, generate plans, and carry out actions.
- *Use cooperative roles that support and assist family members.* Many roles have been identified for social workers to assume when engaging with families from an empowerment approach; they are similar to the roles we take when working with individuals. Some of these roles are listed in Image 5.13; note the prefix "co" in front of many of them, which identifies them as shared with the family and highlights their cooperative and mutual nature. Multiple roles are necessary, as each role adds creativity and responsiveness to the family.

Consider your experiences at your social service agency or internship. What roles have you had the opportunity to embody as a social worker? What were some of the challenges that you encountered within these roles?

Image 5.13 Example of Social Worker Roles in AOP Practice With Families		
Role	*Implementation*	*Goal*
Co-learner	Continuously learn from families about their lived experiences and their knowledge, skills, and strengths	To foster a sense of control, agency, and self-determination in family members
Co-teacher	Incorporate education (e.g., awareness of family power dynamics) into the work; assume that people are already capable or have the capacity to become capable as the experts in their lives	To foster a sense of control, agency, and self-determination in family members
Empathetic listener	Use active and reflective listening skills; convey positive regard, warmth, and respect	To develop a trusting relationship with family members

Role	Implementation	Goal
Co-consultant	Collaboratively provide knowledge and share experiences; provide information and perspective in response to the family's request	To help a family's support networks to be better informed and better able to support the family
Co-investigator	Invite families to participate in seeking information about community resources; assist them in accessing these resources, particularly the resources that are needed immediately	To strengthen the working relationship with the family by adding valuable interpersonal time
Co-creator	Create opportunities for the family to become skilled at obtaining resources and support by acting as an "empowerer," not a "rescuer"; point out that family members help to create the family unit as well as themselves as individuals within the family	To promote family members' ability to see themselves as active agents responsible for change
Co-activator	Promote a sense of cooperation and joint responsibility for meeting family needs; promote partnerships with support personnel and connections with other families and individuals	To help families find new or alternative supports and resources and bring family members together
Mediator	Promote cooperation and collaboration within the family; negotiate tensions if negative experiences have occurred	To support mutually reinforcing interactions among family members and among families and systems and the environment

Source: Adapted from Dunst, Trivette, and Deal, 1998; Wise, 2005.

CHALLENGES OF AOP WORK WITH INDIVIDUALS AND FAMILIES

There are various challenges that emerge when working with individuals and families from an anti-oppressive lens. For instance, it is important to bridge micro and macro practice by maintaining a focus on larger social contexts that can perpetuate oppression at various levels. We also need to be aware of the pathologizing nature of mental health assessments and how they influence individuals and families. When engaging in micro practice, the implications of professionalization and credentialing should be examined, particularly with regards to power and privilege. In addition, it is crucial that we maintain an emphasis on self-care and community care in the work that we do. These challenges are further discussed in the subsequent sections.

Bridging the Micro and the Macro

One persistent challenge in working with individuals and families from an anti-oppressive approach is integrating both a micro and a macro focus. Individual and family processes are inextricably linked to a larger social context, so working with individuals and families must incorporate social systems of accountability and empowerment that move beyond a single person or family (Almeida, Dolan-Del Vecchio, & Parker, 2007). Individual and family patterns of inequality are often unacknowledged, or if acknowledged, they remain unchallenged. It is the role of AOP social workers to connect individuals and families to one another and to help build critical consciousness, awareness, and solidarity which propels action for change. An anti-oppressive approach to working with individuals and families involves personal and collective liberation in order to heal.

Although the social work profession has focused on individual healing, that approach does little to change oppressive systems and structures. We need to provide spaces for family members to come together to address issues of power, privilege, and oppression at the individual, social, and institutional level. We also need to bring them together with other individuals and families in similar circumstances and with shared identities or affiliations. Creating these types of coalitions can alter the boundaries and power dynamics that preserve the status quo of family life (Almeida et al., 2007). Bringing people together with a community of conscientious listeners and responders allows individuals to deconstruct and reconstruct their personal stories and locate themselves within a social and political context.

As social workers, we must challenge ourselves and find ways to expand our work from singular units to collectives. Communal education on the social structures that enmesh participants has the potential to produce social change that benefits the participants and their families.

Depathologizing Mental Health Assessment

Historically, the social work profession has followed the path of other helping professions, such as psychology and psychiatry, by incorporating more sophisticated and complicated assessment designs that focus on pathology. A symbol of this trend is the *Diagnostic and Statistical Manual of Mental Disorders* (DSM), a diagnostic manual produced by the American Psychiatric Association for use by trained professionals to diagnose psychiatric conditions and psychopathology.

Although social workers have a long history of recognizing and acknowledging their service user's strengths, an emphasis on pathology, problems, and dysfunction is now deeply embedded in the culture of social work (Birkenmaier, Berg-Weger, & Dewees, 2011). In addition, through efforts to perceive, analyze, and explain behavior, social workers have borrowed notions of linear causality and positivism (i.e., the reliance on empirical evidence) from traditional science and medicine (Rodwell, 1987). Many social workers still follow a medical model where the social worker is seen as the "expert" who diagnoses the participant and prescribes a solution or treatment that the participant is expected to follow. This traditional, control-oriented way of delivering social services assumes social workers use their professional judgment and expertise to "manage" client information, assessments, planning, and intervention decisions.

Many social workers specifically criticize use of the DSM as an assessment tool, asserting that the process of diagnosing perpetuates dichotomous, "either-or" thinking. The nuances of meaning are lost because the DSM is so restrictive in how it categorizes experiences (Berlin, 1990). Others point to the DSM as dehumanizing participants and ignoring their strengths and resiliency. Some have gone so far as to characterize the diagnosis industry as a form of violence against those most marginalized and oppressed. This type of categorization often affects people of color—perpetuating another form of systemic oppression by the mental health system.

By defining people with labels and diagnoses that perpetuate the shortcomings of individuals, the use of mental health assessments depoliticizes social problems (Baines, 2007). Anti-oppressive social workers argue that what is labeled as "clinical depression" cannot be fully addressed without taking into account poverty, sexism, racism, social alienation, and other oppressive forces experienced by many individuals who are given this label. In fact, oppression is a primary contributor to individual distress (Pritchard, 2006). Within the social work community there is support for moving away from using illness-based models and mental health diagnoses of individuals and moving toward incorporating an analysis of social/cultural and structural/institutional oppression in our understanding of human behavior. Social workers can be trained to deconstruct psychopathology and examine mental health disorders within a social, political, and economic context (Pritchard, 2006). Using an anti-oppressive approach to social work practice entails conceptualizing individual problems through a lens of oppression (considering the effects of racism, sexism, ageism, classism, ableism, heterosexism, and so forth) while examining individual problems within social, political, and economic contexts. However, social workers are facing an uphill battle, because society benefits from pathologizing behavior in order to maintain the status quo, support corporate profits, and promote and expand capitalism.

Nevertheless, it is critical that we remain skeptical of mental health diagnoses, while trying to use these labels in strategic and critical ways. If we do use medical or psychiatric diagnoses to describe a set of problems or symptoms, we need to be aware of how labels oppress and marginalize people. One practical suggestion when using a mental health diagnosis is to counsel the participant about how to use their mental health diagnosis strategically to improve their lives and to obtain access to needed resources (Baines, 2007).

Challenging Professionalization and Credentialing

While many social workers pursue a practice license after receiving a master's in social work (MSW) degree, social workers working from an anti-oppressive practice approach often critique the implications of obtaining licensure, also known as credentialing. Mainstream social work "identifies with professionalism, career advancement and workplace authority rather than with clients, oppressed communities and agendas for social justice" (Baines, 2007, p. 4). Where and to whom our commitments reside is a valid concern. Licensure can be considered a form of "gate-keeping," designed to exclude people with important cultural expertise and life experiences from participating in program and policy decisions.

In an edition of the grassroots, online publication, the *Social Work Activist Reader*, the process of credentialing is explicitly linked with white privilege and white supremacy: Credentialing supports "the idea that white people of European descent unconsciously hold that deep down we are really better and smarter than other groups . . . the ones who define the rules, the terms, the labels, the treatment, the problems and the remedies" (Golden, 2001, p. 4). The key question is whether or not "our profession's commitment to credentials hurt our ability to expand our range of services." The process of licensure among social workers thus brings up issues of power and knowledge.

> Take a few moments to think about credentialing/licensure in the field of social work. What are its benefits? What are the limitations? How do you address issues of power, privilege, and oppression as they relate to credentialing? How might our profession's commitment to credentials hurt our ability to expand our range of services?

Taking Care of Ourselves and Our Communities

In a field where we are continually caring for and caring with others, oftentimes we don't take enough time to care for ourselves. Self-reflection is critical for self-care. Through self-reflection, we are more critically aware of our own responses, biases, and limits to what we are able to do. We can also find our own systems of support, as we do with our participants. Social workers can form and attend support groups or collectives with friends, peers, or coworkers. Supervisors are also an important resource for support. Living a healthy lifestyle through adequate sleep, nutritious food, and exercise also helps us care for ourselves.

As important as self-care is, many assert that "caring" needs to move beyond the self and incorporate others. Among social justice workers, advocates, activists, and organizers, there is a movement to reframe self-care to include the concept of community care. There is a move toward shifting the conversation from the individual to the collective, from independent to interdependent. As one social worker stated:

Too often self-care in our organizational cultures gets translated to our individual responsibility to leave work early, go home alone, go take a bath, go to the gym, eat some food, and go to sleep. So we do all of that "self-care" just to return to organizational cultures where we reproduce the same systems that we are trying to break; where we are continually reminded of our own trauma, or exposed and absorb secondary PTSD, and where we then feel guilty or punished for leaving work early the night before to take a bubble bath. Self-care, as it is framed now, leaves us in danger of being isolated in our struggle and our healing. Isolation of yet another person, another injustice, is a notch in the belt of oppression. A liberatory care practice is one in which we move beyond self-care into caring for each other. (Padamsee, 2011, p. 1)

Revisioning self-care as community care acknowledges that we can find care and healing with others, in unison, instead of in isolation.

> What do you do to take care of yourself? What internal and external signs indicate to you that you need to care for yourself? How do you envision expanding self-care to incorporate community care?

THE HONOR OF OUR WORK

Throughout this textbook thus far, we've discussed the importance of dismantling our own power and privilege associated with our dominant identities in society and our roles as social workers. We aim to shift the concept of privilege to acknowledge and reflect on the advantage we have as social workers to engage in social justice work.

Our role as a social worker offers us access, privilege, and the honor to be part of profound events that happen in participants' lives. Through this position, we have the opportunity to enter and participate in the oftentimes private and sacred affairs of our participants. We are in a place where we can share in-depth human experiences, witness a wide range of emotion, and be present when people are at a crossroads in their lives, searching for direction and meaning. In these cases, we are given a sacred gift: the stories of people's lives and their lived experiences that we carry within us.

We also have the opportunity to be connected to others, to observe people's strengths, and to identify people as resources for each other and for society at large. Being connected to other people offers us a greater sense of connectedness to our environment and to our global community (LeCroy, 2012). Our role as social workers provides us with the opportunity to enter into multilayered relationships with others that are emotional, personal, and intimate, as well as political. Through our connections and connectedness with others, we have the chance to witness participants move from resistance to action, and toward individual and collective change. We have the privilege of participating in the creation of caring communities.

1

DISRUPTING POWER, PRIVILEGE, AND OPPRESSION IN CLINICAL PRACTICE

LYNN PARKER

Many theorists acknowledge that families are inextricably embedded within their larger sociopolitical contexts. Feminists, social constructionists, critical psychologists, postcolonial scholars, and others argue that therapy is political whether the therapist knows it or not. Yet practice methods rarely address how clinical social workers should deal with the interconnecting issues of power, privilege and oppression.

Why this omission? The subjects of power, privilege and oppression (who has it, who does not, and under what circumstances) are often the "dirty little secrets" of family and broader social life. These are the issues we collude to deny, because raising the issues is upsetting. When raised, the status quo, both within relationships and in society generally, is often upset. And, despite our training, social workers too often avoid raising these issues in therapy, championing instead a respect for maintaining therapeutic neutrality. As a result, disparities in privilege and power for the most part remain unchallenged and therefore uninterrupted. Neutrality serves and affirms the status quo.

While power, privilege and oppression may be the last issues that family members (and the rest of us) want to address, they are of central importance to social justice and therefore to social work practice. If the subjects of power and privilege are not on the table, they are invisible, absent, and therefore nonnegotiable. They will not become part of the conversation, and as such are not subject for change.

Raising the issues, then, is the problem: how to raise the issues and not lose the clients—particularly those with more power and privilege who are not so eager to give them up; how to make visible what has been invisible; what has been comfortable, less comfortable; what has been absent, present. The manner by which issues of power and privilege are broached in practice becomes the central challenge. Does the social worker wait for clients to recognize, and then raise, power as an issue? Does the social worker challenge power issues as s/he recognizes them? Is it appropriate for the therapist to educate families about potential power issues? And, with which clients does s/he raise power issues? Does s/he broach them with all clients, or only with those who indicate they are interested—who say they wish for more equity in their relationships?

I suggest three interventions to help clients to begin to consider that their dilemmas may have a basis in power relations: information gathering beyond the usual, cultural genograms, and social education. These interventions are uniquely designed to help broach issues for scrutiny that are outside of the family members' awareness and comfort zone. Raising difficult issues for scrutiny is, of course, not unique to social work practice. What is unique is the focus: issues of power and privilege.

Information gathering beyond the usual: A first session with a family may be structured so that initial assessment questions raise issues of power and privilege for discussion and analysis. Examples include asking how partners negotiate financial decision-making, childcare, and household responsibilities (who manages and arranges it, or has cut back on work to enable them to do it). Discussing the specifics of these and other arrangements, along with other typical first session questions, helps partners begin to move beyond what is likely a denial of power disparities in their relationship.

Examples of information finding questions include, "How do you manage child and home care? How did you come to this arrangement? And, how much money do each of you earn?" When there are disparities in income, "How does the fact that you earn 3 times more money than your partner affect the decision making in your relationship?" Often the partner who earns more will say, "It doesn't affect it at all." But, the partner who earns less will tell you the many ways it affects them.

This line of inquiry introduces family members to the notion that all domestic arrangements are important to and reflect the power structure of the family's relationships. It also opens opportunities to examine the consequences (pros and cons) of current arrangements. Power inequities may be revealed, for example, as couples consider how one partner consistently accommodates to the other's desires or moods, or the repercussions of the way financial, household, and family care responsibilities are allocated. It can also be revealed in who has the privilege of naming (for example, "How did you decide whose last name the family members would carry?").

Cultural genograms: Therapists can help family members examine legacies of power and privilege in a social and political context through the use of three-generation family genograms. Issues that may be difficult to consider in the present seem less charged when once removed—via the past or future.

Clients are encouraged to consider the origins of troublesome patterns in their respective families of origin. For example, "Who were your role models for how to be a man, a woman, or in an intimate relationship? How were housework, income earning and childcare handled? How were disputes expressed and resolved? How was affection displayed?"

Clients may also be asked about their hopes are for their children as they grow up and find partners. Gay and lesbian partners can be asked about their role models for a close relationship as well as the effects of heterosexism and homophobia on their expressions of intimacy, relationships with in-laws, the work world, community, family members, and each other.

Moving back and forward in time—from patterns in previous generations to hopes and wishes for future generations (children)—allows partners to be less defensive. It also provides openings to consider the impact of multigenerational patterns, roles, and norms regarding gender, race, sexual identity and orientation, and immigration status. Patterns of domestic violence, mental illness, and substance abuse are easily tracked. Once introduced, the gathered information allows the therapist to connect family members' pressing concerns with issues of privilege and power, and establishes a respect for inquiry that sets the tone for therapy.

Social education: Critical consciousness is a goal of social education, as clients learn to re-appraise their own private concerns against the backdrop of social and political realities in the broader world. An expanded awareness is critical to meaningful change in family dynamics. Accordingly, clients may be encouraged to read a particular book, watch a popular film or documentary, or get involved in community projects relevant to their own issues as a way of helping them to connect broader social issues to the issues they have brought to therapy.

For instance, a conversation with a middle-age, socially conservative Latina couple struggling with their Americanized teenage daughter might be augmented by showing film clips from the movie *Real Women Have Curves*. The couple would then be asked to connect themes in the film with their own situation. For example, they might be asked to reflect on the depiction of Latinas in film, the relationship between the mother and her daughter, and the meaning of desire and being desired for women of different body types and skin colors. Films can be powerful tools for raising important issues, such as domestic violence (for example, *Sleeping With the Enemy*; *Straight Out of Brooklyn*; and *Once Were Warriors*), familial and societal oppression of gays (*Torch Song Trilogy*), the impact of colonization (*Dirty Pretty Thing*), immigration (*A Day Without Mexicans*), and intersecting social positions (*Quinceanera*).

Another socio-educational tool that is used to raise awareness is the power and control wheel (for examples see: Almeida, Dolan-Del Vecchio & Parker, 2008—or the Duluth Model). The wheel helps clients and therapists locate the social and political aspects of personal experience within family life (such as economic abuse; male privilege; physical, sexual, and emotional abuse; isolation; and intimidation), and within society (such as racism, ageism, colonization, heterosexism, and homophobia). The power and control wheel might assist a family to recognize, for example, how one partner's undocumented citizenship status creates uneven power in the relationship. Incorporating socio-education into the therapeutic process helps clients (and therapists) see that clinical practice is context bound, inseparable from societal dynamics of dominance and subordination. Below I provide a case example of how these issues might be raised in the context of a couples counseling session.

Case Example: Stephen and Megan, a heterosexual German couple in their mid-thirties, initiated counseling with me because they were experiencing, what they called, "constant arguing and conflict." Stephen complained that Megan was "always angry." Megan was upset that "Stephen's work always comes first. Our children and I come second or third. Steven seems to have no time or much desire for me or our children."

Stephen is a liberal, small town minister, revered by his parishioners and the larger community. Megan is a midwife employed by a local family medical clinic. When I asked each about how they had come to these career choices, Megan said her career choice complied with her parents' traditional gender imperative: If wives "have to work it should be 'women's work' since women are more care-giving." Although she "loves her work," for Megan, work is not the central passion that Stephen's is for him, a passion he refers to as a "spiritual calling."

Both express having embraced the notion that, although it is all right for a wife to work, often necessary, the husband's work is primary. It is his work that requires support and accommodation from family members. Megan worries that her "double-shift" complaints seem petty and unimportant next to the "significant" issues Stephen faces. Yet, she is increasingly angry and dissatisfied with his lack of involvement with her and at home.

In the initial information gathering, I asked them to describe their broader societal, church, and family socialization concerning "appropriate" gender roles. Both became aware of strong social messages (at the time it felt to them more like truths) concerning the role of a minister's wife. A "good" minister's wife plays the organ or sings in the choir on Sundays, teaches Sunday school, and arranges potluck dinners. She is at church each Sunday in one of the front pews with well-behaved children listening attentively to her husband's sermon.

Megan, however, expressed that she did not want to have to go to church on Sundays, nor did she want to be expected to carry out any of the other "unpaid" minister's wife roles. As they discussed these expectations and their ramifications, I suggested, "Imagine what it might look like were your roles reversed. For example, what if Stephen was expected to be involved weekly in a subordinate, unpaid role at Megan's place of work?" Both Megan and Stephen were struck that when reversed, the expectation seemed strange. Indeed, Stephen was not expected to come to Megan's place of work. Such reversals often help to illuminate behavioral expectations that do not appear as reasonable when the gender roles are reversed.

Church members grumbled about Megan's lack of attendance on Sundays, and felt sympathy toward Stephen for having a "feminist" wife. Thus, her predicament required careful unpacking. That her feelings could be legitimate was an idea foreign to them both. As Stephen came to understand that if reversed, the expectation would appear silly, he became willing to support Megan's independence—her freedom to choose how she wanted to spend Sundays and what church functions she wanted to attend. He also started to do some "consciousness-raising" with church members regarding Megan's role and, more broadly, women's roles.

I then gave them a homework exercise where I asked each to list the responsibilities they carried daily for home and people-care. When they compared their lists, Stephen was able to acknowledge that the current arrangement was unfair to Megan. I encouraged both of them to notice other behaviors that could be limiting them. For example, I asked Stephen, "What are the consequences of the long hours you put in at work to your relationship with Megan and your family life?" Further discussion revealed that they both assumed it would be Stephen who would take on extra work (for example, weddings, and speaking engagements) to bring in additional income. Neither had considered downsizing their expenses so that both could be more available for family life.

They also learned to make requests of each other. Megan expressed her need for Steven to be more proactive concerning family and relationship issues and responsibilities. Steven requested that when he was assuming a domestic responsibility, she allow him take it—that she would not be micro-managing him in the background.

Steven finally was able to concede that the choice to flee from child and house care was available only to him. Megan had no such "choice." He agreed to my suggestion that he request coaching from a good friend of his, a single father, to improve his domestic abilities. It was important here that Steven take responsibility for improving his domestic skills, versus asking Megan to help him. Also, connecting more intimately with other men takes some of the "emotional burden" off of the female partner to meet all of her male partner's emotional needs and allows them to become more equal in their emotional relationship.

de-construct, challenge the status quo, stand next to our clients, acknowledge this matters—and then we advocate, and advocate and advocate. We take action—we capture our agency and we ignite agency within others to reject this form of systemic oppression. This is what I have learned and this is how I fight, every day, in my social work practice, to break down that gender wall.

One particularly powerful example that comes to mind involves my work with Jacks. When I met him, he was 13 years old, had just been admitted to a children's residential treatment center for severely emotionally and behaviorally challenged children and was screaming at the top of his lungs—he let the whole world hear it, he made sure all of his treatment providers felt it, he made sure all of us could see it. Jacks was not going to quietly submit to gender imprisonment, no matter what he was told. His voice was ready to be heard; it had been ready since he was a little boy living in extreme poverty, subject to neglect and physical abuse by his birth family and his foster families. They could not accept the way in which he was different, and the power dynamics were all against him. But, he would be shamed into silence no longer and, little did I know, he would become one of my social justice heroes.

At 13, Jacks was determined by his family and his society, including most professionals he had encountered in various institutions and systems, that he did not fit; that he did not belong; that he did not conform as he "should." Because he would not change, he was not considered worthy of being seen, heard and valued. He was considered irredeemable and worthy only of being contained in one institution or another until he reached the age of adulthood.

I felt an immediate connection with Jacks even though he tried to push everyone away. As I worked with him in residential treatment and as a member of his daily treatment team, I began to feel he would have success in a home that provided him the outlets and supports he was currently being denied. So my roommate and I applied to become his treatment foster care parents. After he completed residential treatment, he would live with us for one year and learn and practice how to not only function, but thrive in a family setting so that he could ultimately be placed long term in the community with another foster family.

And so it was—the three of us. And it worked. Although we implemented many strategies to help Jacks learn how to function in a family, we knew the most important strategy we needed to implement was acceptance, acknowledgment and love. We created an open environment where he began to talk about his sexual and gender identity exploration. We talked with him about the way society is organized; we let him know that he was not wrong and that many of the feelings of shame and embarrassment that he admitted to us were not indicative of his inherent flaws, but rather of society's.

We also provided him an environment where he could explore his sexual and gender identity appropriate to his age level. He dressed up as a girl regularly and we provided him the tools he needed to do that. We all went shopping for a wig. We went shopping for nails and nail polish, a skirt and some make up.

And we continued to challenge the rest of his treatment team, who argued that Jacks's desire to express his gender, was nothing more than attention seeking. Because they were blinded by their own privilege, because they were indoctrinated themselves by the system, they could only see the gender binary. Precisely because of that, they were rendered blind to Jacks.

Yet, we continued to challenge them. We advocated for him to be provided a therapist who specialized in working with LGBTQ youth. We advocated for him to be able to attend a weekly LGBTQ group in the community—one that we would pay for. We called his out of state caseworker regularly to attempt to get his state, which was also his guardian, to take action. We brought our recommendations to every single member of his team—to the heads of each department, to his psychiatrist, and to the CEO and Director of Operations for the treatment center. Unfortunately, we were met with rejection on every level. Even the few who believed he did need that sort of support were either afraid to challenge the system or bullied by the system to conform.

However, the journey toward agency served him. He watched and learned. He began to recognize that the flaws were with the system and not him. He began to believe that he was inherently good and that the many hues of gender that he explored were beautiful pieces of him that should be celebrated—and were in our home. Jacks began to radiate inside and out. He attached to us and he began to love us as we did him. We were a family. His behavioral problems fluctuated, but his ability to attach, to love, blossomed.

Jacks is one of the most courageous adolescents I have ever had the privilege of knowing. What was so incredibly powerful for me was his rejection of society's socially constructed categories and hierarchies. He would not go down without a fight. He would not be boxed in as a male when inside, he so desperately wanted to be a female. He would not be dictated an identity by institutions and systems that had not only failed him repeatedly, but had also deemed him unworthy of membership, dignity, equality and ultimately freedom to explore, to grow, to learn, to contribute, to be a productive, valued member of society. He identified as bi-sexual and wanted the people he interacted with to not only acknowledge that, but to respect him for it.

What I have learned as a social worker is that you must be ready to wear many different hats—and you must be ready to act—to capture your own agency at any given time for the people you serve. Jacks did well as part of our family and was able to express his gender however he felt was appropriate for his core identity—and he was celebrated for it. Although Jacks did move on and is still in the system, I still hear his voice every single day. He rings that social justice bell for me when I am tired, when I am not doing my best, when I am not clearly seeing my clients and working for them to the absolute best of my ability. To this day, Jacks calls me and tells me he loves me. To this day, I love Jacks with all of my heart. Although we no longer live together, Jacks will always be my social justice hero. His story will always be a critical reminder to me that a supportive family is one that helps you take your own privilege, ignite your own agency and seize your own capacity to act for what is socially just.

Dedicated with the utmost respect and love to all of the Jacks out there still fighting.

1. How does Allison suggest we "break down the gender wall"?

2. 13-year old Jacks is admitted to a children's residential treatment center for severely emotionally and behaviorally challenged children. How do the social workers treat him and perceive his existence?

3. In what ways does Jacks resist oppression? How does his identity challenge mental health diagnosis?

4. As a foster parent, what strategies does Allison implement to nurture Jacks gender identity and gender expression individually, socially and structurally?

5. In what ways do each one of the three family members experience empowerment?

3

SOLIDARITY IN CASE MANAGEMENT

WHITNEY STARK

I've done the job of a social worker, as an outreach specialist and case manager for homeless young people, but I am not one. I am not trained in social work and I would not identify as a social worker. I come from a social justice background, a feminist, queer, and anti-oppression background, and I tried to take all the lessons I had learned, all the things I had been lovingly and/or angrily called-out about, all the models of thinking I had learned to see in social and political structures and bring it to the way I operated in a conflicting and weird position. I am a white, raised Jewish, middle class, queer, visibly able-bodied, cis woman (born and identifying as female) and feminist, committed to anti-oppression work and destabilizing the structures that allow me so much privilege and oppressive possibilities.

I try, but I am also always failing, trying to check myself and get checked, and working to learn to operate in the positions I can and conflicted over what roles I can occupy at differing times. It can be difficult, as many nonprofits are run with institutionally violent structural models. I was lucky and grateful to be able to work with a few organizations that were far from perfect, but acknowledged the need to work differently and were open to shifting practices toward horizontal understandings and leadership.

One of these organizations was a transitional living program for homeless young people in a mid-western city. I am pretty decent at doing this kind of work with young people. I like it when people are bitchy and straight forward like a lot of teenagers, and I am good at reading people and helping people reframe stuff. As a case manager, I was basically a professional lesbian processor— you know, playing to my strengths. Though they hired me for my queer, feminist, anti-oppression, social justice understandings, it took a while for me and my methods to be recognized as legitimate by my colleagues and supervisors. I had to have a lot of conversations about the way I did things and why, and there were a lot of skepticism and a lot of supervision meetings along the way.

Most of my colleagues, all the case managers in the other departments, had clinical educational backgrounds, acquired with social work degrees. The case management they offered was based on a therapeutic and medical model. Therapy can be great, it can be helpful for many reasons, and it can be practiced in critical ways. But, we also have to look at how its framework has been formed. It is not some objective methodology created in a vacuum. If you look at the roots of diagnosis, medical constructions, and research, much of it is based in eugenics. It's basically founded in disgusting ways of testing, forced procedures, and imprisonment. The ways that a lot of that stuff has been played out, in the past and in the present, has been on the bodies of exactly the populations that social workers work with (brown, poor, queer, and so on). Psycho-analytic therapy has also been based in distinctly sexist and homophobic understandings.

These ways of thinking are not removed from the more enlightened models just because people with good intentions practice them. Many times good intentions only hide them better. But, social work is a radical practice. It is work that comes directly from and for social movements. A lot of this gets lost in this move to medicalization, where medical understandings, standards and practices become protocol before anything else can take hold; a lot of structural violence gets re-enabled and perpetuated. I prefer the ways of understanding, organizing and solidarity that come from legacies of critical, intentional and creative activism. There is a movement and discussion about the medicalization of social services, and I have to say I don't know much about the history and the politics of these transformations, but I do know what I experienced.

Consider the way I used the tool of solidarity with survivors of sexual assault while at the living program. I am a survivor too, as way too many people are. With the population of precariously housed young people, in particular, it is pretty safe to say that many of the clients, of any gender identity, were survivors as well. With medical models, especially when talking about sexual violence, incidents, people, and experiences become isolated because 'appropriate' responses are supposed to take place only in private spaces. The medical model prefers that survivors talk about their experience with sexual violence in one-on-one therapy sessions and not talk about their experiences in public or even just assume that the sexual violence is something that the survivor is, and consequently should be, ashamed of. Assigning 'acceptable' behavior is a big part of silencing people. If the appropriate way to handle what sexual violence does to people is to keep it in private, medicalized spaces, then understanding what allows things like this to even be possible is much more difficult, and so is figuring out what you can and want and need to do.

There was a young person, who hadn't been my client, who was living in the program and sticks in my mind. When I came to work one day, I was told that this person had been behaving in some taboo ways that were inappropriate toward other clients. Things were "spilling over," as the practitioners there liked to call it, and this person was sharing aspects of their experience with sexual violence with other folks in ways that were creating an unsafe living environment. I have problems with the idea of "spilling over" and the idea that sexual violence is not something that survivors can or should talk about in public spaces. Others are allowed to talk about it all the time, thinking it's a great joke or something. But, at this time and in this case, in a space where there were a bunch of people in the midst of loads of trauma, I agreed that the ways in which this person's trauma was manifesting in their behavior really was making the space unsafe for the other people living there.

That day, this person was down in the common space, but pretty isolated. They knew that there were problems with their behavior and it was probable that they would no longer be able to live in the program. Of course they were sad about leaving—they really wanted to live there—but they also understood that this decision made sense and accepted it. They told me that they had just started having new flashbacks, memories of sexual violence that they had never remembered before, and it was during those flashbacks that they were behaving inappropriately. The staff at the program were, of course, very concerned about the person's PTSD and the general safety of the space. They had scheduled an emergency meeting with the person's doctor and a few others and met to talk about if and how they could keep the person in the house. And these were important and helpful moves.

While in this conversation, the person told me that they felt the flashbacks were the cause of their complicated behavior. I said "Well, it happens." They responded "I know, I know, sexual violence happens, and I need to . . " I was struck. I couldn't believe that this was how this person was interpreting my comment. This person had worked with so many social workers about this stuff, had talked with doctors and case managers and therapists for years. "No," I said, "PTSD happens and flashbacks happen," and I went on to talk with them about how it was OK and normal to sometimes act in ways you don't understand and can't control and how much it sucks

4

IN THIS FOR THE LONG HAUL:
SELF-CARE WITHIN SOCIAL JUSTICE ADVOCACY

OWEN DANIEL-MCCARTER, GABRIEL ARKLES, AND
ANYA MUKARJI-CONNOLLY

Gabriel: One question I keep coming back to is how we can stay true to our liberatory goals and take care of ourselves in the process. A lot of us at Sylvia Rivera Law Project (SRLP) have read *Trauma Stewardship* by Lauren Van Dernoot Lipsky; I highly recommend it. When I'm having a hard time I try to focus on really basic self-care—eating enough, sleeping enough, and exercising at least some. For me, tabletop role playing games (think Dungeons and Dragons) are also an amazing outlet. Connections with other people doing social justice work have helped me a lot, especially if I'm feeling isolated or hopeless. All of the energy and inspiration out there in the world remind me that I am anything but alone in doing this work and that together we are going to win.

How do you do it?

Owen: I find it extremely difficult to take care of myself while doing this work, especially because of the limitations to self-care brought on by capitalism: lack of health insurance, and lack of coverage for more holistic medicine like acupuncture, radical mental health care, massage, and spiritual work. That said, I have tried to do "trades" with folks who provide this type of care—an exchange for legal advice or other services for holistic health care. I've also learned to be intentional about taking baths, listening to music, reading books that are not about the criminal legal system, and surrounding myself with a loving queer family.

I think one of the hardest things for me is saying no to requests to advocate for folks to collaborate. I am constantly wishing that somehow there could be a few more hours in the day. Bordering at times on burnout, I have learned that it can be really helpful to be transparent with my clients about my capacity and where I am coming from so they understand why I may not be able to help them with a legal or other issue they are having. Sometimes this means explaining that we are an all-volunteer project and what our daily workloads looks like.

Anya: For me, working with youth meant that I needed to be very clear about my role and my capacity. In order to maintain clear boundaries, I didn't share very much about my identity or background. In my experience, many of the youth I worked with had not had strong boundaries in their life. I came to realize that boundaries are a form of protection for youth and I tried to model that for them in my work.

I also think that all public-interest lawyers struggle with managing our work capacities with the high need for services in the communities we advocate for. The problems are so great that there is always more work that can be done. Initially, I wanted to take on as many of my client's problems as possible. I had a difficult time saying no.

At Peter Cicchino Youth Project (PCYP), we decided our clients benefited from us limiting our direct service work. Taking on an issue or a problem that we had little time to work on wasn't helping people. So we limited the cases we took and developed stronger expertise in the areas we focused on and created stronger referral networks for the cases we didn't take.

Gabriel: At SRLP we have had similar struggles with workloads. We all believe deeply in the work that we do and feel its urgency. A lot of people are in terribly dangerous, unjust, and painful situations. It can be easy to say "yes" to new work even when we don't have time to finish the work we've already taken on; to rush to put out fires while neglecting work that is less time-sensitive, but no less important in the long term; or to attend to the needs of a vocal client while overlooking potentially even more urgent needs of a less assertive client. In our co-supervision meetings at SRLP, we help each other address those dynamics and work to create accountability for one another.

We also came up with a number of ways to make caseloads more manageable than they once were—for example, by limiting the types of cases we take and the number we handle at once. We are wary of ranking some of our communities' needs as more "urgent" than others or of focusing only on the "easy" cases. That said, we pay attention to the types of services that particularly large numbers of the most vulnerable members of our communities seek, that they are least likely to be able to find help with anywhere else, and that seem to have a plausible chance of leading to a positive outcome for the client (even if that outcome wouldn't necessarily be identified as "victory" in a traditional legal sense). These types of decisions can be painful to make, but I think they are important to make sure we are following the priorities we believe in, keeping our work sustainable and our workplace just, and improving the quality of our work.

1. What are some of the challenges that Owen, Gabriel, and Anya face with self-care?

2. How does each one negotiate some of the tensions they experience between wanting to pursue their collective activist efforts while needing to engage in self-care?

3. How do you engage in self-care?

4. What are some of the struggles that you face with prioritizing self-care and how do you address them?

5

CHECKING OURSELVES AND CHECKING EACH OTHER: STRATEGIES FOR SELF-CARE

HEIDI GROVE AND JUSTON COOPER (JC)

Heidi: Our main strategy here at The Youth Connection (TYC) for taking care of ourselves is to debrief, which is what a lot of agencies do. But, I think that we debrief a little differently. It's one thing to debrief and respond by "this happened and that happened and blah, blah," when you are disseminating information. We actually take the time to say, "Ok that happened, but how are you feeling about that?"

JC: Anything that we do with the youth, we do with ourselves. We are really clear about when we are overwhelmed, overloaded, drained, or any of those things. The same way that you check the young people is the same way we check each other. "JC, how do you feel, what's going on, do you need to take some downtime, do you need to check out, what do you need?" Same thing we do with the young person.

I think it is important to take care of ourselves. We hang out a lot with each other. We have a very tight group. That's part of taking care of ourselves too—we built a core with each other so we rely on each other for support. We do little things and we make sure that we are ok. We authentically share. "I need some downtime; I need to check out a little bit." That's one way of taking care of each other.

Heidi: And the other piece, too, is that we are very real with each other and when we say "I need downtime," we say "I need downtime and this is why." I am not going to lie that we don't have breakdowns, because we do. We are all human beings, we acknowledge that. We literally had a five-hour screaming fest and at the end of it we were like, "are you done?" "I am done," "yeah I am done" and we walked away just fine.

We use each other for self-care. We really feed on each other. When one of us is down, the rest of the team will spend some time kind of supporting that person and helping them get back on their feet.

JC: Our principles are consistent. We are who we are with young people, just how we are with each other. We don't expect anything from them that we don't expect from ourselves. We create a safe space with each other; we make sure that how we show up is OK. I mean, you can't practice these things with young people and not practice them with each other, and we are adamant about that. Young people are the experts on themselves and no one from our staff is an expert on young people, they are experts on themselves. They know when someone is being real and not real to them. It's similar to us. We know when we are really burnt out and trying to do work and not being there for our team. They will call us on it. They will call me really quick and they will say "yo man, what's going on? You are not there right now and I need you awake." The key piece of self-care is to check in and make sure that you are there. If I am checked out, I am being called out on the field. I will say "are you on the field or in the stands watching?" What that means is that you can be in the stands watching the game being played and criticizing it, what's wrong and what's right. Or you can be on the field playing with us, going for 100%. But, it is a check-in that we have: If I say I am in the stands, that means that I need to step out for a minute because I am not on the field playing. I think that helps us keep our energy and do the work and not get burned out, because people get burned out of what they do and not who they are. Anything that you do, it runs its course. But, who you are never changes it.

Heidi: When you surround yourself with people that are like that, it makes self-care almost seamless—where you have somebody standing next to you, side-by-side, not over you, not above you, not behind you, but side-by-side. "You are a little off today, why don't you do something good for yourself?" Whatever that looks like. I mean, I am the only woman at my agency, and yes, I am the one who gets mani-pedis. But, my co-workers also know me really well and know that those are the things that make feel pampered. So when I am feeling I need that, they are the first to say, "why don't to get a massage, why don't you go to get a mani-pedi, why don't you go to take a walk, why don't you go to meditate," those kinds of things, because they know me that well.

I am so lucky to find such an amazing team where we get each other. We've worked really hard to develop a relationship where we actually function really well and function nonverbally. When we are in a situation that's uncomfortable, when we are in a situation that's potentially dangerous, we don't need to say anything to each other, we read each other.

JC: We are all committed to doing self-work. Even a doctor needs to go to a doctor. What we realize is that it's important for us to do self-work in order to do this social justice work. As far as comfort and safety, we've done the uncomfortable stuff already. We've done the self-disclosure already. We also know that young people see it too—the beauty is the authenticity. The young person in my office is like, "hey JC, what's going on? You don't look good." I am like, "I am not. I don't feel good." Young people respect that trust, that realness and authenticity.

It's important to understand that you when you are doing the work, it is not about you. I think professionals who do the work for themselves end up burning out quickly. They end up stressing, their health deteriorates, and they end up making irrational decisions with clients. That can lead to the oppression of the client. That can lead to having power over.

When I first started doing some work with LGBTQ youth, I was frustrated because, as a heterosexual black man, I really could not connect with them. I knew what I had to do, so I listened and then I went to Heidi and said, "I am really struggling with the LGBTQ youth." My initial response, my initial justification and rationale, was that it was not because they identified as LGBTQ, but because I didn't know how to relate. And Heidi was able to able to engage in dialogue with me while I did the self-reflective work on myself. I had an uncle who identified as LGBTQ who died from AIDS. With that trauma, I had created a story about the LGBTQ community and what it does to people.

I didn't know that there was a block in the work that I was doing. I knew that I was culturally competent. I knew that I was accepting. If I didn't have my partner, if I didn't have my teammate, Heidi, to do that work with, then I would continue getting burned out and unhealthy and not doing a service to the young people who identify as LGBTQ. When I had Heidi to do the work with, it was powerful and transformational for me. I was able to let go of the story I had made up.

Eventually, I worked in a class with a local agency that engaged LGBTQ youth. We created programs around the support of LGBTQ youth. It was interesting that I initially thought that I could not connect with them. So as social workers, we need to do work on ourselves, we've got to take care of ourselves, and we've got to be there for each other so we don't have internal barriers preventing us from being effective.

1. How do Heidi and JC keep each other "in check" in order to prevent burn out and maintain awareness?

2. How does working as a team contribute to maintaining honesty and authenticity?

6

FROM SURVIVING TO THRIVING, FROM SELF-CARE TO VICARIOUS RESILIENCE

CRYSTAL TENTY

A huge part of my job as an advocate is responding to crisis and providing support to people who have often experienced a lot of trauma throughout their lives. You see their struggle. You witness their pain and suffering daily. You observe all the injustices within our systems—the structural oppression in our institutions and how that plays out in the lives of these survivors. This work is difficult sometimes. Rewarding—yes, sometimes. But, mostly it is difficult.

It's nice to know you are there to help people in need, but sometimes it feels like you are simply putting Band-Aids on open wounds. The opportunities for vicarious trauma are all around, and it is easy to fall into a feeling of hopelessness. We all experience it. And self-care only goes so far. What I think is more effective than self-care, and more healing for us as providers, is the concept of vicarious resiliency. The process of observing and even being a part of a survivor's healing process and their personal transformation from surviving to thriving is what sustains me. That is my self-care.

I believe in the power of domestic violence and sexual assault survivors sharing their stories to influence policy-makers and effect change. This year I asked a survivor that I had been working with for over a year to go with me to City Hall and to give her testimony regarding potential budget cuts to domestic violence services offered at the Portland Police Bureau's Family Services Division. She was nervous at first and asked me to help her develop some talking points. That was an amazing experience—to brainstorm talking points together, to help prepare her to speak with policy-makers.

This individual was someone who referred herself to our program a year before. She was in crisis after being sexually assaulted by her partner and not knowing what course of action to take. And here she was, a year later, addressing City Council members in a crowded room, sharing her story and demanding continued funding for vital life-saving services. I don't even think she had ever attended a City Council meeting before, but I was impressed with how brave she was. And she was so articulate, too. After giving testimony, we left the room and one of the city council members ran out after us to shake her hand and thank her for sharing her story.

As domestic violence advocates we try not to set agendas for our participants. We want to support all survivors no matter where they are in their experience. We want them to know that whatever they choose on their path is ok. But, I can't deny that my secret agenda for all my participants is to see them realize their true potential as human beings. To see them grow strong and heal.

1. How does Crystal define self-care for her and what does this entail?

2. In what ways does the transformation and empowerment of this participant play a role in understanding the concept of vicarious resilience?

3. According to Crystal, how is vicarious resilience a form of self-care?

DISCUSSION QUESTIONS

1. What feelings and thoughts came up for you in response to these stories?

2. Describe the common themes that emerge throughout these stories of AOP with families.

3. How do these stories demonstrate concepts presented in the chapter, such as working with diverse families, attending to issues of power, incorporating visual tools, engaging in self-care, and de-pathologizing individuals?

4. How do these stories speak to the possibilities and challenges of doing AOP work with families?

5. Consider your current internship or social work agency. How might you incorporate visual tools to represent families, family dynamics, and the lives of families over time?

6. Think about the various ways in which this chapter proposes that we bridge micro and macro practice. What are the strengths and limitations of these proposals?

ACTIVITIES

1. The purpose of this exercise is to prompt you to reflect on your own family and the internal and external forces that impact it (Lundy, 2011; Strom-Gottfried, 1999).

Internal Forces

a. *Power:* What was the power structure in your family? Who had the most influence? Were there different domains of influence for different people? How was the balance of power maintained? How did gender, age, culture, ability status and other markers of difference play a role in who held power?

b. *Decision-making:* How were decisions made in your family? Were the needs of all your family members considered or were there family members that participated in the decision-making by agreeing, submitting, or discounting their own needs? Was there a dominant figure or subgroup that made decisions with no room for negotiating or consideration of the needs of others? Was there a style of decision making in your family where no one's needs were considered and decisions were avoided? Was there a participatory decision making process where everyone's voice had equal value and all had an equal say? Who allied with whom?

c. *Expression of Feelings:* How were feelings expressed in your family? Was it safe to talk about feelings or was it taboo? What was the range of feelings expressed in your family?

d. *Communication:* How did your family members communicate with one another? Was it effective? How were differences or disagreement discussed?

e. *Strengths:* What are the strengths of your family?

External Forces

f. *Neighborhood resources:* Did needed resources exist in your neighborhood (for example, day care, youth centers, after-school programs, health care, places of worship). If so, were these resources accessible, affordable, and appropriate?

g. *Sense of community:* How did you feel living in your neighborhood? What was your family's relationship with the neighbors? Could neighbors be counted on for support? What kind of support? If not, why?

h. *Home:* What was your home like in terms of type of housing and housing space for your family members? Did your family own or rent their living space?

i. *Work:* What types of jobs did your parents hold while you were growing up? What hours did they work? Were these permanent or contract positions? What were the salaries and benefits?

2. To do a power analysis of the members of your family, start by making a list of all your family members over three generations (Wise, 2005).

a. Think about each person and that person's interactions with each of the other family members. Indicate whether their relationships are "power with," "power over" or "power under." Note the relationships that you are a part of within your family and the power dynamics that exist. Observe any power relationships defined by age, gender, ethnicity, socio-economic status, ability status, language, spiritual beliefs, or developmental stage.

b. Based on these power dynamics in three generations of your family, identify strengths and resources that can be used when working with other families. Identify potential barriers that might emerge when working with other families.

3. Map out your family in a genogram. Make sure to present at least three generations of family members. Incorporate dates of birth, marriages, deaths, ages of family members, gender, race, mental health issues, and any other descriptive factors that are important to your family life.

4. Create an eco-map that identifies your family members and wider social networks, community resources, and agencies or social service institutions that you and members of your family have contact with.

5. Map out your major life experiences in the form of a lifeline. Make sure to also list your emotions corresponding to important moments in your life.

ADDITIONAL RESOURCES

Websites

The Icarus Project: Navigating the Space Between Brilliance and Madness

http://www.theicarusproject.net/

Films

A sentence apart (2012). T. Rigby

Crooked beauty and the embodiment of 'madness' (2010). K. P. Rosenthal

Family matters: Surviving the bipolar journey (2010). M. M. Frymire

My family, Mi familia (1995). G. Nava

New Year baby (2006). S. Socheata Poeuv

Red without blue (2007). B. Sebold & B. Sills

Revolving door (2006). M. Braverman

Saving face (2004). A. Wu

Stages (2009). Meerkat Media Collective & J. A. Sterrenberg

The wedding banquet (1993). A. Lee

Welcome to the dollhouse (1995). T. Solondz

Books

Bechdel, A. (2004). *Fun home: A family tragicomic*. New York: Mariner Books.

Fadiman, A. (2012). *The spirit catches you and you fall down*. New York: Farrar, Straus and Giroux.

Franzen, J. (2002). *The corrections: A novel*. New York: Picador.

Grissom, K. (2010). *Kitchen house: A novel*. Austin, TX: Touchstone.

Redfield Jamison, K. R. (1997). *An unquiet mind: A memoir of moods and madness*. New York: Vintage Books.

Walls, J. (2006). *The glass castle: A memoir*. New York: Scribner.

Walls, J. (2010). *Half broke horses: A true-life novel*. New York: Scribner.

6

Anti-Oppressive Practice
With Groups

Group work has a long history in social work practice, particularly as reflected in the Settlement House Movement (SHM). Working with groups can provide an opportunity for increased participation from the population or community, which is a significant factor in AOP work. Often a jumping off point for community or social movement mobilization and activism, groups can target systemic social justice issues. Groups can take a variety of forms for a variety of purposes, including personal growth, psychotherapeutic, task-centered, mutual-aid, self-help, support, educational, psycho-educational, structured, specific activity, self-directed, and social action/social change. The purpose and organization of a group can also be a blend of types.

HISTORY OF SOCIAL GROUP WORK

The development of individual work and casework is typically attributed to Charity Organization Societies, while group work stems from the Settlement House Movement. Writing on the "Value of Social Clubs," Jane Addams (1990) recounts the history of various clubs at Hull House. She notes that the opportunity to socialize and learn with and from one another supports members of the community to grow emotionally, to become more accepting of difference, and to prompt engagement in social action:

> Thus the value of social clubs broadens out in one's mind to an instrument of companionship through which many may be led from a sense of isolation to one of civic responsibility, even as another type of club provides recreational facilities for those who have had only meaningless excitements, or, as a third type, opens new and interesting vistas of life to those who are ambitious. (Addams, 1990, p. 365)

Initially, social group work was seen as community-focused, as recreational, and as a venue for self-improvement. Philosophically, it was based on the idea that social relationships benefit human development. It was not until the influence of psychodynamic theory that groups began to shift toward a therapeutic model. These early groups were located in settlement houses, the YMCA/YWCA, and 4-H. The function of these groups was social development and education, which was often tied to creating well-rounded individuals who would be more likely to participate in the community and engage in social action.

While there was a common theme in these earlier groups, variations developed which contributed to the development of a more diverse range of group work. Some of these differences were based on physical location—some groups were centered in one building (such as a YMCA), while other groups utilized shared spaces—and groups were both locally and nationally organized. Additionally, groups utilized a combination of volunteer leaders and paid leaders; provided services to disadvantaged and middle class members; focused on specific racial/ethnic groups or were open; catered to various age groups; and had "healthy" versus "problem" memberships (Alissi, 1980; Lee & Swenson, 2005).

Early group work developed from various ideological foundations. The SHM workers and YMCA/YWCA were influenced by Christian theology and often had the goal of rescuing groups from sin and inculcating Christian beliefs in newly arrived immigrant populations. Additional influences of humanism were seen in the SHM where there was a primary focus on the living and working conditions in the poor areas rather than a direct focus on religion. As groups developed, there was also a focus on self-help and the growth of mutual aid philosophies. Group work was also influenced by Emile Durkheim, a French sociologist, social psychologist, and philosopher who is considered by many to be the father of sociology. It was Durkheim who suggested that groups are greater than the sum of their parts, and by creating attachments and relationships, groups can counter alienation and isolation (Alissi, 1980). The SHM groups also drew on theories of John Dewey (an American philosopher, psychologist, and educational reformer) and the progressive education movement which stressed that people learn best by doing and that education must take into account the whole person, including social and emotional factors. In this movement, education was seen as a pathway to participatory democracy. Dewey served on the first board of directors of Hull House and often attended groups held there.

The SHM was active in both educational groups and recreational groups, and successfully established the first public playgrounds and recreation programs in addition to starting many summer camps. The social action work of the SHM movement, including labor movement activity, was often supported through group work, which then translated into community organizing (Alissi, 1980; Lee & Swenson, 2005).

Group work became more professionalized in the 1930s, during which time some of the variations in the goals and approach became more contested. In 1935, the National Conference of Social Work (NCSW) group work section was created and they began to debate preventative and educational goals versus therapeutic and corrective goals. The next year, the 1936 American Association for the Study of Group Work (AASGW) formed. The activities of these new organizations contributed to an increase in both training of professionals in group work and research on group work, which began in earnest in the 1930s. Despite debates about function, there did seem to be primary agreement that group work was "a service for individuals who, through normal satisfying group activities, are encouraged to grow and develop socially and emotionally and to participate responsibly in society" (Alissi, 1980, p. 17). Grace Coyle, one of the early proponents of social group work, believed that it was an "educational procedure" that could lead to social change (Alissi, 1980, p. 17). However, group workers in the 1930s tended to downplay the programmatic, educational, and therapeutic elements of group work as they did not want to overshadow the relationship elements, which they believed to be more foundational to the purpose of groups.

In the 1940s and 1950s, the focus returned to the therapeutic purposes of groups, influenced in part by the alignment of social work with psychodynamic theories as a way to gain increased professional legitimacy, and by the impact of McCarthyism in the 1950s, which seriously hindered group work focused on social action. Additional shifts included the increased development of technical skills and research on group work as well as the development of non-voluntary groups, which in many ways was counter to the original purpose of social group work. In 1943, Bertha Reynolds, a progressive social worker, stressed that group and community work should be at the forefront of the social work profession (Lee & Swenson, 2005). In 1946, ten years after forming, the AASGW became a professional organization renamed the American Association of Group Workers (AAGW). At that point, divisions occurred and some members moved to the newly formed American Association for the Study of Community Organization.

These divisions were directly related to the rifts developing between social action and community focused group work and therapeutic and treatment-focused group work. In 1949, the AAGW published this official definition: "the group worker enables various types of groups to function in such a way that both group interaction and program activities contribute to the growth of the individual and the achievement of desirable goals" (Coyle as cited in Alissi, 1980, pp. 23–24).

In 1955, the AAGW merged with six other organizations to become the NASW, solidifying group work as one social work method. Following this shift, in 1956 the NASW definition of group work was drafted:

> A service to groups where the primary purpose is to help members improve their social adjustment, and the secondary purpose is to help the group achieve objectives approved by society . . . The definition assumes that the members of groups receiving social group work services *have* adjustment problems. It further assumes that there is a diagnostic process through which the worker is aware of the nature of the problems of the members, and that the programming in the group is determined by the findings of the diagnosis . . . The skills used in this process are acquired through application of a wide variety of knowledge in clinical training of social group work field instruction (Alissi, 1980, p. 24).

Less than one-fifth of the membership of the group work section actually agreed with this definition. In response, the group work faculty at the University of Pittsburgh drafted a position paper stressing the social action component of group work.

238 Anti-Oppressive Social Work Practice

Writing in 1959, Grace Coyle, a settlement worker, teacher, and leader in developing a scientific approach to social group work, reiterated what she saw as the primary benefits and purposes of group work, stressing that group interactions contributed to human maturation and development. While she believed society should be set up to provide these experiences naturally, she suggested that a highly urban and mobile society does not always provide these experiences. She also asserted that group work should be initiated to provide this social skills training for adult relationships, stressing the importance of groups for youth to instill these skills. She viewed group work as a supplement to other relationships, particularly for the elderly. However, she also believed that the critical role for group work was, and should continue to be, preparation to participate in democratic society and to build community (e.g., to cope with neighborhood tensions related to intergroup/interethnic/interracial tensions). Coyle acknowledged that group work could be used for institutionalized populations, but she suggested that this form of group work should focus on the social issues related to psychological distress and the impact of being institutionalized. A group worker's role is to be able to "establish a relationship with a group as a group" and to enjoy and be at ease with the "social interplay among members and to be able to perceive both individual behavior and its collective manifestations" (as cited in Alissi, 1980, p. 46).

In the early to mid-1960s, the group work section of NASW suggested five purposes of group work, which appeared to have moderate agreement among members (Hartford, 1980):

- Corrective
- Preventative
- Normal growth and development
- Personal enhancement
- Citizen responsibility and participation

THEORETICAL PERSPECTIVES IN GROUP WORK—MUTUAL AID AND EMPOWERMENT

The concept of mutual aid—the idea that group members learn from one another—is a significant component of group work and is viewed by many as one of the primary benefits of groups. The settlement house workers stressed that support and learning is a two-way process; not only do group members benefit from the knowledge and experiences of the other members and group leaders, the group leaders also learn from the group members. This notion is particularly evident in the teachings of Dewey regarding the role of mutual discourse in groups and in the educational process.

While mutual aid can be a component of any type of group, self-help groups that are peer-led are often seen as a primary example of a mutual aid group. Self-help groups began to blossom in the 1960s, during which time there was a reevaluation of the role of professionals in personal and social change endeavors. Self-help supports egalitarian relationships, provides a common ground, supports collective action, and relies on knowledge-based personal experiences. This group format can conflict with groups led by professionals, however, who respond to self-help groups with a mixture of hostility, disinterest, co-optation, or excessive enthusiasm (Lee & Swenson, 2005, p. 586).

The term *mutual aid* became more commonplace after William Schwartz introduced it in 1961 (Steinberg, 2010). Schwartz suggested that individual and societal needs are symbiotic. An individual needs health, belonging, and growth; society needs to integrate these individual parts into a whole. As Schwartz stated:

> The group is an enterprise in mutual aid, an alliance of individuals who need each other, in varying degrees, to work on certain common problems. The important fact is that this is a helping system in which the clients need each other as well as the worker. This need to use each other, to create not one but many helping relationships, is a vital ingredient of the group process and constitutes a common need over and above the specific tasks for which the group is formed. (1961, p. 18)

Image 6.1 presents nine processes in group work that can be considered "mutual aid processes."

Image 6.1	Nine Mutual Aid Processes in Group Work
Process	*Group Activities That Can Be Facilitated by Social Worker*
Sharing data	Offering ideas, resources, and beliefs about coping—for example, sources of helpful community services and resources, ways to alleviate stress, and ways to navigate local institutions
Dialectical process	Discussing two opposing viewpoints with the possible goal of synthesizing them; deconstructing false dichotomies and thinking critically about contested issues
Airing taboo subjects	Broaching a sensitive or "hidden" subject; not shying away from taboo subjects
"All in the same boat" phenomenon	Sharing stories about similar experiences and emotions in order to break down feelings of isolation and alienation
Offering mutual support	Demonstrating empathy for a challenge or trauma faced by another group member; providing comfort and connection for group members, which contributes to a sense of belonging to the group
Demanding accountability	Holding one another accountable for their actions
Individual problem solving	Addressing members' individual problems
Rehearsal	Role-playing a difficult situation to support a group member who is anticipating or planning an interaction
Strength in numbers	Harnessing group members' strengths to pursue social action

Source: Adapted from Gitterman and Shulman, 2005, p. 21.

Empowerment theories (see Chapter 3) stress the importance of group work as a pathway to personal, interpersonal, and sociopolitical change. To maintain an empowerment perspective, groups need to include a focus on socioeconomic or political oppression and cannot be simply psychotherapeutic (Lee, 2001). As evidenced from the brief history of social group work, there are a variety of views on the function of groups in social work. In AOP practice, group work is considered an important mode of intervention, potentially providing an optimal environment to work on both the individual and the group or community levels, connecting the personal to the larger political arena.

GROUP SKILLS AND DEVELOPMENT

AOP group work practice depends on strong skills in facilitating groups. The basic AOP values and methods all apply, including self-awareness and commitment to social justice. In addition, group practice requires knowledge of group structure and how to develop group processes and goals that integrate social justice throughout.

Group Structure and Dynamics

When it comes to organizing the group, there are a number of variables and many possibilities. The "lifetime" of a group is one of them. Research suggests that for some issues, such as a temporary life transition or an orientation group, short-term, time-limited groups provide helpful structure and focus. Alternatively, a long-term or open-ended group may better serve members who require support for chronic or "intractable" conditions (Gitterman, 2005).

Group work literature often conceptualizes groups through a stage model in which there is a beginning, middle, and end of a group. During each stage, the group undertakes typical "tasks" (see Image 6.2). One group session can also contain elements of the

Image 6.2 Stages of Group Development

Stage	Group Tasks
Engagement	Boundary setting, trust building, goal setting
Work	Individual and group decision making, planning, action and implementation, conflict resolution
Reflection	Analysis of group's work, celebration, planning for termination or evolution of group

engagement-work-reflection stages. When creating a group, determinations about the length of group sessions and the entire group lifetime should take into account the stages of a group and the purpose of the group.

Another important element in organizing group work is the potential dynamics regarding group membership. A homogeneous group may be desirable—for example, a women's group on domestic violence. Some research has suggested that some types of homogeneous groups are more effective, such as groups structured by gender categories, particularly women's groups, and groups structured by racial/ethnic categories, particularly groups that are specifically focusing on issues related to oppression or racial identity (Brown & Mistry, 2005).

Many groups, by either choice or circumstance, will be heterogeneous—for example, a community group that formed to oppose gentrification in the neighborhood. There is certainly evidence that heterogeneous communities can contribute positively to reducing prejudice and racism, but it is important to avoid an expectation that traditionally marginalized and oppressed groups members will "teach" those with privilege.

Principles for engaging in anti-oppressive group work include the following:

- It is helpful for group workers to work within an organization that is empowering and supportive so that they feel more able to create empowering group settings.
- A group that is heterogeneous regarding race/ethnicity, gender, class, sexual orientation, religion/spirituality, ability status, and so on should have a relative balance of members so that individual members do not feel alienated or singled out.
- The location should be as easy as possible for all members to access.
- The group plan or program should be flexible and negotiable.
- Rules about group behavior should be based in anti-oppressive principles.
- Group workers should be prepared to respond to oppressive or discriminatory remarks or behaviors, whether overt or subtle—for example, when historically privileged members, such as males or whites gradually begin to dominate the discussion.

Leadership

While it is imperative that an anti-oppressive practitioner develop an ability to engage in critical self-evaluation regardless of the arena of practice, working in groups is more "public" than working with individuals and families and thus is more likely to bring the practitioner face to face with her or his values and identities. A group practitioner must be able to be vulnerable in front of the group, to be flexible in the face of ever-changing group dynamics, and to effectively handle conflict (Drumm, 2006). The practitioner's personal understanding of her or his own attitudes, values, and history will assist in recognizing how one is engaging with co-facilitators, group members, and the group as a whole.

Before the group begins to meet, important decisions are made about whether a group will be led by a single facilitator or a co-facilitation team, will have shared/rotating leadership, or will be leaderless. A group may be facilitated by a "professional" (social worker) or be a peer-led, self-help group. Regardless of the initial leadership structure that is established, groups may evolve and develop different leadership over time.

Co-facilitation of a group has several benefits, including shared responsibilities, varied experiences and knowledge, and the opportunity to model balanced and equitable relationships. But, there are challenges as well, including the extra time that is often needed for joint planning, potential rivalries and power imbalances, and lack of clarity regarding roles and responsibilities. Some recommend that a co-facilitation team should be heterogeneous (Brown & Mistry, 2005), which provides on-going opportunities to disrupt privilege based on gender, race/ethnicity, sexual orientation, and class, among other categories of difference.

What are some of the dynamics to pay attention to in a co-facilitation team? What are some of the ways that privilege and oppression may be demonstrated in a group setting that you are co-facilitating with a facilitator who is

    a. a different gender;

    b. a different race/ethnicity;

    c. a different SES (socioeconomic status) background;

    d. a different age (and there is a large age gap);

    e. a previous group participant (and you are an "outsider"); and

    f. a nonnative English speaker.

What are some ways that a co-facilitation team may overcompensate for oppressive dynamics or differences?

Shared leadership—with the group as a whole rather than simply a team of co-facilitators—presents another opportunity to develop an anti-oppressive practice. Collective leadership can contribute to a sense of group cohesion and belonging. Leadership can be shared from the start of a group—for example, with individual group members in a psychosocial educational group rotating responsibility for providing an educational component each week. Or a group can shift from sole or co-facilitated leadership to collaborative leadership as it matures or prepares to become a self-help group. In either case, group members need to be cognizant of roadblocks to collective leadership, which include the following:

- Dominance by one or a small group of members, which may be based on power and privilege
- Development of "factions" of group members, which makes collective leadership and group progression stall out

- Silencing of group members for holding dissenting views
- Lack of engagement by some members due to previous history (within group or in other situations), fears, or lack of self-confidence

---

What are some additional issues that may develop in a group that is structured as a collectively led group?

SOCIAL JUSTICE AND ANTI-OPPRESSIVE PRINCIPLES IN GROUP WORK

Reclaiming the historical imperative that group work incorporate and inspire social action, in addition to promoting self-awareness and self-development, is at the heart of anti-oppressive group work. Prioritizing the development of critical consciousness is one way that AOP group facilitators can demonstrate a commitment to social justice and action. Paolo Freire (1970/2009) called the process *conscientización*. In social movement work in the 1960s, conscientización work was at times integrated with empowerment group work, and that method continues (Lee, 2001). This blending consists of the workers "tuning-in" to the language and experiences of people in the group and then the group using their life experiences to create visual understandings (drama, pictures, charts) of these experiences. Thus, "silenced" groups become "conscious makers of their own society" (Lee, 2001, p. 307) and they can use this developed consciousness and understanding to create action.

To apply this concept to group work, it is important to be clear initially about the "contract" with the group: what is the purpose of the group, what stake in the group do the agency and the social worker have, and what are the participants' stakes? In an empowerment group, "the *purpose* is multilevel empowerment; *the process* is dialogical encounter and mutual aid in the process of working on concerns, discussion, debate, action and reflection; *the worker's role* is as a coequal teacher/learner/participant in dialogue who also has specific tasks in facilitating the work" (Lee, 2001, p. 313).

The tuning-in process typically takes place in the initial group meetings. The group leader engages in participant observation and group engagement to begin to understand experiences and "distill" themes for the group. In the group's early stages, the leader may bring in issues of oppression, discrimination, prejudice and "pride in peoplehood," but as the group coheres, they can work together to determine the empowerment purpose of the group (Lee, 2001, p. 308). As the group proceeds, the group worker continually asks critical questions, using social work skills to attend to group dynamics and to help develop the potential for mutual aid and power sharing in the group.

In the working phase of the group, the group develops "codes," which are tools to evoke narratives and storytelling. These "codes" are used to get the group to approach and examine a problem. A code is a way to capture the themes that the group worked on in the previous stage. For example, if the group focused on the problem of accessing quality education in a low-income community, they develop symbols and scenarios that represent this experience which allows them to translate the themes into a material representation of the issues. An important part of this process is translating a personal issue into a political issue. Using pictures, photos, music, poetry and other means that evoke emotion, these codes contribute to developing consciousness, which then allows the group to develop personal, institutional, and cultural/political action plans. These codes "stimulate thinking, feeling, and acting" (Lee, 2001, p. 322). Group members then take action and reflect on actions taken. In addition to promoting action, codification promotes group cohesion and belonging among group members (Lee, 2001).

Another tool in the development of critical consciousness is the Freirean process of *problematización*, in which individuals "develop their power to perceive critically *the way they exist* in the world *with which* and *in which* they find themselves; they come to see the world not as a static reality, but as a reality in process, in transformation" (Freire, 1970/2009, p. 83). The 10 conditions that can support the practice of problematización include listening; dialogue; care for the ways to participate in dialogue (equalizing language); communication; humility and respect; critique; silence (time for self-reflection); concretization of current and specific situations; reflexivity; and openness to possibilities (Montero, 2009).

Building on these principles and concepts, the group leader can pose questions to contribute to the development of critical consciousness.

- What did I learn from the group today?
- What did I teach others in the group today?
- How are we oppressed by society and others?
- How do we oppress each other?
- How do we allow ourselves to be oppressed?
- How did the group help me re-enforce or liberate the oppression I experience? (Brubaker, Garrett, Rivera, & Tate, 2010, p. 128)

Image 6.3 outlines the Dimensions of Social Justice Model which provides a framework for integrating AOP into social group work (Ratts, Anthony, & Santos, 2010). The model can be applied to a variety of group types. The model delineates five different "dimensions." Although they are numbered here, these dimensions do not necessarily take place in this order and may be used to varying degrees based on the trust and comfort level developed in the group.

Since AOP group work is not directly served by the dimension of naiveté, AOP groups usually begin with Dimension 2, multicultural integration. Four of the five dimensions detailed in the image can be challenging and often require a genuine and continual commitment to rethinking and reinventing social group work. In the final dimension, social justice advocacy, honest appraisal regarding both gains and potential losses is an important component of this dimension. Facilitators must also be prepared for challenges from other professionals who take a more intrapsychic approach to social work and group work and who may be uncomfortable with challenging the status quo.

Image 6.3	Dimensions of Social Justice Model	
Dimension	*Focus*	*Tasks and Challenges*
Naiveté	Focuses exclusively on intrapsychic work; does not attend to social, political, economic, and cultural factors.	A group that operates on this dimension tends to generate self-blame in group members and does not contextualize individual challenges, strengths, histories, and stories within categories of gender, race/ethnicity, class, sexual orientation, ability, and so on.
Multicultural integration	Considers the uniqueness of individual experiences based on a variety of sociocultural factors. Group members are supported in developing self-awareness and group-awareness through the lenses of each member's unique social locations and worldviews.	Groups at this level examine and develop a greater appreciation of diversity. It is important for group members to recognize the influence diversity has on their own personal experiences and on the group's developing dynamics. A model of power sharing begins to develop at this stage.
Liberatory critical consciousness	Focuses on the sociopolitical context that surrounds individual lived experiences. This is the level at which Freire's critical consciousness is developed.	Group members are encouraged to examine the ways in which systemic disparities—racism, sexism, classism, heterosexism, ableism, ageism, and so on—contribute to their life histories and experiences. Once they develop critical consciousness, they can move beyond self-blame and acknowledge the significance of environmental factors. The group's work on this level can lead directly into a desire to take action to dismantle oppressive social structures.
Empowerment	Supports development of advocacy skills and action planning; builds increased sociopolitical awareness and the desire for action.	At this stage, the group may discuss how to identify allies, how to build coalitions, and how to identify potential goals and challenges in creating advocacy action plans. Brainstorming, roleplaying, and research are important activities in this dimension.
Social justice advocacy	Motivates group members and leaders to move outside the bounds of the group to engage in action and advocacy.	Group work in this dimension continues to be an exploration of goals and challenges so that group members can troubleshoot before, during, and after they take action. It is important for group facilitators to step back and support the group members to develop and execute their own plans.

Source: Ratts, Anthony, and Santos, 2010.

CONTEMPORARY ISSUES IN GROUP WORK

In an impassioned plea for social work to reprioritize group work as central to the discipline, Kris Drumm (2006), a social group worker and activist, points out that since 1969 there has been a decline in social work education in group work and a danger of group work being absorbed into a generalized practice model. She posits that this decline has led to struggles for social workers who engage in group practice to find legitimacy in agencies where group work is pushed to the periphery. Stressing that group work can challenge "the dominant political sensibilities of individualism, competition, dualism, and authoritarianism" (p. 19), she sees group work as holding a key position in a "natural progression of social work services" (p. 24).

Group work has maintained a place in a number of arenas, including work with persons living with HIV/AIDs, and such subgroups as heterosexual women, teens, and HIV negative partners of HIV+ persons; LGBTQQI individuals; elderly persons; caregivers; and with persons affected by war, terror, or ethnic strife. It is often helpful for these groups to be nontherapeutic to counter the tendency to pathologize members merely due to group status. For example, group work with older adults can include a broad spectrum of types, such as reality orientation groups to help deal with disorientation to time and place; remotivation groups; psychotherapy groups; and reminiscing groups to "enhance sense of belonging and renew their sense of community" (Pandya, 2005, p. 601).

Additionally, technology is now incorporated into group work. For example, phone groups or computer groups provide support for isolated individuals, ill individuals, and individuals who request a level of anonymity not afforded in a face-to-face group. Although these technologies have the potential to support people who may not be able to participate in a group in person, they also pose some disadvantages. For example, using technology for group work may delay group development because of limited personal contact; moreover, techniques for balancing technological and personal contact need to be developed. In addition, it is important to acknowledge that anonymity may also pose unforeseen risks that have yet to be determined (Pandya, 2005).

STORIES FROM THE FIELD: ANTI-OPPRESSIVE PRACTICE WITH GROUPS

1 Promoting Survivor Leadership Within a Support Group Setting, by Crystal Tenty   p. 248

This story involves the process of how a domestic violence advocate formed a support group for and with survivors of domestic violence who were involved in prosecuting their domestic violence cases. The support group environment provided the women with a place to express frustrations about the criminal justice system, a place where survivors could talk about their feelings and experiences, vent their frustrations if needed, and also get accurate information about the criminal justice system to help empower them in their decision making. This group was facilitated and led by the survivors of domestic violence themselves, not by the social work advocates at the agency. The survivors, who had already experienced the prosecution process, served as facilitators, co-facilitators, and peer mentors to other group participants.

2   Woman-Centered HIV Prevention—Women on Top: Loving Ourselves to Love Others, by Carly Goldberg   p. 251

This story highlights the process of forming a group workshop that was aimed at raising awareness and encouraging empowerment among women about women's health, as well as HIV (human immunodeficiency virus) prevention in a local community. This interactive workshop provided women of all ages a safe and open space to assess their knowledge of HIV/STI (sexually transmitted infections) and risk reduction behaviors, as well as voice their concerns as they pertained to their sexual health, growth and development as women of all ages. The goal of this group was to enable and support women to feel empowered around their sexual behaviors and choices.

3   Support Groups: Manifesting the "Spaces Between" Through the Power of Relationship, by Emmy Ritter   p. 253

In this story, Emmy Ritter shares her first experience as a group facilitator for survivors of domestic violence. She locates herself and her feminist approach in the work that she does, while discussing some of the challenges of group work with survivors of domestic violence and her strategies for navigating them. Emmy highlights the importance of relationships within and between group members and the transformation that occurs in the "spaces between."

4   And All Voices Shall Be Heard: The Illumination of the Intersections of Privilege and Oppression in AOP Group Work, by Allison Sinclair   p. 256

In this story, Allison Sinclair shares her experiences as a co-facilitator of a group of older adults who volunteer in schools located in rural communities. Allison describes her transformation as a group facilitator from embodying a space of power and privilege to how this social location prevents her from engaging in authentic social justice group work. She shares the voice of one of the group members, whose self-reflection and marginalized status served as a catalyst for change, creating the space for a group discussion about privilege and oppression and shifting the dynamics of the group.

5   We Are Leaders: Women Working for Change, by Jean East   p. 259

In this story, Jean East describes her experiences as a group facilitator with women who are financially vulnerable, isolated, and striving for empowerment of themselves and others in the community. She highlights five key components of the group's format of activities that promote a social justice agenda. Jean locates herself in the group work that she does and shares the ways in which she has been transformed by her experience.

1

PROMOTING SURVIVOR LEADERSHIP WITHIN A SUPPORT GROUP SETTING

CRYSTAL TENTY

I had been advocating for survivors of domestic violence who were involved in the prosecution process for about a year when my little "ah ha!" moment arrived. I had been listening to my participants' frustrations with the criminal justice process and found many similarities in the struggles they experienced. Their expectations were often very different from the reality. Sometimes that meant feeling like the criminal justice system was not doing enough to protect them or their children, or enough to hold the offender accountable. Other times it meant feeling like the consequences for the offender were too severe.

And it's frustrating for me as an advocate sometimes too because I don't always understand how the criminal justice system works or feel satisfied with the outcome of prosecution either. The prosecution process is not as victim-centered as I'd like to see it and I don't believe that it is always the safest option for survivors. So it can be difficult to support survivors through a process that I don't even believe is very effective sometimes.

At my agency's Holiday Program, where our participants get to pick out gifts for themselves and their families, one survivor I had been working with for a while struck up a conversation with another survivor that my coworker had been working with. The two women just hit it off instantly and were venting about their experiences in prosecuting their abusers. It was so awesome for me to see these two women connect over a common experience—not just the experience of being survivors, which can create strong connections between women, but also the shared experience of dealing with a very frustrating and daunting legal system.

My coworker noticed the women's instant connection too, and she and I talked about it later and how great it would be to create an environment where that kind of personal connection between the various participants we worked with could take root and grow. That gave me the idea to create a support group specific to survivors who were prosecuting domestic violence cases. They have to face things that I don't think anyone else can really understand unless they have been through it.

One common issue I was hearing about a lot in conversations with survivors was a lack of understanding about how the criminal justice system works. And there were a lot of mixed feelings too, such as fear, guilt, anger, and sadness. They were further complicated by the witness tampering that occurs, either directly by the offender or by offenders' families and friends. Then there is the coercive nature of the criminal justice system. Finally, survivors don't typically get a lot of support from their own friends and family, and they are sometimes even discouraged from prosecuting.

When it is all said and done, no matter what the outcome of the case, I have found that survivors rarely feel fully satisfied. What they are really looking for, in addition to accountability, is restorative justice and healing, but those things rarely come out of prosecution. What survivors want is for the offender to say sorry, to apologize and be sincere. What they want is for the abuse to have never occurred. They want their families restored, and some sense of normalcy in their lives. So survivors often experience a deep sense of loss throughout the entire prosecution process, and sometimes it is even more pronounced because of the prosecution. The intensity of emotions stays with survivors long after prosecution ends.

I wanted to create a supportive group environment where survivors could talk about these feelings and experiences, vent their frustrations if needed, and also get accurate information about the criminal justice system to help empower them in their decision-making. But, I didn't just want the group to be facilitated by advocates. And even though I have been working as an advocate for a few years and "get it" to an extent, I myself haven't had to personally go through such an exhausting process. I can only speak to what I have witnessed. I wanted survivors who had already experienced the prosecution process serve as facilitators, co-facilitators and peer mentors to other group participants—to provide emotional support and encouragement and to share information and personal experiences of working with the criminal justice system.

Before starting the group up, I had a lot of conversations with survivors I had worked with for a while. I have one participant in particular who I frequently turn to for "advice." She jokingly tells my colleagues that I am always asking her for "favors" because she is my go-to person, my "survivor informant" to an extent. I go to her for feedback regarding various ideas for services or projects related to domestic violence and sexual assault because she is intelligent, strong, and open to sharing her story and has expressed interest in doing advocacy and activism work as part of her healing process. And she is very vocal about her experience with prosecution. So I approached her in the beginning and asked her if she thought doing a group specific to survivors going through prosecution was a good idea. I really wanted her feedback about how the group should be structured and what types of topics she thought were important and ran some of my own ideas by her. I asked her if she would ever be interested in co-facilitating the group at some point or serving some sort of mentor role and she was totally into it.

Now the group has been going for about a year, and this participant, as well as a few others who have been attending regularly this whole year, are guiding the group structure. They are not afraid to speak up about how the group process is going and make suggestions for change and offer support to one another outside of the group. It is refreshing to be able to work with survivors who are comfortable giving you their honest opinions about how you are doing as an advocate and group facilitator and telling you when they are feeling like group meetings are "getting too boring" and suggesting solutions.

I value the perspectives of survivors and believe their feedback should be used as much as possible in the design and implementation of programs and services created for them. And I believe they feel empowered by knowing that their lived experiences give them unique knowledge and insight, that their voices are valid and that their opinions matter.

Soliciting feedback from survivors also changes the power dynamic from strictly service provider versus service consumer to co-creators of knowledge and mutual empowerment. This new approach allows reciprocity. People always want to feel like they are contributing something, that they are giving back. So I try, when appropriate, to provide opportunities for individuals to do that. This entire movement was led by survivors, and I want to honor that. Even when soliciting feedback from survivors, there still exists a power dynamic because I am still their service provider and the "expert." But, when survivors are in a place of healing, where they longer need immediate support services or crisis intervention, when they no longer are in desperate need of something from the provider, the power dynamic can be shifted and survivors can use their own experiences, knowledge and skills to provide leadership or mentorship to others, if they choose.

I love it when participants teach me. They will recommend a new book they are reading about trauma or domestic violence or share some new insight they had about abuse dynamics or will tell me something about their experience that really shifts my lens and perspective about something, and I can say "wow, that is really cool, I never thought of that!" It is very inspiring to witness this transformation. So this is my approach to advocacy.

1. What are some of the "mutual aid processes" exemplified in Crystal's story?

2. How does the author of this story develop empowerment and shared leadership within the group?

2

WOMAN-CENTERED HIV PREVENTION—WOMEN ON TOP: LOVING OURSELVES TO LOVE OTHERS

CARLY GOLDBERG

I've worked in the field of HIV and AIDS for over 10 years. The last few years I've worked in HIV and AIDS prevention. At the agency that I was working for, which was in a major urban area, I received funding from the Center for Disease Control (CDC) and the state to implement a new prevention department. We were a team of seven women, including myself, assigned to create a new way to provide outreach. The two types of populations that we generally worked with were individuals who were HIV negative and at high risk for acquiring the virus and individuals who were already HIV positive and at risk of infecting or becoming re-infected.

Even though we were catering to approximately 60% women and 40% men, at the time there wasn't an intersectional lens from which to understand the services that we were offering these individuals. So, we would say, "We are meeting with women. Let's make sure they understand how to use this female condom or let's try to talk to them about negotiating safer sex practices because we know that could be a barrier." Or "maybe she is a sex worker. How do we help her understand her behavior in terms of risks?" But, in my mind, that's not enough. We really need to talk about women's understanding of agency and of self, and take the prevention one step further. HIV prevention among women must be closely examined and redefined. I wanted a group workshop to be aimed at raising awareness and encouraging empowerment among women about their health, as well as HIV prevention in our local community.

When I proposed my thoughts and ideas, I got a lot of backlash from the people in charge at organization, who said, "Carly, you can't develop that." Then, when we actually did develop physical materials to use as a collaborative tool to learn about women's experiences and co-create knowledge, the people with power in the organization would say, "You are going to too far afield, that's not prevention." I resisted their responses and discouragement, because I firmly believe that if we don't acknowledge all of the intersecting identities that inform women's lives and their experiences, then we cannot understand what kind of prevention services they need. It wasn't the same for every woman and it certainly wasn't the same for the male population that we were seeing as well.

Out of my resistance and desire to re-conceptualize what prevention meant and really looked like, various things manifested. The first was a specific group for women that I and my colleagues at the agency developed. We facilitated a workshop at various locations around our city—community colleges, a local cosmetology college, and conferences of providers of HIV/AIDS services-where we tried accessing different populations of women. We also accessed other communities of marginalized women.

The name of the workshop was Women on top: Loving ourselves to love others. "Women on top" meant we are giving you space to access your power and authority, but then, you can literally be sexually on top. We used the title of the workshop to pose questions like: Do you want to be on top? Is that the position you are putting your body in? Are you on top of the knowledge? If women don't love themselves and acknowledge themselves in the world then they can't love others and they can't be safe in HIV prevention.

This workshop was designed to assess, educate and empower women's understanding of HIV and safer sex. This interactive workshop provided women a safe and open space to assess their knowledge of HIV/STD and risk reduction behaviors, as well as voice their concerns as they pertained to their sexual health, growth and development. The goal of this workshop was to enable and support women to feel empowered around their sexual behaviors and choices.

In the group workshops with women we all talked about a continuum of mostly heterosexual behaviors from "no risk," such as holding hands or snuggling with your partner, to "high risk." Now, we know that unprotected anal penetration is a really high risk behavior. But, we didn't tell the women that it was no risk or high risk at first. We would say, "Here is the list of behaviors, what would you feel comfortable doing? What feels right for you?" Women wouldn't get very much past the "low to medium risk" column. The very high risk, seemingly dangerous sexual behaviors like anal penetration weren't something women wanted to engage in.

In this moment, this exercise at least gave the women in the group the opportunity to begin thinking, "I'm willing to do this and this is where my comfort zone is. Should I find myself in a position where one of the less comfortable options is being suggested to me, I can take a minute to think about if I'm ready to do this or not." When a woman didn't have time to think of what she wanted for herself or figure out how to negotiate her safety, she could simply tell herself, "Wait, I already acknowledged that's something I don't want to do." This activity empowered the women and gave them the power to think for themselves. The workshops were safe places to think and decide what to do; they could receive information and carry it with them as a tool in order to make decisions down the line.

So, the group workshop went on in this manner. I think that if we hadn't acknowledged the range of intersectional experience and various locations of the women and men who were receiving the information, the women wouldn't have received HIV and AIDS prevention information in a way that honored their agency and choices. The group activities encouraged the women to think about their personal and sexual comfort zone, increased self-awareness regarding the limits of their personal choices, and assisted them in negotiating and discussing these limits with their partners and within the context of their relationships.

It was important bringing this workshop into various communities throughout our city and seeing how transferable it is to the multiple intersecting ways women experience themselves. The group activities were about providing a safe space to think through potential sexual choices and giving the participants the agency to make decisions on their own. I would describe the process as giving them a cognitive behavioral anchor. We even had bracelets that we gave out that the participants could wear to remind themselves that they had given their sexual choices some thought.

What was powerful about the group workshop was the opportunity for participants to experience and discover new ways to think about their own sense of boundaries and safety. Also, the group workshop was a chance to provide our organization, the workers and the participants with the ability to broaden their definition of HIV prevention from a strengths-based perspective.

1. How does the author of this story re-conceptualize HIV prevention through a collaborative group process?

2. Why does the author believe that this redefinition is more in line with an anti-oppressive approach to working with groups?

3. How does the author examine the role of intersectionality as informing the direction of the prevention and empowerment group?

3

SUPPORT GROUPS: MANIFESTING THE "SPACES BETWEEN" THROUGH THE POWER OF RELATIONSHIP

EMMY RITTER

In 1995, I facilitated my first support group for survivors of domestic violence. I spent most of the day before group memorizing, word for word, the group guidelines. "Confidentiality. Confidentiality means that what is said in here stays in here . . . " and planning a very structured psycho-educational activity that included the power and control wheel, a tool for understanding the dynamics and patterns of battering.

The site supervisor assigned to me by my MSW program had allowed me to shadow her groups for a few months and I was in awe of how she wove a magical spell, creating a playful and safe space for women. I remember vividly how she used an "ice breaker" of 101 ways to use a paper clip; I thought she was brilliant. New to group work and studying the different group theories in school, I did not think I could pull it off and felt very dependent on her guidance. Then she moved across the country. Even in that first round of panicked memorization, I realized that the magic had very little to do with my supervisor or me, and I began learning from the experts: the women that began joining me three to four times a week, all with potent stories of abuse and survival.

I realized that providing and maintaining a safe space was my essential role, and it had different components. Those group guidelines were fundamental and deserved repeating at each group, redundant as that is. That said, I did not need to preach them; the group needed to create them, buy into them and hold themselves and each other accountable for them. The emotional safety relied on how well I prepared people before they entered the room and the gentleness I used to interrupt and redirect when the energy shifted away from safe communication. The physical safety was always a risk; although we met in confidential spaces, we all wandered into dark parking lots behind churches after the meetings. What were we thinking?!

The balance of having an open group, which all my groups were, but not opening the door to chaos, proved to be a constant dance between structure and flexibility. Some nights thrived with the ideal group size of 5-8 women, and other nights we brought in extra chairs. Tuesday night group busted at the seams at times and no convincing could bring the women to move to a different day. Overall, I probably leaned too far toward flexibility. Sometimes the openness compromised the sense of boundary, an important concept for women moving away from abusive or controlling relationships. Over a decade later, I have gotten more "strict" about allowing in new group members.

But, something seemed to be going right in that room each week on Tuesdays at 7:00 pm, despite the bits of chaos. The group participants felt safe and heard, and I watched the empowerment process flow. Women went from feeling isolated, self-shaming and confused about their role in the abuse, to feeling compassion that extended to their fellow group members and back to themselves. They became mentors to newer group members and active advocates within our agency, as well political advocates for the cause.

The energy of the group had a potency. As a facilitator, I manipulated just enough to help energy flow in and through each woman who was either contributing to the dialogue with words or quietly listening. Interrupting and reeling the conversation back on topic became my place in the relationship. To be sure, often I would find myself on my domestic violence/feminist educational soapbox and would have to catch myself and toss ideas out to a group member or the group as a whole to bring the real relevance to the theory. Truly, the more I was doing less, the better the group. And each week, I would end the night with a stomachache and euphoria.

What was happening within that circle that exhausted and energized me, that challenged me and felt so organic all at the same time? I knew something amazing was happening, and I needed to examine this with a lens outside my facilitator role.

As a social work student and a feminist, I was fascinated by how these two closely linked philosophies influenced my work with survivors. I knew that my personal was my political, and that is what drew me to become a social worker over other career choices. In fact, even writing the words, "career choices" seems to be outside what drives this work for me and many of the social workers whom I deeply respect. I also knew that building a relationship with women in a therapeutic setting is as much, if not more, about the space between the counselor and the client as it is about the skills brought to the table. Groups manifest that "space between" while simultaneously, silently allowing the "counselor" to fade into the background and let the relationships take over.

Relationships. As women, we thrive in relationships. I acknowledged that my facilitator role was merely to provide safety, streamline the flow of information and, tease out the commonalities. These responsibilities nurtured relationships, and thus, each woman's sense of self flourished.

The group form allowed for women of varied identities to build this mutual support, though slowly and self-protectively. This is not to say that all the women of color who opened the door to a room full of white women left the group at the end feeling understood. Or that women experiencing violence in their lesbian relationships used pronouns. One young African American woman reminded me of the obvious disconnect I had because of my white privilege. She told me that she did not have as great a sense of safety in this particular group as she had in another one that was smaller, yet with greater diversity. At the time, I was still blinded by my position of privilege. Although I actively listened and worked through options with the women, I did not have an understanding of the nuances and power differentials that come with who I am in the group. The manner in which I facilitate safety through the use of language, awareness of oppression, and a humble approach to individual's life experiences sets the stage, to the best of my ability, in providing the relationships that hopefully transcend the differences.

I began researching and reading about the ideas behind what I was experiencing as a group facilitator. I stumbled across the Stone Center writing piece, Women's Growth in Connection (The *Stone Center* for Developmental Services and Studies at the Wellesley Centers for Women (WCW) where I found my feminist theory illuminating the power of group. One chapter articulated a theory of women's development as "an experience of emotional and cognitive intersubjectivity:

the ongoing, intrinsic inner awareness and responsiveness to the continuous existence of the other or others and the expectation of mutuality in this regard" (Surrey, 1991, p. 61). Not only did this feel like the heart of why support groups for women who have experienced intimate relational abuse are so potent, but it also explains that despite the devastation of an abusive partner, women seek mutual ground in intimate relationships. There is an expectation that mutuality should exist. When mutuality doesn't exist in an intimate relationship, a woman will first see the missing element as a reflection on the failing relationship, likely a reflection on themselves, before they see it a reflection on the abusive partner's behavior choices.

In another spot in the Stone Center book, another contributor writes about how, "when empathy and concern flow both ways, there is an intense affirmation of the self and, paradoxically, a transcendence of the self, a sense of the self as part of a larger relational unit" (Jordan, 1991, p. 82). Again, the power of group is invoked; women grow in relationship. Having sought out that self-growth in the intimate relationship and finding just the opposite, women were able to begin rebuilding that damage through the relationships that were fostered in the group. I would even go so far as to say that the relationship each woman had with the group itself would be reparative.

Though these were my epiphanies over a decade ago, the truth of this gender-based philosophy still rings true today, through all my group experiences since those early years. Now when I train new advocates about support group strategies, structure and guidelines, I intentionally infuse these values into my presentation. Now when I supervise group facilitators I am privileged to glimpse their exhilaration as they witness the magic.

1. How does Emmy's approach to group facilitation change from what she was trained to do and how she felt a group should be facilitated?

2. What are some of the challenges of group work with survivors of domestic violence?

3. How does Emmy share power with the group members?

4. Discuss the importance of relationship, particularly for survivors of domestic violence.

5. When Emmy discusses the "spaces between," what is she referring to?

6. What are some of the key features of group work from a feminist AOP approach?

4

AND ALL VOICES SHALL BE HEARD: THE ILLUMINATION OF THE INTERSECTIONS OF PRIVILEGE AND OPPRESSION IN AOP GROUP WORK

ALLISON SINCLAIR

Anti-oppressive group work is critical in the field of social work. In fact, I would argue, it can be one of the most illuminating and healing shared experiences one can participate in—richly beneficial, regardless of the role you play. Understanding aspect of groups is critical to ensuring you are conducting AOP work. Understanding that you are there to participate as a group member ensures that you are not letting your own privilege get in the way. It ensures you remember you are a member of that group, ready to engage and learn, just like everyone else.

You must walk where it is you want the group as a whole to walk and you must do so with grace and with the intention of hearing everyone's story; with the intention of encouraging the illumination of each person's experiences with the intersections of privilege and oppression. This is where all voices shall be heard.

Dropping Your Cloak of Privilege

A colleague and I conducted a presentation about bullying to a group of older adults who volunteer in rural community schools. The older adults' goal is to help provide support to kids, reduce bullying, and provide an extra outlet for struggling children. What began as a narrow presentation on how to both help support the bullied in school and help identify and stop those who bully turned into a conversation with breadth and depth that addressed multiple issues—racism, sexism, ageism, bullying, systemic shortcomings, multiple differences in cultural backgrounds, socioeconomic status, and white privilege—that stretched to touch every single member in that room.

We began with our scripted AOP lecture, drowning out almost every person in the room and really missing the point, the issues and the people altogether. My privilege had me by the throat. I was the co-facilitator, the one brought in to educate this group on AOP work, and I was making one of the most critical errors: not locating myself in the room in its entirety. I was allowing my lens of privilege—a mental health professional with degrees and a wealth of experience—to both blind and hide me, at least parts of me. I was running from my intersecting identities.

And then a very brave, incredibly courageous woman placed her heart on the table. In the midst of our coverage of many intersections of privilege and oppression and how they impact and influence the problem of bullying, this woman attempted to express her feelings about her own experience. And she took my breath away. And, for a brief moment, I began to panic.

This very brave Hispanic woman spoke out, announcing it was the first time she ever felt safe and visible enough to speak. She talked about how she had felt invisible in the group because of cultural differences and how that has impacted her ability to work with the kids and address instances when their voices, too, had been silenced by those with privilege. She told the group "Look around. I am the only person of color in this group. I have felt invisible this entire time. I have felt out of place. I have felt judged. I have felt as though I do not belong, as if I do not fit. And I have felt embarrassed every time we meet."

The remaining intersections of my own identity within the group revealed themselves, and I felt naked, unprepared, and inadequate. I could feel the hostility and denial quickly blow up in the room: "I have never been racist—I have never even acknowledged your color; I don't see color, I see people." Amongst the building chaos and the reinforcement of this woman's message about invisibility via comments that denied her experience and identity, it hit me—so hard I lost the ability to swallow momentarily. I realized what I had been doing wrong.

I remember clearly my co-facilitator turning around and looking over at me and I could feel her fear as strongly as I could feel my own. Here it was, smacking us both in the face—the moment to conduct AOP work—real, in the heat of the moment, AOP group work in the midst of the intersections of privilege and oppression. And we were scared to death. Why? Because we were going to have to stop hiding behind our own privilege and illuminate our own intersections if we were going to address, not just this immediate situation, but AOP group work in its most genuine form. We needed to locate ourselves in the room. I finally found my voice and joined the group.

I began to calm the mumbling and address this woman's experience of oppression in the group. I used an example from my own life to help bring myself into the group, as well as locate and illuminate my own experiences with the intersections of privilege and oppression. I shared a recent experience I had with my grandmother. She was talking about immigration, the economy and the upcoming presidential election. She said to me "I have always been someone who goes to church and I strongly believe in helping other people. But, not before our own. We must always take care of our own and put our own first." It was as delicate a situation as the one I was facing in that room. I told the group what I told my grandmother. "We have to recognize that sort of mindset is what has led to the oppression of large groups of people for centuries. We have to acknowledge that our systems, our institutions are built on that very premise—to put our own first. In this country, that has meant white heterosexual people from a primarily European background. Our systems inherently benefit that particular group, with the most privileges being afforded to the males in that group. Every other group, depending on their intersections, are oppressed on various levels."

I highlighted my intersecting identities to the group: my white privilege and my gender oppression because I am female. I linked another intersecting identity, my periodic nontraditional gender expression and the way society's prescribed gender boxes further my oppression, to the experiences of many middle school children these days. I highlighted how being a "tomboy" has been a sort of accepted form of gender expression for girls, but that society condemns any boy who steps out of their prescribed gender box. This, I explained, is part of the structural oppression the children you work with face every day. This is what lies at the root of the problem of bullying—structural forms of oppression.

My partner joined and we talked, as a group, about the comment "not seeing color." We discussed the notion of ignoring a part of someone's identity. A man in the group spoke up and talked about how he felt his words and ideas in the group were often overlooked because he was shy and quiet. He did not fit into the traditional "macho" box the systems in society reward and that impacted his experience in the group. We acknowledged this statement, and he linked how his identity has impacted his work with the children. He admitted he walked away from many of the more overt bullying incidents because his voice felt invalidated in this group. We continued to dissect the intersections, person-by-person, group-by-group, until we had made everyone in the room visible, until all voices were heard.

Why the Recognition of This Deconstruction Is So Critical

The Hispanic woman's courage opened up an entire conversation about social justice, racism, sexism, ageism, privilege and oppression. In order to help effect change in these children's lives, this group needed to start from their own experiences in this group and in life in order to truly become AOP social justice advocates for these children. In other words, they could not grasp the root struggles of the population they were working with until they could understand the injustices occurring in their own group. And we could not participate and provide a framework for all of us to learn and grow and explore our intersections of privilege and oppression, if my partner and I did not do the exact same thing.

When all our voices are heard, we learn that AOP work cannot truly occur unless we are part of the movement. We learn that, in order to conduct AOP work in the social work field, we must, as social workers, acknowledge and illuminate our own intersections of privilege and oppression. We learn that, no matter where you are, group AOP work can occur. We learn that it is imperative to create an atmosphere where all voices shall be heard, by locating ourselves in the room as a member and identifying our own intersecting identities. And, we learn that we are still learning.

1. In what ways does the one participant's voice in the group create a space for deeper dialogue on issues of racism, classism, sexism, and forms of oppression?

2. How do we see Allison's transformation throughout the process and what form does it take?

3. What stands outs for you in this group experience?

4. In what ways do members of the group connect individual oppression to structural oppression?

5. What are some of the lessons learned?

5

WE ARE LEADERS: WOMEN WORKING FOR CHANGE

JEAN EAST

"Above all, we all had a voice—we were all heard." This quote aptly describes the experience of women who have participated in the "We Are Leaders" group at Project WISE, a nonprofit organization working with women who are financially vulnerable, isolated and striving for the empowerment of themselves and others in the community. The philosophical and theoretical foundation of Project WISE is a feminist empowerment model of practice. This model supports empowerment as a process for individuals and groups to gain a sense of control over matters of concern to them. The model also takes into consideration key feminist principles, such as the personal is political, the validation of the non-rational, the understanding of power and oppression in the lives of women, and women's development in a self-in-relation model (Brinker-Jenkins & Hooyman, 1986; Gutierrez & Lewis, 1999; Jordan, 2010).

The overall goal of Project WISE is for women to experience empowerment at three levels: personal, interpersonal and community/political. Services include individual counseling, groups, community leadership development and action for social justice. Participation in groups is encouraged as a way to learn new skills, decrease isolation and act collectively for change in the community.

The group model at Project WISE is based on the premise that empowerment groups work for both developing group power and meeting individual needs. The empowerment group "is not a support group or a mutual group, nor a therapeutic group, a consciousness-raising group or a critical education group, or a political action group. It is all the preceding, but in its unique combination of these it is more" (Lee, 1994, p. 224). The social justice group described here meets this definition.

The We Are Leaders Groups

Several *We Are Leaders* groups are started every year. Each one is composed of 12 to 15 women between the ages of 20 and 50. They are racially diverse, approximately 20% African American, 30% Anglo, 49% Latina and 1% Native American. The structure of the groups can vary, but generally they have 3-4 meetings and a final all day or weekend retreat. Members self-select and are referred by Project WISE staff and other community partners.

Co-leadership is an important component of the group. Staff at Project WISE take an important role in creating and facilitating the group activities and process, but the women participants are also part of this process. As a group is being planned, women who have participated in previous years are selected to be co-creators of the group. Generally 3-4 women are paired with a staff member to plan and facilitate sessions. They meet, prepare materials and activities, and lead those activities for the group's duration.

7

Anti-Oppressive Practice Within Organizations

Organizations where social work practice takes place include public/governmental, private nonprofit, and, perhaps, for-profit organizations, each with their own distinct cultures and challenges. A majority of social workers currently work or will be working in such an organization. This fact presents the question: in what ways can organizations support anti-oppressive practice and challenge oppressive practices? This chapter provides a brief overview of the thinking behind the development of an anti-oppressive or transformative organizational structure and culture.

CRITICAL AND TRANSFORMATIVE PUBLIC ADMINISTRATION

Public administration is one public/governmental arena where social work practice is prevalent. It is typically seen as an applied field where practitioners are tasked with the implementation of public policy, for example child welfare policy. As a result, practitioners within public or governmental organizations are not often seen as agents of social change. Rather, they are seen as constrained by institutional structures; the expectation is that that they simply carry out the presumed will of the public.

The "will of the public" contains within it a complex set of theoretical considerations as to whether policies are made in a pluralistic fashion (through the input of citizens for the "common good") or made by the elite with little or no consideration of the needs of the public. While these considerations are critical to assess (see Chapter 9), regardless of how current policies are created, public administration practitioners are bound by the U.S. Constitution, state constitutions, state laws, local laws and ordinances, and administrative regulations and operating procedures. Within this complex landscape, it may be difficult to imagine transformational work. Yet, public administration practitioners and scholars do acknowledge "administrative discretion," which allows for some freedom to act.

Whenever possible, public administration practitioners can also embrace and apply progressive values in their work (Box, 2008). Five pairs of regressive and progressive values are shown in Image 7.1. It is possible for the progressive values of cooperation, knowledge, economics as means, limited inequality, and the earth as home to be developed and applied in the field, at times supported by a progressive political milieu or the general public.

Image 7.1 Competing Values in Organizational Social Work Practice		
Regressive Values		*Progressive Values*
Aggressiveness	←--------------------------→	Cooperation
Belief	←--------------------------→	Knowledge
Economics as end	←--------------------------→	Economics as means
Great inequality	←--------------------------→	Limited inequality
Earth as resource	←--------------------------→	Earth as home

Source: Adapted from Box, 2008.

These are some of the actions that a practitioner can take to advance progressive values:

- Gathering information to present to others;
- Initiating assessments (for example, of neighborhood conditions);
- Changing how policy is implemented; and
- Advocating for programs and policies.

While acting as a social change agent in public administration is fraught with difficulty and challenge, progressive values can be developed in the field. By *gathering information to present to others*, using discretion about what information to gather, in addition to *initiating assessments* (e.g., of neighborhood conditions), a practitioner can advance progressive values, provide knowledge to the public, and work to engage the public in the social change process. It is also possible to *change how policy is implemented* using discretionary freedom and to *advocate for programs and policies* through political channels and through public forums.

Image 7.4 Characteristics of Anti-Oppressive Organizations	
Objective	*Organizational Implementation*
Locality development	Grounds its work in the needs of the immediate community; creates a sense of community among those served and participating in the organization
Social development	Engages with the individuals and communities it serves from a holistic and strength-based perspective
Active participation	Encourages authentic, open participation among participants and staff
Structural definition of the situation	Leads participants to understand the social, political, and economic factors related to their experiences
Consciousness raising	Encourages participants to locate themselves within systems of oppression
Social action	Partners with participants to protest, lobby, and mobilize around critical issues

Source: Adapted from Karabanow, 2004.

are interested in developing youth participation—for example, an organizational assessment checklist that helps organizations to examine where the organization stands in terms of resources, attitudes, and issues related to fully engaging youth participation (YOB, n.d. b).

The Youth Connection (TYC), a nonprofit organization in Denver, Colorado, that works with disconnected youth, also embraces participant engagement within the organization. In the Stories From the Field sections in this book, Juston Cooper and Heidi Grove share a dialogue about their work in TYC and provide a snapshot of their organization. At the close of this chapter, the TYC story *"Power With" Youth: Empowering Youth Leaders in the Organization* demonstrates how valuable active engagement can be and how successfully it provides an opportunity to share power with participants.

CRITICAL MULTICULTURALISM IN ORGANIZATIONS

A five-year qualitative research project of youth participation in a variety of grassroots community organizations by Dobbie and Richards-Schuster (2008) served as the foundation for a developing framework for anti-oppressive practice in organizations. The critical multiculturalist approach was developed as an alternative to a mainstream multiculturalism, which often pays lip service to diversity, but does not actually address structural issues. In contrast, critical multiculturalism examines how difference is related to structural and material conditions, recognizes the complexities of multiculturalism, and supports the dynamic nature of cultures. Its framework includes five avenues for changing an organization (Dobbie & Richards-Schuster, 2008, p. 325):

1. Form inclusive leadership and organizational structures: genuinely incorporating the program participants (in this case, the youth) into the organization and organizational decision making instead of involving them simply as "tokens."

2. Develop "bridge-building" leaders: hiring previous participants, individuals who reflect the organization's constituency, and individuals who speak multiple languages "literally and metaphorically" (Dobbie & Richards-Schuster, 2008, p. 328).

3. Strengthen educational programs to support critical consciousness-raising about the issues that the organization is addressing—workshops on capitalism, gender and sexuality, and social change (for example, a workshop titled The Sweatshop Economy That Rules the World of the Poor and How We Contribute to It.).

4. Create spaces for informal interactions: for example, hosting dialogue sessions, art events, and other events "off-site" that support relationship-building.

5. Work on cross-cutting issues through coalition building.

The researchers ultimately proposed a series of questions that organizations can use to evaluate and assist in the development of critical multicultural organizing. Image 7.5 presents this checklist.

Image 7.5 Critical Multiculturalism Assessment for Organizations

- How do we pay attention to the differences within our membership in terms of organizational structure and leadership development?
- Do we explicitly search for "bridge-building" staff by looking beyond the usual suspects and valuing experience in a wide range of movements and venues?
- What are we doing to help our current leaders and staff become better bridge builders?
- Does our internal education program help people learn to discuss their cultural differences, to link them to material conditions, and to find common ground?
- Are we creating welcoming (physical and metaphorical) spaces for people to "hang out" and get to know each other?
- When working in coalitions, to what extent do rank-and-file members develop meaningful connections with members of other organizations and movements?

Source: Dobbie and Richards-Schuster, 2008, p. 334.

We met with different local community groups and organizers that worked on transformative justice, harm reduction, trans justice, and antiracist organizing in Chicago. We asked them what they needed from a law project that wanted to support, not co-opt, community-based organizing. And, in doing so, we began building long-term, trusting political relationships with movement-building groups in Chicago.

We also focused a significant amount of time in our infancy to studying the internal structures of organizations we admired both in Chicago and across the country. We looked at SRLP's collective model and compared it to organizations like TGIJP (Transgender, Gender Variant & Intersex Justice Project) and JusticeNOW in the San Francisco area. We met with FIERCE, a membership-driven organization building the leadership and power of lesbian, gay, bisexual, transgender, and queer youth of color in New York City and the Young Women's Empowerment Project. We met with legal organizations doing essential legal advocacy here in Chicago like the People's Law Office.

The set of values we hold today came almost organically from that process. Core to our work are three main principles:

- First, we believe that everyone has the right to gender self-determination—meaning, we all have the right to full power over our lives and freedom from the state, medical, legal, and social systems that restrict or control our gender expression.
- Recognizing the way that the U.S. criminal legal system is rooted in profound oppression, we also maintain a commitment in our legal services to a long-term goal of prison abolition. This means that we demand lasting alternatives to state-sponsored punishment and see prisons as inherently violent spaces. As abolitionists, we maintain a commitment to actively working against reinforcing systems of injustice in our legal and organizing work.
- Our second value necessitates our third: we believe in transformative justice models as necessary alternatives to the current system of mass incarceration. Using transformative justice strategies as legal advocates means we actively think about how we can support liberation from violence through individual empowerment, community empowerment, dialogue, and support.

These models are truly beautiful because they both reject state regulation and actively work to address the root causes of real problems in communities we work with, such as violence.

Our collective operates on a consensus basis and functions, in part, to hold us accountable to our values. Like SRLP, we are still working out the kinks, but feel that as a law project actively trying to dismantle the law, we'll always be working out kinks. It is the ongoing process of working out these kinks that holds us accountable to our values. There are so few models for the important work we're doing!

When I think about boundaries, transparency, and accountability I think about the impact of the "nonprofit industrial complex" (NPIC) (a term made popular by INCITE Women of Color Against Violence). I question what aspects of the boundaries we are taught to uphold and the systems of accountability we are taught to honor and how they are tied in with oppressive funding structures rooted in power dynamics that work to maintain the status quo instead of challenging it. TJLP tries hard to resist the nonprofit industrial complex that encourages us to be the experts in what we are doing in order to get the funding to keep doing it.

Instead, we support more transformative models, where folks who are more directly affected by the criminal legal system are the experts in their own lives. In all honesty, our own financial sustainability has been a struggle because we are not a 501(c)(3) nonprofit. But keeping true to this value, we only grow when we are ready to grow, not because funding expects us to, and we don't allow our funders to dictate our politics. We don't want to become just another oppressive legal services organization.

I wonder if you all have strategies for navigating the sometimes oppressive impacts of the nonprofit structure. Does your funding ever dictate the way you work? How do you tell it not to?

Gabriel: I have so much respect for the ways that TJLP is resisting the nonprofit industrial complex. At SRLP, our collective structure and consensus-based decision-making help us stay accountable to our communities even within the nonprofit structure. When making big decisions about priorities for our work, we seek broad input from clients, members, and community organizing groups and we strive to apply our core values to the decision. We all have to agree before we move forward and we never assume that funders will hold us back.

We also do a lot of donor education, which helps us develop funders who understand and buy into the decision-making model that we use. We don't seek money that comes with major restrictions on the types of work we will be able to do, unless the restriction matches what we as a collective had already committed to doing. We've avoided almost all government grants for this reason. It also helps that we deliberately maintain diverse sources of funding and prioritize grassroots support, which makes us less dependent on the inclinations of any single funder.

Still, funding pressure can lead us to grow in some ways that are not what we would otherwise want. For example, legal fellowships are an amazing source of money for recent law school graduates to start doing work at nonprofits, but they are only for one or two years and almost always require that the fellow's project be "new." No one will fund us to bring in a fellow to sustain existing work, even if that is really what we need most to meet community demands. While we only take on work that we think is important and consistent with our values, I think we do sometimes end up prioritizing new projects in ways that make it harder to do our existing work sustainably. Once we have invested in a new project with support from a fellowship, it would be damaging to just withdraw from it when the fellowship ends in a year or two, so we need to raise even more money to sustain it. It exacerbates some of the problems we were discussing earlier about workload.

Anya: I think you raise a critical issue here, and one that can be hard to answer carefully given most organizations' dependence on foundations and government agencies. The NPIC has shifted power and resources from communities to respond to problems and into the hands of organizations to solve. The work has been "professionalized" so that now it requires social workers and lawyers and people with degrees. The foundations and government hold the power to set community priorities and strategies.

So I do believe funding can have a big impact on the work we do. In order to keep their doors open, many organizations find themselves at one time or another reframing or reshaping their work and their strategies based on what funding is available or at a funder's direction. Each funder is different. Some understand that they are far removed from the issues and communities they support and leave the prioritizing and strategizing to the organization. But, others have a very specific idea about how the work should be done and who it should impact, and they make compliance with those ideas a condition of support.

1. Owen, Gabriel, and Anya discuss the ways that their experiences at SRLP and TJLP are reflective of organizations that seek to be anti-oppressive not only in the work they do outside the organization, but the work they do inside the organization. Discuss some of the ways you see their organizations exemplifying some of the concepts from this chapter.

2

ACTUALIZING OUR POLITICS:
BUILDING QEJ FROM THE GROUND UP

JOSEPH NICHOLAS DEFILIPPIS

I am a bi-racial gay man, raised in New York City, the son of two immigrants. My work has always been informed by Marxism, black feminism and queer theory. In particular, I have always used an intersectional lens in my work (as articulated by women like Kimberlé Crenshaw and the Combahee River Collective), looking at the ways that classism, capitalism, racism, sexism and homophobia have impacted my life and the lives of the people I work with.

In 2003, a group of community activists came together to discuss building an organization that would work on issues of queer poverty. When we decided to start planning the project, which would become Queers for Economic Justice, we knew that the people building the organization had to reflect the issues and mission that would shape the work. We were determined to build an organization that was multi-racial, multi-gender and multi-classed. We immediately realized that our group of activists on the steering committee was too white and middle-class. We did not want to move forward with our planning in this way. We had seen all too often organizations that began with relatively affluent activists who built organizations that reflected their values and concerns. They then claimed to be surprised when they subsequently failed in their "outreach" to low-income people or people of color (who were invited, after the fact, to join organizations whose values, goals and tactics they had no role in shaping). We did not want to replicate these mistakes.

So we stopped the process completely in order to make sure that before we moved forward we represented the identities and issues that were central to our vision and mission. We spent months conducting meetings and enlisting community members and activists representing diverse race, gender and class identities and backgrounds to work with us to build an organization. We actually built an elaborate matrix that forced us to examine a wide range of qualities that we were looking for in a Founding Board. In addition to particular skills (advocacy, community-organizing, fund-raising, program development, legal expertise, fiscal management, and so on), the qualities we examined also included a mix of professional, volunteer, academic and lived experiences with the social issues we were working on, as well as a mix of racial, gender and class identities.

This effort took a long time, extending the planning process by an additional year, but eventually we had a steering committee that brought together a seasoned group of activists and community leaders with personal experience and expertise in various poverty and economic justice issues (like welfare, homelessness, prison reform, and labor) or experience working in LGBT communities. In the end, the majority of the steering committee was people of color or people with first-hand experience of poverty. These were the right people to now begin the long, difficult work of creating this new organization together.

Learning from feminist organizations, our Board adapted a consensus model of decision-making. Although we knew that standard majority rule might make decision-making faster, we also believed that being simply overruled by the majority serves to alienate and disempower the minority. This can lead to tensions and high turnover rates. The belief of our board was that consensus decision-making, while sometimes more time-consuming, helps to create stronger group cohesion and more sustained, long-term commitment to the organization.

As someone who tends to be very task oriented, and less process focused, I was originally skeptical about the practicality of adopting this model. I was quickly proven wrong. The first two years of creating and building QEJ was a remarkable experience for many reasons and one of those reasons was watching the Board engage in consensus-based meetings. I was part of numerous long, difficult discussions, decision-making and debates that were conducted in respectful, engaged and, yes, efficient ways. It was incredible to watch 20 opinionated, passionate activists talk, think, explain, deliberate and end up finding compromises that worked for everyone. Years later, I still look back at those early meeting with awe.

We first identified the issues that we hoped would become our first programmatic work—welfare reform, immigration, and homelessness. But, there were also other issues that we wanted to address, such as prison reform, access to health care, labor/employment issues (including "underground" labor like sex work), access to education, class tensions within the queer community (such as the kind of gentrification conflict that is taking place in the West Village), poverty in transgender communities, reproductive freedom (beyond the narrow focus on abortion), and sexual liberation. We committed to starting small, but always keeping all of these issues—and their interconnections—in mind.

After coming up with a vision for what our first programs would do, we set about trying to raise funds to start our programs. Raising money for these issues in our communities was not easy, but as the months, and years, passed, we were able to build some of those programs and hire some wonderful people to staff them. When we first began building our staff, we were determined to develop personnel policies that were in keeping with our values and to build an anti-oppressive organizational structure.

One of the first decisions we made was to maintain an equal pay structure. We decided that all staff would be hired at the same base salary rate, regardless of position or title. Part-time staff was pro-rated at the same salary as full-time staff. Salary increases were awarded to senior staff, but seniority was defined by length of employment at QEJ and not by hierarchal rank. I was very proud of the fact that I worked at an organization that recognized all work equally rather than creating a hierarchy. Such salary hierarchies usually end up reinforcing society's class stratification by rewarding people whose economic privileges have provided them with access to the qualifications needed for those higher paying jobs. We were also able to provide health insurance and other benefits to staff (including part-time staff), but we did not have the money to cover the family members of staff members. This shortcoming always troubled me and we were always trying to find ways to increase our insurance coverage to family members. But, since we were a small struggling organization, we were not able to do so during my tenure. I often felt as if I had to prioritize growing the organization (building new programs and hiring more staff). Looking back, I wish that I had, instead, concentrated more of my energies on supporting and expanding the existing infrastructure. Not having done so definitely feels like a failure on my part.

Another personnel policy decision we made early on was to implement a plan for unlimited sick days. I thought this policy demonstrated a trust in the employees (not to abuse the policy), as well as a desire to support their health and well-being. When we were considering this policy, most of the Board was enthusiastic about the idea, but a few board members had reservations. These people were finally convinced when someone brought in research that showed that companies with unlimited sick days did not have high rates of absenteeism. And although this is useful information to have (and I wish more corporations knew this), I also remain troubled to this day about the fact that this research was needed to persuade anyone. It speaks to the tendency in our society to mistrust workers and to the ways in which productivity is valued above all else.

Another issue worth commenting on is QEJ's decision about whether to become a membership organization. We knew that we did not want to become one of those organizations that claim to have a membership, but where membership was limited to donating and receiving a membership card for your wallet. To us, those "members" were really donors. Instead, we debated becoming a membership organization where the members had control of the organization—where they voted on major decisions and elected people to the Board of Directors. There were many thoughtful and nuanced arguments for and against this plan, but they can be indelicately summarized as falling into one of two camps. Those who wanted to become a membership organization felt that it was an important way of assuring that the organization represented the voices and interests of the communities most directly impacted by the issues we were working on. Those opposed to the idea were concerned about the infrastructure resources required to maintain such a structure (we did not have them). There were also a few people worried about control of the organization falling into the hands of 'the wrong people,' such as a group like the International Socialist Organization (which was very active in certain circles of New York City, and they were not viewed favorably by many Board members). Although we never decisively resolved the question (and, for all I know, it may still remain a topic that the current Board discusses), our inability to decide meant that we remained at our default structure of non-membership. Personally, I was torn about my own feelings. On the one hand, I theoretically support the idea. But, on the other hand, I had no interest in personally spending the time to build and maintain such a structure.

To me, this issue was a good example of the real tensions that exist between believing in certain politics and having the ability to enact them. And this seems to be a common theme when doing this work. Negotiating that tension is the challenge of engaging in anti-oppressive practice.

1. Joseph details some of the ways that the founders of QEJ built the organization to reflect the mission and values. What are some of the ways that they explicitly and consciously built an organization that was anti-oppressive?

2. Have any organizations you are a member of approached organizational structure from an anti-oppressive perspective and, if so, in what ways do they actualize these politics and values?

3

"POWER WITH" YOUTH: EMPOWERING YOUTH LEADERS IN THE ORGANIZATION

HEIDI GROVE AND JUSTON COOPER (JC)

JC: I think it is important to understand the difference of "power with" rather than "power over." I often think about how I, as a professional, deal with the barrier of that power dynamic with young people, especially when I am in a position as professional of responsibility, with mandates and so on. But, how do I leverage it to where the young person feels empowered and so that I don't have power over rather power *with* the youth? Power over is usually really force and what we do is try not to be forceful in our positions and in our roles.

For example, I have had situations where I got to say that I was a cofounder and director of the organization, and sometimes the young person I was working with perceived that to be intimidating or authoritative. I had a young person tell me, "You know, JC, I don't give a damn who you are, what you are, and what your position is." That young person was escalating, so as I allowed the space for that young person to express himself and deescalate from his anger, I felt compelled to share with the young person what my position really means. So I disclosed to him my story of what led me to do this work. This was interesting because after the conversation, he asked me how I became a director. So our discussion went from "I don't care about your position" and his being intimidated by that, to a situation to where I had to check myself and realize, ok, how do I reframe this? So I reframed and told him "Ok let me talk to you about the fact that I was involved in these types of situations when I was a young person and I was associated with gangs. My best friend was killed in front of me. I have been through some of these things and I found that it was important for me to get my education, and in a way the title doesn't mean anything. But, what the title does mean is that I am committed to helping you. I am committed to being here for you. And that's why I have this title."

After this conversation, that young person asks, "How do I become a director, what do I need to do that?" So our conversation was transformational. But, first I had to understand the distinction of power with versus having power over (being forceful).

This youth ended up being the chair of the youth advisory board, so my story meant a lot to him and he took it seriously. It was real for him because he felt empowered to be responsible for helping others. And that's what I told him: "All this title does is hold me responsible for helping you guys. It holds me accountable." When he became the chair of our youth advisory board for a while, he really owned this position. It gave him a sense of purpose.

We make sure that, once young people have identified that they want to be in a responsible leadership role, we support them being there. So first they have to self-identify like this youth did. He said, "I want to be in the youth advisory board of TYC." We don't force young people to do to service providers. I think the philosophy behind that stems from what I mentioned earlier, the need for healthy boundaries and safe spaces for advocates and our program participants.

I understand that information about domestic and sexual violence can be really triggering sometimes for survivors. In some situations, it may not be appropriate to have trainings both for providers and consumers to attend side-by-side. But, I would love to create more opportunities for our participants to attend these trainings along with their advocates when appropriate. I think survivors would benefit a great deal if they could hear information from the experts themselves and ask questions that directly relate to their lived experiences. I would prefer that survivors have access to educational trainings that are traditionally an option for agency employees, instead of trying to relay the information myself.

If appropriate safe-space guidelines are set up and the survivors feel comfortable attending, then there is no reason that they should not be allowed to do so. It would even be great to have training topics specific for our participants on subjects, such as how to communicate your needs to service providers, and how to navigate challenging systems, as well as anti-oppression trainings. Information is power and what better way to empower our participants than to provide them with the same training opportunities we get as service providers?

1. How does Crystal believe that access to information and educational trainings addresses issues of power?

2. What are some of the organizational struggles that Crystal identifies in this story?

3. What is the role of healthy boundaries when working with survivors of domestic and sexual assault as it relates to challenging the service provider/consumer paradigm?

4. Crystal highlights educational training for domestic violence survivors as a way to break down barriers between service providers and service users. What are additional ways that these barriers can be addressed?

5. Have you attempted to share professional information and education with participants in any way in your organization(s) and, if so, how did staff and participants respond?

6. If you have not attempted to share information and education with participants in the past, how could you do this in your current organization? What are the challenges, who could be your allies, and how could this change strengthen the organization?

5

DISMANTLING THE DOUBLE STANDARD

CHOYA RENATA

When I began working in a domestic violence shelter in 2006, the detailed level of control imposed by the program rules surprised and disheartened me. I had never heard of anti-oppressive practice, but much of what I've since learned to call by that name came naturally to me; I was shocked to see it wasn't the norm in service programs. Although our stated mission and philosophy were about empowering women and providing survivor-centered services, in reality we were managing what sorts of clothing people wore in their own home (shelter is a home, first, and a program second), expecting complete sobriety, and defining success and the steps to reach it rather than following their lead.

I remember a situation three or four months after I started working in the shelter. One woman had reached the end of her shelter stay and taken up residence in a hotel. A friend of hers, still a shelter participant, went to visit her there. During the visit, one of the women's abusers showed up and created a confrontation, trying to kidnap the children. Both women survived this terrible, traumatizing experience with their kids looking on in fear. Afterward, they went to the hotel bar and had a drink to cope with the stress of the situation and to deescalate. When the participant returned to shelter, she shared with us exactly what had happened, trusting us with this information, which technically violated our dry program policy. One of my coworkers said, "We've got to kick her out, she can't stay since she had a drink and then came back to shelter."

I was appalled, worried. For me, it was clear we are so much harder on people experiencing poverty and trauma than we are even on ourselves—and that it's a problem. How common, how normal, is it for any of us to have a drink after a stressful day of work? Drinking and drug use have become culturally accepted ways to relieve anxiety or trauma (whether or not we believe they are healthy or ideal), and yet we expect people receiving assistance of any kind to abstain, to be more virtuous than we are. In our program, we expected 100% of the people in shelter to be 100% clean and sober 100% of the time they stayed with us. We had the freedom to drink or use drugs; who were we to say, "But, you don't get to relieve your stress that way."

We argued for a while, in this particular situation. In those days, the conflict we had internally among staff was very painful for each of us; we were all committed to doing what's best, and our preferred routes to getting there differed greatly. In the end, for this particular woman, justice won out. She was permitted to stay in our program. Others, throughout my four years working in shelter, were not so lucky.

This situation represented the beginning of a rigorous revision to our rules and policies. It was my first concrete experience of program staff striving to recognize our power and learning to use it in less-oppressive ways. Clarity was on our side: we knew abusers were controlling, indeed that control was the foundation of intimate partner violence. We knew we didn't want to adopt the recently vacated role of controller in each woman's life; quite the contrary. We wanted to support each woman in regaining power in her own life. That meant us doing our best to set aside arbitrary or unnecessary power that comes along with hierarchy and with privilege.

In the new policy, we focused on safety and behavior. We agreed that, if there were unsafe behaviors in shelter, we would talk with the person, help them understand the impact of their behavior, and support them in modifying it if they wanted, or support them in finding another place to stay if that worked better for them. This practice is, of course, as rife with challenges in its own way. But, it was a big step for us in the right direction, at the time. We were advocates. None of us were therapists, drug and alcohol counselors, or psychiatrists. We stepped out of the role of trying to infer, from someone's behavior, what their "problem" might be. We made observations, and did our best to be collaborative.

One woman I worked with had a lot of behaviors that staff and other residents found concerning. She nodded off in public spaces and had slurred speech; we really became worried when she starting falling asleep when she was using the stove. Instead of saying "We think you have a drug problem and we're going to kick you out," the conversation focused on our concern for her and her daughter's safety, as well as the well-being of the house community. "It's scary for other people to see you nodding off, especially at the stove; would you like to talk about what's going on there?" And she was able to share with us that she wasn't using her medication properly. We encouraged her to check in with medical practitioners and provided resources for that, and she agreed to try to go into her room if she was nodding off in public spaces of the house.

This change to a behavior based model was occurring all around us in our professional community. It was an exciting time. I assumed the transition was also happening regionally and even nationally, that we were part of a sea change of becoming less oppressive in our response to survivors of abuse. And yet, once again I was gravely disappointed.

One woman in the shelter decided she needed to move to southern California for safety and to be nearer her family. She and I began calling programs to find out who might have space, where she could end up, at least as a landing place. We discovered that all the shelters in the area had curfews, and many had other paternalistic, restrictive policies. One even had a 30 day lock-down period during which people were not permitted to leave the shelter! Another required women to quit their jobs. I was so angry. I had to put on my "politely assertive" voice and say, "Our programs up here are a little different. Can you help me understand your rules and practices so I can support this woman in her transition?" Their responses were one-dimensional and always parroting something about it being "for her safety." But no one could tell me how a curfew or a lockdown period ensured a woman's safety. There was no analysis of the power dynamics, no deeper understanding of what was really going on. It was very troubling.

At some point, I had a deep realization. For those of us with any kind of class privilege, when we have a need, what do we trade for the thing we need? We trade money. So what do people without money trade for things they need, such as shelter, food, and support? They trade, among other things, dignity, privacy, autonomy. These are massive sacrifices being made for essential survival. Recognizing that someone with so little to give up is nonetheless giving up even more for the privilege of being in our programs, in our presence—this is vital to building trusting working relationships. It's crucial that we continuously check the bar to which we're holding people we work with; is it higher than the bar to which I hold my family, my friends, myself? In actuality, it should be a completely different bar—one defined entirely by the person we're serving. That would be true service. And so, if the goal she sets for herself is to remain clean and sober while in our program, we can support her compassionately in accountability to her own goal—at her request. If her goal, on the other hand, is to find counseling for her kids, we need not concern ourselves with her drug or alcohol consumption.

1. What does the author of the story identify as problematic and unjust within her organization?

2. Are there ways in which your organization seems to be operating under a double standard similar to what Choya observed in her organization?

3. If there does seem to be a double standard in your organization, what changes could be made to organizational structure and policy to address the inconsistencies?

6

FROM THE INSIDE OUT: DEVELOPING ANTI-OPPRESSIVE ORGANIZATIONAL PRACTICES

JOSÉ MIGUEL PAEZ

Personal Journey

In 2007 a former social work teacher called me and asked if I had any interest in working with social work students at the University of Southern California and the surrounding South Los Angeles community. The job was to develop an internship field placement for first year graduate social work students.

My first task would be developing a collaborative partnership between the USC School of Social Work and The Neighborhood Academic Initiative (NAI), which was designed to help local low-income minority students succeed in college (USC Neighborhood Academic Initiative, 2009). The goal of this initiative was to create opportunities and access to resources for marginalized individuals. My next task was to build a field placement that could accommodate the needs of the community that NAI served while fulfilling the academic requirements of the social work students. My third task was to accomplish this within one week. That's right—one week. I expressed interest and agreed to a meeting with all of the principal organizations.

I had worked the previous 6 years delivering mental health services at a Department of Mental Health contracted outpatient clinic in Pacoima, California. The population we served was predominately Latino and African American, mostly low income, with high exposure to violence, substance abuse, and severe and persistent mental illness. Our clients experienced overt and covert forms of oppression ranging from having limited access to adequate health care, nutritious food, and basic safety, and too much experience with racial profiling, racial and gender discrimination, and homophobia. In my role as a bilingual clinician, I had the opportunity to facilitate individual, couples, family, and group therapy.

This was the bulk of my experience as I walked into a meeting that would undoubtedly require me to state exactly how I planned to pull off this task of developing a first year field placement. I didn't think I was the right fit. I'd never done anything like this before. Most of my practice experience was as a clinician, referring to people as "clients," and abiding by very specific (some would argue oppressive) DMH (Department of Mental Health) county approved treatment guidelines.

But, I did have a few things going for me. For one, I had attended USC to earn my MSW and while there developed strong relationships with faculty and staff. I was also familiar with the surrounding community of South Los Angeles. In fact, this area had many similarities to the marginalized community of Pacoima.

Maybe most importantly, I am a male of color, educated, bilingual, heterosexual, and able-bodied. Within the context of helping disadvantaged and marginalized groups, my diversity markers offer me privileges—an unearned boost. True, my former teacher could vouch for me and I'm sure that carried a lot of weight. But, I'm equally sure that my appearance fit the dominant narrative about men being "natural" leaders, strong communicators, and heroes. Being a male of color and educated could be viewed as an example of someone who had overcome structural barriers; thus if I could do it, so could our future clients of color. Heterosexual privilege meant that it was assumed I was "straight" like everyone else. There would be no questioning, explicit or implicit judging, or awkward conversations about how to bring "it" up. My heterosexual orientation is the default. I'm viewed as "normal." And as someone who is able-bodied, I am immediately considered physically and most likely emotionally fit for this job; there's no concern about "special accommodations" and how that would affect my performance.

The benefits I gained from privilege provided me with power and authority. In this way I benefit from preserving unequal hierarchies of power and privilege that disadvantage others. To stay silent on the matter, in my mind, would be to consciously contribute to the various mechanisms of oppression, reinforcing systems of domination. However, practicing from an anti-oppressive lens would be central to all of the work I would engage in with NAI.

Getting Started

In my initial meeting with USC and NAI, it was immediately obvious there was not a representative from the community present. I was worried that maybe this project would be relying on a "normative" or "standard" model of practice that emphasized individualism over collectivism and solidarity. However, as I learned more about the NAI program it became clear to me they were emphasizing equity, partnership, and collaboration, and placed high importance on treating people with dignity and respect.

Since their inception in 1989, NAI has developed a strong alliance within the community and especially with its participants. Almost all of the NAI staff lived in the area and were painfully aware of the barriers that the families in South LA faced on a daily basis. I recall that early on in the initial meeting, an NAI representative stated that they had been advocating for mental health services for the last 5 years or so. NAI indicated that their families were victims of harassment by police and gangs; most were living well below the poverty line and experienced all of the associated stressors. Additionally, concerns were brought up at the meeting that I attended that the NAI staff (in attempting to manage all of this) were stressed, dealing with vicarious traumatization, and in need of support. Thus, whatever program we developed would need to address community concerns as well as staff needs.

Evidence of a strong alliance between NAI and the community was clearly demonstrated when I attended my first Family Development Institute (FDI) meeting. The FDI offered seminars for parents/guardians and advocates of NAI scholars. The topics were developed with input from parents, staff and teachers. The community meetings took place three Saturdays of every month and lasted for 3½ hours. During this time, students attended Saturday classes in English, Math,

SAT preparation, and History or Science. At the FDI meeting, I witnessed close to 200 parents engaged and attentive to an educational presentation on diabetes and prevention. I was informed that this turnout was the norm, that even though parents were expected to come they still ultimately had a choice not to attend. In other words, 200 parents showed up voluntarily 3 times a month so that their kids could get a good education. Talk about commitment. I was moved and humbled by the experience.

Planning

Since I only had a week's time to meet with USC and NAI and to develop a proposal, I worked quickly and developed a preliminary sketch of what the field placement would be like. However, since I was going to be assigned 5 students (all first year graduate level social workers) I decided that it might make more sense to include them in the planning stages. On their first day of graduate school field placement, they were literally going to build their field placement.

These students were nervous, unsure, and anxious about the opportunity. I spent our first meeting together explaining all that I knew about NAI and what was expected of us. I also began the process of making explicit how power would be distributed and shared. I asked if they would be willing to share power through decision-making. They looked at me like maybe I misspoke. One of them asked, "Are you sure you want us to make those kinds of decisions?" Traditionally interns have been considered "followers," relegated to a "lesser-than" status. I wanted to change that. For instance, I strongly advocated that all the interns receive a stipend (free intern labor has always seemed exploitative to me). I also recognized that all 5 interns were women of color and young looking. What would they expect? What had their experiences with male authority figures been like previously? What stereotype threats were they facing? What were their hopes and wishes for this field placement? These were just a few questions that we tackled during our first few meetings.

I was not at all sure how I would address my privilege or how it would manifest in the planning phase. I did know that I wanted to avoid designing a program that continued to privilege and preserve unequal power hierarchies that marginalize people. My thinking was that we needed to continue with what NAI already had established and not enter their space as "knowers" (experts). For starters we absolutely had to take into consideration the cultural context of the institutions and community. Whose interests were being represented here? Who had power? Who had privilege? What were the historical precedents of the University and the community? Did community members want services to address specific needs? If so, did they have a voice in the type of services they wanted? And what specific needs did they have or want to be addressed? Indeed there were many more questions that needed to be answered, and that meant I was going to have to give up my initial ideas.

As we started developing the structure of our program, interns began by reaching out to staff and community members. We reviewed ways to introduce ourselves and considered how we hoped or wanted to be viewed. We spent the first few weeks connecting and building these relationships; we made a point to be respectful since we were entering an established space.

We wanted to avoid being seen as "the other" or as a "threat" to their existing order. We referred to ourselves as social workers and invited discussions about stereotypes people may have held about our profession. When concerns arose about social work's history with removing children disproportionately from communities of color, we acknowledged this. We validated this experience; there was no sense in denying social work's legacy of racial, gender, and class oppression. Dominant streams of social work absolutely upheld white supremacist, patriarchal, heteronormative, and capitalistic ideology manifested through unjust policies, practice methods, and curricula of social work education.

We communicated to families and staff that our job was to move away from oppressive practice norms, to invite participation, advocate, help create spaces where people felt safe and empowered. We gathered information from families and staff as to what they wanted, what they hoped for, what would be most beneficial given their lived experience. From there, we would meet, review, discuss, and debate possible routes of action. What emerged from these dialogues was a format that sought to be as inclusive as possible of community and staff needs. Our first conception of what this field placement would look like consisted of anti-oppressive clinical case management and therapy (no fees) to all those associated with NAI, regular presentations at FDI (based on parent interests), facilitation of teen groups (addressing issues related to poverty, exposure to violence, stressors related to stereotype threats, and the like).

Beginning Our Practice

Within one month of starting their field placement, interns began facilitating FDI presentations (always in Spanish and English) based on topics that parents had requested (subjects like stress related illnesses, healthy food access, substance abuse, mental illness, suicide prevention, inequality, communication and power dynamics within families, and racial and gender discrimination). Understandably, these interns were nervous about presenting to such a large audience. To their relief, I facilitated the first presentation by myself so they could get ideas on how I present, plus they would be able to offer critique of what I could improve on. Additionally, I would be available to join in on their presentations (if needed) while regularly offering support and ideas in developing content. This notion was consistent with our underlying belief in creating an environment that is collaborative, allied, supportive, and open. Our style of presentation emphasized interaction. For example, we generally started a presentation with questions that parents or staff had raised about a particular topic; that was our basis for moving forward. Next we would elicit statements about lived experiences with the understanding that we were all practicing the skill of respecting difference of opinion. In some cases, we would offer information from the research literature; other times we would use film clips to convey a certain idea.

This format initially was nerve wracking for the interns. There were many times when we were overwhelmed by the process and content. They had to concede the power that adheres to the role of "knower" and "expert." They were to be listeners first and foremost, learning to identify themes or patterns, finding ways to connect thoughts and responses. They also had to learn how to take feedback and criticism. From my perspective, this process was essential to disrupting traditional hierarchies of power. It was difficult and uncomfortable at times, yet parents, staff, and interns alike consistently remarked that the presentations were engaging, fruitful, and empowering.

One other major theme we continued to emphasize in all of our work was the impact of inequality. In one example we were addressing "communication" issues within the family; this topic was framed around a perceived lack of verbal dialogue and rarely focused on non-verbal response. After eliciting comments about "communication" issues, we began to address the socio-cultural norms about gender roles and the impact they may have on communication style. I recall a few confused glances from the audience. We examined socialization (conditioning) of people to accept males as "bread winners" and women as "nurturers." We challenged the idea that men "don't share feelings" versus women "share lots of feelings." Parents quickly caught on that gender socialization may have an impact on the way we speak to one another. In essence we were challenging dominant norms and values, explicitly examining the role of inequality on relationships.

Even with a large group we could begin to expand critical conscious and empowerment. I recall moments where a mother would stand up and address the entire audience with comments like "Why have we been thinking like this for so long? It's crazy. I'm not going to teach my daughter to be weak." We had fathers openly disclose feelings of shame and not feeling "man enough" to deal with an out-of-control son. Again, we always steered the conversation back to norms and values that limit our range of expression, leaving us vulnerable and ineffective in dealing with the complexity of relationships. In essence, we were making attempts to connect "personal" problems to a larger social and cultural context.

We also set up an anti-oppressive, informed style of therapy. In line with this approach, our focus was developing relationships between individuals that aimed to empower them by addressing the negative effects of hierarchy found within social relationships (Dominelli, 1998). For example, I encouraged interns to openly address power hierarchies and to help families examine how these internal structures helped or interfered with overall family functioning. We also looked at how the family hierarchy mirrored (or did not mirror) external structures. We subscribed to the notion that family development is affected by the cultural context, which includes past and present socio-cultural-political history (Hernández, Almeida, Dolan-Del Vecchio, 2005). Interns also found ways to direct and facilitate team building activities into sessions with families; these activities were also rooted in empowerment and accountability.

We were all challenged to confront our biases and judgments and privileges. Our ability to address prejudicial thinking was key to being able to connect with others in an authentic and vulnerable way. Quite possibly this was one of the most transformative components to our experience. In both individual and group supervision, we experienced growth, and a deeper understanding of what it means to hold power and privilege.

Evaluating Impact

I would say that this field placement was never truly completed; it was an evolving process that required flexibility, patience, and regular practice of self-examination and accountability. And although we hadn't initially thought it would have happened, we were all humbled by the experience. Within the first 2 months of this program, we had a higher number of referrals for our therapy services than we could actually accommodate. We connected people to outside community resources; in other cases we developed group meetings to accommodate need.

We also sought feedback about the program services we had developed. We used surveys, gathered information from personal testimony, and used variations of informal focus groups. What we found was that parents and staff connected and resonated with our approach. They would remark that they felt included and part of the process; those who received direct therapy services felt supported and empowered.

As a result, the field placement program at NAI continued to develop and grow. Now in its 7th year, there are now 7-10 interns serving the community not only at the NAI offices, but also at neighboring schools. When I left 4 years ago, we were extremely fortunate to find a licensed clinical social worker who shared the same vision of anti-oppressive practice. She has continued to uphold the values of empowerment, dignity, respect, and the need to challenge the dominant narrative.

When I look back on the work we did, I feel incredibly fortunate for the opportunity. The experience radically shifted my worldview of social work and human relationships. I had started from a traditional conception of social work, due to ongoing support from important mentors I was able to change. The staff and community of NAI who were gracious and patient with me during those first days, weeks, months and years are my inspiration. Their commitment to one another, to developing kinship and community, have shaped my understanding of what it means to develop anti-oppressive organizational practice from the inside out.

1. In what ways do Jose's intersecting identities provide him with power, privilege and access to resources?

2. What are some of the challenges that Jose faced prior to immersing himself in the project of developing a field placement through community collaboration?

3. How does Jose share power and with whom?

4. What strategies did Jose and his interns implement with the community to address power, privilege, and oppression?

5. What are some of the lessons Jose and the interns learned about anti-oppressive approach to organizational practices?

DISCUSSION QUESTIONS

1. What feelings and thoughts were brought up for you in response to these stories?

2. Describe the common themes that emerge throughout these stories of AOP in organizations.

3. How do these stories demonstrate concepts presented in the chapter, such as flattening hierarchies and participation, inclusivity, and funding challenges within social work and social service organizations?

4. How do these stories speak to the possibilities and challenges of doing AOP work within organizations?

ACTIVITIES

Organizational Analysis

1. Using your practicum, internship, or field placement as the subject, answer the following questions:

History of the Organization

a. What is the history of the formation of the organization (who, what, where, when, how)?

b. What was the community's definition of the problem and need to be addressed that contributed to the formation of the organization?

c. Describe the stakeholders who were supportive of the organization and the stakeholders who challenged its formation (if any).

Funding and Resources

d. How is the organization funded?

e. What resources are available to the organization and what resources are scarce?

Organizational Structure

f. Describe the system of governance in the organization.

g. Describe the decision-making process in the organization. How much does it vary depending on the issues or decisions at hand?

h. Describe channels of communication and information flow within the organization.

Relationship with employees

i. How is space defined and allocated within the organization?

j. How are grievances addressed?

k. In what ways are staff involved in the organizational decision-making, program development, evaluation, and policy-making processes?

Participants

l. What forms of access do participants have regarding services provided and documentation of their receipt of services?

m. What role do participants play with regards to services received and the quality of services?

n. How are grievances addressed?

o. In what ways are participants involved in the organizational decision making, program development, evaluation, and policy-making processes?

Power

p. How is power defined and distributed within the organization (among employees, between programs, among providers and participants, between organizations and community, among similar community organizations)?

q. How is dissent addressed? Is silence presumed to be assent?

r. In what ways does the organization have "power over" and "power with" participants?

s. What types of legal authority or sanction does the organization have over participants?

Ideology

t. What values are expressed by the organization, and how well are they manifested through the services provided?

u. Describe value tensions that exist.

v. Describe the theoretical approach that informs organizational practices.

Relationship within Community

w. Describe the channels of communication between the organization and the larger community.

x. How does the community view the organization and participants?

ADDITIONAL RESOURCES

Websites

Youth on Board:

http://www.youthonboard.org

Youth for Justice/Chuco's Justice Center:

http://www.youth4justice.org/

Free LA School:

http://www.youth4justice.org/yjc-high-schools/free-l-a-high-school

A New Way of Life:

http://anewwayoflife.org/

South LA Community Coalition:

http://www.cocosouthla.org/

LA Community Action Network:

http://cangress.org/

Films

Black Rain (1989). R. Scott.

Boiler Room (2000). B.Younger.

Brazil (1985). T. Gilliam.

Cry Freedom (1987). R. Attenborough.

Dead Poet's Society (1989). P. Weir.

Death of a Salesman (1985). V. Schlondorff.

Patton (1970). F. Schaffner.

Rashomon (1950). A. Kurosawa.

Wall Street (1987). O. Stone.

Books

Gautney, H. (2010). *Protest and organization in the alternative globalization era: NGOs, social movements, and political parties*. New York: Palgrave Macmillan.

INCITE! Women of Color Against Violence. (Eds.). (2007). *The revolution will not be funded: Beyond the non-profit industrial complex*. Boston, MA: South End Press.

Kingston, M. H. (1975). *The woman warrior*. New York: Vintage Books.

8

Anti-Oppressive Practice
With Communities

A number of terms are used to describe practice at the community level, including *community practice, community intervention, community organization,* and *community organizing.* While they are sometimes used interchangeably, a distinction is usually made between *community organizing* and *community organization.* In the social work field, community organizing is often identified as a subcategory of community organization, yet some community organizers, often from the labor movement, see their work as squarely outside of the field of social work (DeFillipis, Fisher, & Shragge, 2010). Social workers have typically embraced a number of different models and processes in community work, which are often identified as community organization work.

For clarity, we use the term *community intervention* or *community practice* to describe the social work practice of intervening at the community level. Community intervention falls between micro-level work with individuals and families and macro-level work in large-scale movements and state or federal policy practice.

> What does the term *community* mean to you? Before reading on, we encourage you to think about the various ways you identify community. What is encompassed in the term? What is excluded? What community or communities do you see yourself as being a part of—has your community identity changed over time?

Community is a contested and complex concept. A common way to conceptualize community is either by geography/place or by interest/identity. Clearly these two categories are not mutually exclusive—some communities that are bound by "place" may also be bound by "identity." For example, consider a neighborhood that is inhabited mostly by a particular racial/ethnic group or an intentional community that is drawn together in a particular place by certain values or practices, such as a religion or sustainability. Additionally, communities

297

that are defined by geography may be populated by individuals who share little, if any, affiliation beyond proximity. By the same token, communities that are defined by identity or interest may have widely divergent views on what that identity or interest means, and will also have multiple, intersecting identities.

Nevertheless, community is an important aspect of our daily lives. Geographic communities are typically where the day-to-day interactions and experiences of our lives occur. For social workers and consumers of their services, community is also important because social services and housing provisions are typically delivered at the community level (DeFilippis, Fisher, & Shragge, 2010). Communities also tie us to larger societal forces: They influence labor markets, and they are where most people learn about politics and become involved in political life. All these factors support the potential for collective action at the community level.

COMMUNITY INTERVENTION

Theorizing about "community" has a long history in various disciplines. In sociology, the work of German sociologist Ferdinand Tönnies is often cited as foundational to the understanding of community. Tönnies distinguished between *Gemeinschaft*, which represents reciprocal, informal, and mutual relationships, and *Gesellschaft*, which represents formal, industrial, and bureaucratic relationships (Weil, 2005a). A related theory can be seen in German philosopher Georg Wilhelm Friedrich Hegel's earlier concepts of "family-society" (comparable to *Gemeinschaft*) and "civic-society" (comparable to *Gesellschaft*) (Sorokin, 2002, p. 8). Image 8.1 summarizes the two concepts.

Tönnies also applied these two "ideal types" (that is, types not necessarily found in pure form) to the development of social structures over time. As societies have shifted from agrarian to industrial and postindustrial, many theorists, including Marx, Hegel, and Tönnies, saw *Gemeinschaft* as giving way to *Gesellschaft* and the eventual demise of what they considered a more functional type of community (DeFilippis, Fisher, & Shragge, 2010).

Image 8.1   Theoretical Types of Community

Gemeinschaft	Gesellschaft
Agrarian	Industrial
Informal	Formal
Reciprocal and mutual relationships	Bureaucratic relationships
"Family-society"	"Civic-society"

Source: Adapted from Sorokin, 2002.

Modes of Community Intervention

One additional way to understand the various models and forms of community organization work is to look at variations in the work that is undertaken. A community intervention model, first developed in 1968 by social worker Jack Rothman, outlines three modes of effort (Rothman, 2001): locality development, social planning/policy, and social action. Of course, in "real life," these approaches intersect and overlap.

- *Locality development:* A broad spectrum of community members work together to address certain goals or simply to support community well-being and civic participation. The prototype is "community development," defined by the United Nations (UN) as "a process designed to create conditions of economic and social progress for the whole community with its active participation and the fullest possible reliance on the community's initiative" (as cited in Rothman, 2001, p. 29). Locality development typically focuses on community building and leadership development. This mode can be equated with certain feminist perspectives related to democratic participation and consciousness-raising (Rothman, 2001). Community development has often been co-opted by conservative and business interests, which strongly support privatization and the devolution of the welfare state and pass the onus of social development and services onto the community. Some have observed that, although the goals and processes of locality development are laudable, the hoped-for changes are often not attained and the process can be slow.
- *Social planning/policy:* This mode is typically more routinized and technical than locality development, with much less focus on community participation and community building. Social planning/policy often encompasses detailed needs assessments to support the creation and organization of services and programs in a community. It also fosters coordination among agencies in an attempt to avoid duplication of services and to aid in filling in any service gaps in the community (Rothman, 2001). It is important to note that, although planning and policy are combined into this one mode and do overlap, they also have distinct features. Social planning has more resonance on the local level (although it can be done via national and international development organizations) and social policy is often more macro in nature (although it can be developed by local organizations and governments). We examine social policy in Chapter 9.
- *Social action:* This mode encompasses local, national, and international social movement and advocacy work. The focal point is structural change, which likely includes the redistribution of power and resources; the focus is on groups that have been historically marginalized and oppressed. Tactics used in social action include demonstrations, picketing, civil disobedience, and other disruptive actions. This form of practice is one of the primary topics in Chapter 10.

Rothman applies 12 practice variables to each mode and examines the manner in which each mode employs these variables. Image 8.2 specifies these variables. Each mode has its own distinct focal areas and intervention techniques. Locality development is based on engaging the entire community (however defined) through group efforts to problem solve and create collaborations through consensus. Social planning/policy uses data collection to develop and implement programs and policies that address community needs. Social action focuses on shifting power relations via conflict rather than consensus, and works to mobilize disenfranchised community members.

Image 8.2   Practice Variables for Three Community Intervention Modes

	(Locality Develpoment)	(Social Planning Policy)	(Social Action)
1. Goal categories of community action	Community capacity and integration; self-help (process goals)	Problem solving with regard to substantive community problems (task goals)	Shifting of power relationships and resources; basic institutional change (task or process goals)
2. Assumptions concerning community structure and problem conditions	Community eclipsed, anomie; lack of relationships and demographic problem-solving capacities; static traditional community	Substantive social problems, mental and physical health, housing, recreation, etc.	Aggrieved populations, social injustice, deprivation, inequality
3. Basic change strategy	Involving a broad cross section of people in determining and solving their own problems	Gathering data about problems and making decisions on the most logical course of action	Crystallizing issues and mobilizing people to take action against enemy targets
4. Charcteristic change tactics and techniques	Consensus; communication among community groups and interests; group discussion	Consensus or conflict	Conflict conformation, direct action, negotiation
5. Safer practitioner roles	Enabler-catalyst, coordinator; teacher of problem-solving skills and ethical values	Fact gatherer and analyst, program implementer, expediter	Activist, advocate, agitator, broker, negotiator, partisan
6. Medium of change	Guiding small, task-oriented groups	Guiding formal organizations and treating data	Guiding mass organizations and political processes

	(Locality Develpoment)	(Social Planning Policy)	(Social Action)
7. Orientation toward power structure(s)	Members of power structure as collaborators in a common venture	Power structure as employers and sponsors	Power structure as external target of action; oppressors to be coerced or overturned
8. Boundary defnition of the beneficiary system	Total geographic community	Total community or community segment	Community segment
9. Assumptions regarding interests of community subparts	Common interests or reconcilable differences	Interests reconcilable or in conflict	Conflicting interests which are not easily reconcilable, scarce resources
10. Beneficiaries	Citizens	Consumers	Victims
11. Conception of beneficiary role	Participants in an interactional problem-solving process	Consumers or recipients	Employers, constituents, members
12. Use of empowerment	Building the capacity of a community to make collaborative and informed decisions; promoting feeling of personal mastery by residents	Finding out from consumers about their needs for service; informing consumers of their service choices	Achieving objective power for beneficiary system the right and means to impact community decisions; promoting a feeling of mastery by participants

Source: Rothman, J. (1996). The interweaving of community intervention approaches. *Journal of Community Practice,* 3(3-4), 69–99. Taylor & Francis Ltd. http://www.informaworld.com

As can be seen in Image 8.2, there are some areas of overlap between modes. For example, a blending of locality development and social action can be seen in practices that combine education and consciousness-raising with social action. Social action organizations like the United Farm Workers may primarily focus on advocacy (social action) for farm workers, yet mutual aid and community building (locality development) may be a component of the organization. It is also possible that community practice can incorporate all three modes at once.

Can you think of other examples of community practice that illustrate these intersections?

Rothman's classic three-mode schematic has been expanded into an eight-mode model of community practice that can be understood and practiced through the contexts of multiculturalism, feminism, human rights, and globalization:

- Neighborhood and community organizing: defined by geography
- Organization of functional communities: defined by characteristic or goal (such as members of the LGBTQA community organizing across geographical boundaries around a common goal or an international organization working on anti-poverty initiatives)
- Community social and economic development: primarily focused on impoverished communities
- Social planning: primarily concerned with planning and integrating various services
- Program development and community liaison: addresses a specific service or program that the community requires
- Political and social action: seeks social justice via policy change at a local or state level
- Social movement: addresses larger societal and structural changes that result in paradigm changes among the general public
- Coalition building: brings together multiple organizations to develop a stronger power base for enacting social change (Gamble & Weil, 2010)

A Brief History of Community Practice

Social work sees community practice as historically connected with the settlement house movement. However, labor organizers and other community organizers tend to align their history with Saul Alinsky and his organizing work in the 1930s—ignoring or even disdaining social work examples. Activists of color often have yet another frame of reference, focusing on W. E. B. Du Bois and Marcus Garvey's work in the 1920s. Despite these differences, these organizing efforts are still located in similar political or historical moments (DeFillipis, Fisher, & Shragge, 2010).

When examining the history of social work in communities, one helpful framework is to distinguish between dissensus—periods of progressive community efforts—and consensus—periods of conservative or retrenchment efforts (Piven & Cloward, 1979). No era is wholly one of either dissensus or consensus, but there are clearly dominant movements based in the political and historical climate. Most social worker theorists identify three progressive "heydays" of dissensus in U.S. community work: 1900–1920, 1930–1946, and 1960–1975 (DeFillipis, Fisher, & Shragge, 2010). Image 8.3 shows these periods, as well as the periods of conservative community work (discussed later).

Image 8.3 Social and Political Developments and Predominant Type of Community Practice			
	Social and Political Developments	*Conservative Community Practice*	*Progressive Community Practice*
1900			Progressive Era
1910	World War I		
1920	Great Depression, Red Scare	Social Planning Era	
1930	New Deal		
1940	World War II		Depression and Post-Depression Era
1950	McCarthyism	Neighborhood Associations Era	
1960	War in Vietnam, Antiwar movement		Civil Rights Era
1970	Oil embargoes	Anti-Abortion, Christian, and New Right Era	
1980	Trickle-down economics		
1990	Gulf War		
2000	9/11 attacks, Iraq War, Great Recession		
2010	Tea Party Movement		

Progressive Era (1900–1920)

During the Progressive Era, the more progressive settlement houses, particularly in New York City and Chicago, developed a community-based practice with four essential elements (DeFillipis, Fisher, & Shragge, 2010, p. 45):

- Focus on social and economic conditions: Settlement workers rejected the attribution of poverty to individuals' actions, which was common to charitable work, and instead emphasized the conditions that oppressed workers and immigrants.

- Integrated approach: Settlement workers sought to provide services, engage with residents and the community, and develop "cross-class solidarity" between residents and settlement workers.
- Communitarian perspective: Settlement workers placed high value on building community, getting recent immigrants to participate, and developing local networks within the community.
- Advocacy: Settlement workers were willing to participate in political campaigns and movements in the pursuit of "social, political, and economic justice at the local, state, and even national level."

Settlement houses also created the National Federation of Settlements in 1911 so they could harness their collective power together to advocate for larger political and structural changes.

The work of Lugenia Burns Hope and the Atlanta Neighborhood Union is another example of Progressive Era organizing. Hope had worked in social service and advocacy organizations in Chicago, where she met Jane Addams and was influenced by the work being done at Hull House. When she moved to Atlanta she was drawn into community work. In 1908, the death of a young local woman motivated Hope to call a neighborhood meeting to assess the community's interest in settlement work. This was the beginning of the Neighborhood Union, which would be at the forefront of activism in the Black communities of Atlanta. Using community surveys and assessments, the Union identified numerous concerns to members of these communities, such as lack of proper lighting and sewage facilities, poor housing, and dilapidated school buildings. The Union was instrumental in providing health services through a health clinic and public health education programs, improving housing conditions, and supporting the development of recreational areas; it also advocated for improvements in the public education system (Rouse, 2004).

Depression and Post-Depression Era (1930–1946)

During the Depression/post-Depression era, dire economic conditions prompted critiques and dissent regarding capitalism and the manner in which the economic system had failed. Local and national organizing became much more radical than was apparent during the more conservative 1920s. The strategies and tactics at this time became more militant. For many historians, this period is seen as the foundation of conflict-based organizing work (DeFillipis, Fisher, & Shragge, 2010).

This more dynamic organizing period was based on a burgeoning and vibrant radical union movement and the creation of New Deal social welfare policies. Some of the primary organizing groups at this time included the Communist Party, the Catholic Worker Movement, and Saul Alinsky's early Back of the Yards project in the slums behind Chicago's Union Stock Yards. Organizing work, particularly through the Communist Party, was a combination of local and state and national organizing. For example, the Unemployed Councils, developed through the Communist Party, were local groups that addressed evictions, unemployment, hunger, and racism. While some of the organizing work was broader in scope, Alinksy tended to privilege local organizing in his work and maintained a suspicion of ideological organizing, seeing it as undemocratic.

Civil Rights Era (1960–1975)

From 1960 to 1975 there was an upsurge in large-scale social movement activity, which developed from local community organizing and sparked new community organizing efforts. In the 1950s, *Brown v. Board of Education* and the bus boycotts initiated by the Montgomery Improvement Association laid the groundwork for the Civil Rights Movement, supported by groups like the Student Nonviolent Coordinating Committee (SNCC), the Black Panthers, and others. Drawing on the tactics of these groups, other groups, such as the Students for a Democratic Society (SDS), the Brown Berets, the American Indian Movement (AIM), and the Gay Liberation Front (GLF), engaged in organizing and activism throughout this period. Other contributing factors during this era included the federal Great Society programs initiated through Lyndon B. Johnson's War on Poverty and the creation of the Office of Economic Opportunity, which required the "maximum feasible participation" of community members experiencing poverty in the development of anti-poverty programs (however, this program was short-lived).

The primary sites of organizing work also shifted from industry and factory organizing to college campuses and poor local communities, as the activists were not connected to factories in the same way as they had been in the previous periods. Specific to this time was the framing that social movements provided to organizing—that community was framed as "inherently alternative and oppositional to mainstream society" (DeFillipis, Fisher, & Shragge, 2010, p. 53).

Conservative Responses to Community Organizing

While community organizing is seen as a liberal or progressive endeavor during periods of dissensus, organizing has also been pursued by conservative organizations, especially during more conservative eras of consensus. The Red Scare in 1918 was one significant barrier to progressive activism in the 1920s. Socially, there was an increased focus on individualism and materialistic pursuits, and a business ethic replaced community organizing (DeFillipis, Fisher, & Shragge, 2010).

Social planning developed significantly in the more conservative era post 1920, which was heavily influenced by Frederick W. Taylor's work in scientific management regarding efficiency in organizations. At the same time, there was a growing trend toward professionalism in the social work field. The focus among practitioners shifted to planning services and developing funding sources—essentially the bureaucraticization of community organizing to create the umbrella field of community organization. As social planning was taking hold, community work began to encompass interorganizational coordination and social work administration—precursors to the United Way. Funding also became more dependent on local community chest campaigns, which tended to require standardization of operations. While there was action oriented, "radical" organizing in the form of labor strikes and the formation of self-help groups, social work moved toward the more regimented and bureaucratic developments.

Previous organizers, those in settlements for example, shifted programming in this conservative political climate. Jane Addams noted that social work at that time reflected the "symptoms of panic and with a kind of protective instinct, carefully avoided any identification with the phraseology of social reform" (as cited in DeFillipis, Fisher, & Shragge, p. 59). It is also during this time that religious fundamentalism grew and the second iteration of the Ku Klux Klan and other racist and nativist organizations developed (Austin & Betten 1990; DeFillipis, Fisher, & Shragge, 2010).

Post WWII through the 1950s was another era steeped in conservatism, idealization of material gains, the "nuclear" family structure, and nationalism. Community work was seen within the growth of neighborhood homeowner's associations, whose goals were to protect property values and maintain community. Their work was typically related to racism and "white flight" into the suburbs. These neighborhood associations helped enforce deed restrictions, which were restrictive covenants that enabled communities to maintain racial/ethnic segregation. As with the 1920s Red Scare, anti-Communist fervor in the form of McCarthyism had a chilling effect on progressive community change efforts (DeFillipis, Fisher, & Shragge, 2010).

Of course, even in this period there was important work being done, specifically crucial civil rights advocacy. The Montgomery (Alabama) Improvement Association and the National Association for the Advancement of Colored People (NAACP) were active in legal advocacy leading to *Brown v. Board of Education*.

There were also social workers who actively spoke out about the repression of progressive and radical activism. Most notably, Bertha Capen Reynolds, who had been blacklisted due to her association with the Communist Party, presented a paper in 1953 titled "Fear in our Culture." She was not allowed to speak at the NASW conference because of her political views so she spoke at the Cleveland Council of Arts, Sciences, and Professions that was held the same week. She closed her speech with an entreaty to social workers and activists to re-engage:

> What kind of country will we have? What kind of people will we be, as we live in this most critical time of all history? Once we get into motion with other courageous men and women, fear will dissolve in the outpouring of living energies. The point is to get to work with others, where we are, and now. (as cited in Reisch & Andrews, 2002, p. 116)

In the post-1975 conservative, consensus era, Community Development Corporations (CDCs) expanded. CDCs are nonprofit organizations that provide programs and services geared toward economic development with a primary focus on affordable housing projects.

The CDCs grew out of the community control movement, which was a movement that began in the 1960s to shift control of public education to community and away from teachers and administrators. CDCs were originally created to address civil rights and economic empowerment, but became more conservative in subsequent years.

A number of conservative, regressive groups developed in response to the progressive gains and movements of the mid-1950s to early 1970s. For instance, ROAR (Restore Our Alienated Rights) was opposed to school busing and integration efforts. Other conservative organizing efforts were undertaken by anti-abortion groups and the Christian and New Right movements. Some argue that the New Right has been the most "successful social change initiative" since the mid-1970s (DeFillipis, Fisher, & Shragge, 2010, p. 65).

This era of conservative organizing has been accompanied by Cold War politics and a free-market economic stranglehold. Much of it has been top-down organizing, with elites funding conservative groups that promote ideologies that help them remain in power. In terms of organizing by more liberal groups, the last 35+ years have been strongly affected by political climate, and community work has become primarily a matter of community building and consensus work rather than community organizing in the tradition of the conflict model.

Approaches to Community Organizing

There are a number of ways to conceptualize community practice and intervention at the community level; one is on a continuum from progressive to conservative. In broad terms, community organizing has historically been the more progressive and radical practice, while community development has been more neoliberal and conservative. Since the mid-1970s, community practice has shifted into the hands of more conservative and neoliberal practitioners (DeFilippis, Fisher, & Shragge, 2010).

It is particularly important to understand how strongly neoliberal politics, which its adherents consider a more pragmatic form of traditional liberalism, has influenced community practice. Neoliberal practices tend to focus on finances and economics, partnerships with business entities, relationships with other organizations, and the development of community assets (DeFilippis, Fisher, & Shragge, 2010). Neoliberal community practice privileges the consensus model over the conflict model. In many ways, it has co-opted community work for the benefit of capitalism, the free market, and further retrenchment of the state.

Anti-oppressive practitioners need to be mindful of the ways in which community work can be harnessed for emancipatory social justice goals, but also the ways in which the language of community practice can be used to further promote the mythology and ideology of "bootstrap capitalism" (see Stoesz, 2000). In the following sections, we discuss several approaches to community organizing that focus on social justice instead of social control. These approaches are grounded in historical community organizing models and in anti-oppressive theoretical frameworks.

imagination, a sense of humor, "a bit of blurred vision of a better world" (p. 75), an organized personality, "a free and open mind, and political relativity" (p. 79). He also stressed the need for an organizer to have confidence in the form of a strong "ego." An organizer should be "a well-integrated political schizoid" (p. 78), which is a person who can commit to the need to polarize an issue 100%, yet also know there may come a time for negotiation. He situated his brand of organizing solidly within the conflict perspective, which holds that "all new ideas arise from conflict" (p. 79). It is also interesting to note that Alinsky and other organizers of a similar propensity felt that social work training in community organizing does not truly get at the source of community problems and has the effect of turning an exciting field into a boring one (Fisher, 1999).

The Alinksy tradition has been critiqued on a number of fronts, such as privileging the role of the outsider, essentially subscribing to an "end justifies the means" approach, prioritizing a utilitarian "winning" approach, and focusing on "organizing for power" without determining what power was to be used and how. However, Alinsky and those who followed in his footsteps made a significant impact on the field of community organizing. Placing a premium on mobilizing communities by developing leaders and building on successes while consistently viewing community issues through a lens of power relationships are valuable contributions that continue to be an important influence on community work for social justice.

Popular Education

Popular education approaches share some common features, many of which resonate with anti-oppressive goals and practices. One of the core components of this form of community organization is the belief that the individuals and communities most affected by the issues at hand are the ones who can best identify the issues and the solutions—they are the "experts" (Baker & Williams, 2008; Pyles, 2009).

Popular education approaches are based in the work of Brazilian educator and philosopher Paulo Freire (see Chapter 3), Myles Horton's work at the Highlander Research and Education Center (formerly the Highlander Folk School), and participatory research methodologies, such as participatory rural appraisal. Horton's work, like Freire's, is firmly grounded in participatory dialogue as a way to engage community members to tap into their own knowledge through their lived experiences. Both Horton and Freire saw this as the groundwork for social change, calling this type of knowledge "people's knowledge" (Horton & Friere, 1990, p. 98).

The Highlander Research and Education Center, co-founded in 1932 by Horton and Don West, used popular education philosophy and techniques in their trainings and workshops, hosting grassroots leaders working in labor unions, the Civil Rights movement, and anti-poverty, environmental, LGBTQ, immigration, and prison reform movements, among others. The mission statement of the center sums up the center's approach:

> Highlander serves as a catalyst for grassroots organizing and movement building in the Appalachia and the South. We work with people fighting for justice, equality and

sustainability, supporting their efforts to take collective action to shape their own destiny. Through popular education, participatory research, and cultural work, we help create spaces—at Highlander and in local communities—where people gain knowledge, hope and courage, expanding their ideas of what is possible. We develop leadership and help create and support strong, democratic organizations that work for justice, equality and sustainability in their own communities and that join with others to build broad movements for social, economic and restorative environmental change. (Highlander, 2012, para. 1)

Participatory Action Approach

Another style of intervention that sees the local community as the source of wisdom and skills is Participatory Rural Appraisal (PRA), which emerged in the late 1980s and early 1990s from the global South, particularly South Asia and sub-Saharan Africa. The focus of PRA is community development and the integration of community organizing and development through PRA. PRA typically begins when an outside practitioner/facilitator is invited into a community to assist with a development project (Chambers, 2002). Based on an approach that is seen from the very start as a partnership, PRA is founded on the following principles (Castelloe & Gamble, 2005):

- Hand over the stick—turn over the process to the community so that they can do the research and planning needed for their own project; eventually, they become the facilitators of their own process;
- Regard locals as the experts;
- Respect local knowledge;
- Be inclusive;
- Believe in local capacity;
- Let the people create the data; and
- Behave in ways that may be contrary to formal training—for example, knowing when to sit back and listen and letting go of a "blueprint" of how to facilitate.

Thus, PRA is an example of Rothman's bimodal development/planning and, from the eight-mode model of community intervention, a synthesis of neighborhood/community organizing and community social/economic development.

Robert Chambers, who contributed extensively to the development of PRA's principles and approaches, developed a number of exercises for participants in the process (Castelloe & Gamble, 2005). For example, participants map social, health, or demographic conditions. These maps can be created with whatever tools are accessible and applicable—chalk, pens, seeds, or powders. Participants can also create timelines of community events or changes that they have witnessed or that have been documented in the community. In another exercise designed to examine issues of poverty and marginalization, participants identify and make cards representing individuals or groups of individuals in the community and then sort the cards into groups of most well off and most deprived (Castelloe & Gamble, 2005, p. 270).

While PRA is primarily situated in development in the global South, the principles and tools used are transferable to other community development projects. For example, the Advancement Project's HealthyCity.org program in Los Angeles provides a computer platform for community organizations and community members to create maps of their communities. Users can search through a directory that contains data on services, demographics, economic indicators, health and safety, and housing. They can use this information and their own knowledge to develop a map of their community and supplement the map with personal stories and videos (Healthy City, n.d.).

As with any model, approach, or tool in social change work, PRA can be used for progressive social justice and social change, and it can also be co-opted as a way to maintain the status quo of those in power. For instance, three types of tyranny can be found in participatory development models (Cooke & Kothari, 2001):

- power that multinational agencies and funders continue to wield, even if a project is labeled as "participatory";
- local power dynamics that may continue to play out during a participatory development project and may actually be strengthened by the approach; and
- popularity of the participatory method since the 1990s, which resulted in limiting conversations about other possible approaches (Christens & Speer, 2006; see also Cooke & Kothari, 2001; Hickey & Mohan, 2004).

Sustainable Development

Community development can be seen as having three components: social, economic, and environmental development (Gamble & Weil, 2010). All three forms of development intersect to support sustainable development. The term *sustainable development* is linked to the 1987 World Commission on Environment and Development. The Commission Chair, Gro Harlem Brundtland, defined sustainable development as "a path of human progress which meets the needs and aspirations of the present generation without compromising the ability of future generations to meet their needs" (as cited in Gamble & Weil, 2010, p. 214).

Since the 1980s there has been increased attention to the interconnection between environmental degradation, racism, and poverty. The term *environmental racism,* coined by Dr. Benjamin Chavis, refers to

> racial discrimination in environmental policymaking that results in the deliberate and disproportionate exposure of racial and ethnic minorities to toxic and hazardous environmental conditions. These conditions include residential proximity to toxic and hazardous waste sites, unsafe toxic emissions and pollutants in air, water and soil, public and private incinerators, landfills, and other prolonged harmful exposures that

have an adverse impact on the health and wellbeing of persons, families and communities. Environmental racism is also the systematic exclusion of minorities from participating in the regulatory bodies or agencies, forums, institutions, and organizations that determine remedies and enforcement of environmental laws, regulations and public policy. Environmental racism is a devastating manifestation of environmental injustice and inequality. (Chavis, 2009, para. 1)

While social work often promotes viewing the individual in a "person-in-environment" context, ironically there is a significant neglect in attention to the actual physical environment. Certainly, social workers have been involved in addressing issues related to housing and housing conditions and have also addressed sanitation and public health issues (as exemplified in the work of Hull House and other settlement workers). What has been missing is an understanding and prioritization of environmental issues—deforestation, environmental degradation, and climate change, to name just a few.

Think for a minute about how environmental issues affect the people you selected as the focus of your work.

The effort to encourage sustainable development does face interference from outside the communities that need environmental relief. There is a conservative backlash against the wealth of scientific data that compels us to see that the impact of humans on the biosphere is significant and that we are weakening humanity's chances for survival if we ignore this data. In addition, what is sometimes referred to as community development is often "code" for corporate development as a way to sustain a system of unregulated, unfettered capitalism with little or no attention to its real impact on the environment, and on the structural origins of poverty. Since the terms *sustainability* and *sustainable development* are now more commonplace, businesses often co-opt the language of "green" and "sustainable" as a catchy public relations and profit-enhancing maneuver. That being said, there are also many organizations devoted to a progressive vision of environmental justice and sustainability.

For example, in Huntington Park, California, a town southeast of downtown Los Angeles and home to 60,000 residents, 21% are living below the poverty line and a majority are Latino. Huntington Park is also a site of toxic emissions from local industries, exhaust from nearby heavily used highways, and a 110-acre "brownfield"—an expanse of vacant land. Using participatory strategies and a focus on both environmental and economic sustainability, the Communities for a Better Environment "Brown to Green Project" was formed to assess, safely clean up, and sustainably reuse brownfields and is an example of participatory sustainable planning and development.

Image 8.4   Guiding Steps for Community Organizers

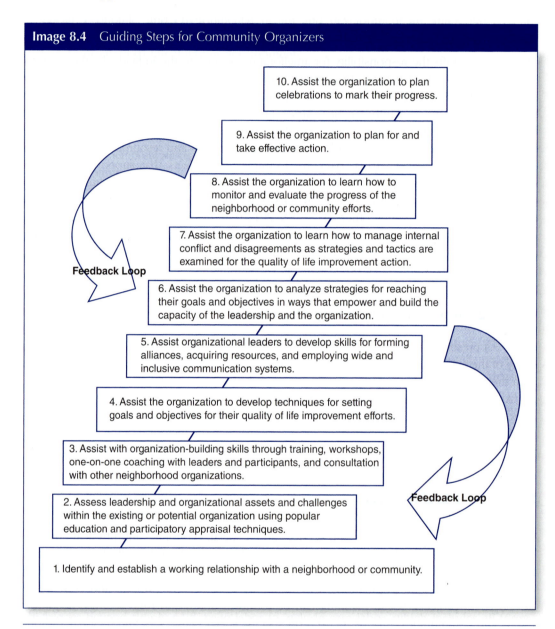

10. Assist the organization to plan celebrations to mark their progress.

9. Assist the organization to plan for and take effective action.

8. Assist the organization to learn how to monitor and evaluate the progress of the neighborhood or community efforts.

7. Assist the organization to learn how to manage internal conflict and disagreements as strategies and tactics are examined for the quality of life improvement action.

6. Assist the organization to analyze strategies for reaching their goals and objectives in ways that empower and build the capacity of the leadership and the organization.

5. Assist organizational leaders to develop skills for forming alliances, acquiring resources, and employing wide and inclusive communication systems.

4. Assist the organization to develop techniques for setting goals and objectives for their quality of life improvement efforts.

3. Assist with organization-building skills through training, workshops, one-on-one coaching with leaders and participants, and consultation with other neighborhood organizations.

2. Assess leadership and organizational assets and challenges within the existing or potential organization using popular education and participatory appraisal techniques.

1. Identify and establish a working relationship with a neighborhood or community.

Feedback Loop

Feedback Loop

Source: From *Community Practice Skills* by D. Gamble and M. Weil, p.127. Copyright © 2010 Columbia University Press. Reprinted with permission of the publisher.

- planning to address physical or infrastructure changes: such as building a new hospital or solar-powered electricity generators; and

- participatory neighborhood or community planning: driven by community members with the support of professional planners who serve in a consulting role.

Social planning can arise from community organizing efforts or from the efforts of a nonprofit, public, or even business organization whose purpose is to plan improvements to a community or to coordinate and develop services (such as the United Way, a local or regional aging council, or an international NGO, such as UNICEF). However, although social planning has potential for social change and participatory, anti-oppressive practice, it also has the potential to merely extend the existing social order and maintain dominant values and structures. It has often been the province of "experts" and is often done "to" and "for" people. Instead, the focus here is on the models and efforts at social planning that are participatory and strive to be "community driven."

Historical Development of Social Planning Practice

Historically, social planning developed through the work of Charity Organization Societies (COS), which focused on rational planning and service delivery. The assumption was that services needed to be rationed due to a greater need than available resources and thus efforts to provide effective and efficient services needed to be coordinated.

The COS developed into the Community Chests, which had two focal points: social planning and federated fund-raising, which is fund-raising through a primary organization that then allocates funding to member organizations. The Community Chests eventually became Health and Welfare Councils, which were instrumental in social planning and resource distribution. The significant need for resource development was the impetus for the development of United Way programs, which were formed to undertake both planning and fundraising, but ended up being primarily involved in community funding. More recently, the United Way is beginning to renew their focus on social planning (Gamble & Weil, 2010).

Planning Councils, originating from Health and Welfare Councils, typically engaged in one or more of the following activities:

- problem-solving planning, typically related to service development and implementation;
- inter-agency program development and coordination;
- agency administrative planning, typically via consultation with a specific agency to assist with agency-specific programming; and
- community policy planning.

There was a significant decrease in the number of planning councils between the late 1960s and 1980s due to increased social planning by the federal government during that time; the growth of specific needs-based organizations; expansion of the United Way; and the need for greater policy planning expertise.

Since the late 1980s, the resurgence of planning councils was marked by the incorporation of the National Association of Planning Councils (NAPC) in 1992 (National Association of Planning Councils, 2012a). It is interesting to note that the resurgence of planning councils occurred during a time of increased focus on community building, which was strongly influenced by the neoliberal political climate.

The National Association of Planning Councils (2012b) delineates the following values, strategies, and methods for planning councils if approached with a critical, participatory, and ground-up perspective:

- An openness to involvement of a wide constituency in decision making throughout its board and committee structures, supporting community sanction for council actions.
- A "big-picture" perspective on community needs, problems, and possibilities for improvements, generating a broad agenda of work.
- A plan of work based on an objective review of data and information from a wide variety of sources, such as census reports, sponsored task forces and coalitions, public surveys, focus groups, and consumers' views.
- Action based on consensus among those most concerned about a particular issue.
- A planned approach for involving those directly affected by critical problems and needs in organizational decisions—in other words, a strong emphasis on a "bottom-up" approach to planning.
- An effective working relationship with all sectors—voluntary, public, and private—to help promote effective community-wide action.
- A close connection at the neighborhood level to provide strong links for community-wide action and to support effective integration of helping resources where people are—in their homes, schools, churches, and neighborhoods.
- A recognition that, for the comprehensive community planning function to occur, organizations, such as councils at the community-wide level, are the critical link—the "intersection" between the neighborhoods and the state and nation.

Participatory Planning

The three primary objectives of participatory planning are to engage the individuals, groups, and communities most affected by the issues at hand; to promote power sharing; and to create a bottom-up process. Participatory planning can range from extremely limited participation (for example, providing a seat on an advisory or consulting board for a community member) to more inclusive, ranging from participation in the initial problem and needs assessment stage through the implementation and evaluation stages of a project.

Community participants can be incorporated into all stages and components of program development (Nicols, 2002, pp. 11–12).

- *Participatory input:* Potential program participants are identified and encouraged to provide input regarding their experiences.

- *Stakeholder check-in:* The program development team includes groups and individuals who may provide resources, mobilization, and support or create roadblocks to the program plan. Joint collaboration may evolve if the stakeholders are brought to the table early, although it may turn out that they are not willing to share power, create consensus models, or truly listen to the participants.
- *Definition of need and program purpose*: Community needs and program purpose are identified.
- *Resource and asset mapping:* Individual resources, program and organization resources, and community resources are identified.
- *Ecological environment assessment:* An ecosystems approach is used to assess micro, mezzo, exo, and macro contexts.
- *Program design or replication* (of an existing program): A new program is developed or decisions are made about how to replicate existing program.
- *Program theory:* All programs are ideally theoretically based, even if the theory is not explicitly stated.
- *Program goals:* Decisions are made regarding the explicit and implicit goals of the program.
- *Policy considerations:* The political environment and funding possibilities that influence the potential program are examined.
- *Evaluation plan*: Plans are made to evaluate program, such as when to evaluate, what tools to use, and what type of evaluation (process and/or outcome).

A common pitfall throughout the process relates to power sharing and stakeholders' opinions of the input of other participants. Anyone on a planning team—whether they are stakeholders (e.g., funders, community leaders, and other service providers), facilitators, or potential program participants—can discount the knowledge and wisdom of the other participants. However, typically the potential program participants hold less power in the planning process than anyone else. They are often representing a historically oppressed and vulnerable group, so their knowledge is more likely to be marginalized. Interestingly, the agency personnel organizing a program development team often become the mediators in power struggles (Nicols, 2002). Also, participatory planning often taps into the community for their feedback and lived experiences, yet does not pay them for their work, which brings up additional considerations related to the question of "who participates?"

> Imagine that a program is being developed for survivors of domestic violence. Is it likely that the most affected individuals have the time, support, resources, and feelings of safety that they need in order to volunteer hours of their time to community meetings? What are the ways that volunteers can be disempowered or exploited? How can power sharing be strengthened in a program development team?

STORIES FROM THE FIELD: ANTI-OPPRESSIVE PRACTICE WITH COMMUNITIES

1 Social Justice Lawyering: How Legal Services Can Fit Into a Broader Movement for Social Justice, by Gabriel Arkles & Anya Mukarji-Connolly   p. 325

In this community intervention story, Gabriel and Anya engage in conversation as they examine how their work in transformative justice fits into larger AOP work through community collaborations. As a staff member at the Sylvia Rivera Law Project, Gabriel mostly advocates for imprisoned trans, intersex, and gender nonconforming people around conditions of confinement. Anya represents homeless LGBTQ youth in New York City and discusses her work with FIERCE!, an organizing project in NYC serving LGBTQ youth of color.

2 When Urban Renewal Strikes Home, by Cheryl Distaso   p. 329

In this story, Cheryl Distaso describes her work with the Fort Collins Community Action Network (FCCAN), a social and environmental justice nonprofit. She shares an example of a small housing community that experienced forced relocation and her role in bringing together the community and mobilizing the people of the neighborhood to advocate for themselves.

3 Transformative Organizing through Collective Living: El Hormiguero in Pacoima, CA, by Marcos Zamora-Sánchez   p. 332

In this story, Marcos Zamora-Sánchez describes the formation of a collective living space in an urban community, El Hormiguero. It began with six individuals from various lifestyles joining in a journey to relearn and reclaim the traditional ways of their indigenous ancestors. Marcos's story exemplifies how community organizing at a micro level transforms those involved and how this collective reaches out to engage in the greater community where it is located.

4 Listening to Community Voices, by Daniel Moore   p. 335.

In this story, Daniel Moore describes how community canvassing with a specific political goal turned into a larger community action project. Daniel and his fellow organizers decided to seize on the momentum gained from mobilizing disenfranchised voters to create a platform for the community to voice their concerns. Building on a shared sense of hope in the community, they were able to work together to address policy within the local school system and support the families who were most affected by inequitable policies.

1

SOCIAL JUSTICE LAWYERING: HOW LEGAL SERVICES CAN FIT INTO A BROADER MOVEMENT FOR SOCIAL JUSTICE

GABRIEL ARKLES AND ANYA MUKARJI-CONNOLLY

Below, Gabriel and Anya discuss their experiences as attorneys working collaboratively within broader liberatory and anti-oppression movements.

Gabriel: The last three years that I worked at Sylvia Rivera Law Project (SRLP) as staff, I mostly advocated for imprisoned trans, intersex, and gender nonconforming people around conditions of confinement. That type of work is hard to do because of all of the horrific institutional violence that imprisoned people face all the time. Often, I think that a particular experience both is and isn't completely shocking. It should be shocking, but some of the most terrible things in the world can come to seem depressingly mundane given sufficient repetition. One of my clients said that she was sexually assaulted around 80% of the times she got searched and that she got searched several times a day. She shrugged and said, "You can't really do anything; you just got to get used to it."

I've learned a lot of things from a lot of people over the years about how to do this work and about why it matters. Organizers have taught me to talk about legal problems in a way that is not isolating and disempowering. Instead, I try to highlight to clients that a lot of people are getting hurt by the same rules, and I try to provide openings for involvement with others who are fighting to change those rules. Attorneys have shown me that information about the law is a kind of power and that sharing that information also shares power. Colleagues, co-workers, and comrades of all kinds have taught me about linking direct services with direct action and shown me that with vision amazing things are possible. Again and again, clients have shown me what fearless advocacy and commitment to community looks like, as they have stick up for each other everywhere from welfare offices to holding cells.

I believe that if we can support people in attaining the "small victories"—fewer months in prison, a name change, lower risk of rape, access to hormones, a filled tooth cavity, meds for diabetes or HIV, clothes consistent with their identity—they will have more resources available to them to keep doing work that is ultimately world-changing. Of course services alone are not enough, but I do think they can be an important part of social change work. So I try to value the "small victories"—the victories that are actually momentous in terms of harm reduction.

But, some of those battles shouldn't have to be won at all and they still leave our community members in awful situations. For example, I had a client who, like almost all imprisoned transgender women, was being held in a men's prison. She wasn't allowed to take a shower because the prison administrators thought having a woman in a shower with men might be "disruptive" and they wouldn't give her time to shower alone. She couldn't even wash in her cell because her sink was broken. After I wrote and called the superintendent of the prison a few times, my client finally got access to a shower and eventually they also fixed her sink. This client had suffered the harm of not having access to basic hygiene for a long time before I got involved so that was a huge victory! At the same time, why is it that this woman needed a lawyer to fight for her just to be able to take a shower? And how great a victory is it when she is still a captive of the state and endures violence every day?

One of my favorite parts of my job at SRLP was coordinating the Prisoner Advisory Committee, which is a group of incarcerated people who participate in and advise SRLP on our work. The members decided they wanted a newsletter, so I got to read all of their submissions of inspiring poetry, beautiful artwork, heartbreaking narratives, and visionary essays and put them into a format that would get the newsletter back into the prisons. I also got to work with incarcerated people when we were trying to push government agencies to make things less terrible for trans people in prison, educate lawyers on how to work with trans people in prisoners' rights cases, and share self-advocacy tips with other trans people in prison.

I learned a lot from members, who helped me and others to understand what changes would be helpful, what changes would do nothing, and what changes would actually make things worse. Those types of collaboration I think helped us all to feel less alone and more positive about the potential for change. Getting to do legal observing and other work for and with community organizers also helped me to feel connected and inspired.

Anya: It's an honor to be engaging in this conversation with you. I appreciate the opportunity to think through what it means to be a radical lawyer fighting for liberation from state oppression. In law school, we spent time reading the work of progressive lawyers and thinkers who paved the way for many of us and inspired us to study the law. The day to day work as attorneys, with the high volume of intense cases, can leave little room most days to consider how critical legal theories can be incorporated into our work. But, it is essential to take a step back every now and then to reevaluate our work, our relationship to the communities we work with and our role.

I believe I had just graduated from law school when I first met you, Gabriel. Immediately after law school, I received a fellowship to work as a lawyer at the Peter Cicchino Youth Project, a small law project representing homeless LGBTQ youth in NYC. In fact, we may have even shared the same work space, since SRLP was housed with this same law project very briefly at its inception. What an incredible way to begin working as a lawyer, surrounded by radical, queer attorneys who were challenging the way we thought about direct legal services. Those first few years were filled with so many questions; we were learning how to be lawyers and also questioning what it meant to be progressive lawyers connected to a larger movement for social justice. It was this connection to a greater movement that inspired me.

Like many lawyers, there were moments when the work also felt very disconnected from the larger social justice movement. As an attorney, I provided legal services to LGBTQ youth who were homeless or marginally housed. The vast majority of the youth I served were youth of color who had experienced violence or trauma at home or in the institutional settings where they were living. By the age of 18, most of these young people were living in shelters or on the streets and struggling each day just to find their next meal. Most of the youth I worked with were not in school and spent their days trying to access services to survive. Local and state laws fall short of guaranteeing those in need with adequate housing, a source of income, health care and education, all which are necessary not merely for survival, but to live with dignity. And yet my work many times focused on survival—working to ensure that these young people were not illegally denied foster care services, shelter, public assistance, health care and other desperately needed services. For many trans youth, survival meant having government-issued identification that matched their identity. In a highly policed city like New York, youth need ID just to enter most buildings. I advocated on behalf of individual youth and when necessary, engaged in systemic reform efforts to ensure that these systems were safe and accessible to homeless LGBTQ youth.

Yet there is always this tension that exists because we are often working for individual goals within a broader, unjust system. The system itself is often the problem. One example is advocacy work in the juvenile justice system. It operates to punish and rehabilitate youth who have committed crimes. As an advocate, I have worked to make these facilities safer for LGBTQ youth. However, I believe this system is inherently violent and punitive. And yet, so many marginalized youth have to be involved in this system and efforts to protect them are critical.

The bulk of my day-to-day work was fighting for the rights of LGBTQ youth to have a safe place to sleep and a source of income. The legal system is not well equipped to handle the realities of homeless and low-income people of color, especially youth. When we saw patterns of discrimination or mistreatment, we considered legal action, but often these issues were more effectively addressed through advocacy or education. The realities of pursuing a lawsuit were challenging for homeless youth since most of the youth I worked with did not have a regular address or phone access and were living very transient lives. At times I worried that the legal process felt too alienating for the young people I worked with. Advocating within the legal system also required a re-victimization of these young people. The legal system pathologizes low-income LGBTQ youth, requiring them to emphasize a physical impairment, mental health diagnoses, and traumatic experiences in order to access services and benefits. While the end goal can be empowering, the process is often a disempowering one. It maintains a system of inequality while benefiting those already in positions of power. It's no wonder then we keep asking ourselves how is it that we can responsibly navigate this unjust system for our clients' advantage without compromising our contribution to the fight for liberation.

Ultimately, change through litigation is slow and often unfulfilling. Even a successful lawsuit requires enforcement. Defendants don't always comply with court orders. Partly for these reasons, I focused a lot of my efforts on working in coalitions to try and change the culture and the understanding within the local systems that most impacted my clients' lives. As lawyers, we went into shelters and drop-in centers where youth sought other services and offered them legal assistance. Through our legal services we were able to see patterns of discrimination and used our clients' experiences to engage in systemic advocacy and policy change efforts. But, over time we realized that we were using our own personal and professional privilege to interpret these problems and to try and resolve them. Rarely were youth involved in the problem solving.

Some of my most important lessons were learned while working with FIERCE!, an organizing project in New York City designed to serve LGBTQ youth of color. In 2000, FIERCE! launched its Save Our Space campaign to challenge the displacement and criminalization of LGBTQ youth of color from the West Village. The West Village is the community where the modern LGBTQ movement was born in response to police repression and where homeless and LGBTQ youth of color gather today. As this neighborhood gentrified, the community and police intolerance for youth of color increased. The youth were targeted for "quality of life" offenses, such as turnstile jumping, loitering for the purposes of prostitution or sex work, noise violations, and things like that—minor crimes that have historically targeted the poor, homeless and people of color in many urban communities. In fact, this neighborhood in New York was the testing grounds for many of the current quality of life policies that we have on the books today.

The LGBTQ youth of color in this community were considered outsiders, despite having strong roots in the community. But these young people were not property owners and were not considered valuable stakeholders. Decisions affecting their ability to access public space were being made without their input. In response, the youth organized a multi-year campaign to gain recognition and a stake in decisions made by the community that directly affected their lives. I recall some of those early community board meetings and was shocked at the blatant racism and classism that was shared by members of the local community. But, the youth stood strong and persisted. After all, their lives and homes were at stake. And over time, the community of LGBTQ youth of color has achieved incredible victories. They were recognized as a stakeholder in the neighborhood and had the ear of many of the local decision makers. The youth, through sustained organizing efforts, had gained a level of political power that they had been previously been denied.

As lawyers, we did not set the campaign priorities and we did not create the strategies on our own. We used our privilege to support the campaign in ways that did not co-opt the organizing efforts. We conducted legal research, secured meetings with local officials and provided Know Your Rights trainings for youth and youth service providers who were being targeted by the police. This was a strong lesson for me in the power of community organizing and supportive role that lawyers can play in these efforts.

Internally in our law project, we began to discuss the absence of low-income and homeless LGBTQ youth in our advocacy work. Involvement in the criminal (in)justice system was by far the most common legal issue these young people faced on a daily basis. As low-income and homeless LGBTQ youth of color, nearly all of the young people I worked with were targeted by the police. They were targeted for their gender expression, engaging in sex work, and jumping subway turn-stiles. Their schools and shelters and public assistance offices are all heavily policed. Youth often asked us what their rights were when they encountered the police on the street. Many of the youth were involved in sex work and had formed informal networks in order to share safety information and to support one another.

As lawyers we were providing advice regarding these issues to individual young people through our legal clinics, but we knew that this information would be more valuable when more young people could access it and could share with their peers. We also knew that young people were hungry to be a part of broader advocacy efforts to change the systems that impacted their daily lives. In order to participate, they needed to be compensated and supported. And this is how our youth development project, "Streetwise and Safe," was born. Working with lawyers who shared their knowledge and understanding of the criminal legal system, an inaugural group of LGBTQ youth of color studied the information and worked to collect it in a format that they believed would be most useful to their peers. Over the course of a few months, these young people created a media project that was used as a Know-Your-Rights tool for other LGBTQ youth to learn about their rights during street encounters with the police.

1. What are some of the community organizing tactics that Gabriel and Anya mention in their story?

2. What are some of the intersecting issues that required collaborative approaches?

2

WHEN URBAN RENEWAL STRIKES HOME

CHERYL DISTASO

"I want a flower on my cheek, Say-wo!"

Emma, not yet 3, pushed an index finger, muddy from playing in her yard, onto the precise spot on her chubby cheek where she insisted I paint a flower. With her other hand, she very diligently pointed to each color she determined I should use from a face painting kit, which I had in my car as a stroke of luck, on the first of many visits to her home. She was, fortunately for me, more interested in process than product, and quite forgiving of my inept artistic skills. Looking at the creation in the bathroom mirror became part of our ritual, and when she nodded approvingly at what was, in reality, barely recognizably a flower, I knew I had a friend for life.

Emma is one of seven children who lived on Grape Street in Fort Collins, Colorado. I first met her, her family, and her community on a brisk October day in 2008. The previous spring, before I met Emma or her neighbors, I expressed concern to Fort Collins City Council members about what might become of the tenants in what I only knew to be a small mobile home park, slated to be demolished for a mega-shopping center. I was told that the residents were transient single men, typically renting there for only a few weeks, who were satisfied with the relocation assistance ($2,000 per household) offered to them by the City of Fort Collins and the developer. Having talked to no one who actually met the neighbors directly, I decided to go out to the neighborhood, along with a volunteer from the Fort Collins Community Action Network (FCCAN), a social and environmental justice nonprofit, where I work as a coordinator.

The first thing that caught my eye when we pulled onto the dusty dirt road on that autumn day was a tire swing hanging from a branch of a large elm tree in a fenced yard. My eyes followed the trunk of the tree to the ground, where a bright yellow pedal car was parked among other toys. Halloween decorations playfully embellished the porch. This was a neighborhood of families.

After we introduced ourselves, the neighbors poured out their stories. The landlord and owner of the mobile home park, Stan Hoover, had just given them 30-days' notice to move that morning. Emma's father, Jack, shared concerns about finding a new home for his family, changing schools for his children, and finding money to move, all on short notice in a city lacking in affordable housing. I asked them if Hoover had informed them of the financial assistance. He had not. I suggested that I learn specifics about their relocation package, and that we meet again later that week.

Although there was confusion about timelines and details, the City did confirm with me that each household would be compensated $2,000—half to come from the city and half to come from the developer. I told the neighbors everything I learned, including how the money would be distributed and who they could contact at the City. We began to meet regularly at Grape Street to discuss rental possibilities and to brainstorm different solutions.

The 24 neighbors that made up Emma's neighborhood ranged in age from 3 months to 60 years old. They would have put our local co-housing communities to shame because of their

3

TRANSFORMATIVE ORGANIZING THROUGH COLLECTIVE LIVING: EL HORMIGUERO IN PACOIMA, CA

MARCOS ZAMORA-SÁNCHEZ

Our collective goal began with an idea. Our idea was to create and live in a space that embodies the world we want to live in. The intention was to build in the community of Pacoima, California, located in the San Fernando Valley, simply because some of us grew up and worked in the area in various capacities.

Pacoima is no paradise, no hotbed of community organizing. It is a forgotten community that is part of the City of Los Angeles. We are surrounded by three freeways: I-5, the 210, and the 118. Most of the city's trash comes to Pacoima; we have three active landfills and thirteen are believed to be around the area. There are roughly 1,000 registered auto dismantlers in Pacoima and the near neighborhood of Sun Valley that emit toxins for our community to breathe. Pacoima also has an airport (ironically called Whiteman!) even though none of the residents in the area own an airplane to park at the airport. Yet, the community has to inhale the fuel toxins emitted by the planes. Because of the industries and toxins located in the area, Pacoima is considered a "toxic hot spot" in the City Of Los Angeles (Liberty Hill Foundation, 2013).

At this point, even considering the many atrocities occurring throughout the world, we understood that it would be best to use our energies in creating a new world rather than attempting to "fix" the one we already live in. It was an idea many of us already shared, but one that only a few can see flourish in everyday practice. Implementation of this idea is often limited and obstructed by social and popular media and those who own them. To begin with, we asked ourselves, "What is autonomy? What is collectivity? What is mutual aid? What does living with dignity look like? What is sustainability?" It looks like this: Six individuals from various lifestyles joined in a journey to relearn and reclaim the traditional ways of our ancestors in the urban community setting. We knew we wanted to live collectively because:

We want to live free of hate.

We want clean neighborhoods.

We need access to healthy food.

We want to depend on ourselves and each other.

We want to live with dignity.

We want a supportive household.

We have the right to live with dignity.

We want to learn and preserve our own music and art.

We have the right to defend our community.

We want to create something out of nothing.

And because "we didn't cross the borders, the borders crossed us."

We knew we had to reclaim and relearn the traditional ways our ancestors once lived, simply because they were wiped out by colonialism and hatred toward indigenous communities for the past 520 years. However, we knew there was not a formula that would result in reclaiming our ancestral ways of living. So we opted to emancipate together, as we knew we would have each other for support. We understood this would not be an easy process, but we all agreed to embark on this learning opportunity for the betterment of ourselves and our community.

Early on, we talked about our individual skills and pet peeves—what we were good at and what our challenges were. We knew that combining our skill-sets increases our ability to incorporate and strengthen what we've gained from the capitalistic arena and put it into practice. Some of the skills and areas of interest for our collective are transformative community organizing, education, gender and sexuality, collective living, arts and media, music, photography, talking circles, urban Zapatismo (a movement promoting community action to make a better world), and urban participatory planning, to name a few. Because all of the members have a university degree, graduate degree, or all but the degree, we expected our collective to offer a space that can question systems of power, privilege and oppression.

As a result, our collective aimed to integrate traditional indigenous customs like autonomy, mutuality, relationship building, and sustainability into our lives. Indigenous people work with what they have, and distribute labor that acknowledges people's roles in their community. Indigenous work follows non-hierarchical, consensus decision-making, an ideal structure to follow as we embarked on building a home. Understanding the idea that people have roles and responsibilities in their community, we actively articulated what exactly responsibilities meant, as well as work. Work for many of us is the notion of a nine to five job. Though some of the collective have nine to five's, coming home would include work as well.

El Hormiguero, which translates to Anthill in Spanish, was founded in 2011. We have opened our home as a community space. We have opted to relearn and unravel our role in community by adopting the concept of work done by the ant, bee, and spider: *el trabajo de hormiga, abeja, y araña*. The work of the ant is collective underground work. It is work that often goes without recognition, but it is essential work for the anthill's well-being: community building, collectivity, and mutual aid. Bees are pollen-carrying creatures, transferring the nectar they gather to other flowers, as they grow. The work of the bee keeps spreading information. The work of the spider is to build webs and networks.

Work from below: El Hormiguero acknowledges that community change occurs within the community. So unlike charitable and nonprofit organizations, which hire outsiders and often involve the community only by asking for tax-deductible donations, El Hormiguero is focused on building community and sharing roles and responsibilities. Our projects are self-sustaining, and people share their skills and knowledge to build community and not to win recognition. Our projects have included the skill sets of all collective members: Urban Regeneration, Queer Healing Oasis, The People's Musiq, The Berry, La Otra Berry, Bikesan@s del Valle Collective and Co-op, La Abeja, Art in Resistance. Our projects range from independent media productions to a lending library, music and art classes, gardening, and healing talking circles. El Hormiguero has also hosted several events, such as an opening ceremony for the space, an anniversary celebration, several community gatherings, and movie nights.

The philosophical ideas of building from the underground, germinating seeds and coalescing networks with other groups and ideas are the foundation of our work. El Hormiguero provides a meeting space to organizations that are doing similar work in the area. Organizations like the San Fernando Valley Dream Team and Young Warriors, a youth group in Pacoima, meet regularly at El Hormiguero. So the work at El Hormiguero not only illustrates *el trabajo de hormiga, abeja, y araña*, but is the epitome of building rapport in community. We believe that by opening our doors, we will essentially become autonomous and not depend on others to keep doing our work.

The nature of our projects makes it feel good to come home and work there. We know and understand the importance of creating a safe space and being each other's support system. However, there are times where people have felt unsafe in our space. Challenges, such as issues with security, open hours, under aged youth, and alcohol and drugs have risen and been addressed collectively at El Hormiguero. Transformative organizing lets us build on the idea of including all parties and understanding our autonomy when resolving the issue. We do not include the police, as in the past they have stripped us of our autonomy. Instead, we attempt to provide a space for people to share and provide suggestions to move forward. For example, alcohol and drugs are not allowed during El Hormiguero projects and events because our events are open to everyone, though we often have a beer for a personal birthday gathering.

Living at El Hormiguero has allowed me to really understand community and the idea of reclaiming space. We know we live in a collective space open to the community, but El Hormiguero is also our home. El Hormiguero is where we cry, scream, share, heal, learn, reclaim, relearn, teach, and much more. It is a space we continue to build, as we share our experience and encourage others to do the same.

In an attempt to also share our stories about our collective work and transformative organizing in Pacoima, we present at various local community spaces and have been asked to share at several universities as well. Sharing and being asked to share about our work is humbling. We are happy people recognize our work and want to attempt the same in their communities. Imagine if we all lived this way? What could the world be? What would our connections with other people look like?

As a professional macro-social worker, my skill-set has allowed me to aid in strengthening collectivity, mutual aid, and sustainability. The ability to understand people in their communities is one of the fundamentals of social work practice. As a social worker, I am privileged to assist in elaborating and building community assets by focusing on people's strengths and skills and not dwelling on weaknesses. Our work at El Hormiguero attests to the validity of ideas of reclaiming, relearning, and living in a dignified world that we create together.

1. What are some of the tools of community organizing being cultivated at El Hormiguero?

2. How does El Hormiguero's work within the microcosm of their collective represent transformative community organizing?

4

LISTENING TO COMMUNITY VOICES

DANIEL MOORE

In the months leading up to the November elections in 2012, I spent most of my time registering voters, organizing civic engagement clubs at our local community colleges and canvassing for the passage of Proposition 30, a bill that would temporarily raise income taxes on persons earning $250,000+ in order to stop deep cuts to education and provide billions in education funding. In California, the budget was seriously out of balance, and the education system was shouldering a disproportionate share of the pain. Classes were being cut, teachers were being laid off and tuition was increasing consistently and this was only what was happening at the college level. Nearly all public K-12 schools were still feeling the effects of the housing market meltdown that had affected the whole country. Foreclosed homes were not providing support to community schools.

The pain of austerity was being felt among almost all income brackets and races, but most disproportionately by the group of citizens that have the least amount of representation and who have the lowest voter turn-out rate: low-income Latino/a students and their families. In Ventura County, California, as in the rest of the country, the voter turnout rate for college age students, Spanish speaking citizens and low-income neighborhoods is significantly lower than for older (55-64), English speaking, middle-high income citizens. In effect, decisions being made for the entire county are based on a fraction of the population.

Having Proposition 30 on the ballot that fall provided CAUSE (Central Coast Alliance United for a Sustainable Economy) with a way to connect people to policy in a way that had been lacking for many years. We organized hundreds of volunteers every weekend to work phone banks and walk door to door in those communities that are ignored every election cycle. We spoke with thousands of families and registered nearly 700 new college age voters. High school and college students and their families and friends all came out to speak to their neighbors and peers about Proposition 30 and what it meant for their community. Through these efforts and others like them across the state Proposition 30 was successfully passed and tuition hikes and teacher layoffs were put on hold. This was a victory for college students and their families across the state, but there was something bigger and more powerful to be gleaned from the results of the elections.

In the November 2012 elections the United States saw an increase in the Latino vote like it had never seen in history and our community was part of that. Thousands of Latino voters mobilized in Ventura County, which is considered very conservative, and passed a progressive piece of legislation. The implications were enormous. Politically, the increase in Latino voters meant a potential shift in policy, specifically with regards to immigration reform, but at the grassroots level, where community organizing takes place, these results meant so much more. The election turnout combined with the prop 30 victory not only provided CAUSE with something we could point to in order to encourage engagement, it also gave people hope and courage to speak out against other injustices they face on a daily basis. People were beginning to sense their power and policy makers had to listen. As organizers we wanted to nurture this sense of power and hope and use the momentum from this victory to further advance the needs of the community. So CAUSE began the year 2013 by asking the community what they needed and what they would like to focus on to change. While immigration reform is an important issue for this country it was not necessarily on the top of the list for Ventura County residents. Instead, we heard about the need for affordable housing, healthier grocery stores, safe parks for the children, and school assistance to improve graduation rates of high school students. Many of these issues had been raised in the past and CAUSE was already working on some but now we had leverage.

In February 2013, I began working with the local high schools regarding their English Learner programs. Graduation rates for Spanish-speaking students had dropped significantly as of late and a recent ACLU investigation found that some of the schools in our district had some of the worst performance records. In California, English Learner programs, supported in part by government grants, assist students for whom English is a second language. This funding is intended to pay for extra classes, Special Programs counselors, college prep events and other supplemental assistance these students may need in order to be successful. As I began going to the schools and talking to counselors and administration I learned that, in fact, most of the "supplemental" programs and special programs counselor positions had been eliminated. Students were no longer receiving that extra help they needed and were only given the guidance services that were standard for English speaking students.

The parents of these students, meanwhile, were only minimally aware of the available services for their children and when they tried to get involved they became frustrated by the bureaucracy of the district administration. One counselor revealed that at the high school where he worked the office administrator did not speak Spanish. This meant that in a high school where most of the students identify as Hispanic, the first person a parent would come in contact with would be someone who probably would not be able to understand what the parent was saying. Needless to say, parents who speak only Spanish had enormous difficulty getting involved in their children's education.

At this point, there was enough external pressure on the school board from the passage of Prop 30, the report from the ACLU, and the newly proposed budget from the governor to appropriate funding to public schools based on the number of English Learners. It would be possible to effectively create change, so long as enough internal pressure was applied. This meant mobilizing the students, their parents and the special programs counselors to attend school board meetings and make their needs and desires known.

At one of the high schools a group of English Learner students wrote a letter to the Superintendent requesting the reestablishment of the English Learner Coordinating Council. The ELCC was originally established with the intent of improving the EL program in the district. It consisted of special programs counselors, administration, teaching staff and parent liaisons. One of its major accomplishments was the development of the "Master Plan," which was a comprehensive approach to improve the EL program that provided accountability for both the staff and the administration. Unfortunately, two years prior, with the hiring of a new Superintendent, the

ELCC was eliminated and the "Master Plan" never was enacted. The students delivered the letter at a school board meeting and a month later the reestablished ELCC had its first meeting. The "Master Plan" was again the main focus.

It was important from an organizing standpoint that the school board not see this as an isolated problem at the one high school from which the letter came. Therefore, we had to ensure that parents, counselors and students from all the schools in the district were aware of the ELCC meeting and were free to attend. The attendance of students, teachers, counselors and parents from the other high schools in the area, highlighted that this was a district-wide issue and that there were a lot of problems with the EL programs at the schools. The ELCC reestablished the tenets of the Master Plan, but the real work of ensuring that the EL programs at the schools were meeting the needs of the students and their families would be an ongoing process that would require consistent participation and vigilance from all parties. The Master Plan does not address all the issues with the EL programs and each high school individually will need to address some problems like hiring bilingual staff.

For these efforts to be effective, there needs to be open and fluid communication between the school, student and the parents, but how can that be established when the front office staff is unable to direct parents' calls due to their inability to speak Spanish? Many of these parents are monolingual Spanish speakers who want to be engaged, but are unsure about how to navigate the public school bureaucracy. In speaking with a parent liaison, who happened to also be the college prep event coordinator, I discovered that many parents call her directly when they have concerns about their child's education, instead of calling the school. The parent liaison/college prep event coordinator speaks Spanish and can direct parents to the right people. It may not seem like a huge barrier, but it is part of a systemic problem that is perpetually preventing people of color from advancing and engaging in society.

Community organizing in this capacity is about addressing oppression on multiple levels. Through our efforts to engage the Latino community by registering voters and providing information about policy that directly affects them we addressed national disenfranchisement on a macro level and oppression in the educational system on a mezzo level. In turn, those efforts provided us an opportunity to address oppression on a micro level with students and their families directly in their community. This is what drew me to community organizing work and is what is so effective about the AOP approach to social work. Oppression and discrimination occur on multiple levels and often concurrently. Likewise, the approach to address oppression and discrimination needs to be comprehensive and individualized. For example, all of the high schools in our district are failing to provide the necessary resources for students in their respective EL programs, but each student is going to need assistance in different ways and at different levels.

1. Apply the basic intervention strategies shown in Image 8.2 to Daniel's example. What form(s) of intervention modes and practice variables are being used?

2. What steps in Image 8.4, Guiding Steps for Community Organizers, do you believe may have been implemented in Daniel's example? Since the story ends as a work in progress, hypothesize next steps using the feedback loop.

DISCUSSION QUESTIONS

1. What are some of the common themes and characteristics found in each story?

2. What are some of the qualities that you believe would be helpful for a community organizer to possess?

3. What are some of the challenges you can imagine facing as a community organizer?

ACTIVITIES

Community Mapping

The purposes of this exercise are to:

- assess and evaluate your experiences as part of a community;
- tell a visual story of your experience;
- teach and learn about your community;
- provide a vision for the potential of your community; and
- identify resources and ways to create a desired community.

1. Either individually or as a group, identify a community you know well—for example, you could use your university/college.

2. What current elements consist in your community and what does your community look like? Identify:

   a. Assets and limitations

   b. Physical structures or place

   c. Demographic characteristics of all individuals

   d. Associations, clubs, organizations, alliances, and so on.

   e. Community links and collaborations

3. What does an ideal community setting look like?

   a. Strengths and resources

   b. Areas for improvement

4. What are the uses of a community mapping approach of teaching and learning about the community?

5. What are some of the strengths of this approach?

6. What are some of the challenges you might confront?

ADDITIONAL RESOURCES

Websites

Global Footprint Network (ecological impact tool) http://www.footprintnetwork.org/en/index.php/GFN/

Healthy City (California mapping tool) http://www.healthycity.org/

National Priorities Project http://nationalpriorities.org

Films

Bread & Roses (2000). K. Loach.

Building hope (2011). T. Pipkin.

Business as usual (1987). L. A. Barrett.

City of hope (1991). J. Sayles.

Erin Brockovich (2000). S. Soderbergh.

Freedom song (2000). P. A. Robinson.

Fundi: The story of Ella Baker (1981). J. Grant.

Harlan County U.S.A. (1976). B. Kopple.

Holding ground: The rebirth of Dudley Street (1996). M. Lipman & L. Mahan.

Hull House: The house that Jane built (1990). T. Ward.

Live nude girls unite! (2000). V. Funari & J. Query.

Man of iron (1981). A. Wajda.

Matewan (1987). J. Sayles.

Milagro beanfield war (1988). R. Redford.

Norma Rae (1979). M. Ritt.

Northeast passage: The inner city and the American dream (2011). S. Wolf & C. Swart.

One day longer (2000). A. Williams.

Roger and me (1989). M. Moore.

Silkwood (1983). M. Nichols.

Store wars: When Wal-Mart comes to town (2001). M. X. Peled.

The Democratic promise: Saul Alinsky and his legacy (1999). B. Hercules.

The fenceline (2009). B. Rasmussen.

The fight in the fields (1997). R. Tejada-Flores & R. Telles.

The Global Assembly Line (1986). L. Gray.

The long walk home (1990). R. Pearce.

The organizer (1963). M. Monicelli.

The take (2004). A. Lewis.

The times of Harvey Milk (2004). R. Epstein.

The uprising of '34 (1995). G. Stoney.

The Willmar 8 (1981). L. Grant.

This black soil: A story of resistance and rebirth (2004). T. Konechne.

We were here (2011). B. Weber & D. Weissman.

Books

Alinsky, S. (1989). *Rules for radicals*. New York: Vintage.

Crass, C. (2013). *Towards collective liberation: Anti-racist organizing, feminist praxis, and movement building strategy*. Oakland, CA: PM Press.

Horton, M. (2003). *The Myles Horton reader: Education for social change*. Memphis: University of Tennessee Press.

Miller, M. (2009). *A community organizer's tale: People and power in San Francisco*. Berkeley, CA: Heyday.

9

Anti-Oppressive
Policy Practice

In many ways, it is at the macro level that anti-oppressive practice comes full circle. While many practitioners focus their energies on micro or mezzo work, social change work requires that some practitioners examine the oppressive structures that perpetuate the social conditions that we aim to ameliorate or extinguish. Macro practice work can be reformist or transformational, but policy practice is more solidly positioned in reform work.

Similar to the history of social workers in community-based practice, the history of social workers in macro practice ebbs and flows in relation to larger social, political, and economic factors. As with community/mezzo practice, the periods of greater activity in macro practice were during periods of social unrest and greater economic and political upheaval—the Progressive Era (the early 1900s), the Depression and post-Depression era (the 1930s into the 1940s), and the Civil Rights era (the 1960s into the 1970s). During these times, social movement activity and legislation expanding the welfare state were particularly marked.

At the center of policy practice is social policy, which may be defined as strategy for collectively addressing social problems (Jansson, 2003, p. 11). Social policies may attempt to solve, ameliorate, or avoid problems. Often social welfare policies are considered to be a subset of social policies, focused specifically on regulating benefits for the needy (Jimenez, 2010, p. 18).

Social policies affect all of us every day, from the policies that structure our workplace to those that shape the healthcare, criminal justice, and education policies as well as a myriad of other organizations and institutions. Regardless of the focus of our work, social workers and the participants we work with both interact with policies. Thus, social workers must gain an understanding of policies, particularly policies that are specific to our field of practice, such as policies related to poverty, domestic violence, child welfare, mental health, and aging.

It is also important to distinguish between policy practice and policy advocacy (Jansson, 2003). Policy practice aims to change policies within legislative, community/local, and organizational settings by creating new policies, amending current policies, or defeating policy proposals. Policy advocacy is a subset of policy practice that centers on the needs and experiences of groups that have been oppressed and marginalized.

Coursework in the history of social problems, the development and implementation of policies, and policy analysis is one of the primary components of social work education and typically constitutes one or more separate educational courses. This section serves as a preliminary introduction to policy advocacy, highlighting areas of interest specific to anti-oppressive practice.

HISTORY OF SOCIAL WORKERS IN POLICY ADVOCACY

In her series of essays detailing the experiences and accomplishments that took place during twenty years at Hull House, Jane Addams (1990) describes "Pioneer Labor Legislation in Illinois." She begins by describing her first year at Hull House and how she and the other workers were introduced to the dangerous and oppressive working conditions in the local factories. As a result of their organizing efforts, Florence Kelley was appointed by the Illinois State Bureau of Labor to investigate conditions, particularly as they related to child labor.

These early investigations contributed to passage of the Factory Law in 1893, which prohibited child labor and limited women's working hours. Although the law was declared unconstitutional in 1895, the residents of Hull House continued to collaborate with and support labor organizations trying to secure legislation related to safety and fair labor practices. Addams outlines the tensions between labor unions and capitalists, touching on public attitudes toward strikes, gains made for labor over the years, and her dismay regarding violence that took place in a number of high-profile labor disputes, such as the Haymarket and Pullman Strikes. In closing, Addams states, "The residents in the Chicago Settlements became pioneer members in the American branch of the International League for Labor Legislation, because their neighborhood experiences had made them only too conscious of the dire need for protective legislation" (1990, p. 135).

Jeanette Rankin, a social worker, was elected the first woman in the U.S. Congress in 1917. She was an active suffragist who was also well-known for her courage to vote "no" regarding the declaration of war in 1917. After her first congressional term (she served again in 1941–43), she was active in the pacifist movement, joining the Women's International League for Peace and Freedom and lobbying for the National Council for the Prevention of War from 1929 to 1939. In addition, she worked as a field secretary for the National Consumers League and was an influential lobbyist when the Sheppard-Towner Act (a short-lived act that provided federally funded maternity and child care from 1921 to 1929) was passed (Women in Congress, n.d.).

The influence of social workers Frances Perkins and Harry Hopkins in the development of policies and programs of the New Deal is typically noted in social work policy and history texts. Lesser known is that in 1934, as the director of the Federal Emergency Relief Administration (FERA), Harry Hopkins hired 15 reporters, journalists, and novelists to document the stories of the individuals and families who were recipients of federal relief so that they could better assess the policies and programs that were part of FERA. Hopkins indicated he didn't want statistics; he wanted the stories of "ordinary citizens" (as cited in Burnier, 2008, p. 213).

While Frances Perkins has the distinction of being the first female to be appointed to a presidential cabinet as the Secretary of Labor from 1933 to 1945, she was one of approximately 30 women in the federal government during the development and implementation of the New Deal. Frances Perkins and Grace Abbott, who was active in government and had been nominated for the cabinet, but not confirmed, had both lived at Hull House and were influenced by the philosophies that were part of the settlement house movement. Other groups that influenced these administrators' perspectives were the National Consumers League, headed by Florence Kelly, and the Women's Trade Union League. Kelley's approach to mitigating social problems, which she shared with these administrators, was to "investigate, agitate, and legislate" (as cited in Burnier, 2008, p. 414).

Social work also played a prominent role in the policies encompassed by Lyndon B. Johnson's War on Poverty legislation. Whitney M. Young, Jr., a coauthor of the legislation, was a social worker, civil rights activist, past president of the National Urban League, founder of the Urban Coalition, and president of NASW from 1969–1971 (NASW, n.d. a.).

POLICY ADVOCACY TODAY

The social work tradition of involvement in policy advocacy continues today. In the current neoliberal and conservative environment, many are in fact calling for a strengthening of policy practice in social work and a stronger understanding of the impact of politics and economics on social work and social justice issues (Dempsey, 2008). Trends in public policy analyzed by the American Political Science Association from the mid-1970s to 2005 reveal that while direct spending to the elderly remains somewhat "vibrant," there is a continued retrenchment of social provision for disadvantaged non-elderly. Compared with other wealthy democracies, in the past 30 years this country has also seen little public policy change reflecting current economic risks, structural family changes, and declining civic participation (Dempsey, 2008).

Goals and Modes of Policy Practice

As we describe, policy practice is a rich field and encompasses a wide variety of activities. The aims of policy practice work include the following (Jansson, Dempsey, McCroskey, & Schneider, 2005, p. 320):

- Analyzing social problems, fashioning policy proposals, placing policies on decision makers' agendas, enacting (or blocking) policies, shaping implementation of policies, and evaluating policies;

- Influencing how resources are allotted in human services;
- Changing informal (unwritten) policies that influence policy formation and implementation, including the beliefs, prejudices, definitions, and perceptions of decision makers and policy implementers. Examples include legislators' or administrators' negative stereotypes of welfare recipients, views of line staff that make them insensitive to specific populations, and administrators' proclivity to create turf boundaries when clients need coordinated services (p. 320);
- Changing formal (written) policies, such as legislation, court rulings, administrative regulations, mission statements, and budgets; and
- Changing the cast of decision makers who make policies.

The four models of policy advocacy shown in Image 9.1 are based on these aims. Each model potentially addresses a number of the goals of policy advocacy, although the models tend to have a specific focus area. For example, a practitioner could work in social planning, a form of implementation advocacy, which could shape the implementation of policies, influence how resources are allocated, and influence informal policies, including the beliefs, prejudices, definitions, and perceptions of decision makers and policy implementers.

It is also important to note that legislative advocacy is currently the "default" model of policy practice, it is, in and of itself, too narrow to solve our large social problems. We also need to focus on electoral politics (a feature of the ballot-based model) by running for office and working to revitalize the political arena by supporting a greater variety of political parties

Image 9.1 Models of Policy Advocacy

Model	Goal	Means
Ballot-based advocacy	Changing the composition of government	Participating in political action committees, organizing campaigns, and creating or joining electoral coalitions
Legislative advocacy	Securing or blocking a specific piece of legislation	Establishing or participating in interest groups, community-based organizations, and professional associations
Analytic advocacy	Engaging in research and analysis of policies	Establishing or participating in think tanks, universities, and government agencies
Implementation advocacy	Increasing the effectiveness of programs and supporting the integration of policies and programs into social life	Engaging in social planning, legal monitoring, and activism in consumer-based organizations or community groups

Source: Adapted from Jansson, Dempsey, McCroskey, & Schneider, 2005.

and candidates (Dempsey, 2008). We can also help the people we work with become better equipped to engage politically. One way to do this is by opening up conversations about "political values, such as inclusion, participation, solidarity, and social justice and how to implement them without talking about Republicans or Democrats or Greens or Libertarians" (Dempsey, 2008, p. 103).

The Role of Think Tanks

Participation in think tanks is another historically underdeveloped area of practice for progressive social workers (Miller-Cribbs, Cagel, Natale, & Cummings, 2010), which falls into the analytic advocacy category or model. When think tanks were developed in the early to mid-1900s, they were typically nonpartisan, with the goal of conducting research and advocacy on a variety of issues, including social policy issues. Since the 1970s, there has been significant growth in partisan think tanks, particularly conservative think tanks. The social policy agendas for these conservative think tanks include (but are not limited to) the following categories:

- Anti-diversity—anti-LGBT, anti-feminism, anti-affirmative action, anti-multiculturalism and immigration
- Media/censorship—pro-government censorship of the arts, anti-pornography, and Internet restrictions
- Life/choice—anti-abortion, anti-euthanasia
- Civil and religious rights and liberties—gun rights, religious liberty, school prayer, school vouchers, and school choice
- Government reform—limited government, privatization of services, restrictive health care and welfare reform, social security reform, sex education reform, and anti-sex education
- Social issues—marriage incentives, domestic violence, and crime

Currently, some of the most influential conservative think tanks are the Heritage Foundation, American Enterprise Institute, Free Congress Research and Education Foundation, Cato Institute, and Citizens for a Sound Economy. These think tanks heavily fund research by conservative academics while at the same time proclaiming that conservative students are oppressed in university settings.

Conservative foundations contribute significant funding to these think tanks. In contrast, left-leaning organizations and individuals are more likely to contribute funds to improve social service delivery and infrastructure, leaving less money for progressive research and think tank activity. Liberal and moderate foundations attempt to avoid partisan implications in their work, while conservative foundations actively seek out researchers and organizations that popularize a conservative ideology. The conservative think tanks are also media savvy, flooding airwaves and social media with a repetition of simple messages. Thus, they become the "go to experts" on an issue (Miller-Cribbs et al., 2010; see also Lakoff, 2002).

While social workers were prominently involved in public policy development and analysis during the Progressive Era, the New Deal, and Lyndon Johnson's Great Society, more recently, the profession has contributed minimally, if at all, to the national political debate. To shift this dynamic, social workers must become part of the political dialogue again.

> At this critical point in history, complacency from progressive advocates is perhaps the greatest threat to advancing a socially, politically and economically just society. (Miller-Cribbs et al., p. 304)

Feminist Perspectives on Policy Advocacy

An additional element of analytic advocacy is the type of framework within which policy analysis occurs. Frameworks include such values as social equality, collectivity, interdependency, spirituality (from an Afrocentric perspective), and various political ideologies. Another common framework is gender neutrality, from which the bulk of policy analysis is presumed to arise. In reality, men traditionally dominated policy analysis and women dominated direct practice. However, there is a growing shift in this gender distribution of social workers, which has opened up space for the development of a feminist policy analysis framework.

Acknowledging the need for multiple feminist frameworks to encompass the variety of feminist perspectives, McPhail (2003) proposed an action-oriented model of analysis that can be embraced by most feminist perspectives. This model focuses on ending gender oppression of women and includes the following goals:

- centering women in the analysis;
- identifying the manner in which women and men are treated either the same or differently;
- uncovering gendered assumptions and stereotypes; and
- examining the ways that policy regulates women's lives.

In this model, a series of questions can be posed to prompt analysis of the gender implications embedded in a policy. Image 9.2 lists the types of questions to ask when examining the social control by the state or the market inherent in the policy. For example, we could pose a question that asks how the policy affects gender relationships among the state, the market, and the family: "Does the policy increase women's dependence upon the state or men?" (McPhail, 2003, p. 55).

This model posits crucial questions related to making women visible in policy analysis. However, we suggest that the examination also include an expanded understanding of gender

Image 9.2   Questions for Feminist Policy Analysis

1. How well does the policy reflect feminist values?

2. What is the policy's effect on gender-based state and market control?

3. How well does the policy account for multiple identities?

4. Does the policy further gender equality?

5. What special treatment or protection does the policy offer for the oppressed gender, namely women?

6. How well does the policy embody gender neutrality?

7. What is the gender-related context of the policy?

8. Is the language used in the formal policy gender-neutral?

9. Does the policy support gender equality in rights and responsibilities?

10. To what degree does the policy promise material and symbolic reform?

11. What sorts of role changes and role equity does the policy address?

12. How are power relationships addressed by the policy?

Source: Adapted from McPhail, 2003.

to avoid a simple dichotomous male/female analysis. For example, a question that looks at context by asking, "Are women clearly visible in the policy? Does the policy take into account the historical, legal, social, cultural, and political contexts of women's lives and lived experiences, both now and in the past?" (McPhail, 2003, p. 56) could be expanded to include individuals who identify as transgender.

BALLOT-BASED ADVOCACY

The policy advocacy arena is traditionally seen as the province of "experts," particularly in analytic, implementation, and legislative work. Ballot-based advocacy may appear to be more accessible to participants, yet it is interesting that thus far, there is limited research regarding whether and how social workers promote the political participation of their constituents. The communities and individuals specific to social workers' work are more likely to be disproportionately affected by social policies that can be misguided or Draconian, particularly at this time when we are deeply embedded in neoliberal policies and the continued devolution of social welfare policies in the United States.

One exception is a study based on a random sample of 3,000 "regular" NASW members (Rome, Hoechstetter, & Wolf-Branigin, 2010). The researchers examined the role of social workers in facilitating political participation. Overall, they found that relatively few social workers actively engage in conversations related to public policy and politics with their clients or participants. For example, only 22.1% of the social workers who were surveyed responded "often or always" to the statement "I inform my clients about public policy developments that are likely to affect them." Of those who responded affirmatively, social workers in nonprofit and public settings had higher rates of response than those working in private clinical practice. This finding could point to either social workers' lack of information about public policy or their belief that public policy is not relevant to the participants' needs and situations. Additionally, 75% of the respondents indicated that they either rarely or never "encouraged clients to participate in political marches, rallies, or demonstrations" and 63% rarely or never "encouraged clients to participate in community groups that seek to influence policy" (Rome, Hoechstetter, & Wolf-Branigin, 2010, p. 208.)

Based on study results, the researchers speculate that in addition to the possible lack of interest in or disconnect from public policy, social workers may also be uncertain about the ethics of discussing policy and politics with their constituents. Particularly on the part of clinical social workers, when answering open-ended questions, there was a tendency to view any discussion of policy and political action as an imposition of their views on their client. One social worker stated, "Because of the nature of psychotherapy, I believe it would be unethical and inappropriate for me in this role to engage in any political discussions with clients" (Rome, Hoechstetter, & Wolf-Branigin, 2010, p. 214). On the other hand, some of the respondents shared examples of ways that they did engage participants in dialogue about policy, which included encouraging media advocacy, supporting individuals to advocate for increased funding for programs, and including participants in lobbying efforts.

Running for local, state, and federal political office is another component of ballot-based advocacy. A survey of political beliefs, previous political participation, and motivations for running for political office identified 416 social workers who had run for a political office (Lane & Humphreys, 2011), which is more than twice the number identified in previous research. A majority of the social workers were recruited into candidacy by peers, elected officials, or nonelected political activists. The social workers who ran for office were concentrated in positions related to education, such as town boards of education, and positions related to health care and mental health. Study participants were asked to identify their political and community involvement prior to their first run for office, revealing a common commitment to voting, serving on nonprofit boards, and political campaigning for other candidates.

NASW supports ballot-based advocacy through its political action committee, Political Action for Candidate Election (PACE). This group works to mobilize social workers to vote, endorses candidates who support the policy agenda of NASW, and provides financial support to candidates. PACE also provides information regarding the voting records of U.S. Senators and Representatives and information on social workers elected to office (NASW, n.d. b.)

PARTICIPATORY POLICY ADVOCACY

Policy development, implementation, and evaluation, which are aspects of legislative and implementation advocacy, are more than ever driven by a top-down model that excludes the voices of the communities most affected by public policies. The mental health survivor/consumer movement and the movement to involve parents in child welfare policy decisions are two examples of efforts to shift this paradigm to engage participants more fully in the policy process.

The mental health survivor/consumer movement began to gain momentum in the early 1970s, influenced significantly by other social movement activity in the 1960s and early 1970s. Individuals and family members with experience in mental health diagnosis and treatment began to question the prevailing pattern of deferring to mental health professionals to develop and implement mental health policies. The National Mental Health Association (now Mental Health America) was created in 1901 as the National Committee for Mental Hygiene and traditionally had an overreliance on "expert" voices (MHA, 2012). In response, groups like the Oregon Insane Liberation Front, the National Association of Mental Patients, and the National Alliance on Mental Illness were founded in the 1970s and 1980s to prioritize consumer/survivor and family voices.

These advocacy groups varied in focus and ideology, which manifested in a variety of disagreements among activists. They debated whether the focus should be on individual treatment through a peer approach or whether the focus should be policy advocacy. Additional questions were raised about whether the medical model should be embraced or rejected; whether groups should consist solely of consumers/survivors or include allies; and whether consumer/survivor advocates should be paid for their work as consultants or peer support (Tomes, 2006).

The role of consumers/survivors in the development and implementation of mental health policy has increased since the 1970s. In 1978, they played a small role when the Community Support Program (CSP) of the National Institute of Mental Health was tasked with examining issues related to deinstitutionalization and consumer/survivor activists were invited to share feedback during annual CSP "Learning Conferences." In 1984, the CSP incorporated a more participant friendly focus in their mission by highlighting "self-determination" and "consumer empowerment." In 1986, the State Comprehensive Mental Health Plan Act and the 1992 creation of the Substance Abuse and Mental Health Services Administration required that planning councils responsible for policy planning ensure equal representation of consumer/survivors and family members to receive federal funding. Consumer/survivors were also incorporated into outcome research and as peer service providers in local and state mental health agencies. While there continue to be differences in the movement, particularly regarding positions on involuntary treatment and the more recent funding of consumer groups by pharmaceutical companies, there is a consensus that self-determination is paramount for consumer/survivor advocacy (Tomes, 2006).

Similarly, until recently, parent participation in child welfare policy has been almost non-existent. Parents are often stigmatized and seen as the problem rather than potentially part of the solution, and most often are relegated to passive roles as recipients of services driven by state and federal child welfare policies. However, given increased emphasis on accountability, standards, and competency in the child welfare system, and an increased recognition of the systemic factors that contribute to child neglect (such as poverty, drug abuse, domestic violence, discrimination, and lack of child care), there is a subtle shift in attitudes toward parents. Additionally, the Adoption and Safe Families Act passed in 1997 and other child protection laws now include parents as one of the "consumer" groups who should be included in state planning and consultation. Citizen Review Panels are also mandated to evaluate state and local child welfare agencies and are required to include community representation, although biological parents are typically not chosen to participate on these panels (Mizrahi, Humphreys, & Torres, 2009).

An example of parent participation at the local level is evident in the work of the Child Welfare Organizing Project (CWOP). As an advocacy group for parents involved with the NYC child welfare system, CWOP staff and board members are primarily parents who have successfully navigated the child welfare system and reunited with their children. Some of their policy successes include mandated parental participation on citizen review boards and on case conference teams. Their work also influenced the development of a Parent Advisory Council that meets with the NYC Commissioner of the Administration for Children's Services and influenced legislation that requires agencies to provide contract services for child welfare to hire parent advocates (Child Welfare Organizing Project [CWOP], n.d.; Mizrahi, Humphreys, & Torres, 2009).

Policy advocacy has a long history in social work, dating back to the Settlement House Movement. While there has been a trend toward provision of direct social work services over the years, there continues to be a significant need for social workers to bring a critical, anti-oppressive lens to the arena of social welfare policy. Regardless of the focus of an individual's social work practice, policies—at the micro, mezzo, and macro levels—have a profound impact on the lives of all of the social workers and their participants. In fact, social work professionals and academics describe social work as a "policy-based profession" (Popple & Leighninger, 2011, p. 12). To truly contextualize our work and develop our understanding of the intersecting nature of social issues, it is important to not only analyze the policy system, but also to bring our critical analysis to the policy advocacy arena in hopes of creating longer term systemic change.

STORIES FROM THE FIELD: ANTI-OPPRESSIVE POLICY PRACTICE

1 The Human Right to Housing, by Deborah Burton and Steve Diaz   p. 352

In this policy practice story, Debbie and Steve, longtime members and community organizers for Los Angeles Community Action Network (LA CAN), recount how they became involved in LA CAN. They detail the policy advocacy work that they participate in regarding housing policies in downtown Los Angeles, California.

2 Bursting My Privilege Bubble Through Policy Advocacy, by Natasha Surendranath   p. 355

Natasha describes how during her senior year internship some of her assumptions and fears about the Skid Row community were confronted through her work with LA CAN. She highlights a few projects that she was able to work with during her placement and her observations about how the organization is perceived within the community.

3 Summer of Safety, by Heidi Grove and Juston Cooper   p. 358

Heidi and JC recount policy/program advocacy led by the youth at The Youth Connection (TYC) during an extremely violent summer in Denver, Colorado. One of their clients was killed in a drive-by shooting. Heidi and JC describe how the youth from TYC became engaged in program development with Colorado State Senator Mike Johnston during this Summer of Safety.

4 Creating Policy and Programming With Input From Affected Stakeholders, by Leslie Colwell   p. 361

This story about the Summer of Safety in Denver, Colorado, is written from the perspective of Leslie, the Legislative Director. She also recounts her experience of working with the disconnected youth from The Youth Connection. Leslie discusses how they addressed gang violence by involving the youth in planning community activities for young people in order to deter them from participating in violence.

1

THE HUMAN RIGHT TO HOUSING

DEBORAH BURTON AND STEVE DIAZ

The mission of the Los Angeles Community Action Network (LA CAN) is to help people dealing with poverty to create and discover opportunities. LA CAN is a vehicle to ensure they have voice and power in the decisions that are directly affecting them. We focus on community organizing and leadership development as core strategies for promoting and defending human rights and contributing to long-term social change.

Our membership includes homeless people and extremely low-income people living primarily in Downtown and South Los Angeles. We have a special focus on the Central City East region of downtown Los Angeles, commonly known as Skid Row, which is home to about 15,000 homeless and extremely low-income people.

Both of us lived in Skid Row for many years. We joined LA CAN because of the pressing issues we were facing related to gentrification and displacement, as well as hunger and food access. We both also moved through LA CAN's leadership development process and after becoming members, engaged in training opportunities. Eventually we became full-time community organizers within our organization. The following dialogue highlights our contributions to LA CAN's human right to housing project and how this low-income resident-led work challenges multiple forms of oppression and, at the same time, helps people heal from the effects of oppression.

Steve: I joined LA CAN in 2003. I was living in the Frontier Hotel with my family and it was targeted by the City and the owner for a loft conversion—including an unfair crackdown by law enforcement that labeled us all as criminals. I came to a tenant rights workshop and never left the organization. I was drawn to our organizing model—one that created opportunities for people like me not just to be involved as volunteer members, but also to get education and training to become organizers and contribute more to the long-term social justice struggle.

Debbie: I joined LA CAN in 2004 when my neighbor, who was already a member, knocked on my door and asked me to go to Sacramento for Hunger Action Day. She started talking to me about food justice and I quickly realized that our community was in great need of healthy food sources. This issue went hand in hand with our housing issues. I went to Sacramento and have been involved with LA CAN ever since.

Steve: The entire organization is reflective of people like myself and Debbie. Other leaders that have emerged from our membership make up the majority of every decision-making body that we have: staff, Board of Directors, and project committees. Before LA CAN, our community had recognized "leaders" who were not truly representative of us as low-income residents but who spoke on our behalf anyway. We have changed all that.

Debbie: We have both been working on our human right to housing project for many years. Housing is a fundamental right—not a privilege—and all rights are interrelated, interdependent, and indivisible. Therefore we promote and defend the human right to housing, in conjunction with our interrelated projects focused on civil rights, healthy food access, women's rights, and equitable development.

Steve: Human rights principles require participation and inclusion of impacted residents. Our human right to housing project ensures that opportunities for meaningful participation in all aspects of our work are made available to directly impacted residents. LA CAN's organizing model includes a decision making process that ensures impacted people are making every decision that directly impacts their lives and communities. The model also places deep emphasis on leadership development activities, which develop the political analysis and practical skills of impacted persons.

Debbie: We believe these principles have led to our successes. When the City passed a redevelopment plan that called for the elimination of almost 4,000 extremely low-income homes in Downtown LA and included very few direct benefits for the low-income residents that would have remained in the community, we were one of the only organizations to say, "No way."

Steve: LA CAN and our partner organizations challenged these plans with a lawsuit. Then we started going door to door, every day, to build up a strong membership of hundreds of extremely low-income residential hotel tenants—those who were directly targeted for displacement. This work culminated in the strongest housing preservation ordinance in LA's history. In 2008, the City of Los Angeles enacted a Residential Hotel Preservation Ordinance, permanently preserving more than 15,000 homes for LA's lowest income tenants across the City with more than 8,000 of those homes located in the Downtown community.

Debbie: While we worked on the hotel ordinance, we fought all kinds of other battles as they arose. We ended "the 28-day shuffle," the practice of moving people in and out of their homes every 28 days. The 28-day shuffle was identified and named by LA CAN members during their outreach and recruitment efforts. It had been used for decades in Downtown LA to prevent people from establishing full tenant rights. We also started a community-based weekly legal clinic that has expanded every year and is run by community residents in partnership with Legal Aid Foundation of Los Angeles.

Steve: After this set of neighborhood housing campaigns and victories, LA CAN helped form the Los Angeles Human Right to Housing Collective in 2009. The Collective brings together similar neighborhood-based organizations building indigenous leadership and organizing for systemic changes. We have a membership base in nine low-income neighborhoods as well as 8 of the 15 public housing communities across the City. Members work on neighborhood- or issue-based committees, with all of the committees working in solidarity across issues and geography.

Debbie: The Collective's work has led to many victories as well, such as preventing the privatization of public housing in LA—at least temporarily. But, it has also helped us build bridges between communities, across race and language barriers, and learn about people and neighborhoods that are struggling just like us. Because of this work, I was invited as the LA CAN representative to speak at the 2010 United Nations' Universal Periodic Review hearings in Geneva—at 59 years old, the first time I had ever been out of the country. I was proud to represent our Collective work, and was motivated to tell these world human rights leaders that the U.S. has a lot of human rights violations to address in their own backyard. This was one of the things I said:

> We are building power. We will make progress. We can win. But, the task is huge and we need the international community to join us in pressuring the U.S. to do better within our country and throughout the world.

Steve: The real challenge is that despite all of our hard work and success, the "powers that be" are promoting gentrification in LA, and the removal and/or punishment of poor people and people of color, every day. Neo-liberalism is thriving—as we see with shrinking wages and benefits and increased privatization of housing, schools, health care, and other human needs. Because of this trend, LA CAN is always working to expand and improve community organizing efforts to fight the national and local forces that do not support our people. And our communities are responding—we are growing in numbers and power every day.

1. How do Debbie and Steve locate themselves in the work that they do?

2. What types of policy practice are described here (using the model depicted in Image 9.1)?

3. How do you see the work of LA CAN as fitting into anti-oppressive practice work?

2

BURSTING MY PRIVILEGE BUBBLE THROUGH POLICY ADVOCACY

NATASHA SURENDRANATH

When I went for my interview for an internship at Los Angeles Community Action Network (LA CAN), I was nervous—not because I didn't think I'd get the position, but because I had my own preconceived ideas about the community. When the opportunity to intern there was presented to me, I was immediately drawn to it. This was my chance to work with a community that has been extremely stigmatized. Numerous stereotypes often come to mind when we think of people who are homeless. Homelessness is often assumed to be a result of laziness, personal choice, or drug and alcohol addictions—assumptions I also held. I was afraid of people who were homeless, particularly the residents of Skid Row in downtown Los Angeles. Even though I had worked with high risk, homeless young adults the year before, I knew this experience would be completely different.

Due to gentrification, there has been an increase in homelessness on the streets of downtown Los Angeles. Many of LA's homeless population reside in a section called Skid Row, which is where LA CAN is also located. The sidewalks of Skid Row are packed with tents, shopping carts, and trash. The people who live there are struggling due to poverty, drug issues, and mental health issues. Skid Row has always been painted in a dark light, with people warning that the streets are filthy, the people there are dangerous, and you should never walk through there alone, day or night.

I felt like an outsider when I started at LA CAN because of my privileged upbringing. As part of an upper middle class family, I never had to worry about where I would be sleeping, when or where my next meal would come, and whether I could access health care. I was sent to private schools until I finished high school, and during that time I was extremely sheltered from life outside this privileged bubble. I felt very disconnected from the issues and the people who had no choice but to put up with them.

As an outsider, I was unaware of the numerous problems the community was facing. The stereotypes surrounding this group of individuals were wrong; there was so much more to their homelessness. Through my policy advocacy work I discovered how systemic oppression and discriminatory policies play out in the lives of individual Skid Row residents and how important it is to always look at the big picture.

At LA CAN, I was involved with several groups, each of which addressed a different community concern in Skid Row. For example, gentrification is a pressing issue. Investors were coming into the community and buying the hotels and apartments where community members lived. The rent would be raised, and residents could no longer afford to live there. Residents were evicted from their homes and forced to find another place to live. Given the lack of affordable housing, many of the former residents either used the resources from homeless shelters or actually started living on the streets of Skid Row.

3

SUMMER OF SAFETY

HEIDI GROVE AND JUSTON COOPER (JC)

Heidi: In Denver, Colorado, we started off with a pretty violent summer in 2013. We actually lost one of our young people in May, right before Memorial Day weekend. We were called to the scene when he was killed in a drive by shooting. After the shooting, JC and I went to a meeting where the participants had come up with a list of activities to keep young people off the street. JC and I kind of looked at each other at the meeting and kind of challenged the other people, asking if they had asked any young people what they wanted. Some of the lists that they had created included things like "yoga in the park." Our population don't want to do yoga in the park.

So we scheduled a private meeting with California State Senator Mike Johnston. He was talking with us about what we do need to do to curb the violence. He talked about the calendar they had put together with all the different activities. Our response consisted of two questions: "What conversations are we not having?" and "Who is not at the table?" Senator Johnston sat back and thought about the questions and said, "I don't know, who is not at the table?" We told him that the young people he was trying to serve were not at the table. We asked him, "If you are not incorporating and including them, how are you going to impact them and involve them in participating? If they're not going to do yoga in the park, then how are you going to keep them out of the streets?"

So we challenged Senator Johnston and he invited a group of young people to the state capital to meet with him privately in chambers to ask them their opinion. We took a group of about eight young people to the capitol the day after the Fourth of July (see Image 9.3). He brought a calendar of the planned youth activities to the meeting with him and asked the young people to look at it. This is, verbatim, what they said: "Sir, we mean no disrespect, but this list is crap." He just kind of looked at them and threw the list over his shoulder and said, "What do you guys want?"

So through that encounter we created what we titled the Summer of Safety, which was four events:

- A graffiti arts class, which Senator Johnston housed at his office;
- A flag football tournament, housed at Manual high school, one of our local high schools;
- An open mike night held at Civic Center Park; and
- A fishing trip, which the young people did, even though a lot of people don't expect them to want to go fishing.

The Senator sponsored every one of those events, and he allowed the young people to design them. They designed the flyers promoting those events and distributed 1,300 of them in 5 days. So the young people really made the events their events.

Image 9.3 Youth Representatives From TYC Meet With Colorado State Senator Mike Johnston to Discuss Youth Policy

JC: It was very exciting. What TYC staff found in our preplanning for the meeting with Senator Johnston was that we were really taking a policy advocacy approach. So in our staff meetings we discussed what some of the gaps were in the Senator's approach to bridging policy with a youth voice. We found that one of the critical components to youth policy reform was having the youth voice at the table. This was policy advocacy. Heidi and I were able to truly advocate for having the youth voice involved from the beginning of the project to the actual implementation phase.

As it relates to social justice, we really wanted to be able to mobilize and build an advocacy coalition for true policy reform. Senator Johnson agreed, based on our philosophical approach, to really look at what the next steps might be in meeting with the young people. He and his staff wanted to play an instrumental role in mobilizing young people, getting them to meet with the Senator, talk about the issues, and truly talk about how young people wanted programs to be implemented from the grassroots level. We hoped that Senator Johnston and Mayor Hancock would incorporate the Summer of Safety activities into some kind of legislative reform.

This experience encouraged us to look at how you mobilize grassroots efforts to truly impact policy. We were able to mobilize the youth in this case because of the level of violence that had happened and their personal relationship to it. We predicated our work with them on relationship; that was the common thread, what brought them all to the table.

In some ways, our ability to mobilize the young people also related to our understanding of trauma. That is one reason the work of TYC is so important. We were able to help the youth draw the correlation between the trauma that they had all experienced and their background, their experiences with rival gangs. This fact—that they had all experienced the same level of trauma—was part of the focus group experience as we mobilized their efforts to go speak with the senator.

Another thing we were able to do collectively was really important: being able to understand the importance behind their advocacy as a collective message. The senator was very excited to see that we had prepped them to understand why they were doing what they were doing and why it was important for them to advocate on young people's behalf. We didn't want it to become just a "vent" session. We were very proud of our young people in that meeting with their ability to advocate very strategically. They had a wholehearted understanding that it is important for government to look at how in the future they will work on policy and programs to prevent violence in the community. From that, the young people who attended the meeting all took a stand and accepted an individual accountability and responsibility to say, "I'm going to take this back to my community and push this as a peer leader."

Heidi: And we were so proud of them. They ran the meeting with the senator. They point blank said, "Honestly, the first thing you cut when the budgets are bad is programs for us, and then you wonder why young people are out in the streets now." They challenged policy as it is. And Senator Johnston said, "You know, you're right. Youth programs are the first to go—youth programs and education." And their response was, "And you wonder why people are dropping out and you wonder why people are struggling to survive and you wonder why people are selling dope on your doorstep. Let's walk outside and talk to the people selling dope on the streets; you'll get a whole new perspective and see what is really going on."

1. What types of policy practice are described here (using the model in Image 9.1)?

2. How do you see the work of TYC during the Summer of Safety as fitting into anti-oppressive practice work?

4

CREATING POLICY AND PROGRAMMING
WITH INPUT FROM AFFECTED STAKEHOLDERS

LESLIE COLWELL

I work as a Legislative Director for Colorado State Senator Mike Johnston, who represents northeast Denver, an area of the city that unfortunately has a long history of gang violence. In the summer of 2013, there were several high-profile shootings in our district, many involving youth—two shootings in one day on the corner across from our community office and the fatal shooting of a police officer at a well-attended jazz in the park event.

Mike and several other community leaders hosted a meeting at our office to bring folks from the community together and ask the hard questions: Why were we seeing this gun violence, and what were we all going to do to stop it?

We decided to put together a calendar of positive events happening all over the city geared toward young people, with the idea that if there were ways to engage them during the long summer days, they would be diverted from trouble. At that meeting, I met Heidi Grove and Juston Cooper from The Youth Connection, a relatively new nonprofit providing career training for disconnected youth. We set up a time to get coffee. In that meeting, Heidi suggested we meet with TYC youth to get their feedback on the ideas presented at the community meeting.

We came into the meeting with the calendar in hand. I'll never forget the reactions from some of the youth: "Yoga in the park? For real? No one's going to go to that." There was a lot we hadn't considered as we built the calendar, things like what areas of the city made sense as locations for programming, since many of the youth we were targeting were formerly gang-involved and didn't feel safe entering certain "territories." We had created the calendar by aggregating what was already being done for youth—in most cases, not the disconnected youth we were targeting—instead of asking those youth what they actually wanted and then tailoring the activities to them.

We threw the calendars in the trash and the meeting turned into a brainstorm. If they could create their own programming, what would it be? What were the activities we could get Denver youth to turn out for? We took their list—which included graffiti classes, flag football games, an open mike night, and fishing trips—and partnered with TYC to start planning. A few weeks after our first meeting, we hosted about 10 youth at our community office for a graffiti art class and DJ lessons. We ended the "Summer of Safety" event series with an open mic night in Denver's Civic Center Park, situated right between the City and County Building and the Capitol. Between what most would consider the city's traditional "seats of power," youth were empowered to have their voice heard through hip-hop and spoken word poetry.

When I was in college, I interned with an education nonprofit called Critical Exposure, whose mission is to teach youth to use the power of photography and their own voices to become

Losing Isaiah (1995). S. Gyllenhaal.

Scout's honor (2001). T. Shepard.

Sentenced home (2006). D. Grabias.

Sicko (2007). M. Moore.

The house I live in (2012). E. Jarecki.

The shock doctrine (2009). M. Whitecross & M. Winterbottom.

Books

Klein, N. (2007). *The shock doctrine: The rise of disaster capitalism*. New York: Picador.

Lakoff, G. (2004). *Don't think of an elephant: Know your values and frame the debate—the essential guide for progressives*. White River Junction, VT: Chelsea Green.

Ravich, D. (2010). *The death and life of the great American school system*. New York: Basic Books.

Reid, T. R. (2009). *The healing of America: A global quest for better, cheaper, and fairer health care*. New York: Penguin.

10

Social Movements

Where do social movements come from? And how are they formed? Their roots are in the fundamental injustice of all societies, relentlessly confronted by human aspirations of justice . . . social movements always have an array of structural causes and individual reasons to rise up against one or many of the dimensions of social domination. Yet, to know their roots does not answer the question of their birth. And since, in my view, social movements are the sources of social change, and therefore of the constitution of society, the question is a fundamental one. (Castells, 2012, p. 12)

Social movements are the foundation of social change. Indeed, the primary goal of a social movement is to elicit some form of change or to halt change. In addition, social movements are a form of collective action, which also includes riots, looting, crowd behaviors (such as at large events), special interest group campaigns, and revolutions. A basic element of collective action is that it consists of goal-directed activity by two or more people, and it often takes place within institutionalized channels. One thing that distinguishes a social movement from discrete collective behavior is the element of time—a social movement has some continuity. It can be episodic and brief, such as a "not in my backyard" (NIMBY) movement that attempts to oppose a particular neighborhood development, or it can be generations long with ebbs and flows, as demonstrated by the feminist movement (Snow, Soule, & Kriesi, 2007). Other types of collective behavior, except for revolutions, generally occur at one particular point in time.

Social movement activity is most likely to overlap with interest group behavior; yet, most often interest groups are defined in terms of their relationship with government and are embedded in political arena and legitimized. Also, interest groups primarily use institutionalized means to pursue goals, such as lobbying, and as such are more relevant to policy practice than social movements (Snow, Soule, & Kriesi, 2007). Some examples of interest groups are the American Civil Liberties Union, Defenders of Wildlife, the Feminist Majority, the Grey Panthers, and the National Alliance on Mental Illness (NAMI). While social movements and interest groups can work together on defined goals, social movement actions are more often extra-institutional and include direct action tactics, such as protests, boycotts, marches, and encampments.

In the United States, the social movements of the late 1950s through the early 1970s are typically held up as the pinnacle of social movement activity—from the Civil Rights, the women's feminist, anti-war (Vietnam), American Indian, gay and lesbian, and Chicano movements, among others. This period was dramatic, and for many, life-changing. While there has not been the same volume of social movement activity in the United States since that time, social movements continue to fluctuate and shift throughout the world.

Social movement scholarship has proliferated since the increased activity of the 1960s, with a significant increase in sociological journals publishing research on social movements and collective action. The field of study is vast, but there are common characteristics that aid in conceptualizing social movements. Most research and theorizing contend that each social movement incorporates three or more characteristics from the following list (Snow, Soule, & Kriesi, 2007, p. 6):

- collective or joint action;
- change-oriented goals or claims;
- collective action outside of institutions;
- some degree of organization; and
- some degree of continuity over time.

For our purposes here, we concentrate on social movement activity that is progressive, anti-oppressive, and focused on social justice goals. Yet, it is important to note that social movements can be regressive, attempting to halt political, social, economic, or cultural gains. Often countermovements develop to dispute the claims and actions of a social movement. In other words, social movements can either challenge or defend institutional authority (political, corporate, religious, or educational) or cultural authority (systems of beliefs or belief-based practices) (Snow, Soule, & Kriesi, 2007, p. 9).

ORGANIZATIONAL STRUCTURE IN SOCIAL MOVEMENTS

One particularly contested aspect of social movement research and theory is the role that organization (as a process) and organizations (as entities or institutions) play in social movement activity. Some suggest that social movement organizations (SMOs) should be the focus of the study of social movements (McCarthy & Zald, 1977). Indeed, research indicates that the more centralized and hierarchical the organizational structure of a social movement, the more success it has in changing policy (Gamson, 1990).

Others see organizations as antithetical and potentially damaging to social movement activity (see Piven & Cloward, 1977). Over time, organizations become more bureaucratic and hierarchical and become subsumed into the existing system rather than accomplishing their goals of changing the system. The classic model of an SMO is grounded in Max Weber's and Robert Michel's models of bureaucratization and the "iron law of oligarchy"

(Zald & Ash, 1966). These models suggest that SMOs move from a more loosely formed, dynamic structure that is led by charismatic leaders, to a bureaucracy that becomes increasingly conservative and where the focus becomes maintenance rather than change.

A third perspective is that organizations are only one possible component of social movements and that interaction for social change may or may not include formal organizations as circumstances shift (Della Porta & Diani, 1999). Theorists who take this perspective point out that networks within social movements encompass both formal and informal structures and that the interpersonal networks within these structures may be more durable than the structures themselves (Tarrow, 2011, p. 123). Thus, we can conceptualize three different forms of movement organization:

- The organization of the actual movement activity, which can be directed by a formal organization, a coalition, or "no one in particular" and occurs at "the point of contact with opponents"
- A formal group or organization that specifically makes claims with and on behalf of constituencies regarding the promotion or resistance of social change
- The "connective structures or interpersonal networks" (Tarrow, 2011, pp. 123–124).

The challenge for social movements is to create organizational structures that are both robust enough to survive the effort and flexible enough to cope with changing circumstances (Tarrow, 2011). Networks often bridge the two conditions. Whether those networks should be weak or strong in relation to the organizational structure may depend on the form and function of the social movement. Sometimes weak ties can promote larger networks, as strong ties are often premised on exclusivity and exclusion.

One contemporary example of challenges among organizational networks is set within the context of the global justice movement. Polarization has occurred between nongovernmental organizations (NGOs) and direct action groups. Many NGOs that are working on issues of environmental protection, development, and climate change are viewed as relatively sedate compared to more radical direct action groups, such as those that took to the streets in Seattle at the 1999 World Trade Organization (WTO) meetings. Also, at the 2009 UN climate change summit in Copenhagen, two competing networks were represented: SMOs that were challenging delegates to seriously examine the ramifications of climate change rather than state and national interests versus NGOs that were working directly with the delegates through informal ties. These divides suggest the ways that strong networks can advance some aspects of a social movement while also alienating certain factions of movement supporters, causing rifts.

Certainly SMOs can be beneficial. They can provide movements with leaders and resources and can also be a focal point for activists and an arena for building a base and recruiting supporters. But, mainstream SMOs tend to develop into either service delivery or advocacy groups rather than organizations that focus on protest. Organizations that develop in a nontraditional fashion may overcome that tendency. For example, some feminist social movement organizations began as grassroots organizations, but have not

social work in social action activities. During demonstrations at the National Conference on Social Welfare, the NWRO and their allies demanded support from the NCSW for interns to address poverty-related issues. On the final day of the conference, about 500 social workers joined NWRO in a direct action protest (Reisch & Andrews, 2002).

During this period of direct action and activism, the National Association of Social Workers (NASW) was lukewarm in their support of this form of direct action/activist social work. However, social work radicals influenced NASW to make changes in the late 1960s and early 1970s to include "social action" as one of a social worker's roles (Reisch & Andrews, 2002). As it currently reads, the NASW Code of Ethics states that the activities of social work include "social and political action" (2008, para. 6).

A Call to Action

From the mid-1970s through today, despite multiple issues—conservative administrations in the United States and allied countries; a retrenchment of social welfare gains; a rise in neoliberalism in many Northern and Western countries (particularly the U.S., Great Britain, and Canada); and limited social movement activities—a segment of social workers continue to prioritize social action. The formation in 1974 of the group the Radical Alliance of Social Service Workers is one such example. They included in their vision and goals statement that "social action, in concert with others, is necessary to bring about basic changes" (as cited in Reisch & Andrews, 2002, p. 189). Various other position papers highlighted social action, including everything from "letter writing and lobbying to mass demonstrations and rallies" (p. 193).

Social workers have still not embraced social action to the level that they once did. A decade ago, around the time of the demonstrations against the World Trade Organization (WTO), social work scholars commented on the place for radicalism in social work, and, as an extension, engagement in social action and social change efforts. Their call to action stated:

> We believe that significant numbers of social workers would be receptive to alternative, radical theoretical orientations and open to a critical examination of capitalism as an economic and social system. Recent demonstrations in Seattle and Washington, DC, against the WTO may reflect the possibility of bridging racial, gender, and ethnic barriers around a common agenda. Are we, as a profession with a historical commitment to social justice and social change, willing to go beyond bold statements in official documents? Are we capable of developing forms of practice that respond effectively to contemporary issues while working to create a socially just and non-oppressive environment? (Reisch and Andrews, 2002, p. 226)

THE ROLE OF SOCIAL WORKERS IN SOCIAL MOVEMENTS

While social workers have played a part in the history of social movements, for the past 50 years or so this history has a rhythm of ebb and flow, driven by the politics of fear and reflected in the overreliance on micro practice and limited large-scale social movement activity. It is also likely that there are untold stories of social workers participating in social movement work. Unfortunately, however, social workers are often isolated from movements and left to deal with neoliberal trends that result in increasing privatization of services, increasing bureaucratization, and a "race to the bottom" (Brechner, Costello, & Smith, 2000, p. 5; see also Mullaly, 2001, 2007). As long ago as 1980, one scholar commented that if [structural] social workers did not "strive to build a revolutionary social movement" they would "rightly be accused of failing to take seriously our own analysis of the need for fundamental change" (Galper, 1980, p. 114).

Some suggest that social work could be "reinvented" by once more becoming actively engaged in the sort of community organizing work that links to social movements (Shepard, 2005). Creativity, play, and joy are important components of contemporary social movement activity in the global justice movement and in local social movement actions. This playfulness and creativity can open up new possibilities for social justice and social change, because it encourages us to dream and think outside the box. If we do not, our ability to confront intractable problems is compromised.

Involvement in Social Movements Throughout Practice

By their very nature, social movements address macro-systemic change, but social workers can be involved a movement throughout the micro to macro spectrum of interventions (Hyde, 1994). On a micro level, social workers can support individuals to engage in movement work as a way to link their individual concerns with larger systemic problems. This involvement can be empowering to the participant and can increase skills, hopefulness, and social connections. As discussed in previous chapters, this type of work is an important element of popular education and the development of critical consciousness. However, social workers also need to understand the possible negative impact that participating in activism can have on individuals, including stress and trauma reactions that result from police brutality and despair, discouragement, and hopelessness if the movement is a "failure" (Hyde, 1994; Pyles, 2009).

On the mezzo level, there are direct links between community organizing and social movements. Indeed, a great deal of community organizing is situated in larger social movements. In addition, organizations can engage in both service and advocacy work; for example, the Housing Works community based in New York City provides a variety of prevention, housing, medical, and support services for individuals living with and affected by HIV/AIDS. Yet they also state that their mission is "to end the dual crisis of homelessness and AIDS through relentless advocacy, the provision of lifesaving services, and entrepreneurial businesses that sustain our efforts" (Housing Works, 2012, para. 1).

Lately, there is also renewed emphasis on the importance of coalitions to social movements. A study of factors related to the formation of social movement coalitions found that a common set of beliefs, values, identities, or strategic orientations are sufficient for coalitions to be created (Van Dyke & McCammon, 2010b). Threats to an issue or policy may also be sufficient reasons to create a coalition even if there are not preexisting ties among organizations. Given this upsurge in coalition activity related to social movements, another important role for social workers is to link their organization to larger social movement coalitions as a way to engage more fully in macrosystemic change work.

Bureaucratization: The Battered Women's Movement

We can use the battered women's movement as a cautionary example of how social workers participated in a social movement that became increasingly bureaucratized. What started as an anti-oppressive impulse has transitioned, for the most part, into the "family violence industry" (Kanuha, 1998, p. 10).

In the United States, the battered women's movement was originally linked to the feminist movement and the rape-crisis movement (for a detailed history, see Pleck, 2004; Schecter, 1982) and was deeply rooted in a feminist analysis of patriarchy. Grassroots advocacy focused on safety and services, however, it was also concerned with dismantling patriarchal structures that sustained violence. Peer support was an important foundation of the grassroots movement. Collective identity formation within the movement related initially to common experiences as women or as women who had experienced domestic violence. The connection with women's lives drew activists to commit to the movement.

A number of social workers were directly involved in the early battered women's movement, including Susan Schechter, who was an activist and historian in the movement for over 25 years; Barbara Hart, who developed concepts for civil protective orders and mandatory arrest; Ginny NiCarthy and Karen Merriam, who authored self-help books for battered women and advocates; Beth Ritchie, an activist, professor, and researcher on battering and the experience of Black women; and Barbara Mikulski, who proposed domestic violence legislation in Congress in 1980 (Kanuha, 1998).

Between the 1970s and the present day, the battered women's movement turned from a "radical, feminist-based, activist movement to a viable, mainstream, bona fide institution in American life" (Kanuha, 1998, p. 10). Rather than a social movement, it is now a service industry. Its focus has shifted dramatically from changing a system of patriarchy that perpetuates gendered oppression to offering licensure for therapists and treatment for posttraumatic stress disorder (PTSD). The solutions have become about management of the social problem and incremental systemic changes. An astute observation pointed out fifteen years ago is still relevant today:

> While social workers can and should be engaged in clinical interventions with battered women and their families, for those social workers who are feminist activists, the more profound analytical question is at what cost to transformative social change do we implicitly maintain the structure for and thereby valorize our micro-level interventions. (Kanuha, 1998, p. 11)

One important change that activists continue to demand is reintegration of the knowledge, wisdom, and expertise of battered women themselves into the field. The movement has become professionalized to such a degree that organizers, activists, and particularly domestic violence survivors, have been all but eliminated from the movement. Fortunately, activists who work from a feminist or critical theory perspective continue to question whether the field is or could be a social movement again. It is women of color and organizations that serve women of color that have been, and continue to be, at the forefront of the conversation about reinvigorating the movement (see Incite!, 2006).

Coalitions: Occupy Wall Street and Global Justice

The global justice movement has been one of the most enduring and widespread movements in the late 20th and early 21st centuries. It comprises a diverse array of individuals and organizations and has spread throughout the world, in large part through digital media and improved transportation systems (Castells, 2012). But there are some common threads in this tapestry of priorities, needs, and visions. The central elements are a rejection of neoliberal economic policies, a demand for truly participatory democracy, and a belief that "another world is possible"—the clarion call of the World Social Forum.

One of the largest social movement coalitions in history was in evidence during the Seattle World Trade Organization (WTO) protests in 1999, when over 500 participating organizations worked together (Van Dyke & McCammon, 2010a). In 2001, the first World Social Forum (WSF) was held in Porto Alegre, Brazil with approximately 20,000 people in attendance. Hundreds of NGOs were represented, from 117 different countries. Some see the WSF as evolving from the WTO protests. Others place the origins of the WSF in the earlier 1990s with the parallel NGO forums during UN conferences and the *encuentros* (encounters or gatherings) staged by the Zapatistas (Conway & Singh, 2009). Although the participants at the initial WSF and those that followed may not be a coalition in the truest sense of the word, the WSF has developed a network of organizations throughout the world that are brought together through their commitment to the global justice movement.

Beginning with the 2010 political uprising in Tunisia, there are numerous social movements across the globe that are connected by communication processes and by a link to the global justice movement. These movements were responses to grave economic disparities, corrupt governments, lack of participatory democracy, austerity measures, police brutality, and censorship—both overt and covert.

Occupy Wall Street and the subsequent Occupy movements that sprang up throughout the United States and the world in 2011 provide a direct link to the global justice movement. Fueled by the mortgage crisis, bank bailouts, the student loan crisis, and high rates of unemployment that began with the Great Recession and have shown little improvement over the years, the Occupy movement captured the attention of the world.

Were social workers there? Certainly as individuals they were. Rank and Filer, a website dedicated to "political analysis for radical social service workers" (2012, para. 1), provides a picture of social workers at Liberty Square—formerly Zuccotti Park—the Occupy Wall Street (OWS) encampment in New York City. A few months prior to the OWS encampment, there was an extended encampment christened Bloombergville (in "honor" of Mayor Bloomberg) to protest austerity cuts in New York City (NYC). Social workers were present and took leadership roles in this action. Some of the same social workers that were involved in Bloombergville were also involved in the OWS protests and actions. These social workers saw that building a movement to demand services from the state was a way to work with working class and poor people to get their needs met. They viewed the OWS encampment as a place to meet and to organize campaigns.

Radical social workers from NYC were aware of the violence and oppression that have been a significant aspect of mental health care—from cuts in mental health care, to an increase of individuals on the streets, to increases in incarceration of mentally ill. It was under these conditions that homeless individuals also began to move into Liberty Square because it was a safer place than the streets. Some of these individuals became activists; some simply sought safety. Police began to drop homeless individuals off at the encampment, some of whom had untreated, serious mental illnesses.

In response, a group of social workers began to organize to effect a full-time presence at Liberty Square. These social workers saw an opportunity to address issues of mental illness, drug abuse, and homelessness in a deliberate community. They began to monitor the park, check on people, help solve problems, and deal with the impact of police trauma; often, the social workers served as first-responders. They also attempted to engage some of these residents in activism and collective decision-making and sometimes served as a buffer between these residents and the "others."

This development of a community to care for community members was, for some social workers, a prefigurative political act, an opportunity to develop an alternative mental health response that would challenge existing services. Yet for others, this presence was seen as contentious, and the social workers who participated in this act of community care were referred to as the "social work cops" or "mental health cops" (Rank and Filer, 2012, para. 6).

This experience raised what is, in many ways, the ongoing question, conflict, and conundrum in social work: Should social workers primarily be in the streets demanding better public services, or should we be

the mental health providers in prefigurative, alternative institutions that could one day replace an oppressive state? Should we prioritize how we do our work, or what we can demand and win? Is our work primarily making change through putting pressure on others, or demonstrating what we can do on our own? (Rank and Filer, 2012, para. 27)

There is another question: Can we do both? Can prefigurative communities also fight for government reform? From some ideological perspectives, it is counterproductive to make demands of a broken state; others see the act of developing alternative services as narcissistic "and deeply distracting for the need to win real political gains" (Rank and Filer, 2012, para. 28).

> How do you feel about this dilemma? Can social workers engage in both prefigurative work and reform work?

Whether as individual actors or as members of an organization, coalition, or network, social workers have a role to play in social movements. The conditions of injustice, such as poverty, racism, sexism, and violence (to name a few) are the very conditions that progressive social movements seek to ameliorate or eliminate. Thus, the question is not whether social workers should engage in social movement work; it is: How should they engage?

STORIES FROM THE FIELD: SOCIAL MOVEMENTS

1. Sharing Our Stories of Social Change, by Gabby Santos   p. 379

   In this story, Gabby Santos describes her work of addressing domestic and sexual violence within historically marginalized communities. She describes how she builds social capital through various organizations within communities and effectively builds a movement for sustainable change. Gabby identifies key partners in the movement building and highlights the process of expanding social networks to include experts and leaders from diverse

   (Continued)

(Continued)

communities. Her goal is to build collective power to address interpersonal, cultural and structural violence. Gabby's efforts balance power, develop leadership, and engage with historically marginalized communities. This work demonstrates diverse ways to create collaborations and build networks for social justice and change.

2. Toward a Prefigurative and Transformative Praxis, by Jeff Kim   p. 384

In this story, Jeff reflects on the development of his politicized self and his social justice work. Through his initial exposure to community organizing and his subsequent work as a paid immigrant rights organizer, Jeff analyzes and critiques the role of the nonprofit industrial complex and identifies a vision for prefigurative social justice movements.

1

SHARING OUR STORIES OF SOCIAL CHANGE

GABBY SANTOS

As a change agent for a domestic and sexual violence prevention coalition in Oregon, my role is to work to undo oppressive social norms and power structures that lead to and maintain the over-all culture of violence. Building social capital that drives effective movement building for sustainable change is a natural fit with my work. Community engagement is a way of life for me, not just a nine to five job.

Mi Historia, My Story

Growing up in a migrant farm-worker family, lessons of survival and healing in the midst of adversity came as early as my existence in the womb of my madre. My mother was a survivor of domestic violence; her firstborn, a survivor of family violence since inception; both of us, survivors of historical trauma, community violence and institutional power and control, all of which ran pervasively in our familia y comunidad.

Adolescence was not any less painful, though it was far more victorious. Over the years, my identities began to flow freely with the hard-core cadence of a norteño corrido. Quite paradoxically and metaphysically, both the societal oppression and my core resilience intensified, battling each other at the intersections of racism, poverty, transphobia, and all things related to colonization and re-colonization vs. decolonization. The battle brought me closer to a stronger analysis: What happened? What is happening now? What can we do? Who needs to be included? And, how do we electrify and infuse this transformational work across communities in order to create safer spaces for all?

For nearly twenty years now, my corrido is one that promotes putting theory into action by applying an intersectional framework. It addresses the root causes of all relevant issues in order to prevent all forms of violence. Although the fact is oftentimes overlooked, I have learned that the most radical change is one that interrupts the social micro-aggressions, the subtle acts of indifference and oppression that lead to a build-up of unhealthy norms and violence toward historically marginalized communities—like people of color, Tribal Nations, LGBT folks, and people with disabilities.

Sola No, Not On My Own

Working to end oppression while working in an oppressive system requires community engagement. We cannot do this work in isolation. Expanding networks to include experts and leaders from diverse communities has helped to build collective power and a broader analysis. Reaching out to them works to meet the unique cultural needs of individuals living with the most disparities. By promoting and supporting the great work happening outside of the anti-domestic and sexual violence movement in which I work, we can strengthen our intercommunity relationships and learn how to include culturally specific approaches happening in other social justice groups. We also need to remember to remain humble and to take a step back so that we may listen and be reflective of where the gaps exist in resources and where the lack of institutional power and privilege remains.

We also need to acknowledge who is already doing transformational work in their communities and honoring their leadership by reaching out, learning from them, and partnering with them. Our collaboration is based on balancing power and sharing, developing leadership, expanding support systems for advocates who work on the ground, and looking to historically marginalized communities as resources for change. All are key components necessary to build a diverse network of activists and allies.

Nuestras Historias, Our Stories

The key partners in building this movement are the Communities of Color Task Force, A Call to Men Oregon, The Gender Positive Systems Advocacy Committee, and other community partners, statewide and national. Although there are many highlights to share, here are some of those stories.

Language Access

The domestic violence and sexual assault prevention coalition has actualized our commitment to providing language access. The coalition is able to conduct domestic violence awareness campaigns in English, Spanish, Russian and Vietnamese, the four primary languages in Oregon. We have begun to accept annual conference proposals from presenters who wanted to facilitate workshops in their native language. Additionally, our language access plan includes making our social marketing efforts linguistically accessible in the primary language communities of Oregon as well as in deaf and hard of hearing communities. As a member of ALAS (Alianza Latina en contra la Agresión Sexual) a cyberactivism workgroup of Arte Sana, a national Latin@ Sexual Assault training and technical assistance provider, we are committed to prevention efforts that engage immigrant monolingual communities as agents of social change. We have also partnered with the Immigrant Refugee Community Organization on translation services for various initiatives.

Training and Technical Assistance

Supporting programs and community partners in addressing the needs of historically marginalized communities is at the heart of this program. We have always done this through an anti-oppressive framework in order to effect the social change needed for the prevention of domestic and sexual violence, particularly with and within communities of color, people with disabilities, elders, LGBT and gender non-conforming folks, and survivors with criminal histories.

A popular area of training since the inception of our youth violence prevention program has been training in technology and social media. As a member of the National Network to End

Domestic Violence Safety Net Team, we were able to infuse technology safety and social media into the traditional youth bullying, teen dating and sexual violence curricula.

Another prevention effort that addressed youth was our collaborative position paper with Arte Sana's ALAS, a national Latin@ cyberactivism group. Outraged by the Miramonte Middle School tragedy and the lack of proper response, we partnered on writing "Preventing Sexual Abuse of Latin@ Children." Most of the children victimized were Latin@ immigrants who had disclosed their abuse several years before, but were not seen as credible until a photo lab technician reported the pornographic photos of children taken by their teacher. Our position paper is in Spanish and English. It has circulated in many state and national prevention circles and has been read by people from the general public and school officials.

We were also able to partner with 1-in-6 on a media advocacy campaign that promoted the re-airing of the *Law & Order SVU* episode, "Personal Fouls." The episode was a project of 1-in-6, A CALL TO MEN, The Joyful Heart Foundation, and *Law & Order SVU*. "Personal Fouls" presented the realities of male athletes sexually abused and raped as youth by their coaches. It also shed light on the barriers to disclosure due to societal norms that can maintain unhealthy power models in athletic communities. Our collaboration with 1-in-6 resulted in a national kit, "Media Advocacy Works." It included a public awareness letter about male sexual abuse that explained how ending oppression helps to prevent sexual violence against everyone and announced the re-airing of "Personal Fouls"; other pieces in the kit included a Timeline of Media Advocacy and Public Engagement of Male Sexual Abuse, a "Personal Fouls" Discussion Guide, and a list of local and national resources.

Outreach to Tribal Communities

Reaching out to tribal communities has been an invigorating experience. For example, we partnered with the Confederated Tribes of Warm Springs in developing a regional training that gave voice to the realities of survivors of sexual abuse and domestic violence from Tribal Nations. The conference also brought up community solutions for addressing the gaps in services and prevention. Tribal leaders and other speakers shared their understanding across the region and the state about the need for progressive collaborations between Tribal and nonprofit advocates.

Workgroups and Systems Advocacy

A Call to Men Institute is our newest workgroup, which developed from a partnership of the Communities of Color Task Force and the national A CALL TO MEN organization. The Institute helps build capacity for anti-violence organizing efforts across Oregon, with leaders from historically marginalized groups engaging their communities in domestic and sexual violence prevention. Diverse initiatives have flourished under the leadership of faith-based leaders, people of color, youth, grandparents, people with disabilities and LGBTQ folks.

One lasting outcome of the Men's Institute has helped enhance what we call 'community engageMENt,' recognizing that men have always been part of the activism within communities of color. As an anti-violence movement, we need each other to collectively address the dispari-ties that lead to violence in our communities. Men as allies are welcome, are valued, and are held accountable by women, youth, the community and each other. This coalition continues to build capacity through A Call to Men statewide listserv, technical assistance calls, leadership development and promotion of member projects.

The Communities of Color Task Force (CCTF) is another multi-community, statewide work-group. It is made up of anti-violence advocates, community members and allies who address the specific concerns of domestic violence and sexual assault survivors from a racial justice perspective. The CCTF is very intentional about our work at the intersections of oppression. Our efforts are geared toward decreasing the struggles of communities of color within mainstream systems that do not offer culturally relevant resources. Systems advocacy is also a way to give voice to advocates of color, who are often tokenized and assigned roles that ignore other fea-tures of their identities. The CCTF amplifies the voices of all people of color so that issues of racism, poverty, sexism, transphobia, homophobia, ageism and ableism can be addressed simultaneously.

Recent initiatives of the CCTF include submitting input to the National Prevention and Health Promotion Strategy and the National Prison Rape Elimination Act. Our input supports our mission to promote a prevention strategy that supports the needs of communities of color and all of their intersecting identities. The CCTF members participate in criminal justice policy reform, including issues of community alternatives to policing and immigration reform.

We also partner with the Center for Community Engagement on the Healing-Based Liberation Conference. This is a peer-led group that shares roles in all activities ranging from meeting facili-tation to legislative advocacy to public speaking and community education. This leadership development is what fuels movement building among members of the CCTF.

The Gender Positive Systems Advocacy Committee (GPSAC) is another multi-community workgroup, this one composed of transgender and gender non-conforming advocates and allies. GPSAC was formed as a response to advocates needing assistance in supporting sexual-abuse survivors who didn't identify as cisgender women and to address the needs of transgen-der survivors, who are often silenced in lesbian and gay communities. For example, GPSAC members developed a transgender specific SANE (Sexual Assault Nurse Examiner) training called "Getting the Exam Right." This training gives nurses the ability to use a Sexual Assault Forensic Exams (SAFE) kit in a manner that is culturally relevant to transgender survivors. Service providers often overlook gender identity and the different needs of transgender survi-vors. GPSAC seeks to work collaboratively with other anti-violence programs and community organizations.

GPSAC began as a technical assistance and training provider, but continues to evolve into a group that extends services with the goal of impacting systems change. For example, it has con-tributed comments to the National Prison Rape Elimination Act Standards, working to influence policies about housing transgender people in prisons. Through educational components that have not been historically welcomed by mainstream organizations, GPSAC aims to raise awareness of how organizing and creating change around violence against females silences people with other gender identities. The ultimate goal is systemic change.

National Work

On a national level, the Coalition continues to partner with In Our Own Voices, an organization located in Albany, NY that serves the needs of Lesbian, Gay, Bisexual and Transgender People of Color. One project of collaboration is Unity Through Diversity: Living at the Intersections, a National LGBT People of Color Health Summit held in 2011. The National Health Summit aimed at promoting health and well-being. It featured presentations, workshops, and panel discussions on the importance of meaningful involvement of LGBT people of color as leaders in policy development and implementation, physical and mental health issues, and innovative interventions and research that address and educate people about the health and well-being of this community throughout the nation.

Coalition workgroups and In Our Own Voices also submitted recommendations to the American Psychiatric Association's DSM-5 Gender Identity Disorder Committee. We advocated for the removal of gender dysphoria as a diagnosis.

Paso a Paso y Mano a Mano, Step by Step and Hand in Hand

Violence is a public health issue, and environments that promote and enable the marginalization of diverse communities are a public health hazard. We must hold institutions and communities accountable for changing these conditions. We must work to eliminate the risk factors that exist for historically marginalized communities by increasing protective factors that support and promote the safety and equity of all identities and expressions. It is evident that people of color have fewer societal resources for good health and life itself. This is a health epidemic affecting millions of people of color, particularly those who are immigrants, transgender, two-spirited, lesbian, gay, living with a disability or all the above.

Each one of us has a story of survival, healing and transformation. Alone we are great, but together we are electric. We work together through big efforts and small efforts because we recognize that change is incremental. But, by the same token, outcomes are never ending and ever so life-changing. Theory to action is a movement in which everyone can participate.

1. How does Gabby locate herself in the work that she does in the community?

2. How does building social capital through various organizations affect social movement building for addressing domestic and sexual violence in marginalized communities?

3. What are some of the ways in which the various programs and organizations work in an anti-oppressive way with marginalized communities?

4. What models of community organizing are evident in Gabby's examples?

5. Gabby outlines a number of collaborations that the Coalition has been a part of. In what ways do you see this work as exemplifying the strengths of coalition work?

6. What are some of the intersecting issues that these collaborations are addressing (rather than "single issue" work)?

focused on making sure the quantifiable numbers on the quarterly report were satisfactory to the funders instead of critically assessing whether we were on the right path to attain substantive justice for the immigrant community. Even though I desired to be an organizer with radical politics, the demands of the nonprofit industrial complex forced me to be just another bureaucratized office-worker. I had minimal contact with immigrants except for those who came into the office seeking our services.

Another way that the nonprofit industrial complex manifested itself during my experience in the immigrant rights movement was the nonprofit organization directors' admonishments barring their staff from critiquing U.S. foreign policies. Any condemnation of regressive foreign policies—such as the North America Free Trade Agreement, which compelled millions of people from Mexico to enter the United States in search of a better life—was effectually censored by the directors. They saw these critiques as self-defeating rhetoric that would make the movement seem anti-American when the immigrant community needed to display their love and allegiance to this country in order to earn their papers. To make demands for ending the inhumane warfare at the U.S./Mexico border was also denigrated as a utopian stance, as something that only sounds good in theory and would not be supported by the politicians.

So, while my praxis reflected a radical stance involving a critique of capitalism and the exploitation of borders as the root causes of the immigration "problem," the directors instead demanded that I parrot moderate talking points thickly veiled in patriotism and nationalism. Instead of recognizing that we inhabit a land that was appropriated and preserved through war and violence, we formulated a defensive stance that begged for forgiveness on behalf of those whose "crime" was crossing over a social construction of a border. These moderate to conservative talking points were so detached from my personal politics that I mostly avoided participating in press conferences and other speaking opportunities. The reform-driven movement stalled waiting for a bill to be introduced while collecting millions in grants from elite foundations that demanded professionalization and a moderate political stance.

My experience in navigating the tensions caused by the nonprofit industrial complex within the immigrant rights movement is not unique. As activists, our collective failure to resist the nonprofit industrial complex presents yet another challenge. Are we able to stop the machines of the nonprofit industrial complex and foster a revolutionary movement based on community, mutual aid and horizontalism? Can we as activists truly make the claim that an "another world is possible" when our own milieu is modeled on capitalism? These critical self-inquiries must be honestly answered through horizontal dialogues among those who participate in the social justice sector.

I take the position that as organizers, we do have a choice. We can continue to cooperate with the nonprofit industrial complex and the elites by focusing primarily on grants, foundations, evaluations and policies; or we can reimagine our roles in society and become those invigorated to strive for social change, consciousness-building and liberation of the oppressed communities. We must start scrutinizing ourselves through asking a crucial question: To whom are we accountable? Our solution must be analyzed through the tangible effects that our work has on the most marginalized sectors of our society. It is possible to do social justice work toward achieving radical social change while serving the needs and interests of the working class, people of color, women, the queer community, and those with disabilities.

Many of us need to figure out ways to organize outside of the boundaries of the nonprofits, as it is almost natural that we become disconnected from our communities when we are inside offices and buildings. Instead, social justice activists must support all forms of public spheres and localized resistances in our communities through which people can mobilize to realize their collective power. We should not be content with providing services and helping a few people get ahead while the majority of the communities we supposedly want to organize are constantly oppressed, criminalized and exploited. As activists, we must not internalize any forms of supremacy over the community we organize with, privileging ourselves and our opinions over those who have less political and social capital than many of us possess. Instead, we must acknowledge that those who are oppressed know their way to freedom the best and allow them to lead their own movements.

Vibrant, progressive and radical social movements focused on radical social change can and do flourish in every community outside of the nonprofit industrial complex. Therefore, our work must be accountable to these groups struggling outside the traditional boundaries and we must work together to seize power and achieve justice for all communities. Social change can happen when we recognize that we share mutual wants, needs, interests and hopes for a better future for all. We must dedicate ourselves to creating, defending and multiplying community-based prefigurative spaces where people can come to understand the interrelatedness of our struggles, develop their political praxis, and reject the hegemonic model of organizing that forces us to compete for grants and money, effectually barring us from mobilizing together to challenge the dominant ruling class. Our obligation is to create the world we want to live in and then to display it by fostering community networks. We must acknowledge that we exist to meet each other's basic needs, which have been so neglected in modern capitalist society: housing, food, medical care, mental care, community protection, and redistribution of wealth and resources. As activists, we must always speak truth to power, even be willing to lose our livelihoods instead of perpetuating the status quo by remaining silent. Together, we can and must reject the hierarchical accountability to the foundations, funders and the State and instead be responsible to those who most need our solidarity and commitment.

1. What are prefigurative social movements?

2. What are some of the challenges Jeff faced in his immigrant rights work that he suggests are inevitable impacts of the nonprofit industrial complex?

3. How could the tensions that Jeff describes play out in your own work and personal life? How would you navigate them?

DISCUSSION QUESTIONS

1. What feelings and thoughts came up for you in response to these stories?

2. How do the stories reflect some of the concepts and issues raised in the chapter, such as the place of organizations in social movements, bureaucratization of social movements, and the engagement of coalitions in social movements?

ACTIVITIES

1. Identify a social movement that is active in your community (it can be part of a broader national or global movement).

   a. What are some of the tactics used (for example, direct action, lobbying, strikes)?

   b. Is this social movement tied to organizational networks or more loosely defined? If it is part of a network or coalition, what are some of the organizations or groups represented?

   c. Do you see any evidence of social work as a presence in the movement, and if so, how is social work represented?

   d. How could this movement connect to your work or the populations you work with or are interested in working with?

   e. Have you personally participated with this social movement? If so, in what ways? If not, what are the barriers to your own participation?

ADDITIONAL RESOURCES

Websites

http://www.rankandfiler.net/ (Rank and Filer)

Films

A force more powerful (1999). S. York.

After Stonewall (1999). J. Scagliotti.

Another world is possible (2002). M. Dworkin & M. Young.

Before Stonewall (1984). J. Scagliotti.

Berkeley in the sixties (1990). M. Kitchell.

Bread and roses (2000). K. Loach.

Eyes on the prize (1987). J. A. DeVinney & C. Crossley.

Freedom on my mind (1994). C. Field & M. Mulford.

Iron jawed angels (2004). K. von Garnier.

Jonah who will be 25 in the year 2000 (1976). A. Tanner.

Lives worth living (2011). E. Neudel.

Making sense of the sixties (1991). D. Hoffman.

Matewan (1987). J. Sayles.

Mic check: Shorts from the occupy movement (2012). N. Shimkin.

One woman, one vote (1996). S. Sarandon.

Romero (1989). J. Duigan.

Rosa Luxemburg (1986). M. von Trotta.

Salt of the earth (1954). H. Biberman.

Sisters of '77 (2005). C. S. Mondell & A. Mondell.

Tahrir: Liberation Square (2011). S. Savona.

10,000 Black Men Named George (2002). R. Townsend.

The organizer (1963). M. Monicelli.

The take (2004). A. Lewis.

The times of Harvey Milk (1984). R. Epstein.

The war at home (1979). G. Silber, & B. A. Brown.

The white rose (1982). M. Verhoeven.

This is what democracy looks like (2000). J. Friedberg & R. Rowley.

Union maids (1976). J. Reichert.

Viva Zapata (1952). E. Kazan.

Walkout (2006). E. J. Olmos.

We were here (2011). B. Weber & D. Weissman.

Books

Bobo, K., Kendall, J., & Max, S. (2010). *Organizing for social change*. Santa Ana, CA: The Forum Press.

Castells, M. (2012). *Networks of outrage and hope: Social movements in the Internet age*. Malden, MA: Polity Press.

Goodwin, J., & Jasper, J. M. (2009). *The social movements reader: Cases and concepts*. Malden, MA: Blackwell.

Graeber, D. (2009). *Direct action: An ethnography*. Oakland, CA: AK Press.

Hughes, C., Peace, S., & Van Meter, K. (2010). *Uses of a whirlwind: Movement, movements, and contemporary radical currents in the United States*. Oakland, CA: AK Press.

Mann, E. (2011). *A playbook for progressives*. Boston, MA: Beacon.

McAdam, D. (1988). *Freedom summer*. New York: Oxford Press.

Pleck, E. (2004). *Domestic tyranny: The making of social policy against family violence from colonial times to present*. Chicago: University of Illinois Press.

Polletta, F. (2006). *It was like a fever: Storytelling in protest and politics*. Chicago: University of Chicago Press.

Schechter, S. (1982). *Women and male violence: The visions and struggles of the battered women's movement*. Boston, MA: South End Press.

Sen, R. (2003). *Stir it up*. San Francisco, CA: Jossey-Bass.

Shannon, D., Rogue, J., Daring, C. B., & Volcano, A. (2013). *Queering anarchism: Addressing and undressing power and desire*. Oakland, CA: AK Press.

Shaw, R. (2001). *The activist's handbook: A primer*. Berkeley: University of California Press.

Shepard, B., & Hayduk, R. (2002). *From ACT UP to the WTO: Urban protest and community building in the era of globalization*. New York: Verso.

Shiffman, R., Bell, R., Brown, L. J., & Elizabeth, L. (2012). *Beyond Zuccotti Park: Freedom of assembly and the occupation of public space*. Oakland, CA: New Village Press.

Sitrin, M. (2006). *Horizontalism*. Oakland, CA: AK Press.

11

Global Anti-Oppressive Practice

I n an increasingly interdependent world, global processes are affecting the living standards and the lives of individuals, families, groups, and communities. As we enter the 21st century, various worldwide social issues continue to emerge that require action and attention. These include: the widening global gap between the rich and the poor (within nations and between nations); extreme poverty and social exclusion, exacerbated by the globalization of the economy, which creates a larger divide between people and nations that do not benefit from social and economic progress; the concept of security and the added international efforts to "secure" borders, which brings little security to families facing long-term unemployment, declining social welfare benefits and risk of personal violence; growing interethnic, racial, and religious conflict in the world; and a shortage of resources, which creates an urgent need for sustainable, resource efficient social and environmental interventions (Healy, 2001).

Taking into account these global changes, a global perspective becomes imperative to our work. A global perspective refers to the whole world—the unity of the earth and its interconnectedness (Pawar, 2013), whereas an international perspective specifically refers to interactions between or among two or more nations (Healy, 2008). In this chapter, we use both of these terms, oftentimes interchangeably, to refer to anti-oppressive social work practices that extend beyond the boundaries of the United States. Image 11.1 highlights six elements of a global perspective for social workers.

Four effects of globalization are shaping anti-oppressive global social work practice (Healy, 2001, pp. 2–3):

- Social service agency caseloads and domestic social work practices are increasingly influenced by international social forces and events, including the worldwide movement of people
- Collaborative work and knowledge exchange is more desirable now since social problems are shared by countries across the economic development spectrum, far more so than in previous decades
- The political, social, and economic actions of one country directly influence and affect other countries' social, political, and economic well-being, as well as the earth's environmental health

- Advancements and developments in technology enhance opportunities for global sharing and collaboration

Image 11.1 Elements of a Global Perspective on Society	
Element	*Implications*
Unity	All humans derive from the same origins, inhabit the same planet, and exhibit the same basic needs—meaning that all are affected by happenings in another part of the world.
Diversity	The world encompasses a wide variety of people, cultures, geographies, resources, political arrangements, economic conditions, and social systems.
Interdependence	Identifying our commonalities while drawing on the benefits of diversity helps us to identify and achieve mutually beneficial goals.
Globalization	Global political, economic, social, cultural, institutional, and technological processes are increasingly relevant to social life, in many respects more relevant than local processes.
Localization	Because local processes have the most immediate effect on individuals and are usually less alienating than global processes, many aim to reinforce local processes.
World citizenship	Adequate standards of human welfare and belongingness for everyone, at both local and global levels, depend on equality in individual and human rights, free and universal political participation, and state responsibility for human welfare.

Source: Adapted from Pawar, 2013, pp. 636–637.

The range of actual global social work practice is broad—from social workers practicing in other countries to social workers practicing domestically, but addressing cases with international dimensions. The practices of social workers are influenced by macroeconomic and geopolitical forces and are informed by international conventions and interrelationships between nations and transnational communities (Huegler, Lyons, & Pawar, 2012). Thus, as social workers, we need to be prepared to work with internationally related individuals, families, groups, and communities that arise in our domestic practice and to engage in mutual problem solving of global issues. It is also critical to understand the impact of our nation's policies and practices on people and the environment in other countries.

There are three main bodies that give voice and international visibility to social workers:

- International Federation of Social Workers: 92 national associations of social workers are members
- International Association of Schools of Social Work: schools of social work from up to 100 countries have joined
- International Council of Social Welfare: composed of national nongovernmental organizations as well as international organizations from over 70 countries

These global, interconnected bodies are involved in social development and engaged in developing a global agenda.

TERMINOLOGY IN GLOBAL SOCIAL WORK

Global social work is an emerging field, therefore, the terms that are used within the field to describe it tend to be fluid. When engaging in anti-oppressive global social work practice, it is important to attend to the ways in which language frames our work.

Approach-to-Practice Terms

There is no single definition of global social work accepted by the majority of people. In the literature, the terms *international, transnational,* and *global* are often used interchangeably. All refer to social work practice that extends beyond the boundaries of the United States. All include the core elements of practice listed in Image 11.2. However, these terms have distinctive connotations that emphasize different aspects of the work (Pawar, 2013):

- *International social work:* a comparative, cross-cultural approach that involves interactions between two or more nations (Healy, 2008). It includes "intergovernmental work on social welfare, concern and action on global social problems, a worldwide collegiality among social workers, professional exchange activities, and a general worldview" (Healy, 2001, p. 5). At the core of international action are internationally related domestic practice and advocacy, professional exchange across national borders, international practice, and international policy development and advocacy (Healy, 2008).
- *Transnational social work:* an emerging field of practice that requires the strategizing of solutions that incorporate more than two nation-states. It is designed to serve populations that cross borders, "whether physically or through new technologies," and to address complex cross-border "problems and dilemmas" (Furman, Negi, & Salvador, 2010, p. 8).
- *Global social work:* a focus on social work education and practice that take place both locally and around the world. It assumes a unity and connectedness of the earth and its inhabitants (Pawar, 2013). Its purpose is to promote "social work's capacity to respond appropriately and effectively, in education and practice terms, to the various global challenges that are having a significant impact on the well-being of large sections of the world's population" (Cox & Pawar, 2006, p. 20).

What do you see as some of the differences among these definitions?

Image 11.2   Core Elements of Global Social Work Practice

- The practice of social work in a country other than the home country of the social worker;
- Working with individuals, families, and communities whose origins are in a country other than where the social worker is practicing;
- Working with international organizations;
- Collaborations between countries in which social workers exchange ideas or work together on projects that cross national borders; and
- Practice that addresses local issues that originate in globalized systems.

Source: Adapted from Hugman, 2010, pp. 18–20.

Geopolitical Terms

In the 1960s, the terms *first world, second world*, and *third world* were commonly used to distinguish between countries and geographical locations linked by similar political, cultural, and economic status. The "first world" consisted of the United States, Western Europe, and other economically developed, capitalist countries; the "second world" comprised the Soviet Union and its satellites and allies, which were communistic. The "third world" was everybody else, particularly countries that were underdeveloped economically and were located, primarily, south of the equator. The term *fourth world,* which is not seen as often as the other terms, was used to refer to the estimated 6000 groups of indigenous people, usually the poorest of the poor in the countries where they lived. None of these terms are seen as often as they once were, however. With the transformation of the Soviet Union to Russia, and the fall of its communist government, the term *second world* is much less relevant. And the term *third world* is increasingly viewed as a negative term, implying a hierarchy among countries in which those that are not part of the "first" or "second" world are inferior.

Other terms have emerged to distinguish between countries with different levels of social and economic development. Two commonly used terms are *developed country* and *developing country*. The terms imply differences in living standards, infrastructures, industrial base, and human development (measured by life-expectancy, infant mortality, literacy rate, and so on). However, critics assert that these terms also assume a desire to "develop" along the traditional "Western" model of economic development. A few countries, such as Cuba and Bhutan, deliberately choose not to follow that model. The terms also imply homogeneity within developed or developing countries when, in reality, the wealth and well-being of the most and least affluent groups varies widely within each category. In addition, the term "developed country" incorrectly implies that economic development and growth is static and does not continue in more developed countries. Consequently, the terms *global North* and *global South* emerged. They indicate geographical locations north and south of the equator, but also have implications for socioeconomic and political differences between countries. These terms serve as a main organizing principle for understanding the world economy. Generally, countries in the global North are better developed and countries in the global South are in early stages of socioeconomic and political development. However, countries like Australia, South Africa, and Angola, which are located in the global South, are considered to be developed.

In this chapter, we use the terms *developed/developing* and *global North/global South* to refer to differences between countries and regions in the world. We acknowledge the problems and limitations of these terms and do not advocate for a binary of differences. Rather, we need a way to acknowledge the global status of countries in relation to one another.

HISTORICAL BACKGROUND OF GLOBAL AOP

Social work has a long history of international involvement, through the first exchanges between individual social workers and then the congresses leading to the formation of international associations (Huegler, Lyons, & Pawar, 2012). The roots of global social work are European and North American in their origins (Healy, 2001), with "social work interventions" through religious institutions and philanthropic activities having been implemented as early as the 19th century in various countries around the world.

The particular histories of social work in individual countries vary in length and degree. These histories largely correspond to the role of European countries in colonialization and the influence of U.S. economic and political power. As a result, there are many countries where social work has been molded and shaped by colonial or hegemonic influences.

Some of the earliest international exchanges among social workers consisted of individual Americans' visits to other countries within Europe or across the Atlantic to learn about social work in other parts of the world and to share their experiences (Huegler, Lyons, & Pawar, 2012). For example, Jane Addams (U.S.) and Alice Solomon (Germany) met at an International Congress of Women that took place in Germany in 1904 (Healy, 2001). The First International Conference on Social Work took place in 1928. International conferences became the basis for the formation of the three international social work bodies previously mentioned in the introduction: the International Federation of Social Workers, the International Association of Schools of Social Work, and the International Council of Social Welfare. Not surprisingly, the early definition of international social work included the exchanges of ideas by social workers at international meetings, as well as through intercountry work, intergovernmental work, and relief work (Huegler, Lyons, & Pawar, 2012).

By the end of the 19th and early 20th centuries, international social work was associated with individual and group exchange programs, the establishment of cross-national professional networks, and organizations concerned with "exchange" through conferences and research programs (Huegler, Lyons, & Pawar, 2012). This internationalist movement was concerned with issues, such as social justice, world peace, human rights, environmental protection, and other global subjects. These concerns led to the establishment of the League of Nations, the United Nations, and a host of international nongovernmental organizations, such as the Red Cross, Amnesty International, Save the Children, and Greenpeace (Ife, 2000).

The establishment of international social work education, research, and altruistic volunteering in many countries of the global South was driven by the efforts of missionaries, religious organizations, and other influences from the global North. It did not develop from indigenous roots and local people's knowledge, which has led to critiques like this one by Mel Gray, a leading researcher in social work:

> Driven by altruistic intentions, social work has promoted the kind of missionary zeal in colonial and postcolonial situations where inherent power imbalances and the relevance of Western models went unquestioned. . . . Underpinning this "professional imperialism" was the implicit assumption that developing countries were incapable of finding their own models. (2005, p. 235)

Many researchers critique these earlier approaches to global social work, pointing out that social workers from the global North engaged in such oppressive practices as imposing their own cultural lenses and approaches as universally applicable. Oppressive practices also included imposing Western culture, languages, and religions on indigenous peoples in Australia, Canada, New Zealand, and the United States, removing indigenous children from their families and communities, and denying them their culture (Grande, 2004).

Some critics have pointed up the role of the English language as a tool of oppression. Imposing a dominant language embodies power relations, cultural assumptions, and worldviews that can become expressions of unjust international social work practices (Dominelli, 2008). Currently, access to the discourse on international social work is dependent on the ability to speak with the conceptual and linguistic capacity of those in the global North, who are the same people who are constructing the conversation (Haug, 2005).

ISSUES AFFECTING GLOBAL SOCIAL WORK

In order to understand global anti-oppressive social work, it is crucial that we understand the concept of globalization and its impact on countries, welfare systems, communities, and people around the world, as well as how it informs our social work at home and abroad. In this section, we look more closely at globalization and at a few particular issues that it raises in terms of economic and cultural oppression, transnational migration, and damage to the environment.

Economic Globalization

Globalization is a complex and contested phenomenon. Used broadly, this term describes socioeconomic processes that transcend national boundaries. However, the term is often used without clear explanation, and there is no consensus on what it actually means (Ife, 2000). Here are a few additional definitions of *globalization*:

- The "compressing of the world through economic and technological means" (Fook, 2002, p. 19).
- A geopolitically informed process promoting a single economy unevenly across time and space.
- The blend of national and international capital that controls global, regional, and national economies.
- A "complex set of multiple processes rather than either a singular process of an end state. These processes operate very unevenly across both time and space, and above all are politically mediated." (Khan & Dominelli, 2000, p. 100)

There are three essential elements of globalization:

1. *Information technology:* a means of digitally transmitting information around the world. Information technology has transformed communication and economic transactions (Drover, 2000). Flows of capital and monetary transactions can take place in a matter of seconds. While those at the center of the new information-based movements of power have an advantage, those who are not wired into these networks are inevitably at a disadvantage, becoming more marginalized and excluded (Ife, 2000). In social work, there are some positive aspects of technological changes, such as easier and more accurate monitoring and reporting and more effective clinical services (Drover, 2000, p. 12); however, technological advances have also increased the surveillance and supervision of clients. Technology has also redefined education in social work and has the potential to dehumanize social work (Hick & McNutt, 2002).

2. *Neo-liberalism:* a political ideology that embraces the free market as the best way to allocate goods and services (Drover, 2000). Neo-liberalism believes in the removal of trade barriers to capital mobility. Without such barriers, corporations are free to operate globally—the essence of globalization. The rise of neo-liberal ideology influenced social work practice by shifting the idea of "service" from doing what another person desires to conducting a transaction with that person (Ife, 1997). This quasi-economic approach influences the power relationships, and the purpose and meaning in social work practice. More to the point, neo-liberalism maintains that the government's protection of people and redistribution policies (the "welfare state") hinder economic growth. The result is the privatization of services and a decline in

collective responsibility for social problems. For example, some new public services, such as home health care for individuals with disabilities and the elderly, will not be instituted because they are already under the auspices of private, commercial providers who would not cede their livelihood to the government (Dover, 2000). Furthermore, the values of individuality, competitiveness, and progress that are central to the ideology of neo-liberalism are in direct opposition to the values of a social work practice committed to social justice (Bishop, 2001; Ife, 1997). This clash in values poses contradictions and tensions for social workers.

3. *Free trade:* a system in which goods, capital, and labor flow freely between nations, without barriers that could hinder the cross-border flow of money and products. Under free trade policies, governments do not discriminate against imports by applying tariffs or quotas or interfere with exports by providing subsidies to local producers. The interpretation of international free trade agreements is actively debated. Critics maintain that public services are not sufficiently protected under these agreements and that as a result governments will gradually phase out the delivery of public social services (Barlow, 2003). This would mean that governments would be constrained in providing social services and instead, transnational corporations would facilitate the access of social services in a multitude of areas, such as child care, elder care, mental and physical health care, and education. Another major concern with free trade policies is the lack of rules about working hours, fair rates of pay, working conditions, and so forth. Corporations often take advantage of other countries' cheaper labor, inexpensive supplies, and lax regulatory systems in order to increase their profit.

The problem with economic globalization isn't with global interdependence, but rather with the effects of globalization that perpetuate unequal structures and policies. Many of these disparate programs are created by countries in the global North and negatively impact the lives of people in the global South. For example, the International Monetary Fund, World Bank, and the World Trade Organization set up the economic rules. These organizations impose standards on nations for making loans and determine where products are manufactured, how rapidly the products are made, the working conditions under which they are produced, and the product price (Van Wormer, 2010). The Western-dominated world banks impose structural adjustments or requirements on countries owing lots of debt (predominately countries of the global South), which necessitates cuts in their domestic spending to pay off creditors. The result is less spending in the global South on health care, education, and other social services. The effects are reflected in local communities through maternal and infant mortality, the spread of disease, mass unemployment, and degradation of the land and environment, among other forms of oppression. An anti-oppressive lens is critical in global social work since it focuses on the structural origins of an individual's problems and seeks to transform unequal social and power relations between groups (Mullaly, 2007).

Why is an anti-oppressive lens useful and relevant to a discussion of the impact of economic globalization?

Cultural Globalization

The effects of globalization aren't only economic, but also cultural. Increased migration and the smooth flow of global capital results in the homogenization of culture, so people in disparate places eat the same food, speak the same language, watch the same television programs, and so on. Humans who do not participate in this culture risk marginalization and exclusion from economic development (Ife, 2001). The culture of the global North dominates, so signs of the globalization of culture include "the reproduction of mass-produced quasi-American culture in the form of McDonalds, Levis, basketball, Coca-Cola, television sitcoms, and other cultural symbols, perhaps the most important being the English language" (Ife, 2001, p. 52).

Take a moment to consider the impact of this trend on global cultural diversity. What are some of your thoughts and concerns?

The complex phenomenon of the globalization of culture can be seen through four different lenses, as shown in Image 11.3. Globalization often has negative connotations, but

Image 11.3	Lenses for Critiquing the Globalization of Culture
Lens	*Consequence*
Globalization as destroyer	Leads to cultural fragmentation, dwindling social ties, and the end of certainty and sustainability
Globalization as homogenizer	Perpetuates cultural imperialism and domination by the global North, particularly values, such as individualism, rationalization, and standardization
Globalization as instigator	Leads to a backlash against dominant values of the global North, resistance, division, and conflict fueled by growing disparities
Globalization as incubator	Fuses ideologies and practices to create new, hybrid cultures, values, and patterns of life

Source: Adapted from Midgley, 2008.

some have noted that cultural identities are continually changing and evolving anyway and that variations exist within specific cultures regardless of the degree of globalization (Gray & Allegritti, 2003). Image 11.3 shows that globalization can have various effects on culture.

When considering the effects of globalization, we need to examine our definition of culture. Consider the following questions, intended to guide us in articulating the meaning of culture:

> Are we seeing culture as a context-specific and "historically created system of meanings and significances" (Parekh, 2000, p. 143) relating to basic activities and social relationships that remain fairly static, such as "how one mourns and disposes of the dead and how one treats one's parents, children, wife, neighbors and strangers" (Parekh, 2000, p. 144)? Or are we seeing it in postmodern terms as "continually changing and evolving" (Dean, 2001, p. 625)? Do we agree that "every culture is internally varied, speaks in several voices, and its range of interpretive possibilities is often indeterminate" (Parekh, 2000, p. 144)? Do we share [the] idea that cultures "are continuously contested, imagined, reimagined, transformed, and negotiated both by their members and through their interaction with others" [(Tully, 1995, p. 11)] or are we using culture to refer to "a nation" or "a people" and do we agree that most nations have a dominant culture and a "relatively small number of minority cultures"? (Gray, 2005, p. 32)

Consider these questions about the definitions and notion of culture. How would you answer these questions? How does globalization influence our understanding of culture?

Transnational Migration

One aspect of globalization that directly influences social work is transnational migration. Globalization results in an increase in the flow of people back and forth across national borders. There are two main reasons: the integration of economies, which sets workers in motion from one country to another, and the displacements of people due to changing economic and social conditions (Li, 2003). Transnational migration predominately takes place from poorer countries to richer countries, as workers cross borders in search of work opportunities and better working conditions than what is available in their home country (Van Wormer, 2010). Often those same immigrants seek social services.

Two main factors involved in the displacement of people are economic crises and war. Asylum seekers migrate to Europe, but usually only temporarily, whereas asylum seekers in Canada and the United States often settle permanently (Van Wormer, 2010). Refugees from certain designated war zones are given a special status that results in increased benefits.

Immigration is often desirable from the perspective of manufacturers, employers, and governments. Countries of the global North need imported workers to satisfy labor shortages, specifically in difficult or strenuous working conditions. Simultaneously, countries of the global South are eager to have people leave so that they aren't placing a burden on their social services (Van Wormer, 2010). Highly skilled workers who enter countries of the global North are in a special category and are often granted privileged immigration status; however, once they migrate they are often pushed to the lower ends of the labor market in their profession.

Various scholars have written about the feminization of migration and the use of poor, mostly young female employees who endure 12-hour work days in arduous working conditions. These women can be found working at export processing plants (maquiladoras), sweatshops, farms, in homes as domestic labor or childcare workers, or in the sex industry (Hochschild, 2003; Van Wormer, 2010). Some of these women are susceptible to trafficking and exploitation. There are also traumatized female refugees who migrate to escape personal and political violence as well as the ravages of war. With dire economic conditions in their home countries, some women agree to serve as "mules" or couriers to transport illegal drugs across borders, and when caught, end up serving in prisons in the global North.

International forces and events that result in the movement of people have changed the composition of social service agency caseloads and the way we practice. Globalization today is not working for many of the world's poor (Stiglitz, 2004). Aspects of exploitation and marginalization remain attached to the harsh economic realities that the majority of people face all over the world. In a sense, economic globalization is a complex system of oppression that reinforces more familiar forms of oppression—such as racism, ethnocentrism, sexism, and classism (Van Wormer, 2010).

Environment and Sustainability

The environment and ecological sustainability are growing concerns in social work, especially as they relate to globalization. Exploitation of the earth's natural resources for multinational corporate profit and various environmental events affect communities worldwide. For example, the 2004 tsunami off the Indian Ocean, the 2009 earthquake in Haiti, the 2010 oil spill of Deep Water Horizon, the tsunami in 2011 affecting Japan (Alston & Besthorn, 2012), and the heavy monsoons in 2013 affecting Bangladesh and India are all events that caused billions of dollars in economic and infrastructure damage, displaced millions of people from their homes, and caused damage to our ecosystems. Human beings are responsible for a wide range of circumstances that affect our ecosystem: overpopulation, global warming, depletion of the ozone layer, wetland and coastal estuarial erosion, water pollution, air pollution, species extinction, loss of biodiversity, over-fishing, toxic waste and emissions, poisonous effects of chemical-based fertilizers and pesticides, and desertification; people are also displaced due to environment-related events, such as collapses in ecosystems, famine, and global pandemics (Alston & Besthorn, 2012, 56–57).

There is no longer much debate that Earth's climate is changing. However, a debate continues over whether or not climate change is the product of human activity or a normal (yet extreme) pattern of weather events (Plimer, 2009). If nothing else, we can point to increasing populations in most regions of the world, which contribute to the pressure on our environment and resources (Alston & Besthorn, 2012). These environmental strains result in food and water insecurities, with many of the worlds' poor lacking access to safe, reliable water. Many people are leaving rural areas where access to food and water is unreliable and moving to urban locations and neighboring countries in order to support their families (Besthorn & Meyer, 2010).

Environmental crises evolve in the context of community, society, and historical patterns of production and consumption. Solutions for environmental stresses that affect our local and global communities need to consist of "more than just new international policy agreements, calls for more corporate responsibility, more personal restraint, or the development of a handful of ecologically friendly technologies" (Alston & Besthorn, 2012, p. 57). Meaningful environmental action requires that we transform our consciousness and question our dominant social and economic relationships.

The notion of sustainability is crucial to the discussion of environmental issues. It depends on a balance of environmental, economic, and social priorities. Many focus on environmental and economic sustainability, but do not take into account social sustainability or acknowledge that all three are intertwined. Natural resource depletion has a significant effect on indigenous people, the rural poor, and impoverished women, but their challenges are marginalized when the social aspect of sustainability is ignored (Alston & Besthorn, 2012). For example, polluting factories and industries of the global North are located in the global South where most poor people are silenced by their need for employment. The pollution and exploitation both adversely affect and effect the well-being of marginalized communities.

The idea of social sustainability also raises the issue of social exclusion. Barriers to participation in society include unemployment, discrimination, poor skills, low income, poor housing, high crime, ill-health, and family breakdown. Individuals or communities affected by social exclusion are doubly oppressed when they are subsequently prevented from participating fully in the economic, social, and political life of their society. Refugees, migrants, and displaced people are often excluded from all benefits of citizenship, sometimes for many generations. Social exclusion is also connected to trade, migration, debt policies, human rights, and security (Healy, 2001). The social work profession has been slow to respond to environmental concerns, even as people and cultures throughout the world are experiencing deep alienation from their natural systems.

Another threat to environmental sustainability is loss of biodiversity. The term *biodiversity* refers to the degree of variation of life forms within a given ecosystem or on an entire planet, which maintains the health of all systems. Our unhealthy land and farming practices—monocropping (i.e., an agricultural practice in which the same crop is planted year after year) and using synthetic fertilizers, pesticides, and herbicides—contribute to the depletion of biodiversity (Van Worner & Besthorn, 2010). For example, highly toxic chemical fertilizers seep into rural waterways, drinking water, soil, and air (Despommier, 2009) not only causing health problems for people living in rural communities, but also degrading much of the soil. A global ecosystems report suggests helping to protect biodiversity by changing our consumption patterns, becoming more informed and better educated about our food, employing new technologies, reducing the number of fertilizers and pesticides, and penalizing industry and agriculture for engaging in exploitative practices (Mooney, Cropper, & Reid, 2005).

Many scholars point out that the most harmful abuse of the earth comes from war. Of course, modern industrialism abuses the earth in the process of feeding human consumption, but wars against people involve a deliberate attack on the natural environment. From setting fires to creating oilfields to defoliating jungles to bombing the earth and sea, war has also contributed to the devastation of our natural environment. The chemicals used in toxic weaponry contribute to ongoing mass destruction of human and natural life and long-term radioactive contamination in our bodies and in the earth (Alston & Besthorn, 2012).

From a global AOP lens, it is important to examine structural disadvantage within and between countries based on equitable access to resources and equal accountability and responsibility for resource depletion (Alston & Besthorn, 2012). In this context, social workers can engage with local people to develop locally driven and sustainable solutions to complex environmental problems that emerge from resource depletion and changing environmental contexts (Taylor, Wilkinson, & Cheers, 2008).

INTERNATIONAL AND DOMESTIC GLOBAL AOP

As mentioned at the beginning of the chapter, global social work can take place on both a domestic stage and an international one. The roles that social workers engage in internationally are essentially the same as the roles they assume in domestic settings. The central focus in both settings is empowerment, capacity building, and sustainability.

Herscovitch (2001) identifies eight major social work roles in international and domestic work:

- *Program implementation*: Individual social workers work at the community level and directly with program participants. Usually these positions are held by individuals who understand local culture, language, and values. Some of their tasks might include organizing after-school activities, teaching literacy classes, building a capacity for a women's microbusiness group, organizing communities about reproductive health and HIV/AIDS, or building potable water systems.
- *Casework:* This role tends to be most prevalent in relief work following a disaster or in urban programs. Caseworkers respond to participants' needs for short-term psychological "first-aid," long-term therapy or rehabilitation, or psychiatric interventions for

people suffering from clinically diagnosed posttraumatic stress disorder (Garbarino, Kostelny, & Dubrow, 1991). These interventions can be in the form of direct therapy or group work. In this role, the caseworker is assumed to have a deep understanding of local and cultural issues—for example, the ways in which people from the local community cope and "heal" so that a westernized mental health agenda is not imposed. Sometimes the caseworker might not provide direct service, but rather might support local staff in their own delivery of casework or therapy. For example, communities may be assisted by local resources in the form of traditional healers, shamans, or other religious leaders. In emergency or war situations, program staff may also need support to effectively address any vicarious trauma.

● *Program development and technical assistance:* The individual social worker in this role focuses on the programmatic content of projects (not administration or management). The focus is on strategizing and designing program approaches in a single sector (such as education or health), or in multiple sectors (such as in a project for life skills development for youth). Other tasks might include conducting needs assessments and designing projects, developing and writing program or project proposals, communicating with project donors, giving technical assistance and guidance, documenting program progress, and writing technical publications.

● *Program management:* This role is more administrative in nature and involves representation of the program with partner agencies and donors, oversight of project budget and personnel, oversight of implementation and technical assistance, and assistance with fund-raising. The challenges associated with this role include how to balance decentralized, participatory decision making and management with the need for quick decision making and efficiency (Latting & Gummer, 1994).

● *Program monitoring, evaluation, and research:* Social workers take on this role in agencies where evaluation is being conducted. Tasks include setting up baseline surveys, training field staff in data collection, analyzing data collected, holding focus groups with program participants and program staff, and writing evaluation reports for NGOs, governments, and donors.

● *Training:* Social workers may be engaged in training individuals who provide direct services, individuals who are managing or developing programs, and, in some cases, training other trainers. Their responsibility is to facilitate active learning as well as to model effective training techniques though active participation and dialogue by teachers and learners alike.

● *Organizational development and network building:* This role focuses on two levels of work. The first is building the capacity of one organization by supporting the development of organizational vision and developing positive organizational values, work processes, and learning. The second level is building the capacity of local organizations so they can more effectively conduct their direct implementation of services. Network building involves the linking, connecting, and facilitating of inter-organizational collaboration.

- *Advocacy and policy making:* The social worker can engage at this level in various sub-roles, including lobbying in order to influence legislative actions or the voting behavior of legislators. Individuals can also be advocates, working for an organization that seeks to leverage its field of practice into large structural change. This endeavor involves demonstrating to other organizations, donors, and governments which approaches are most effective and thereby influencing them on what types of activities to fund and support. One can also engage in policy making, leading NGOs, or holding positions within globally influenced institutions, such as the World Bank, a United Nations agency, or a bilateral/multilateral donor organization. Partnerships between donor organizations and countries are vital to national efforts to achieve common goals.

In all of these roles, whether in domestic or international practice, what is important is the degree to which the values of social work fit the context, the effectiveness of the social work to meet human needs, and the extent to which social work contributes to social improvement (Gray & Fook, 2004).

Domestic Social Work Practice

Domestic social work practice refers to social work activities that take place in the United States with a focus on issues of international concern (for example, problems of refugees or ecological issues). It also includes international exchanges between social workers and individuals from different societies and cultures. Examples of domestic practice include work in refugee resettlement, work with international populations, international adoption work, and social work in border areas (Healy, 2001).

One important caution for domestic social work practice is to avoid "professional imperialism," whereby social workers unquestioningly implement Western models of practice and do not examine inherent power differences (Gray, 2005). To accept and incorporate other worldviews into one's frame of reference is difficult, and it is necessary to move beyond "cultural sensitivity" or "cultural competence" to understand the cultural views of others (Brydon, 2011). The idea of cross-cultural awareness tends to imply that the primary challenge for social workers of the global North is to gain "insight," and therefore a better understanding, about other cultures. As important as it is for social workers to gain cultural sensitivity into the views, experiences, and expectations of their participants, they must also gain insight into their own culture and intersecting identities (Lee & Greene, 1999). Earlier chapters present concepts that are key to achieving this insight, such as critical self-reflection, awareness of one's own positionality, values and ethics, inherent power differences, privilege and oppression, as well as structural and global issues that influence individual circumstances.

When discussing domestic social work practice, some scholars draw attention to the values that unify professional social workers on the international level, such as empowerment, justice, human rights and equity (Hokenstad, Khinduka, & Midgley, 1992; Ife, 2001). Others question the universal applicability and superiority of professional, international social work values (Bar-On, 1998; Cossom, 1990). Some point to the need for social work practice to be much more contextually oriented. However, there is also the belief that different types of social work can take place across widely divergent contexts, united by shared human rights and social justice goals.

International Social Work Practice

International organizations concentrate on interventions at different levels and with varied emphases (e.g., environment/natural resources, education, health, or economic development). In addition, international practice, even though its mission may take on one of these typical forms of expression, takes place in different countries and is therefore informed by local practices. The main challenge is to find ways to celebrate and recognize commonalities between the local participants and social workers while at the same time valuing and including differences (Gray & Fook, 2002).

The key to a successful outcome is to work from a multi-sector, multilayered approach (Gray & Fook, 2004; Herscovitch, 2001). For example, if working in education, there may be a community where many children do not attend school in order to help their parents because their labor is needed to support the family income. Even though the children's long-term potential might be higher if they were attending school, the family may not be able to survive without the children helping out in the fields. Or there may be a family that has enough resources to send only one child to school (because of costs associated with books, supplies, school uniforms, and so on). Oftentimes low-income families choose to send sons rather than daughters to school. Thus, education programs might focus not only on quality issues within a school (curriculum development and teacher training), but also on health, gender, and economic issues.

Using environmental issues illustrates another example of the need for multilayered social work. For instance, to demonstrate how issues are interconnected think about how more children working in the fields increases the number of people in the fields, thus further degrading the soil, which then requires more effort to reap the same yields—and so on.

Another important factor in international social work is capacity building and empowerment, meaning that work shouldn't be done *for* people and their communities, but rather in collaboration with them (Herscovitch, 2001). However, it is important to add that participatory approaches are easier to implement with long-term projects rather than in emergency situations, especially when health needs may be at stake or when individuals are experiencing trauma.

In order to achieve a greater impact, programs are encouraged to adopt the concept of praxis that calls for implementing, reflecting, and adapting a program (or activity) based on collective lessons learned about what worked and what did not (Freire, 1992). However, this approach can be challenging when major funders require a project to predetermine program outcomes. One solution is for NGOs to diversify their funding sources and raise funds locally (Edwards & Hulme, 1992). More diversified support is important in creating sustainable change. Another solution is to keep program costs low—perhaps by drawing on locally available materials and resources—in order to support affordability and thus sustainability (Herscovitch, 2001).

Social Development

One important form of international practice is social development. In fact, the second half of the 20th century has been called the "era of development." The origins of this era included the need for global reconstruction in the immediate aftermath of World War II; the evolution of colonialism or "colonization" into globalization; the establishment of new free trade policies between "developed" and "underdeveloped" nations; and with the start of the Cold War, the desire of the United States and its allies to prevent countries of the global South from drifting toward communism.

International development, in its very meaning, was geared toward colonies that had gained independence. The governance of the newly independent states was to be constructed so that the inhabitants could enjoy freedom from poverty, hunger, and insecurity. Today, international social development work involves helping developing countries create the necessary capacity needed for sustainable solutions to issues that arise, with the goal of developing a greater quality of life for individuals, families, groups, and communities. International development projects may consist of a single, transformative project to address a specific problem or a series of projects targeted at several aspects of society.

The five domains of social development work are shown in Image 11.4. Some believe that economic development and infrastructure development to address the widening economic disparities should be the priority; thinking that if a country's economy is healthy, other benefits will follow. Many critique this rationalist lens, however, and advocate for a focus on democracy building, human development, and environmental development.

In the field of social work, many agree about the goals of social development, but disagree about how these visions, strategies, and processes should be implemented in the field. To be consistent with AOP, according to Pawar and Cox (2010) these are the best methods for working toward social development:

- Understanding current and changing global conditions
- Acknowledging the well-being, quality of life, and freedom of everyone to realize their potential

Image 11.4	Domains of Social Development Work
Domain	*Concerns*
Democracy building	Citizenship, local governance, decentralization of government
Economic development	Agriculture, microbusiness, group loan programs
Environmental development	Wildlife, ecology, agriculture, pollution, industrialization, desertification
Human development	Education, early childhood development, health, population trends
Infrastructure development	Water systems, wastewater disposal, irrigation

Source: Adapted from Herscovitch, 2001, p. 171.

- Valuing human dignity, human rights and obligations, diversity, and the human link with nature
- Paying attention to process as participatory and empowering
- Developing and implementing plans and strategies that are multilevel (from local to international) and multidimensional (including cultural, political, economic, ecological, education, health, housing, equity groups and citizens and their institutions) (pp. 27–34)

Some of the critiques about social development efforts center on the idea that social development can be practiced and achieved in the global North, but may not be relevant to the global South or may be significantly more difficult to implement in "developing countries." Others question the very idea of "development," perceiving it as an effort to shape the global South "in the likeness of the global North, with the help and expertise of Northerners" (Gray & Fook, 2004, p. 631). Others believe that the way that national governments and international aid agencies operate is just another way to control the poor (Rozario, 2001). Critics of international social development assert that the way to overcome poverty is through emancipatory social movements and a robust civil society, not paternalistic aid programs, international organizations, or corporate charity.

There is also criticism around the "export model" of intervention, where social welfare theories, practice models, and approaches have been inappropriately and uncritically exported or borrowed (Healy, 2001). Exchanges under these conditions are mostly one-way relationships between the "expert" who holds more power, and the recipient of services, creating unequal or exploitative relationships. True mutual exchange exists only when all participants benefit from the relationship or transaction.

The importance of local people's participation in development rather than a top-down approach, where others (from the global North) come and execute the development for them, cannot be overemphasized (Carr, 2012). It is critical that the local communities' perceived needs and desires are what drives the development rather than the needs perceived by others. Local people with shared and common interests can and should define their own solutions. Shared and agreed ownership over community growth is key. Therefore, in collaboration, development workers and the community should aim for conscientization, or the development of critical consciousness—a critical process in liberatory, anti-oppressive practice for individuals who have historically been marginalized, oppressed, and excluded from decision-making processes.

Disaster Management and International Relief Work

International relief work consists of social assistance and humanitarian aid conducted under emergency circumstances. Disaster, whether from human causes or natural causes, can occur without warning, at any time and at any place. When it occurs, infrastructures and social systems often collapse, affecting thousands of people and sometimes causing major injuries and deaths. According to the *World Disaster Report: Focus on Public Health* (2000), it is striking to note that 96% of deaths from natural disasters have occurred in countries of the global South. This report suggests that the root causes of these deaths include a lack of resources, deforestation, global capitalism, global warming, and political agendas (IFRC, 2000; Mathbor & Bourassa, 2012). Examples of disaster management or relief work include assisting others in a war environment, during a famine or epidemic, and following an earthquake or a tsunami (Herscovitch, 2001). Immense loss results from these events. Relief work involves an immediate response to basic human needs, such as shelter, food, water, safety, and family reunification. Social and psychological interventions are also included in the programming of local, national, and international organizations that respond to disaster. Disaster management focuses on identifying risks and creating strategies that assist people in addressing the negative consequences of a disaster.

Government emergency response policies and procedures can alleviate some of the harmful outcomes that are generated by disasters. However, some national governments are unable or unwilling to provide support, particularly during mega-disasters or during times of civil conflict (Lyons, Hokenstad, Pawar, Huegler, & Hall, 2012). This lack of government support can raise significant barriers to affected communities accessing relief and recovery services, and as a consequence leave thousands struggling to survive.

International relief work also has political dimensions that can produce significant barriers to relief work. In some instances, governments have a difficult time coordinating the services of local and international organizations that offer assistance during mega-disasters. On other occasions, governments use external disaster support as a tool to redistribute power (Lyons et al., 2012). They funnel disaster aid into more affluent communities rather than assisting those most marginalized and impoverished, leaving these oppressed communities even more vulnerable.

On the other hand, excluding local governments from relief and recovery efforts can create combative, even deadly, relationships with international relief organizations. In 2008, reports surfaced of 260 workers who were severely injured, taken hostage, or killed while working in conflict zones that were not secured by government forces (Stoddard, Harmer, & DiDomenico, 2009). In some cases, when adversarial relationships existed the delivery of humanitarian aid was facilitated with military or private security forces (Save the Children, 2010). These types of problems often can be avoided by including all voices in decisions, including government officials, otherwise antagonism can arise toward humanitarian aid workers. Consequently, the coordination of disaster management activities is extremely important so that all efforts are organized and gaps in services are reduced.

Further tensions emerge when deciding how to serve individuals, families, and communities without creating a "handout" or dependency dynamic, but rather working *with* communities to create long-term sustainable solutions (Herscovitch, 20001, p. 171). Humanitarian aid that uses participatory approaches enhances community capacity and sustainability. A grassroots, bottom-up approach, where communities are inspired to participate in the design, creation, and coordination of programs supports empowerment, collaboration, and investment in the process. In addition, incorporating a community's strengths, capacities, expertise, and local resources increases their sense of control over reconstruction (Lyons et al., 2012; Van der Veer, 2006).

Recently, some scholars maintain that international relief work and international development work are interconnected and on a continuum, as opposed to viewing them as mutually exclusive or separate actions. For example, poorly planned agricultural practices (typical development work) can cause soil erosion or deforestation, which can cause a disaster with heavy rains. Similarly, well-executed relief work, conducted through full collaboration and participation with local community groups, can build local capacity to create their own solutions and thus create a path toward sustainable development during non-emergency times (Herscovitch, 2001). Other activities can overlap. For example, land mine education and removal of land mines are connected to war situations (traditionally considered relief work), but also be useful to development efforts in times of political peace.

Faith-Based Social Work Around the World

Throughout the world, there are many religious and faith-based organizations that are responding to the needs of people. These religiously motivated organizations can be multinational like the Salvation Army, or locally based like the Buddhist monks from temples in Thailand (Nye, 2008). These organizations are similar in that they offer socially based services, each with a mission, mandate, and goals to achieve a certain outcome related to human well-being. Financial and political support of these organizations often comes from various governments around the world. These organizations vary in the degree to which they try to convert others to their religion. Some organizations solely provide services; others are remnants of a colonial era, when Christian missions were established in Asia, Africa, and

South America. They often had an enormous impact (often eradicating) on local culture and religious and spiritual practices (Huegler, Lyons, & Pawar, 2012).

Many criticize the motivation of religious development groups, especially in the global North where the majority of organizations are Christian. They combine economic, health, and other types of aid with efforts to convert local people away from their indigenous beliefs and cultural practices. However, due to historical networks, some of these faith-based organizations and missionary groups can reach out to communities in ways that other groups cannot. For example there are some organizations with strong connections to Africa's churches, which in turn facilitates their ability to provide top quality services in health and education. Still, faith-based foreign aid is sometimes regarded as a modern-day extension of religious colonialism. Morality is often dangerously mixed with critical development concerns, especially global health education, prevention and treatment of infectious diseases, economic security, and sex work.

Many of these questions became more intense during President George W. Bush's faith-based initiative. In 2006, the *Boston Globe* newspaper published a special report called "Exporting Faith," which examined the expansion of U.S. foreign aid funding directed to religious organizations. The *Boston Globe*'s Washington bureau conducted an 18-month research project, analyzing more than 50,000 government funding awards by the U.S. Agency for International Development (USAID) during the Bush administration. Based on the findings, the newspaper article reported that the amount of U.S. foreign aid dollars awarded to religious organizations doubled from 2001 to 2005, from 10% to nearly 20%, totaling more than $1.7 billion. Of the funds directed to so-called "faith-based" organizations, 98% went to Christian groups (Stockman, Kranish, Canellos, & Baron, 2006), while only two Jewish and two Muslim organizations received funding. In response to charges of unfair funding, U.S. officials said they had trouble even identifying local religious groups abroad for collaboration.

Federal regulation states that any religious organization can compete for USAID funding for development projects as long as there is no religious discrimination for or against the beneficiaries of this funding, and that the objectives of the organization's project match the objectives of the agency. However, officials say that smaller, decentralized faith-based organizations often do not meet USAID accounting requirements, or they do not have the capacity to deal with the bureaucratic contracting process (U.S. Agency for International Development, 2004). In addition, some have critiqued the politics and practices of American Christian development workers funded by U.S. taxpayer funds as the workers are often placed in locations where there is little to no federal monitoring or evaluation.

Take a moment to consider these perspectives on religious and faith-based organizations. What is your personal view about faith-based organizations and their receipt of government funding to engage in international social work? What are some of the challenges that you can identify that could occur when the U.S. government predominantly supports Christian-based organizations?

Indigenization

In large part, the involvement of faith-based organizations (and other aid organizations) raises questions about respect for local communities. In the context of social work, *indigenization* refers to the extent to which social work practice is in line with local contexts. Social work practice is, in turn, shaped by the extent to which native or resident social, political, economic, historical and cultural factors, including local voices, mold and shape social work responses (Gray, 2005). Indigenization celebrates local traditions, relationships and practices, and allows people to self-define (Grande, 2004).

The process of indigenization involves rediscovering and redeveloping indigenous identities in a postcolonial and postmodern world. These identities are made and remade in a dynamic process of interaction with many diverse groups and structures (Gray & Fook, 2004). Some see indigenization as rejecting cultural hegemony perpetuated through globalization (Gray, Coates, & Yellowbird, 2009), since it entails resistance to domination.

As an empowering practice, indigenization resists injustice and oppression through the imposition of European and Northern American models of social work on non-individualistic and non-capitalistic cultural models of helping (Dominelli, 2008). At the same time, indigenization aims to preserve local cultures, communities, and traditions (Yip, 2005). It also situates indigenous people as active agents in contemporary capitalist societies (Grande, 2004).

It is important to note that the concept of indigenization varies from population to population, and does not capture the complex relationship of interdependence between people and cultures. Indigenous social work involves using the terms "locality specific" and "culturally relevant social work." Using the words of indigenous people to label and understand their own discourses helps to affirm indigenous people's strengths and support their resistance to colonization (Dominelli, 2008). Local players become aware of the forces depriving them of resources, power, and self-determination, and develop the capacity to collectively take action. Thus, indigenization becomes a form of emancipatory, anti-oppressive social work.

LINKS BETWEEN THE GLOBAL AND THE LOCAL

Linking the global to the local is the process of "linking global change to local experience and local programs" (Ife, 2000, p. 58). Global social work isn't about the spread of professional social work around the globe, but rather about the development of practices that are relevant in local contexts (Gray, 2005). It requires initiatives directed at global change and also at local community development. Global AOP embraces the concept of *localism,* which "holds out the promise of empowered local communities, ecological sustainability and cultural diversity; structures that genuinely meet human needs and are able to be controlled by the people themselves, and enrich their quality of life" (Ife, 2000, p. 58).

To link the global and the local requires that social workers begin to concern themselves with policy at the regional and global levels (Ife, 2000). They should seek greater inputs into the deliberations of the key global players, such as the IMF, the World Bank, the WTO, and so on, while also contributing to and promoting the work of NGOs (Deacon 1997). Along with increased attention to global efforts, there should be an emphasis on local strategies to address issues of equity and access. A concentration on global issues focuses on universal human rights, while locally based practice is about needs: assessing the nature and extent of community need, identifying groups in need, working to have human needs met, and so on (Ife, 2000, p. 60).

How might expanding the practice of policy advocacy to international forums and organizations, such as the IMF, the World Bank, and the WTO, assist with linking the global and the local? What are other strategies and ways that build international solidarity? What are your thoughts about incorporating a strong human rights analysis alongside a more traditional social work-based practice?

STORIES FROM THE FIELD: GLOBAL ANTI-OPPRESSIVE SOCIAL WORK PRACTICE

1   Global Meanings in Local Spaces: Rachel's Story in a Global Context, by Carly Goldberg   p. 415

    This story illustrates Carly Goldberg's direct practice work with a female immigrant refugee from Monrovia, Liberia, who had experienced torture and trauma. Understanding globalization offers opportunities for social workers to recognize the importance of the intersection between global and local spaces. Carly is transformed through her interactions with Rachel, who is unlike anyone she had ever encountered. Through this story, we witness the importance of working from an anti-essentialist lens and further understand the role of globalization in social work.

2   Cross-Cultural Explorations of Power and Privilege, by Lynn Parker   p. 417

    This story describes a social worker's journey with teaching a social work course in Cuernavaca, México. Lynn Parker explores power and privilege through her course, Global Relations and Poverty in Mexico. This course for MSW students is based in the community-learning philosophy of Paulo Freire and provides a mixture of experiential and academic learning. Rather than going to books and texts, students learned directly from the local people via lively two-way conversations with peasants, spiritual and civic leaders, squatters, refugees, social workers, human rights activists, and indigenous peoples.

(Continued)

In this story, Lorraine Kerwood locates herself and her experiences in life, providing a context for how she came to engage in anti-oppressive global social work. She describes how she experienced various form of oppression based on her lower socioeconomic status, her sexual orientation, and her disability, among her other identities. When she learns of her diagnosis of Aspergers syndrome, Lorraine realizes her personal computer became an interface between herself and the world. The benefits of having a computer in her life led her to acknowledge the importance of computer access for people in marginalized countries. This story details her collaborative efforts to bring technology to rural villages in Guatemala. She and her colleague found old computers that they could rebuild and then gift to the indigenous children who needed them in Central America.

1

GLOBAL MEANINGS IN LOCAL SPACES: RACHEL'S STORY IN A GLOBAL CONTEXT

CARLY GOLDBERG

I first met Rachel when working as a prevention specialist at a New York City–based HIV/AIDS organization. My initial introduction to Rachel was through her intake sheet, completed by a case manager who had referred her to our organization from a local health center. I learned that Rachel was a 35-year-old mother of three and a recent refugee to the United States from Monrovia, Liberia, via a refugee camp in Ghana. When I first read this I thought, "OK, what do I do with this information" and "Where exactly is Monrovia?" Going immediately to the internet to figure out exactly where Monrovia and Ghana are located, I learned about the first and second Liberian civil wars, the violent atrocities perpetrated during the wars, and the multitude of human rights violations that had been occurring over the course of nearly ten years. I couldn't imagine how this information about my client's background would impact our work together.

Our initial meeting took place in my dimly lit office, which was shared with two other coworkers. The walls were covered in HIV/AIDS prevention pamphlets and posters promoting safer sex education and HIV testing. Although I engaged Rachel in the same kind and warm way as I did all my clients, my initial meeting with her felt terrible. I felt that I lacked, not only the conceptual framework and skills to engage with her, but quite simply and literally the words to even begin a conversation. I remember feeling quite out of place, dislocated from my usual confident and knowledgeable professional self—like I was a foreigner in my own office and in my own job.

Though I didn't realize it at the time, I think that it is fair to say this may describe the way Rachel, too, was feeling, dislocated from the familiar—her homeland, family, friends, and daily way of life. If I had had this insight at the time, I would have begun the initial session very differently. Instead of trying to complete the required psychosocial assessment (which was mandated protocol on meeting new clients), I would have spent our time together simply discussing geography and location.

Thinking about globalization offers opportunities for social workers to recognize the importance of the intersection between global and local spaces. I had come to learn that Rachel was in deep mourning over the loss of her family, who had been brutally murdered in front of her eyes; she had also lost her home, her worldly possessions, her job in Monrovia's bustling market, her dignity (after being violently raped as an act of war), and her health (after learning while in the refugee camps that she was HIV-positive). Now, she comes to find herself in the United States alone with her three young children, with no family or friends, an unwanted pregnancy, and quickly deteriorating health. She is sitting in an unknown office building, with a White woman who is a stranger, being asked questions about her HIV infection, risk behaviors, and prevention practices.

Unfortunately, her journey in the course of a few months from her home to my office was ignored. I later came to find out through our work together that she longed for her dead relatives, friends, work, religious community, home, and ordinary activities of daily living. If I had been able to acknowledge the loss of her homeland and everything that was connected to this loss, and the pain that I could see on her face and the tears in her eyes, I would have validated how she was feeling in our initial few meetings. That acknowledgment would have grounded our work together while honoring her homeland and experiences in West Africa and the new experiences and life she was working hard to forge in the United States.

In my initial interaction with Rachel as a client, I recognized that our work together would be different from the way in which I engaged and worked with other HIV-positive clients, who needed HIV prevention education and counseling. Rachel, unlike many of the American-born clients with whom I had worked, was not familiar with our social service and health care system. Furthermore, for Rachel, navigating an unfamiliar system of physicians and other persons in positions of power and authority may have been overwhelming, confusing, and terrifying. Early on in our working relationship I came to believe that our work could not be confined to the four walls of my office, but would require assisting her to navigate a complex system of care. I felt that accompanying her to her numerous appointments with infectious disease, internal medicine, and OB-GYN physicians would help our work together.

It was in these moments that our relationship began to develop and she began to put her trust in me. This process is called "therapeutic accompaniment," a powerful tool in developing a working relationship with a survivor of trauma and torture (Fabri, 2001). It was in the waiting rooms, in the hallways walking to and from various appointments, in the actual examination room, on the streets of New York City, at fast food restaurants, and in her home in Harlem that she began to develop trust in the therapeutic relationship, allowing for our work to progress. Increasingly she was reaching out to me over the phone, asking for my opinion about things related to her children and their needs in school or calling when she didn't feel well to see if and how I could help her. When she gave birth to her fourth child she wanted me to visit her in the hospital and at home to get to know the baby, in addition to her three other children.

Having reached this point in our relationship, we could return to the initial reason for our meeting and collaboratively work to reduce the risk of HIV transmission to her as-yet-unborn child, reduce her risk of becoming reinfected with HIV, and ensure that she was able to address her overall health needs related to her HIV infection. As a social worker, I was able to recognize that while her needs in the area of HIV prevention were similar to the needs of the many other clients with whom I worked, her needs as an HIV positive woman from West Africa resettling in an urban landscape were quite distinct. Therefore, as a client her particular needs needed to be reframed through a cultural context and not the universal, essential, and positivistic framework through which many of our agencies still demand we view our clients.

In order to address her HIV prevention needs, it was imperative that together we understood who Rachel was in her distinct and intersecting identities: woman, Liberian, daughter, sister, mother, survivor of rape and torture, refugee, person living with HIV, Christian, client, and so on. Though we did not explicitly discuss her identity formation via the concept of intersectionality, in practice many of her intersecting identities and experiences influenced the way in which we worked together.

1. Reflecting back on her work with Rachel, what would Carly have done differently?

2. Essentialism is the belief that things have a set of specific characteristics that make them what they are. It is the practice of regarding something as having innate existence or universal validity rather than as being socially, ideologically, or intellectually constructed. How does incorporating an anti-essentialist lens inform global anti-oppressive social work practice?

3. What are some of the ways in which Carly and Rachel built trust and a therapeutic alliance, leading to moments of transformation in their relationship?

4. What role does globalization play in social work practice?

2

CROSS-CULTURAL EXPLORATIONS OF POWER AND PRIVILEGE

LYNN PARKER

If you have come here to help me, you are wasting your time, but if you have come here because your liberation is bound up with mine, then, let us walk together. —Lilla Watson

Each year I have the good fortune to teach a social work course in Cuernavaca, México, *Global Relations and Poverty in Mexico*. Before taking on this course, I had only a cursory familiarity with the issues and people of Mexico. I inherited my course, or rather, a prior version of it. A colleague who had been leading the course for a couple of years was no longer able to do it, and encouraged me to take it on, saying she thought I would really love doing it. Frankly, I was a bit reluctant because it would take two weeks of my summer. However, I trusted this colleague, and so I said yes.

It was not an outlandish prospect for me, because I did and do have a fervent commitment to issues of social justice. Having been a social work practitioner for many years prior to coming into academia, I also loved group work. And, though I did not know that these attributes would be a good fit for the course when I agreed to lead it, the actual experience of the course felt like I had come home to issues, people, and a sense of solidarity with who I am at my best and at my roots. I felt I was doing what I was meant to do. What had been missing for me in academia was the experience of connection and collaboration—of being engaged in something really meaningful, life changing, transformational—all of which I experienced in the two weeks of the course. My group of slightly acquainted students slowly coalesced within an intense and powerful learning experience, and together began to scaffold a commitment to work for a better world for everyone.

When I arrived in Mexico and realized that we were immersed in issues of justice—in dialogue each day with the people there about shared and respective problems, questions, hopes, and dreams—I knew that I was engaged in making a difference and doing what mattered, that we as a group were involved in a transformational process. There was no dissonance between my values and my work. Moreover, the relationship with the students felt more authentic. I was a learner with them in this process as well as group leader/facilitator. And, I reveled in the opportunity to craft a group process that gently and skillfully deepened the students' relationship with the course, the experiences, the content, and each other. The two weeks were a firsthand experience of praxis: practice in action. I was able to use my skills as a seasoned practitioner to evoke a process of critical consciousness.

Cuernavaca was chosen initially as the site for this course because of its long time roots as a center of emancipatory political, religious, and educational thought and conversation, especially lively in the 1960s, 1970s, and into the 1980s. Ivan Illich's Center for Intercultural Documentation (CIDOC), founded in 1961, was a think tank and meeting place where many American and Latin American intellectuals came together to reflect on education, politics, and culture. Taking place during this time were the famous and vigorously argued debates between Paulo Freire and Ivan Illich on education, schooling, and the awakening of awareness. Many of their students are still living in the city and present to our group.

My course follows the spirit of those times and is based in the community-learning philosophy of Paulo Freire, which provides a mixture of experiential and academic learning. Rather than going to books and texts, students learn directly from the local people via lively two-way conversations with peasants, spiritual and civic leaders, squatters, refugees, social workers, human rights activists, and indigenous peoples. The course is not service learning-based, where we more privileged people come to help those who are less fortunate. Nor do we come to Mexico to study from academics or experts. Instead, the U.S.-based students and faculty come to learn from ordinary, local people with whom we dialogue and to whom we afford great respect. We are the students; they are our teachers.

The course privileges experience through dialogue and reflection. This is the opposite of most academic learning, which mostly leads with knowledge from experts (books, professors) up front. Instead, we participants venture out of our comfort zones to visit remote communities where we gain knowledge regarding Mexican culture; individual, family, and community responses to poverty; historical patterns of oppression; spirituality and liberation theology; global economics and policy; and the role of indigenous movements. It is our intention in this course to enter humbly with a willingness to learn from the people—to enter their homes; sit with them; and learn about their lives, needs, wishes, and dreams. We also answer any questions they might have about us. Included are discussions on the relationship between poverty in Mexico and policies in the United States; the plight of legal and illegal immigrants to the United States and Canada; and international trade policies—whether they help or further marginalize those with less.

The course incorporates Freire's pedagogy for developing critical consciousness. The process we use includes three phases of learning:

1. See—We immerse ourselves in experience.

2. Reflect—We reflect and begin to dialogue with community people and with each other about our experience—our reactions to what we saw, felt, and heard. Within that process, we begin to hypothesize, theorize, and evaluate.

3. Act—We develop action plans based on experience, knowledge, and thoughtful dialogue.

Freire contrasts experiential learning with what he calls, "banking education"—where experts (or teachers) make "deposits" of information that students are to receive, remember, and repeat—a transmission of knowledge from the knowledgeable to those who know less, subject to object.

I will highlight just a few of the people we visit as part of the course:

- Nacho is an indigenous spiritual leader and local veterinarian. We visit him at his family home in Amatlan, a small community that still maintains ancestral customs. He tells the story of the Spanish conquest of Mexico. We also hike with him to a sacred spiritual center where he invites participants into an ancient ritual.

- Maggie is a young woman who tells her harrowing story of crossing the border and entering the United States with her mother and sister when she was a child. She weaves a poignant story of the family's experiences with their "coyote"; of the attempts, failures, and eventual crossing; then of living and going to school in the United States; and finally of her return to Mexico after a U.S. social worker (wrongfully) threatened to remove the children from the home. She tells her story in her grandparents' home, where her extended family now lives. After Maggie tells the story, her grandfather serenades us with music, and her mother and sister lead the group in dance. Students experience the profound love within the family and the dire circumstances that led Maggie's mother to risk a border crossing without documents.
- Ofelia, an exuberant woman now in her 60s, tells of traveling as a young child to México City to become a domestic worker to help provide for her family. Though she hungered to go to school, education was denied her as a girl. As a woman, Ofelia became connected to a liberation theologist, Gerardo Thijssen, in the squatters' settlement where she lived. He helped organize the women to make changes in their community—for example, getting running water into their settlement. Ophelia eventually was able to leave her abusive husband and become self-supporting. She now organizes domestic workers in Mexico.
- Gloria, a T-shirt vendor, tells of her escape from the massacre in El Salvador and the destruction of her family and community there.
- Alfonso, a priest, serves the gay lesbian, bisexual, and transgender community and established a shelter for AIDS victims in Cuernavaca.
- Hector, a Zapatista, tells of the struggles of the indigenous peoples in Chiapas.
- Estella, a spiritual healer, portrays the struggles of women in Mexico.
- Arturo, another teacher, former diplomat, and community activist, challenges the students to feel and embrace the complexities, contradictions, and relationship of the struggles in Mexico with the relative privilege of the United States and to translate their learning into meaningful social action.

The course also incorporates experiential exercises. For example, students compare shopping at the farmers market with shopping at the local Wal-Mart. After the shopping excursion, students deliberate the impact of Wal-Mart type companies on the local culture and economy. This is followed by dialogue with a professor from a university in México City that gives the students more information about the history of México and the implications of trade policies (for example, the North American Free Trade Agreement, or NAFTA). With the accumulating experiences, students begin to comprehend the repercussions of global policies on the 70% of the Mexican population who make only 40 pesos ($4) a day.

With each encounter, the students become aware of the huge and too often painful complexities of poverty, privilege, dominance, and subservience. How are we connected? What actions of mine—of my people—serve the whole, and which actions and decisions serve to maintain my (our) power and privilege while marginalizing others? Students begin to take to heart some of the major dilemmas as they realize how intimately related we all are fundamentally. They leave the experience with the sense that we in the United States hold responsibility for many of the world's problems; our advantage comes at the expense of others. They leave Mexico struggling with their own consumerism and relative privilege. Many vow to buy more consciously in the future—for example, to examine labels to ascertain where the clothing is made so as not to buy brands that farm the work out to *maquiladoras* ("sweat shops") and benefit U.S. factory owners while marginalizing young female workers from third world countries. These are comments by some of the students that reflect their growing consciousness:

Jessica: I thought I was a poor college student who didn't have any money, but then I went to Mexico, and I was like, "Man, I don't realize how much stuff I do have, I mean, compared to the people there."

Aliza: As we attempt to make sense of all of this, we have questions. Everyday concepts suddenly have become complicated and confusing. What do we do with our money? What does it mean to be a consumer? How do we define happiness and poverty? What values do we use to make these judgments?

The students have been welcomed into homes with no beds, dirt floors, little food for the day and been told, "*Mi casa es su casa*" (My house is your house). "Come back and visit."

Jake: I like the idea of standing in solidarity with people. It does not presume that one person knows better or more, or that one group needs to educate or help another. Rather, we stand together in our differences, in our struggles, in our hope for a better future.

We have heard their stories, and, out of hearing another's experience comes the possibility of a different relationship. When we become aware of the other's humanity, so much becomes possible. A transformative connection is built that is carried forward into each of our lives in the United States. Hopefully, we are each moved to work for a better more accommodating world for everyone.

Luke: We have talked a lot about the idea of transformation. Transformation means to evolve, to change, and to grow. Transformation means that we have opened our hearts enough to see the world in a different way. When we change our hearts, our world also changes. We leave this experience a little more awake, and because of this, we are a little freer. This is transformation.

1. In what ways do the students from the global North engage in dialogue and experiential learning through the course?

2. How are the students' experiences unsettling, yet transformational?

3. Consider the different local voices presented. How do their stories and lives serve to create awareness of global issues, power, and privilege?

3

FROM GERMANTOWN TO GUATEMALA

LORRAINE KERWOOD

The very first religious protest against U.S. slavery occurred where I grew up, in Germantown, Pennsylvania. In 1688, a group of Quakers filed a formal petition that, while never acted on, was still significant. During that time Germantown had its own industry, and it was a thriving metropolis for several centuries. After the Civil War, freed African Americans could buy houses anywhere in Germantown; today Germantown is one of the oldest racially integrated neighborhoods in the country.

In the early 1700s, Germans began immigrating to Germantown and for decades spoke their own dialect to hold themselves separate from the English-speaking residents already settled there. Perhaps this is why my father moved my German-speaking immigrant mother there when they arrived in Philadelphia in the late 1950s, thinking she would be most comfortable there. However it was also because by then Germantown was no longer thriving and it was a very cheap place to live. By the 1960s, Germantown was the place that "poor people" lived, and it was here that I grew up with my ten brothers and sisters, scrambling to make a place for ourselves in a pocket of Philadelphia that had become ethnically divided and sometimes quite dangerous—though not as dangerous as my very violent father.

From an early age my siblings and I were warned not to go beyond "our" (read "white") block, onto the blocks where the "Schwartzes" lived. The Schwartzes were dangerous, and they were not "our" kind. But, then the Jews weren't our kind either, nor were any of the other folks in Germantown who were different from our very large, very poor, very Catholic white family. And it's true, I got beat up a lot—not by the "others," but rather by those who believed my family didn't belong. I was "visibly" poor: dirty, disheveled, clad in ill-fitting hand-me-downs, and almost always hungry. I learned to be street smart and tough, and soon punching was my second language of sorts. Often I didn't wait to see whether someone was "safe" or not; I simply punched when someone came too close.

One year, after our house burned, my family moved multiple times in order to stay ahead of landlords to whom we were unable to pay the rent. My mother couldn't always find housing for eleven children, and so sometimes I was sent to live with people we barely knew, and who often resented having another mouth to feed. I remember being locked in bedrooms, once a basement, and given what was left of other people's dinners after they were finished.

I moved to Oregon just as soon as I could figure out how to travel away from Pennsylvania. I had been institutionalized twice for "mental illness," and had lived on the streets more times than I care to remember. In Oregon I found a mental health practitioner with a social justice background and perspective, who helped me to understand that I was neither bad nor crazy, just wounded . . . and not beyond repair.

Healing from the years of abuse, the classism, the homophobia, the damage done in the classrooms into which I was warehoused, the myriad food allergies I discovered—all of this takes time, and much of it is hard and painful work requiring the support and love of many, many fabulous friends and allies. However life is on the other side, and life has never, ever ceased to delight and amaze me. It is worth the work to have my life back.

A pivotal moment came when my partner read *Nobody Nowhere: The Extraordinary Autobiography of an Autistic Girl*, by Donna Williams—and discovered me there, on the pages. Autism. Asperger's. Ah . . . sigh of relief. Yes, that's me. Asperger's. Not "retarded," not crazy, not any of the labels people had called me over the years. People sometimes ask me if it frightened to me to receive an official diagnosis of Asperger's syndrome. On the contrary, it was the final door to freedom for me. Now that I had the final piece to the puzzle that was me, I could move all the way forward. There was nothing at all to stop me except for me, and I was learning to handle me. Labels can be helpful—and they can be harmful—but in this case the label of "Asperger's" got me to think bigger about the challenges and barriers I faced.

I received the official diagnosis of Asperger's (now considered simply part of the Autism spectrum) when I returned to college in 1986. There I discovered that, even at the community college level, computers were now required, and I was terrified that I could never, ever be smart enough to use a computer. I was the kid who sat in the back of the classroom and, one year, didn't speak at all. I was the kid the other kids called "retard" . . . and I believed them. No one ever expected me to succeed at anything when I was growing up—and now I was going to college.

However, I quickly discovered that computers are often good friends to people on the Autism spectrum. Not only did my mind quickly come to understand the way computers worked, computers became an interface between me and the world. It was much easier to work through a computer than communicate in the classroom. Computers made sense to my particular Autism mind and, with typical Asperger's focus, I set about learning everything I could about them—including how to repair and rebuild them.

Shall I interject here that I finished college? In fact, I graduated magna cum laude from the University of Oregon and then went on, later, to get a master's in social work from Portland State University. I say this to give anyone reading this hope. Let nothing stop you, not labels or class structure or any of the systems that oppress almost all of us. Get the support you need, be fearless, and do anything and everything you want to do. But, I digress.

How did this get me to Guatemala in 2008? Well, after receiving my bachelor's degree, I got a job working in child welfare, where I encountered children like me, every day. I understood that, for them to succeed, they needed the technology the world has come to require from students. And I had access to that technology. With a group of volunteer geeks like me, we scoured the second hand stores, dug in trash cans, and shamelessly asked for hardware donations. We went everywhere we could think of to find old computers we could re-build and then gift to the kids who needed them. My partner supported me to create a nonprofit, "MacRenewal." Together we envisioned a community organization that could divert toxic materials from our landfill and provide education and opportunity to community members who did not have access to technology. MacRenewal was born out of my garage.

At about that time I discovered Matthew Rutman. Matthew and I had similar social justice beliefs. In one of our first conversations he said, "You know, as a Jew, I see through the lens of the oppressed and as a white man born in the United States, the lens of the oppressor." This common understanding of oppression, and how vital it is that we always remember both our privilege and our lack thereof, is what brought us together.

After he graduated from the University of Oregon, Matthew lived in Quetzaltenango, a rural area of Guatemala, for seven months. He became incredibly inspired by the work an NGO called INEPAS (Instituto de Español y Participación en Ayuda Social: inepas.org). At that time, most indigenous children in Guatemala did not progress past the 3rd grade, and the schools that exist for this particular group of children are extremely underfunded and very poorly equipped. Matthew founded Partners in Solidarity initially to send medical and school supplies to INEPAS.

In 2005, we began to work together to send computers there as well. All told, over a period of seven years, we managed to send over 1,000 refurbished computers to eight communities, 14 schools, ultimately reaching a total population of 25,000 people. The computers were equipped with a Spanish operating system, English language educational software and Mayan K'iche' (keechay) language and cultural software written by UNESCO that describes K'iche' history and traditions. In a country where it is mandatory to speak and learn Spanish, adding the K'iche' language software was a radical move, a powerful statement that the people we were serving had an integrity and culture deserving of complete respect and inclusion. Traditionally, these are the communities that supplied the unskilled labor required in Guatemalan sweatshops. The Guatemalan government for years refused to fund schools for indigenous people, and even now the schools are underfunded. Without an education, the children in these small places will continue to be locked into a cycle of poverty. "With the access to technology and the school equipment Partners in Solidarity brings down, their chances at economic success has grown," says Maria Antonieta Ixcoteyac Velásquez, director of INEPAS. In Guatemala, just like in the United States, higher education is only available to students who know how to use computers, and this kind of education provides children with choices they would not otherwise have.

What was exceptional about this partnership was that the entire community signed on to support the computer labs. Some schools had to build the rooms to house the labs, run electricity to the buildings, agree to maintain security (which led some parents to sleep in the labs at night, to ensure their children had access to this learning tool). The communities also had to work together to raise the $10.00 per unit to get a lab placed in their schools. And, each community also demonstrated their students' academic successes at quarterly meetings. The commitment these parents showed to their children's education was, and remains, extraordinary.

Every year, we combined efforts to send computers to this very committed community of people. In 2008, I received a small grant that allowed me and my fourteen-year-old grandson to go with the computers, and to meet some of the wonderful people with whom Matthew worked. By then, MacRenewal had morphed into NextStep Recycling, and our board chair, Phyllis Haddox, and one of the members of our Stewardship Committee, also went. It was a wonderful trip. For the first time I could see, up close, the computer labs that our efforts had helped build, and meet the children and their families who benefitted from our work.

Over the years, I've been asked by many organizations to join efforts to "help" some particular group of people with whom they're involved. I chose to work with Matthew because his goal was to empower the people with whom he lived, not to be "gringos who drop goods and run."

There's a brilliant article written by Rachel Naomi Remen (1999), "Helping, Fixing or Serving," in which she states:

> Serving is different from helping. Helping is not a relationship between equals. A helper may see others as weaker than they are, needier than they are, and people often feel this inequality. The danger in helping is that we may inadvertently take away from people more than we could ever give them; we may diminish their self-esteem, their sense of worth, integrity or even wholeness. (para. 3)

When I was a child, there were many people who tried to "help" us, from the position that we were much "less" than they were. Rather than being provided with the resources we could have used to make our own way, we were instead given hand-outs, labeled, condescended to and then dismissed. The helpers rarely stuck around to see whether anything they'd done actually worked, or that we were doing better for their helping. This experience has informed my social work practice from the very beginning, and my dedication to this way of serving people has never wavered. No one is lesser than anyone else, which is what I proved when I got the resources and information I needed to be all of who I was capable of being. It is in all of our best interests to serve our clients from the perspective that they are not deficient, but simply needful of some piece of critical information that will tip them into their true selves—that lifts them out of their "otherness" and into their absolute belonging.

1. How is this story an example of anti-oppressive global social work?

2. What experiences in her life inform Lorraine's journey toward global social work?

3. In what ways does the local community become involved in the process?

4. How does Lorraine differentiate between "serving" and "helping"?

DISCUSSION QUESTIONS

1. Describe the common themes that emerge throughout these stories of global anti-oppressive social work practice.

2. How do these stories speak to the challenges of doing global anti-oppressive social work?

3. Consider your current internship placement or social service agency of employment. How do you currently engage in global anti-oppressive social work?

4. Taking into account issues of privilege and oppression based on your intersecting identities, how do you envision incorporating global anti-oppressive social work in your own practice?

ACTIVITIES

1. Take some time to look up the following faith-based organizations on the Internet. They are some of the diverse religious organizations that are engaged in global humanitarian work.

   • *Salvation Army*: founded in the United Kingdom in 1865. Its work is informed by Evangelical Christianity.
   • *World Vision International*: established in 1950 to administer assistance to impoverished children. Unlike the Salvation Army, it does not try to convert individuals and communities to Christianity. This organization's work has expanded to community development, advocacy, and disaster relief programs.
   • *Church World Service*: formed in 1946, in the aftermath of the Second World War, with a mission to feed the hungry and help those in need. This organization also founded the ACT Alliance, a coalition of more than 130 churches and church-based humanitarian organizations working together in humanitarian assistance and development around the world.
   • *Humanity First International*, formed in 1995. This organization works on human development projects and responds to disasters.
   • *Muslim Brotherhood*, established in 1982 in Egypt: It has a reputation for developing systems of social aid from hospitals to charities and responding to human need during natural catastrophes.
   • *Catholic Agency for Overseas Development*, formed to address social justice issues in the global South. It is well known for its support of the "Make Poverty History" program and for its projects to eliminate landmines and reduce the debts of developing countries. Other areas of global assistance include HIV and AIDS education, peace-building, health, water, sanitation, environment, and livelihoods.

- *Guru Nanak Nishkam Sewak Jatha*: a Sikh organization founded in the United Kingdom in 1974. Their work spans the whole of the globe, with special projects taking place in Africa and India.
- *International Orthodox Christian Charities*: started in 1992. It offers assistance to the poor, either in response to emergencies or for long-term socio-economic development needs.
- *Aga Khan Foundation U.S.A:* established in 1981 to struggle against hunger, disease, and illiteracy, primarily in Africa and Asia. This organization is guided by the Islamic ethical principles of consultation, solidarity with the less fortunate, human dignity, and self-reliance.
- *Islamic Relief International:* founded in the United Kingdom in 1984. It focuses on promoting sustainable economic and social development by working with local communities to eradicate poverty, illiteracy, and disease.
- *Norwegian Church Aid:* rooted in the Christian faith. It focuses on long-term development work, emergency preparedness and response, and advocacy.
- *Pax Christi International:* a nonprofit Catholic peace movement working on a global scale on a wide variety of issues. It is active in the fields of human rights, human security, disarmament and demilitarization, just world order, and religion and violent conflict.
- *United Methodist Committee on Relief:* It is an organization dedicated to alleviating human suffering around the globe by providing humanitarian relief in war, conflict, or natural disaster.

a. Compare and contrast the type of international work that each organization engages in.

b. Consider each organization's agency values, global lens or worldview, and approach to international social work. What parts of the world do they serve? Who are the primary recipients of their services? Where do you see similarities? Where do you see differences? What stands out for you about these organizations?

ADDITIONAL RESOURCES

Websites

AAWORD: Association of African Women for Research and Development http://www.afard.org/indexang.php

FAWE: Forum for African Women Educationalists www.fawe.org/

FEMNET: African Women's Collective Leadership! http://femnet.wordpress.com/

War Resisters' International http://www.wri-irg.org/network/about_wri

International Association of Schools of Social Work http://www.iassw-aiets.org/

International Federation of Social Workers http://ifsw.org/

American Refugee Committee http://www.arcrelief.org

CARE http://www.care.org

Doctors Without Borders/ Medecines Sans Frontiers http://ww.dwb.org, http://www.msf.org

Grassroots International http://www.grassrootsonline.org

Strategic Actions for a Just Economy http://www.saje.org

Ethiopian Community Development Council, Inc. http://www.ecdcinternational.org

Foundation for Sustainable Development http://www.fsdinternational.org

Freedom House http://www.freedomhouse.org

Global Exchange http://www.globalexchange.org

MADRE http://www.madre.org

Sister Cities International http://www.sister-cities.org

Voices on the Border http://www.votb.org

Witness for Peace http://www.witnesssforpeace.org

Foundation for Sustainable Development http://www.fsdinternational.org

Operation USA http://www.opusa.org

Project Concern http://www.projectconcern.org

Films

Afghanistan unveiled (2007). B. Brault.

Black gold (2006). M. Francis, & N. Francis.

Blood diamond (2006). E. Zwick.

Born into brothels: Calcutta's red light kids (2004). Z. Briski, & R. Kauffman.

End of the rainbow (2007). R. Nugent.

Invoking justice (2011). D. Dhanraj.

Maquila: A tale of two Mexicos (1999). S. Landau.

Maquilapolis: City of factories (2006). V. Funari, & S. De La Torre.

Sentenced home (2006). N. Newnham, & D. Grabias.

T-shirt travels (2001). S. Bloeman.

Taking root: The vision of Wangari Maathai (2008). L. Merton, & A. Dater.

The beloved community (2006). P. Calvert.

The big sellout (2006). F. Opitz.

The debt of dictators (2005). E. Borgen.

The end of poverty? (2008). P. Diaz.

We don't play golf here and other stories of globalization (2007). S. Landau.

Books

Beah, I. (2007). *A long way gone: Memoirs of a boy soldier*. New York: Farrar, Straus, and Giroux.

Berry, W. (1996). *The unsettling of America: Culture and agriculture*. San Francisco, CA: Sierra Club Books.

Fuller, A. (2003). *Don't let's go to the dogs tonight: An African childhood*. New York: Random House.

Greenberg, P. (2011). *Four fish: The future of the last wild food*. New York: Penguin Books.

Jackson, W., & Berry, W. (2011). *Nature as measure*. Berkeley, CA: Counterpoint.

Kingsolver, B. (2008). *Poisonwood bible*. New York: Harper.

Mortenson, G., & Relin, D. O. (2007). *Three cups of tea: One man's mission to promote peace . . . one school at a time*. Logan, IA: Perfection Learning.

Said, E. (1997). *Covering Islam: How the media and the experts determine how we see the rest of the world*. New York: Vintage.

Appendix

Aligning the Text With the Council of Social Work Education's Educational Policy and Accreditation Standards

CSWE Educational Policy and Accreditation Standards	Chapter
Educational Policy 2.1.1—Identify as a professional social worker and conduct oneself accordingly. Social workers serve as representatives of the profession, its mission, and its core values. They know the profession's history. Social workers commit themselves to the profession's enhancement and to their own professional conduct and growth.	2
Educational Policy 2.1.2—Apply social work ethical principles to guide professional practice. Social workers have an obligation to conduct themselves ethically and to engage in ethical decision- making. Social workers are knowledgeable about the value base of the profession, its ethical standards, and relevant law.	2
Educational Policy 2.1.3—Apply critical thinking to inform and communicate professional judgments. Social workers are knowledgeable about the principles of logic, scientific inquiry, and reasoned discernment. They use critical thinking augmented by creativity and curiosity. Critical thinking also requires the synthesis and communication of relevant information.	4-11
Educational Policy 2.1.4—Engage diversity and difference in practice. Social workers understand how diversity characterizes and shapes the human experience and is critical to the formation of identity. The dimensions of diversity are understood as the intersectionality of multiple factors including age, class, color, culture, disability, ethnicity, gender, gender identity and expression, immigration status, political ideology, race, religion, sex, and sexual orientation. Social workers appreciate that, as a consequence of difference, a person's life experiences may include oppression, poverty, marginalization, and alienation as well as privilege, power, and acclaim.	1, 4-11
Educational Policy 2.1.5—Advance human rights and social and economic justice. Each person, regardless of position in society, has basic human rights, such as freedom, safety, privacy, an adequate standard of living, health care, and education. Social workers recognize the global interconnections of oppression and are knowledgeable about theories of justice and strategies to promote human and civil rights. Social work incorporates social justice practices in organizations, institutions, and society to ensure that these basic human rights are distributed equitably and without prejudice.	1, 4-11

CSWE Educational Policy and Accreditation Standards	Chapter
Educational Policy 2.1.6—Engage in research-informed practice and practice-informed research. Social workers use practice experience to inform research, employ evidence-based interventions, evaluate their own practice, and use research findings to improve practice, policy, and social service delivery. Social workers comprehend quantitative and qualitative research and understand scientific and ethical approaches to building knowledge.	N/A
Educational Policy 2.1.7—Apply knowledge of human behavior and the social environment. Social workers are knowledgeable about human behavior across the life course; the range of social systems in which people live; and the ways social systems promote or deter people in maintaining or achieving health and well-being. Social workers apply theories and knowledge from the liberal arts to understand biological, social, cultural, psychological, and spiritual development.	N/A
Educational Policy 2.1.8—Engage in policy practice to advance social and economic well-being and to deliver effective social work services. Social work practitioners understand that policy affects service delivery, and they actively engage in policy practice. Social workers know the history and current structures of social policies and services; the role of policy in service delivery; and the role of practice in policy development.	10
Educational Policy 2.1.9—Respond to contexts that shape practice. Social workers are informed, resourceful, and proactive in responding to evolving organizational, community, and societal contexts at all levels of practice. Social workers recognize that the context of practice is dynamic, and use knowledge and skill to respond proactively.	8, 9
Educational Policy 2.1.10(a)–(d)—Engage, assess, intervene, and evaluate with individuals, families, groups, organizations, and communities. Professional practice involves the dynamic and interactive processes of engagement, assessment, intervention, and evaluation at multiple levels. Social workers have the knowledge and skills to practice with individuals, families, groups, organizations, and communities. Practice knowledge includes identifying, analyzing, and implementing evidence-based interventions designed to achieve client goals; using research and technological advances; evaluating program outcomes and practice effectiveness; developing, analyzing, advocating, and providing leadership for policies and services; and promoting social and economic justice.	4-11

Council on Social Work Education (2010). Educational Policy and Accreditation Stanadards. Retrieved October 20, 2011 from http://www.cswe.org/File.aspx?id=13780

References

Adams, M., Bell, L., & Griffin, P. (2007). *Teaching for diversity and social justice* (2nd ed.). New York: Routledge.

Adams, M., Blumenfeld, W., Castañeda, C., Hackman, H., Peters, M., & Zúñiga, X. (2010). *Readings for diversity and social justice* (2nd ed.). New York: Routledge.

Adams, R. (1996). *Social work and empowerment*. London, UK: Macmillan.

Adams, R. (2009). Being a critical practitioner. In R. Adams, L. Dominelli, & M. Payne (Eds.), *Critical practice in social work* (2nd ed., pp. 233–248). Basingstoke, UK: Palgrave Macmillan.

Adams, R., Dominelli, L., & Payne, M. (2009). *Critical practice in social work* (2nd ed.). Basingstoke, UK: Palgrave Macmillan.

Addams, J. (1892). *The subjective necessity for social settlements*. Retrieved from http://www.infed.org/archives/e-texts/addams6.htm

Addams, J. (1990). *Twenty years at Hull-House with autobiographical notes*. Chicago: University of Illinois Press.

Agger, B. (1998). *Critical social theories*. Boulder, CO: Westview Press.

Alinksy, S. (1972a). *Rules for radicals: A practical primer for realistic radicals*. New York: Vintage Books.

Alinsky, S. (1972b/2003). Organizing the back of the yards. Interview with Saul Alinksy, part seven. *The progress report: Empowering people, not elites*. Retrieved from http://www.progress.org/2003/alinsky8.htm

Allison, A. (2005). Embracing diversity and working in partnership. In R. Carnwell, & J. Buchanan (Eds.), *Effective practice in health and social care: A partnership approach*. Maidenhead, UK: Open University Press.

Alissi, A. (1980). Social group work: Commitments and perspectives. In A. Alissi (Ed.), *Perspectives on social group work practice: A book of readings* (pp. 5–35). New York: The Free Press.

Almeida, R., Dolan-Del Vecchio, K., & Parker, L. (2008). *Just families, a just society: Transformative family therapy*. New York: Allyn & Bacon.

Almeida, R., Vecchio, K. D., & Parker, L. (2007). Foundation concepts for social justice-based therapy: Critical consciousness, accountability and empowerment. In E. Aldarondo (Ed.), *Advancing social justice through clinical practice* (pp. 175–201). Mahwah, NJ: Lawrence Erlbaum.

Alston, M., & Besthorn, F. H. (2012). Environment and sustainability. In K. Lyons, T. Hokenstad, M. Pawar, N. Huegler, & N. Hall (Eds.), *The SAGE handbook of international social work* (pp. 56–69). Los Angeles, CA: SAGE.

Andrews, J., & Reisch, M. (1997). Social work and anti-communism: A historical analysis of the McCarthy Era. *Journal of Progressive Human Services, 8*(2), 29–49.

Anzaldua, G. (1987). *Borderlands/La frontera: The new mestiza*. San Francisco, CA: Spinsters/Aunt Lute.

Aron, A. (1992). Testimonio, a bridge between psychotherapy and sociotherapy. *Women & Therapy, 13*(3), 173–189.

Austin, M. J., & Betten, N. (1990). The roots of community organizing: An introduction. In N. Betten, & M. J. Austin (Eds.), *The roots of community organizing, 1917–1939* (pp. 3–15). Philadelphia, PA: Temple University Press.

Baines, D. (2007). *Doing anti-oppressive practice: Building transformative politicized social work*. Halifax, Canada: Fernwood.

Baker, C., & Williams, L. (2008). 75 years of empiricism and empowerment: The Highlander Research and Education Center. *Humanity & Society, 32*, 197–203.

Bakhtin, M. (1981). *The dialogic imagination*. Austin: University of Texas Press.

Banerjee, M. M. (2005). Social work, Rawlsian social justice, and social development. *Social Development Issues, 27*(1), 6–24.

Banks, S. (1997/2001). *Ethics and values in social work*. Basingstoke, UK: Palgrave McMillan.

Banks, S. (2008). Critical commentary: Social work ethics. *British Journal of Social Work, 38*, 1238–1249.

Banks, S., & Nøhr, K. (2011). *Practising social work ethics around the world: Cases and commentaries*. London, UK: Routledge Press.

Barlow, A. L. (2003). *Between fear and hope: Globalization and race in the United States*. Rowman & Littlefield.

Bar-On, A. A. (1998). Social work in "rainbow" nations: Observations of a troubled relationship. *Social Work/Maatskaplike Werk, 34*(2), 150–162.

Bay-Cheng, L., Lewis, A., Stewart, A., & Malley, J. (2006). Disciplining "girl talk": The paradox of empowerment in a feminist mentorship program. *Journal of Human Behavior in the Social Environment, 13*(2), 73–92.

Beck, E. L., & Eichler, M. (2000). Consensus organizing: A practice model for community building. *Journal of Community Practice, 8*(1), 87–103.

Bell, L. A. (2007). Theoretical foundations for social justice education. In M. Adams, L. Bell, & P. Griffin (Eds.), *Teaching for diversity and social justice* (2nd ed., pp. 1–14). New York: Routledge.

Bell, L. A. (2010). *Storytelling for social justice: Connecting narrative and the arts in antiracist teaching.* London, UK: Routledge.

Bellefeuille, G., & Hemingway, D. (2006). A co-operative inquiry into structural social work students' ethical decision-making in field education. *Journal of Social Work and Ethics, 3*(2).

Benard, B. (2006). Using strengths-based practice to tap the resilience of families. In D. Saleebey (Ed.), *The strengths perspective in social work practice* (4th ed., pp. 197–215). Boston, MA: Pearson.

Benhabib, S. (2002). *The claims of culture: Equality and diversity in the global era.* Princeton, NJ: Princeton University Press.

Beresford, P. (2005). Theory and practice of user involvement in research: Making the connection with public policy and practice. In L. Lowes & I. Halatt (Eds.), *Involving service users in health and social care research* (pp. 6–17). London, UK: Routledge.

Berlin, S. (1990). Dichotomous and complex thinking. *Social Service Review, 64*(1), 46–59.

Besthorn, F. H., & Meyer, E. (2010). Environmentally displaced persons: Broadening social work's helping imperative. *Journal of Critical Social Work, 11*(3), 123–138.

Birkenmaier, J., Berg-Weger, M., & Dewees, M. (2011). *The practice of generalist social work* (2nd ed.). New York: Routledge.

Bishop, A. (2001). *Becoming an ally.* Halifax, Nova Scotia: Fernwood Press.

Bornstein, K. (2000). Which outlaws? or, Who was that masked man? In M. Adams, W. J. Blumenfeld, R. Castaneda, H. W. Hackman, M. L. Peters, & X. Zuniga (Eds.), *Readings for diversity and social justice: An anthology on racism, antisemitism, sexism, heterosexism, ableism and classism.* New York: Routledge.

Box, R. (2008). *Making a difference: Progressive values in public administration.* Armonk, NY: M. E. Sharpe.

Braithwaite, J., & Daly, K. (1998). Masculinities, violence and communitarian control. In S. Miller (Ed.), *Crime control and women: Feminist implications of criminal justice policy* (pp. 151–180). Thousand Oaks, CA: SAGE.

Braithwaite, J., & Strang, H. (2002). Restorative justice and family violence. In J. Braithwaite & H. Strang (Eds.), *Restorative justice and family violence* (pp. 1–22). New York: Cambridge University Press.

Brechner, J., Costello, T., & Smith, B. (2000). *Globalization from below: The power of solidarity.* Boston, MA: South End Press.

Brinker-Jenkins, M., & Hooyman, N. (Eds.). (1986). *Not for women only: Social work practice for a feminist future.* Silver Spring, MD: National Association of Social Work.

Bronfenbrenner, U. (1979). *Ecology of human development.* Cambridge, MA: Harvard University Press.

Brown, A., & Mistry, T. (2005). Group work with "mixed membership" groups: Issues of race and gender. *Social Work with Groups, 28*(3/4), 133–148.

Brubaker, M. D., Garrett, M. T., Rivera, E. T., & Tate, K. A. (2010). Justice making in groups for homeless adults: The emancipatory communitarian way. *The Journal for Specialists in Group Work, 35*(2), 124–133.

Bruce, B. C. (2008). From Hull House to Paseo Boricua: The theory and practice of community inquiry. In B. Dicher, & A. Luduşan (Eds.), *Philosophy of pragmatism (II): Salient inquiries* (pp. 181–198). Cluj-Napoca, Romania: Editura Fundaţiei pentru Studii Europene (European Studies Foundation Publishing House). Retrieved from https://www.ideals.illinois.edu/bitstream/handle/2142/13166/cluj.pdf?sequence=2

Brydon, K. (2011). Promoting diversity or confirming hegemony? In search of new insights for social work. *International Social Work, 55*(2), 155–167.

Burke, B. (1998). Understanding and practicing participatory evaluation. *New Directions for Evaluation, 80*(2), 43–56.

Burke, B., & Harrison, P. (1998). Anti-oppressive practice. In R. Adams, L. Dominelli, & M. Payne (Eds.), *Social work: Themes, issues, and critical debates.* Basingstoke, UK: Macmillan Press.

Burnier, D. (2008). Erased history: Frances Perkins and emergence of care-centered public administration. *Administration & Society, 40*, 403–422.

Campbell, C. (2003). Anti-oppressive theory and practice as the organizing theme for social work education: The case in favor. *Canadian Social Work Review, 20,* 121–125.

Capeheart, L., & Milovanovic, D. (2007). *Social justice: Theories, issues, and movements.* New Brunswick, NJ: Rutgers University Press.

Carr, C. (2012). *A song of longing: Anti-oppressive practice in international development work.* Retrieved from http://afritorial.com/anti-oppressive-practice-in-international-development-work/

Castelloe, P., & Gamble, D. N. (2005). Participatory methods in community practice. In M. Weil (Ed.), *The handbook of community practice* (pp. 261–286). Thousand Oaks, CA: SAGE.

Castells, M. (2012). *Networks of outrage and hope: Social movements in the Internet age.* Malden, MA: Polity Press.

Chambers, R. (2002). *Participatory workshops: A sourcebook of 21 sets of ideas and activities.* Sterling, VA: Earthscan.

Chapin, R., & Cox, E. (2001). Changing the paradigm: Strengths-based and empowerment-oriented social work with frail elders. *Journal of Gerontological Social Work, 36*(3/4), 165–179.

Charity Organization Society of the City of New York. (1883). *Handbook for friendly visitors among the poor.* New York: Putnam. Retrieved from http://www.archive.org/stream/handbookforfrie00yorkgoog#page/n6/mode/2up

Charlton, J. I. (2000). *Nothing about us without us: Disability oppression and empowerment.* Berkeley, CA: University of California Press.

Chavis, B. (2009). *Concerning the historical evolution of the "environmental justice movement" and the definition of the term: "Environmental racism."* Retrieved on August 7, 2012 from http://drbenjaminchavis.com/pages/landing/?blockID=73318

Child Welfare Organizing Project (CWOP). (n.d.). *Child welfare organizing project: About.* Retrieved from http://cwop.org/about/

Cho, S. (2000). Selflessness: Towards a Buddhist vision of social justice. *Journal of Buddhist Ethics, 7.* Retrieved from http://www.urbandharma.org/udharma/towardjustice.html

Christens, B., & Speer, P. W. (2006). Tyranny/transformation: Power and paradox in participatory development. *Forum: Qualitative Social Research, 7*(2). Retrieved from http://www.qualitative-research.net/index.php/fqs/article/view/91/189

Cienfuegos, A. J., & Monelli, C. (1983). The testimony of political repression as a therapeutic instrument. *American Journal of Ortopsychiatry, 53,* 43–51.

Clark, C. (2006). Moral character in social work. *British Journal of Social Work, 36,* 75–89.

Clarke, J. (2006). Listening for meaning: A research-based model for attending to spirituality, culture and worldview in social work practice. *Critical Social Work, 7*(1), 250–263.

Clifford, D. (1998). *Social assessment theory & practice.* Aldershot, UK: Ashgate.

Clifford, D., & Burke, B. (2009). *Anti-oppressive ethics and values in social work.* New York: Palgrave MacMillan.

Coates, J. (2003). *Ecology and social work: Towards a new paradigm.* Halifax, Nova Scotia: Fernwood.

Cohen, M. (1989). Social work practice with homeless mentally ill people: Engaging the client. *Social Work, 34*(6), 505–509.

Collins, P. H. (2000). *Black feminist thought: Knowledge, consciousness and the politics of empowerment* (2nd ed.). New York: Routledge.

Comas-Diaz, L. (2007). Ethnopolitical psychology: Healing and transformation. In E. Aldarondo (Ed.), *Promoting social justice in mental health practice* (pp. 91–118). Mahwah, NJ: Lawrence Erlbaum.

Communities for a Better Environment (CBE). (2012). *Greenup Projects.* Retrieved on August 29, 2012 from http://www.cbecal.org/organizing/community-organizing/

Constable, R., & Lee, D. (2004). *Social work with families: Content and process.* Chicago: Lyceum Books.

Conway, J., & Singh, J. (2009). Is the World Social Forum a transnational public sphere? Nancy Fraser, critical theory and the containment of radical possibility. *Theory, Culture & Society, 26*(5), 61–84.

Cooke, B., & Kothari, U. (2001). *Participation: The new tyranny?* New York: Zed Books.

Cossom, J. (1990). *Increasing relevance and authentisation in social work curricula by writing and teaching from indigenous cases.* Paper presented at the 25th International Association of Schools of Social Work, Lima, Peru.

Council on Social Work Education (CSWE). (2008). Educational policy and accreditation standards. Retrieved from http://www.cswe.org/File.aspx?id=41861

Council on Social Work Education (CSWE). (2010). *Educational policy and accreditation standards.* Retrieved from http://www.cswe.org/File.aspx?id=13780

Cousins, J. B., & Whitmore, E. (1998). Framing participatory evaluation. *New Directions for Evaluation, 80,* 5–23.

Cox, D., & Pawar, M. (2006). *International social work: Issues, strategies and programs.* Thousand Oaks, CA: SAGE.

Coyle, G. L. (1980). Some basic assumptions about social group work. In A. Alissi (Ed.), *Perspectives on social group work practice: A book of readings* (pp. 36–51). New York: The Free Press.

Craig, S. (2011). Precarious partnerships: Designing a community needs assessment to develop a system of care for gay, lesbian, bisexual, transgender, and questioning (GLBTQ) youths. *Journal of Community Practice, 19,* 274–291.

Dalrymple, J., & Burke, B. (1995). *Anti-oppressive practice: Social care and the law.* Buckingham, UK: Open University Press.

Dalrymple, J., & Burke, B. (2006). *Anti-oppressive practice: Social care and the law* (2nd ed.). New York: Open University Press.

Danso, R. (2009). Emancipating and empowering de-valued skilled immigrants: What hope does anti-oppressive social work practice offer? *British Journal of Social Work, 29,* 539–555.

Deacon. B. (1997). *Global social policy: International organizations and the future of welfare.* Los Angeles, CA: SAGE.

Dean, R. (2001). The myth of cross cultural competence. *Families in Society, 82*(6), 623–630.

DeFillipis, J., Fisher, R., & Shragge, E. (2010). *Contesting community: The limits and potential of local organizing.* New Brunswick, NJ: Rutgers University Press.

De Hoyos, G. (1989, March). Person-In-Environment: A Tri-level practice model. *Social Casework: The Journey of Contemporary Social Work,* 131–138.

Della Porta, D., & Diani, M. (1999). *Social movements: An introduction.* Malden, MA: Blackwell.

Dempsey, D. (2008). The path to social justice goes through politics and economics. *Journal of Policy Practice, 7*(2–3), 94–105.

de Shazer, S. (1991). *Putting difference to work.* New York: W.W. Norton.

Despommier, D. (2009). The rise of vertical farms. *Scientific American, 30*(1), 80–87.

Dewees, M. (2006). *Contemporary social work practice.* Boston, MA: McGraw Hill.

Dobbie, D., & Richards-Schuster, K. (2008). Building solidarity through difference: A practice model for critical multicultural organizing. *Journal of Community Practice, 16*(3), 317–337.

Dominelli, L. (1988). *Anti-racist social work* (2nd ed.). London, UK: Macmillan.

Dominelli, L. (1996). De-professionalizing social work: Anti-oppressive practice, competencies and postmodernism. *British Journal of Social Work, 26,* 153–175.

Dominelli, L. (1998). Anti-oppressive practice in context. In R. Adams, L. Dominelli, & M. Payne (Eds.), *Social work: Themes, issues and critical debates.* Houndmills, UK: MacMillan Press.

Dominelli, L. (2002a). *Anti-oppressive social work: Theory and practice.* Basingstoke, UK: Palgrave MacMillan.

Dominelli, L (2002b). *Feminist social work theory and practice.* Basingstoke, UK: Palgrave Macmillan.

Dominelli, L. (2008). Globalisation and indigenisation: Reconciling the irreconcilable in social work? In K. Lyons, T. Hokenstad, M. Pawar, N. Huegler, & N. Hall (Eds.), *The SAGE handbook of international social work* (pp. 39–55). Los Angeles, CA: SAGE.

Dominelli, L. (2009). *Introducing social work.* Malden, MA: Polity Press.

Dominelli, L., & McLeod, E. (1989). *Feminist social work.* Basingstoke, UK: Macmillan.

Drover, G. (2000). Redefining social citizenship in a global era. *Canadian Social Work* (Special issue on social work and globalization), *2*(1), 9–49.

Drumm, K. (2006). The essential power of group work. *Social Work with Groups, 29*(2/3), 17–31.

Dunst, C., Trivette, C., & Deal, A. (1998). Guidelines for family empowerment. In C. Dunst (Ed.), *Enabling and empowering families: Principles & guidelines for practice* (pp. 94–97). Cambridge, MA: Brookline Books.

Early, T. J., & GlenMaye, L. F. (2000). Valuing families: Social work practice with families from a strengths perspective. *National Association of Social Workers, 45*(2), 118–130.

Edwards, M., & Hulme, D. (1996). Too close for comfort? The impact of official aid on nongovernmental organizations. *World Development, 24*(6), 961–973.

Enns, C. Z. (2004). *Feminist theories and feminist psychotherapies* (2nd ed.). New York: Routledge.

Fabri, M. R. (2001). Reconstructing safety: Adjustments to the therapeutic frame in the treatment of survivors of political torture. *Professional Psychology: Research and Practice, 32*(5), 452–457.

Ferguson, I. (2008). *Reclaiming social work: Challenging neo-liberalism and promoting social justice.* Thousand Oaks, CA: SAGE.

Finn, J., & Jacobson, M. (2008). *Just practice: A social justice-oriented approach to social work.* (2nd ed.). Peosta, IA: Eddie Bowers.

Fisher, R. (1999). Reflections on the reflections. In J. Rothman (Ed.), *Reflections on community organization: Enduring themes and critical issues.* Itasca, IL: F. E. Peacock.

Fitzgerald, K. J., & Rodgers, D. M. (2000). Radical social movement organizations: A theoretical model. *The Sociological Quarterly, 41*(4), 573–592.

Fook, J. (1993). *Radical casework: A theory of practice.* St. Leonards, Australia: Allyn & Unwin.

Fook, J. (2000). Critical perspectives on social work practice. In E. O'Connor, P. Smyth, & J. Warburton (Eds.), *Contemporary perspectives on social work and the human services: Challenges and change.* Sydney, Australia: Pearson Education.

Fook, J. (2002). *Social work: Critical theory and practice.* London, UK, SAGE.

Fraser, N. (2003). *Redistribution or recognition? A political-philosophical exchange.* New York: Verso.

Freedom Center. (2007). *Welcome.* Retrieved from http://www.freedom-center.org/welcome

Freire, P. (1970). *The pedagogy of the oppressed.* New York: Continuum.

Freire, P. (1973). *Education for critical consciousness.* New York: Seabury Press.

Freire, P. (1985). *The politics of education: Culture, power and liberation.* Hadley, MA: Bergin & Garvey.

Freire, P. (1992). *Pedagogy of hope: Reliving pedagogy of the oppressed.* New York: Continuum.

Frye, M. (1983). *The politics of reality: Essays in feminist theory.* Trumansberg, NY: Crossing Press.

Furman, R., Negi, N. J., & Salvador, R. (2010). An introduction to transnational social work. In N. J. Negi, & R. Furman (Eds.), *Transnational social work practice.* New York: Columbia University Press.

Galper, J. (1980). *Social work practice: A radical perspective.* Englewood Cliffs, NJ: Prentice Hall.

Gamble, D., & Weil, M. (2010). *Community practice skills.* New York: Columbia University Press.

Gambrill, E. (1997). *Social work practice: A critical thinker's guide.* New York: Oxford University Press.

Gamson, W. A. (1990). *The strategy of social protest.* Belmont, CA: Wadsworth Publishing.

Garaway, G. (1995). Participatory evaluation. *Studies in Educational Evaluation, 21*(1), 85–102.

Garbarino, J., Kostelny, K., & Dubrow, N. (1991). *No place to be a child: Growing up in a war zone.* Lexington, MA: Lexington Books.

Garner, R. T., & Rosen, B. (1967). *Moral philosophy: A systematic introduction to normative ethics and meta-ethics.* New York: Macmillan.

Gillette, K. (2008). *Modern progressive values: Realizing America's potential—A Commonweal Institute report.* Menlo Park, CA: Commonweal Institute.

Gilmore, E. (2012). Why resource generation is committed to racial justice. Retrieved from http://www.resource-generation.org/blog/2012/07/14/why-resource-generation-is-committed-to-racial-justice/

Gitterman, A. (2005). Group formation. In A. Gitterman & L. Shulman (Eds.), *Mutual aid groups, vulnerable and resilient populations, and the life cycle* (3rd ed., pp. 73–110). New York: Columbia University Press.

Gitterman, A., & Shulman, L. (2005). The life model, oppression, vulnerability, resilience, mutual aid, and the mediating function. In A. Gitterman & L. Shulman (Eds.), *Mutual aid groups, vulnerable and resilient populations, and the life cycle* (3rd ed., pp. 3–37). New York: Columbia University Press.

Golden, G. (2001). Retooling mental health models for racial relevance. *Social Work Activist Reader, 1.*

Goldstein, H. (1973). *Social work practice: A unitary approach.* Columbia: University of South Carolina Press.

Gould, K. H. (2000). Beyond Jones v. Clinton: Sexual harassment law and social work. *Social Work, 45*(3), 237–248.

Graham, K., & Harris, A. (2005). New deal for communities as a participatory public policy: The challenges for evaluation. In D. Taylor & S. Balloch (Eds.), *The politics of evaluation: Participation and policy implementation.* Bristol, UK: The Policy Press.

Graham, M. (2007). The ethics of care, black women and the social professions: Implications of a new analysis. *Ethics and Social Welfare, 1*(2), 194–208.

Grande, S. (2004). *Red pedagogy: Native American and political thought.* Lanham, MD: Rowan & Littlefield.

Gray, M. (2005). Dilemmas of international social work: Paradoxical processes in indigenization, universalism and imperialism. *International Journal of Social Welfare, 14,* 231–238.

Gray M., & Allegritti, I. (2003). Towards culturally sensitive social work practice: Re-examining cross-cultural social work values. *Social Work/Maatkaplike Werk, 39*(4), 312–325.

Gray, M., Coates, J., & Yellow Bird, M. (2009). *Indigenous social work around the world: Towards culturally relevant education and practice.* Aldershot, UK: Ashgate.

Gray, M., & Fook, J. (2002). Issues in defining "universal social work": Comparing social work in South Africa and Australia. *Social Work/Maatskaplike Werk, 38*(4), 363–376.

Gray, M., & Fook, J. (2004). The quest for a universal social work: Some issues and implications. *Social Work Education, 23*(5), 625–644.

Green, S., & Baldry, E. (2008). Building indigenous Australian social work. *Australian Social Work, 61*(4), 389–402.

Guilloud, S., & Cordery, W. (2007). Fundraising is not a dirty word: Community-based economic strategies for the long haul. In INCITE! (Eds.), *The Revolution will not be funded: Beyond the non-profit industrial complex* (pp. 107–111). Cambridge, MA: South End Press.

Gutierrez, L. M., & Lewis, E. A. (1999). *Empowering women of color.* New York: Columbia University Press.

Gutierrez, L. M., & Ortega, R. (1991). Developing methods to empower Latinos: The importance of groups. *Social Work with Groups, 14*(2), 23–43.

Gutierrez, L. M., Parsons, R. J., & Cox, E. O. (1998). *Empowerment in social work practice: A sourcebook* (pp. 146–162). Pacific Grove, CA: Brooks/Cole.

Hanna, W., Talley, M., & Guindon, M. (2000). The power of perception: Toward a model of cultural oppression and liberation. *Journal of Counseling & Development, 78*(4), 430–441.

Hansan, J. E. (n.d. a). *The social welfare history project: Charity organization societies.* Retrieved from http://www.socialwelfarehistory.com/organizations/charity-organization-societies/

Hansan, J. E. (n.d. b). *The social welfare history project: Settlement houses: An introduction.* Retrieved from http://www.socialwelfarehistory.com/programs/settlement-houses/

Haraway, D. (1988). Situated knowledges: The science in feminism and the privileges of partial perspective. *Feminist Studies, 14,* 575–599.

Harding, S. (2004). *The feminist standpoint theory reader: Intellectual and political conversations.* New York: Routledge.

Harro, B. (2008). Updated version of the cycle of liberation (2000). In M. Adams, W. J. Blumenfeld, R. Castaneda, H. W. Hackman, M. L. Peters, & X. Zuniga (Eds.), *Readings for diversity and social justice* (pp. 463–469). New York: Routledge.

Hartford, M. E. (1980). Frame of reference for social group work. In A. Alissi (Ed.), *Perspectives on social group work practice: A book of readings* (pp. 64–73). New York: The Free Press.

Haug, E. (2005). Critical reflections on the emerging discourse of international social work. *International Social Work, 48*(2), 126–135.

Haynes, D. T., & White, B. W. (1999). Commentary: Will the "real" social work please stand up? A call to stand for professional unity. *Social Work, 44*(4), 385–391.

Healthy City. (n.d.). *HealthyCity: Information + action for social change.* Retrieved from http://www.healthycity.org/

Healy, K. (2000). *Social work practices: Contemporary perspectives on change.* London, UK: SAGE.

Healy, K. (2005). *Social work theories in context: Creating frameworks for practice.* Basingstoke, UK: Palgrave Macmillan.

Healy, L. (2001). *International social work: Professional action in an interdependent world.* New York: Oxford University Press.

Healy, L. M. (2007). Universalism and cultural relativism in social work ethics. *International Social Work, 50*(1), 11–26.

Healy, L. M. (2008). *International social work: Professional action in an interdependent world* (2nd ed.). New York: Oxford University Press.

Hennessey, R. (2011). *Relationship skills in social work.* Thousand Oaks, CA:SAGE.

Hepworth, D. H., Rooney, R. H., Rooney, G. D., Strom-Gottfried, K., & Larsen, J. A. (2010). Roles of direct practitioners. In D. Hepworth, R. Rooney, G. D. Rooney, & K. Strom-Gottfried (Eds.), *Direct social work practice: Theory and skills* (8th ed., pp. 27–31). Belmont, CA: Brooks/Cole.

Hernández, P., Almeida, R., & Dolan-Del Vecchio, K. (2005). Critical consciousness, accountability, and empowerment: Key processes for helping families heal. *Family Process, 44*(1), 105–119.

Herscovitch, L. (2001). International relief and development practice. In L. M. Healy (Ed.), *International social work: Professional action in an interdependent world* pp. 170–119). New York: Oxford University Press.

Hick, S., & McNutt, J. (2002). *Advocacy, activism, and the Internet: Community organization and social policy.* Chicago: Lyceum Books.

Hick, S., Peters, H., Corner, T., & London, T. (2010). *Structural social work in action: Examples from practice.* Toronto, Canada: Canadian Scholars' Press.

Hick, S., Peters, H., Corner, T., & London, T. (2012). *Structural social work in action: Examples from practice.* Toronto, Canada: Canadian Scholars' Press.

Hickey, S., & Mohan, G. (2004). *Participation: From tyranny to transformation?* New York: Zed Books.

Highlander Research and Education Center. (2012). *Mission.* Retrieved from http://highlandercenter.org/about-us/mission/

Hill Collins, P. (2000). *Black feminist thought: Knowledge, consciousness, and the politics of empowerment.* New York: Routledge.

Hinman, L. M. (2003). *Ethics: A pluralist approach to moral theory.* Belmont, CA: Wadsworth/Thomson.

Hochschild, A. (2003). Love and gold. In B. Ehrenreich, & A. Hochschild (Eds.), *Global woman: Nannies, maids, and sex workers in the new economy* (pp. 15–30). New York: Metropolitan Books.

Hodges, V., Burwell, Y., & Ortega, D. (1998). Empowering Families. In L. Gutierrez, R. Parsons, & E.O. Cox (Eds.), *Empowerment in social work practice: A sourcebook.* Pacific Grove, CA: Brooks/Cole.

Hokenstad, M. C., Khinduka, S. K., & Midgley, J. (Eds.). (1992). *Profiles in international social work: Global challenges for a new century.* Washington, DC: NASW Press.

Honneth, A. (1996). *The struggle for recognition: The moral grammar of social conflicts.* Cambridge, MA: MIT Press.

hooks, b. (2000). *Feminist theory: From margin to center* (2nd ed.). Boston, MA: South End Press.

Horton, M., & Friere, P. (1990). *We make the road by walking: Conversations on education and social change.* (B. Bell, J. Gaventa, & J. Peters (Eds.). Philadelphia, PA: Temple University Press.

Housing Works. (2012). *About.* Retrieved from http://www.housingworks.org/about/mission/

Huegler, N., Lyons, K., & Pawar, M. (2012). Setting the scene. In K. Lyons, T. Hokenstad, M. Pawar, N. Huegler, & N. Hall (Eds.), *The SAGE handbook of international social work* (pp. 1–37). Los Angeles, CA: SAGE.

Hugman, R. (2010). *Understanding international social work: A critical analysis.* New York: Palgrave MacMillan.

Hugman, R., & Smith, D. (Eds). (1995). *Ethical issues in social work.* London, UK: Routledge.

Hurtado, A., Gurin, P., & Peng, T. (1994). Social identities—A framework for studying the adaptations of immigrants and ethnics: The adaptations of Mexicans in the U.S. *Social Problems, 41*(1), 129–151.

Hyde, C. A. (1994). Commitment to social change: Voices from the feminist movement. *Journal of Community Practice, 1*(2), 45–64.

Hyde, C. A. (2000). The hybrid nonprofit: An examination of feminist social movement organizations. *Journal of Community Practice, 8*(4), 45–67.

Ife, J. (1995). *Community development: Creating community alternatives—vision, analysis and practice.* Melbourne, Australia: Longman.

Ife, J. (1997). *Rethinking social work: Towards critical practice.* Melbourne, Australia: Addison Longman Wesley.

Ife, J. (2000). Localized needs and a globalized economy: Bridging the gap with social work practice. *Canadian Social Work* (Supplementary Issue), *17*, 50–64.

Ife, J. (2001). *Human rights and social work: Towards a rights-based practice.* New York: Cambridge University Press.

INCITE! (2006). *The color of violence: The Incite! anthology.* Boston, MA: South End Press.

INCITE! (Eds.). (2007). *The Revolution will not be funded: Beyond the non-profit industrial complex.* Cambridge, MA: South End Press.

International Federation of Red Cross and Red Crescent Societies (IFRC). (2000). *World Disasters Report 2000: Focus on public health.* Bellegardesur-Valserine, France: SADAG Imprimerie.

International Federation of Social Workers (IFSW). (2011). *Definition of social work.* Retrieved from http://www.ifsw.org/f38000138.html

International Federation of Social Workers (IFSW). (2012). *Definition of social work.* Retrieved from http://ifsw.org/resources/definition-of-social-work/

Jansson, B. S. (2003). *Becoming an effective policy advocate: From policy practice to social justice* (4th ed.). Pacific Grove, CA: Thompson.

Jansson, B. S., Dempsey, D., McCroskey, J., & Schneider, R. (2005). Four models of policy practice. In M. Weil (Ed.), *The handbook of community practice* (pp. 319–338). Thousand Oaks, CA: SAGE.

Jimenez, J. (2010). *Social policy and social change: Toward the creation of social and economic justice.* Thousand Oaks, CA: SAGE.

Johnson, A. (2006). *Privilege, power, and difference* (2nd ed.). New York: McGraw-Hill.

Jones, K. (2010). Buddhism and social action: An exploration. *Access to insight.* Retrieved from http://www.access-toinsight.org/lib/authors/jones/wheel285.html

Jong, P., & Berg, K. (2002). *Interviewing for solutions* (2nd ed.). Pacific Grove, CA: Wadsworth/Thomson Learning.

Jordon, J. (1991). The meaning of mutuality. In J. Jordon, A. Kaplan, J. Miller, I. Stiver, & J. Surrey (Eds.), *Women's growth in connection: Writings from the Stone Center* (pp. 81–96). New York: The Guilford Press.

Jordan, J. V. (2010). *Relational-cultural therapy.* Washington, DC: American Psychological Association.

Kadushin, A., & Kadushin, G. (1997). *The social work interview: A guide for human service professionals* (4th ed.). New York: Columbia Press.

Kaner, S., Lind, J., Toldi, C., Fisk, S., & Berger, D. (2007*). Facilitator's guide to participatory decision-making* (2nd ed.). San Francisco, CA: Jossey-Bass.

Kanuha, V. (1998). Professional social work and the battered women's movement: Contextualizing the challenges of domestic violence work. *Professional Development: The International Journal of Continuing Social Work Education, 1*(2), 4–18.

Karabanow, J. (2004). Making organizations work: Exploring characteristics of anti-oppressive organizational structures in street youth shelters. *Journal of Social Work, 4*(1), 47–60.

Karls, J. M., & Wandrei, K. E. (1992). PIE: A new language for social work. *National Association of Social Workers, 37*(10), 80–85.

Kekes, J. (1993). *The morality of pluralism.* Princeton, NJ: Princeton University Press.

Khadduir, M. (2001). *The Islamic concept of justice.* Baltimore, MD: Johns Hopkins Press.

Khan, P., & Dominelli, L. (2000). The impact of globalization on social work in the UK. *European Journal of Social Work, 3*(2), 95–108.

King, C. S., & Zanetti, L. A. (2005). *Transformational public service: Portraits of theory in practice.* Armonk, NY: M.E. Sharpe.

Kivel, P. (2006). *Social service or social change?* Retrieved from http://www.paulkivel.com/

Kondrat, M. E. (1999). Who is the "self" in self-aware: Professional self-awareness from a critical theory perspective. *Social Services Review, 73*(4), 451–477.

Lakoff, G. (2002). *Moral politics: How liberals and conservatives think.* Chicago: The University of Chicago Press.

Lamont, J., & Favor, C. (2008). Distributive justice. In E. N. Zalta (Ed.), *The Stanford encyclopedia of philosophy* (Fall ed.). Retrieved from http://plato.stanford.edu/archives/fall2008/entries/justice-distributive/

Lane, S. R., & Humphreys, N. A. (2011). Social workers in politics: A national survey of social work candidates and elected officials. *Journal of Policy Practice, 10*(3), 225–244.

Langan, M., & Lee, L. (1989). *Women, oppression and social work: Issues in anti-discriminatory practice (state of welfare).* New York: Routledge.

Larson, G. (2008). Anti-oppressive practice in mental health. *Journal of Progressive Human Services, 19*(1), 39–54.

Latting, J. K., & Gummer, B. (1994). Can administrative controls and pressure for efficiency and effectiveness be balanced with the staff's demand for decentralization and participation? In M. J. Austin & J. L. Lowe (Eds.), *Controversial issues in communities and organizations* (p. 251–266). Needham Heights, MA: Allyn and Bacon.

LeCroy, C. (2012). *The call to social work: Life stories* (2nd ed.). Thousand Oaks, CA: SAGE.

Lee, J. (1994). *The empowerment approach to social work practice.* New York: Columbia University Press.

Lee, J. (2001). *The empowerment approach to social work practice: Building the beloved Community* (2nd ed.). New York: Columbia University Press.

Lee, J. A. B., & Swenson, C. R. (2005). Mutual aid: A buffer against risk. In A. Gitterman, & L. Shulman (Eds.), *Mutual aid groups, vulnerable and resilient populations, and the life cycle* (3rd ed., pp. 573–596). New York: Columbia University Press.

Lee, M., & Greene, G. (1999). A social constructivist framework for integrating cross-cultural issues in teaching clinical social work. *Journal of Social Work Education, 35*(1), 21–37.

Legge, J. S. (1995). Understanding American Judaism: Revisiting the concept of "social justice." *Contemporary Jewry 16*(1), 97–109.

Li, P. S. (2003). *Destination Canada: Immigration debates and issues.* Toronto, Canada: Oxford University Press.

Liberty Hill Foundation. (2013). *Clean up: Green up.* Retrieved from http://www.libertyhill.org

Lister, P. G. (2012). *Integrating social work theory and practice: A practical skills guide.* New York: Routledge.

Lowenberg, F. M., & Dolgoff, R. (1996). *Ethical decisions for social work practice.* Itasca, IL: F. E. Peacock.

Ludvig, A. (2006). Difference between women? Intersecting voices in a female narrative. *European Journal of Women's Studies, 13*(3), 245–258.

Lundy, C. (2004). *Social work and social justice: A structural approach to practice*. Peterborough, Ontario: Broadview Press.

Lundy, C. (2011). *Social work, social justice and human rights: A structural approach to practice* (2nd ed.). Toronto, Canada: University of Toronto Press.

Lyons, K., Hokenstad, T., Pawar, M., Huegler, N., & Hall, N. (2012). *The SAGE handbook of international social work*. Los Angeles, CA: SAGE.

Maina, W. M. (2008). African communitarian ethics in the theological work of Bénézet Bujo. *Pacifica, 21*, 192–209.

Matahaere-Atariki, D., Bertanees, C., & Hoffman, L. (2001). Anti-oppressive practices in a colonial context. In M. Connolly (Ed.), *New Zealand social work: Contexts and practices*. Auckland, New Zealand: Oxford University Press.

Mathbor, G., & Bourassa, J. (2012). Disaster management and humanitarian action. In K. Lyons, T. Hokenstad, M. Pawar, N. Huegler, & N. Hall (Eds.), *The SAGE handbook of international social work* (pp. 294–310). Los Angeles, CA: SAGE.

Matthies, A., Närhi, K., & Ward, D. (Eds.). (2001). *The eco-social approach in social work*. Jyväskylä, Finland: SoPhi, University of Jyväskylä.

McBeath, G., & Webb, S. A. (2002). Virtue ethics and social work: Being lucky, realistic, and not doing one's duty. *British Journal of Social Work, 32*, 1015–1036.

McCarthy, J. D., & Zald, M. N. (1977). Resource mobilization and social movements: A partial theory. *American Journal of Sociology, 82*, 1212–1241.

McGoldrick, M., Gerson, R., Petry, S., & Gil, E. (2008). Family play genograms. In M. McGoldrick, R. Gerson, S. Petry, & E. Gil (Eds.), *Genograms, assessment and intervention* (3rd ed., pp. 257–274). New York: W.W. Norton.

McLaughlin, H. (2009). What's in a name: "client," "patient," "customer," "consumer," "expert by experience," "Service User"—What's next? *British Journal of Social Work, 39*(2), 1101–1117.

McPhail, B. (2003). A feminist policy analysis framework: Through a gendered lens. *The Social Policy Journal, 2*(2/3), 39–60.

McWhirter, B., & McWhirter, E. (2007). Toward an emancipatory communitarian approach to the practice of psychology training. In E. Aldarondo (Ed.), *Advancing social justice through clinical practice* (pp. 391–442). Mahwah, NJ: Lawrence Erlbaum.

Mental Health America (MHA). (2012). *Mental health America: About*. Retrieved from http://www.nmha.org/

Meyerson, D. (2001). *Tempered radicals: How people use difference to inspire change at work*. Cambridge, MA: Harvard Business School Press.

Midgley, J. (2008). Perspectives on globalization and culture: Implications for international social work practice. *Journal of Global Social Work Practice, 1*(1).

Miller, M. (2010). Alinsky for the left: The politics of community organizing. *Dissent, 57*(1), 43–49.

Miller-Cribbs, J. E., Cagel, B. E., Natale, A. P., & Cummings, Z. (2010). Thinking about think tanks: Strategies for progressive social work. *Journal of Policy Practice, 9*, 284–307.

Min Ha, T. T. (1991). *When the moon waxes red: Representation, gender and cultural politics*. New York: Routledge.

Mizrahi, T., Humphreys, M. L., & Torres, D. (2009). The social construction of client participation: The evolution and transformation of the role of service recipients in child welfare and mental disabilities. *Journal of Sociology and Social Welfare, 36*(2), 35–61.

Mizrahi, T., & Rosenthal, B. B. (2001). Complexities of coalition building: Leaders' successes, strategies, struggles, and solutions. *Social Work, 46*(1), 63–78.

Moch, K. (Trans.). (2009). A critical understanding of social work by Paulo Friere. *Journal of Progressive Human Services, 20*(1), 92–97.

Montero, M. (2009). Methods for liberation: Critical consciousness in action. In M. Montero & C. C. Sonn (Eds.), *Psychology of liberation: Theory and applications* (pp. 73–91). New York: Springer.

Mooney, H., Cropper, A., & Reid, W. (2005). Confronting the human dilemma. *Nature 434*(3), 561–562.

Moosa-Mitha, M. (2005). Situating anti-oppressive theories within critical and difference-centered perspectives. In L. Brown & S. Strega (Eds.), *Research as resistance: Critical, indigenous and anti-oppressive approaches* (pp. 37–72). Toronto, Canada: Canadian Scholars' Press.

Moreau, M. (1979). A structural approach to social work practice. *Canadian Journal of Social Work Education, 5*(1), 78–94.

Moreau, M., & Frosst, S. (1993). *Empowerment II: Snapshots of the structural approach in action*. Ottawa, Canada: Carleton University Press.

Moreau, M., Frosst, S., Frayne, G., Hlywa, M., Leonard, L., & Rowell, M. (1993). *Empowerment II: Snapshots of the structural approach in action*. Ottawa, Canada: Carleton University Press.

Morgaine, K. (2014). Conceptualizing social justice in social work: Are social workers "too bogged down in the trees?" *Journal of Social Justice, 4*, 1–18.

Morris, P. M. (2002). The capabilities perspective: A framework for social justice. *Families in Society, 83*(4), 365–373.

Mullaly, B. (2001). Confronting the politics of despair: Toward the reconstruction of progressive social work in a global economy and postmodern age. *Social Work Education, 20*(3), 301–320.

Mullaly, B. (2007). *The new structural social work: Ideology, theory and practice* (3rd ed.). New York: Oxford University Press.

Mullaly, B. (2010). *Challenging oppression and confronting privilege: A critical social work approach.* (2nd ed). Toronto, Canada: Oxford University Press.

Mullaly, R. (1997). *Structural social work: Ideology, theory, and practice* (2nd ed.). New York: Oxford Press.

Närhi, K. (2004). The eco-social approach in social work and the challenges to the expertise of social work. *Jyväskylä Studies in Education Psychology and Social Research, 243*, 1–107). Retrieved from https://jyx.jyu.fi/dspace/handle/123456789/13326

National Association of Black Social Workers (NABSW). (2012a). *History*. Retrieved from http://www.nabsw.org/mserver/Mission.aspx

National Association of Black Social Workers (NABSW). (2012b). *Mission statement*. Retrieved from http://www.nabsw.org/mserver/Mission2.aspx

National Association of Planning Councils (NAPC). (2012a). *What are planning councils?* Retrieved from http://www.communityplanning.org/planning_councils.htm

National Association of Planning Councils (NAPC). (2012b). *Community planning: The planning council approach*. Retrieved from http://www.communityplanning.org/community%20planning.htm

National Association of Social Workers (NASW). (n.d. a). *Whitney M. Young, Jr*. Retrieved from http://www.social-workreinvestment.org/content/Bio WhitneyMYoungJr.pdf

National Association of Social Workers (NASW). (n.d. b). *PACE: Building political power for social workers*. Retrieved from http://www.naswdc.org/pace/default.asp

National Association of Social Workers (NASW). (2008). *Code of ethics*. Retrieved from http://www.socialworkers.org/pubs/code/code.asp

National Priorities Project (NPP). (2012). *Trade-offs*. Retrieved from http://nationalpriorities.org/en/interactive-data/trade-offs/

Nes, J. A., & Iadicola, P. (1989). Toward a definition of feminist social work: A comparison of liberal, radical and socialist models. *Social Work, 34*(1), 12–21.

Nicols, L. (2002). Participatory program planning: Including program participants and evaluators. *Evaluation and program planning, 25*(1), 1–14.

Norton, C. L. (2012). Social work and the environment: An ecosocial approach. *International Journal of Social Welfare, 21*, 299–308.

Nussbaum, M. (2003). Capabilities as fundamental entitlements: Sen and social justice. *Feminist Economics, 9*(2–3), 33–59.

Nussbaum, M. C. (2011). *Creating capabilities: The human development approach*. Cambridge, MA: Harvard University Press.

Nye, C. (2008). The delivery of social services in northern Thailand. *International Social Work, 51*(2), 193–205.

Oboler, S. (1995). *Ethnic labels, Latino lives: Identity and the politics of (re)presentation in the U.S.* Minneapolis: University of Minnesota Press.

O'Hara, A. (2011). The microskills of interviewing. In A. O'Hara & R. Pockett (Eds.), *Skills for human service practice: Working with individuals, groups and communities* (2nd ed., pp. 145–163). Melbourne, Australia: Oxford University Press.

O'Hare, T. (2009). *Essential skills of social work practice: Assessment, intervention and evaluation*. Chicago, Lyceum Books.

Okun, B. F. (1992). *Effective helping: Interviewing and counseling techniques* (4th ed.). Pacific Grove, CA: Brooks/Cole.

Olivier, C. (2010). Operationalizing structural theory: Guidelines for practice. In S. Hick, H. Peters, T. Corner & T. London (Eds.). *Structural social work in action: Examples from practice* (pp. 26–38). Toronto, Canada: Canadian Scholars' Press.

Orme, J. (2002). Social work: Gender, care and justice. *British Journal of Social Work, 32*, 799–814.

Padamsee, Y. M. (2011). *Communities of care, organizations for liberation*. Retrieved from http://nayamaya.word-press.com/2011/06/19/communities-of-care-organizations-for-liberation/

Pandya, V. (2005). Contemporary group work practice. In A. Gitterman, & L. Shulman (Eds.), *Mutual aid groups, vulnerable and resilient populations, and the life cycle* (3rd ed., pp. 598–613). New York: Columbia University Press.

Parekh, B. (2000). *Rethinking multiculturalism: Cultural diversity and political theory*. London, UK: Macmillan.

Parker, J., & Bradley, G. (2010). *Social work practice: Assessment, planning, intervention, and review* (3rd ed.). Exeter, UK: Learning Matters.

Parker, L. (2004). Bringing power from the margins to the center. In L. Silverstein, & T. J. Goodrich (Eds.), *Feminist family therapy* (pp. 225–238). Washington, DC: American Psychological Association.

Parsons, R. J. (1995). *Empowerment based social work practice: A study of process and outcomes*. Paper presented at the annual program meeting for the Council on Social Work Education, San Diego, CA.

Parsons, R. J. (1998). Evaluation of empowerment practice. In L. Gutierrez, R. J. Parsons & E. O. Cox (Eds.). *Empowerment in social work practice*. Pacific Grove, CA: Brookes/Cole.

Parton, N. (2009). Postmodern and constructionist approaches to social work. In R. Adams, L. Dominelli, & M. Payne, *Critical practice in social work* (2nd ed., pp. 220–229). Basingstoke, UK: Palgrave MacMillan.

Pawar, M. (2013). International community practice: Local-global issues and strategies. In M. Weil, M. Reisch, & M. L. Ohmer (Eds.), *The handbook of community practice* (2nd ed., pp. 633–652). Los Angeles, CA: SAGE.

Pawar, M., & Cox, D. (2010). Social development. In M. Pawar, & D. Cox (Eds.), *Social development: Critical themes and perspectives* (pp. 13–36). New York: Routledge.

Payne, M. (2002). The politics of systems theory within social work. *Journal of Social Work, 2*(3), 269–292.

Payne, M. (2005a). *Modern social work theory* (3rd ed.). Chicago: Lyceum Books.

Payne, M. (2005b). *Social work change and continuity*. Basingstoke, UK: Palgrave Macmillan.

Payne, M. (2011). *Humanistic social work: Core principles in practice*. Chicago: Lyceum Books.

Pease, B., & Fook, J. (1999). *Transforming social work practice: Postmodern critical perspectives*. London, UK: Routledge.

Phillips, C., Palfrey, C., & Thomas, P. (1994). *Evaluating health and social care*. Basingstoke, UK: Macmillan.

Pincus, A., & Minaham, A. (1973). *Social work practice: Model and method*. Itasca, IL: Peacock.

Piven, F. F., & Cloward, R. (1977). *Poor people's movements: Why they succeed, how they fail*. New York: Vintage.

Piven, F. F., & Cloward, R. (1979). *Poor people's movements: Why they succeed, how they fail*. New York: Vintage.

Pleck, E. (2004). *Domestic tyranny: The making of social policy against family violence from colonial times to present*. Chicago: University of Illinois Press.

Plimer, I. (2009). *Heaven and earth*. Victoria, Australia: Conner Court.

Poe, M. A. (2007). Fairness is not enough: Social justice as restoration of right relationships. *Social Work and Christianity, 34*(4), 449–470.

Pollack, S. (2004). Anti-oppressive social work practice with women in prison: Discursive reconstructions and alternative practices. *The British Journal of Social Work, 34*(5), 693–707.

Popple, P. R., & Leighninger, L. (2011). *The policy-based profession: An introduction to social welfare policy analysis for social workers* (5th ed.). New York: Allyn & Bacon.

Poulin, J. (2000). *Collaborative social work: Strengths-based generalist practice*. Itasca, IL: F. E. Peacock.

Pozzuto, R., Angell, G. B., & Dezendorf, P. K. (2005). Therapeutic critique: Traditional versus critical perspectives. In S. Hick, J. Fook, & R. Pozzuto (Eds.), *Social work: A critical turn* (pp. 25–38). Toronto, Canada: Thompson Educational.

Prevey, C. E. (1899). Economic aspects of charity organization. *Annals of the American Academy of Political and Social Science, 14*, 1–17.

Pritchard, D. (2006). Deconstructing psychopathology: Contextualizing mental disorders in teaching psychosocial assessment. *Journal of Progressive Human Services, 17*(2), 5–26.

Pyles, L. (2009). *Progressive community organizing: A critical approach for a globalizing world*. New York: Routledge.

Radermacher, H., Sonn, C., Keys, C., & Duckett, P. (2010). Disability and participation: It's about us but still without us! *Journal of Community and Applied Social Psychology, 20*, 333–346.

Radical Social Work Group (RSWG). (n.d.). *About us.* Retrieved from https://sites.google.com/site/radicalswg/about-us

Rank and Filer. (2012, May). *The role of social workers in Occupy Wall Street: Prefigurative politics and anti-austerity organizing.* Retrieved from http://www.rankandfiler.net/social-workers-in-ows/

Ratts, M. J., Anthony, L., & Santos, K. N. T. (2010). The dimensions of social justice model: Transforming traditional group work into a socially just framework. *The Journal for Specialists in Group Work, 35*(2), 160–168.

Rawls, J. (1971). *A theory of justice.* Cambridge, MA: The Belknap Press.

Reamer, F. G. (1993). *The philosophical foundations of social work.* New York: Columbia University Press.

Reisch, M. (2002). Defining social justice in a socially unjust world. *Families in Society, 83*(4), 343–354.

Reisch, M. (2007). Social justice and multiculturalism: Persistent tensions in the history of U.S. social welfare and social work. *Studies in Social Justice, 1*, 67–92.

Reisch, M. (2011). Defining social justice in a socially just world. In J. Birkenmaier, A. Cruce, E. Burkemper, J. Curley, R. Wilson, & J. Stretch (Eds.), *Educating for social justice: Transformative experiential learning.* Chicago: Lyceum Books.

Reisch, M., & Andrews, J. (2002). *The road not taken: A history of radical social work in the United States.* New York: Brunner-Routledge.

Remen, R. N. (1999, Sept.). Helping, fixing or serving? *Shambhala Sun.* Retrieved from http://www.shambhalasun.com/index.php?option=com_content&task=view&id=2328

Richmond, M. E. (1907). *Friendly visiting among the poor.* Retrieved from http://www.gutenberg.org/catalog/world/readfile?fk_files=1537959&pageno=20

Robbins, S., Chatterjee, P., & Canda, E. (2006). *Contemporary human behavior theory* (2nd ed., pp. 92–125). Boston, MA: Allyn & Bacon.

Roberts, P. (1999). A dilemma for critical educators? *Journal of Moral Education, 28*(1), 19–30.

Rodwell, M. (1987). Naturalistic inquiry: An alternative model for social work assessment *Social Service Review, 61*(2), 231–246.

Rogers, A. T. (2010). *Human behavior in the social environment* (2nd ed., pp. 19–47). New York: Routledge.

Rolfe, G., Freshwater, D., & Jasper, M. (2001). *Critical reflection for nursing and the helping professions: A user's guide.* Basingstoke, UK: Palgrave Macmillan.

Rome, S. H., Hoechstetter, S., & Wolf-Branigin, M. (2012). Pushing the envelope: Empowering clients for political action. *Journal of Policy Practice, 9*, 201–219.

Rothman, J. (1996). The interweaving of community intervention approaches. *Journal of Community Practice, 3*(3-4), 69–99.

Rothman, J. (2001). Approaches to community intervention. In J. Rothman, J. Erlich, & J. Tropman (Eds.), *Strategies of community intervention: Macro practice* (pp. 27–64). Belmont, CA: Wadsworth.

Rouse, J. A. (2004). *Lugenia Burns Hope: Black southern reformer.* Atlanta: University of Georgia Press.

Rozario, S. (2001). Women and poverty: Is Grameen Bank the answer? *Journal of Interdisciplinary Gender Studies, 6*(2), 60–82.

Rubin, S. (2011). Tackling taboo topics: Case studies in group work. *Social Work with Groups, 34*, 257–269.

Ruch, G. (2002). From triangle to spiral: Reflective practice in social work education, practice and research. *Social Work Education, 21*(2), 199–216.

Sakamoto, I., & Pitner, R. (2005). Use of critical consciousness in anti-oppressive social work practice: Disentangling power dynamics at personal and structural levels. *British Journal of Social Work, 35*, 435–452.

Saleebey, D. (1996). The strengths-perspective in social work practice: Extensions and cautions. *Social Work, 41*(3), 296–305.

Saleebey, D. (1997). Introduction: Power in the people. In D. Saleebey (Ed.), *The strengths perspective in social work practice* (2nd ed., pp. 1–18). White Plains, NY: Longman.

Satir, V. (1988). *The new peoplemaking.* Mountain View, CA: Science and Behavior Books.

Save the Children. (2010). At a crossroads: Humanitarianism for the next decade. Retrieved from http://www.savethe-children.org.uk/en/54_12550.htm

Schechter, S. (1982). *Women and male violence: The visions and struggles of the battered women's movement.* Boston, MA: South End Press.

Schwartz, K. (2010). Injustice can happen whether you're psychotic or not: Incorporating structural social work theory in a mental health setting. In S. Hick, H. Peters, T. Corner & T. London (Eds.), *Structural social work in action: Examples from practice* (pp. 106–120). Toronto, Canada: Canadian Scholars' Press.

Schwartz, W. (1961). The social worker in the group. In B. Saunders (Ed.), *New perspectives on services to groups: Theory, organization, practice* (pp. 7–29). New York: The National Association of Social Workers.

Sen, A. (2009). *The idea of justice*. Cambridge, MA: The Belknap Press.

Sewpaul, V., & Jones, D. (2004). Global standards for social work education and training. *Social Work Education, 25*(5), 493–513.

Shaping Our Lives National User Network. (2003). *Shaping our lives—from outset to outcome: What people think of the social care services they use* (Black User Group (West London), Ethnic Disabled Group Emerged (Manchester), Footprints and Waltham Forest Black Mental Health Service User Group (North London) and Service Users' Action Forum (Wakefield). London, UK: Joseph Rowntree.

Shebib, B. (2003). *Choices*. New York: Allyn & Bacon.

Shepard, B. (2005). Play, creativity, and the new community organizing. *Journal of Progressive Human Services, 16*(2), 47–69.

Shulman, L. (2009). The skills of helping individuals, families, groups and communities (6th ed.). Belmont, CA: Brookes/Cole.

Simon, B. (1990). Rethinking empowerment. *Journal of Progressive Human Services, 1*, 27–39.

Smith, R. (2008). *Social work and power*. Basingstoke, UK: Palgrave Macmillan.

Snow, D. A., Soule, S. A., & Kriesi, H. (2007). Mapping the terrain. In D. A. Snow, S. A. Soule, & H. Kriesi (Eds.), *The Blackwell companion to social movements* (pp. 3–16). New York: Blackwell.

Social Welfare Action Alliance (SWAA). (2014). *Who we are*. Retrieved from http://www.socialwelfareactionalliance .org/whoweare.html

Solas, J. (1996). The limits of empowerment in human service work. *Australian Journal of Social Issues, 31*(2), 147–156.

Song, L. (2011). The extent and correlates of the utilization of empowerment strategies: A survey of social workers in the field of partner violence. *British Journal of Social Work, 41*, 1016–1037.

Sorokin, P. A. (2002). Preface. In F. Tönnies (Ed.), *Community and society*. New York: Harper.

Spivak, G. (1988). Can the subaltern speak? In C. Nelson & L. Grossberg (Eds.), *Marxism and the interpretation of culture* (pp. 271–313). Chicago: University of Chicago Press.

Steinberg, D. M. (2010). Mutual aid: A contribution to best-practice social work. *Social Work With Groups, 33,* 53–68.

Stiglitz, J. (2004). Capital-market liberalization, globalization, and the IMF. *Oxford Review of Economic Policy, 20*(1), 57–71.

Stockman, F., Kranish, M., Canellos, P. S., & Baron, K. (2006, Oct. 8). Bush brings faith to foreign aid: As funding rises, Christian groups deliver help—with a message. *Boston Globe Newspaper*, p. 2.

Stoddard, A., Harmer, A., & DiDomenico, V. (2009). *Providing aid in insecure environments: 2009 update trends in violence against aid workers and the operational response*. Retrieved from http://www.odi.org.uk/resources/ download/3250.pdf

Stoesz, D. (2000). *A poverty of imagination: Bootstrap capitalism, sequel to welfare reform*. Madison, WI: University of Wisconsin Press.

Strom-Gottfried, K. (1999). *Social work practice: Cases, activities and exercises*. Los Angeles, CA: SAGE.

Surry, J. L. (1991). The "self-in-relation": A theory of women's development. In J. Jordon, A. Kaplan, J. Miller, I. Stiver, & J. Surrey (Eds.), *Women's growth in connection: Writings from the Stone Center* (pp. 51–66). New York: The Guilford Press.

Sutherland, A. (1995). Getting everyone involved: A guide to conducting participatory evaluations. Calgary, Canada: YWCA of Calgary.

Swenson, C. (1998). Clinical social work's contribution to a social justice perspective. *Social Work, 43*(6), 527–537.

Tarrow, S. (2011). *Power in movement: Social movement and contentious politics* (3rd ed.). New York: Cambridge University Press.

Taylor, C. (1994). *Multiculturalism: Examining the politics of recognition*. Princeton, NJ: Princeton University Press.

Taylor, J., Wilkinson, D., & Cheers, B. (2008). *Working with communities in health and human services*. Melbourne, Australia: Oxford University Press.

Taylor, P. (1993). *The texts of Paulo Freire*. Buckingham, UK: Open University Press.

Tew, J. (2006). Understanding power and powerlessness towards a framework for emancipatory practice in social work. *Journal of Social Work, 6*(1), 33–51.

Thompson, N. (1993). *Anti-discriminatory practice* (3rd ed.). Basingstoke, UK: Palgrave Macmillan.

Thompson, N. (2000). *Understanding social work: Preparing for practice.* Basingstoke, UK: Palgrave Macmillan.

Thompson, N., & Thompson, S. (2008). *The social work companion.* Basingstoke, UK: Palgrave Macmillan.

Tomes, N. (2006). The patient as a policy factor: A historical case study of the consumer/survivor movement in mental health. *Health Affairs, 25*(3), 720–729.

Townsend, J., Zapata, E., Rowlands, J., Albereti, P., & Mercado, M. (1999). *Women and power: Fighting patriarchies and poverty.* London, UK: Zed Books.

Tracy, E., & Whittaker, J. (1990). The social network map: Assessing social support in clinical practice. *Families in Society: The Journal of Contemporary Human Services, 171*(8), 461–470.

Tully, J. (1995). *Strange multiplicity.* Cambridge, UK: Cambridge University Press.

U.S. Agency for International Development (USAID). (2004). *Participation by religious organizations in USAID programs.* In Center for faith-based and community initiatives, 22 CFR Parts 202, 205, 211, and 226. Washington, DC: Government Printing Office.

USC Neighborhood Academic Initiative. (NAI). (2009). *About us: Program overview.* Retrieved from http://www.uscnai.com/about-2

U.S. Solidarity Economy Network (SEN). (2012a). *Solidarity economy news.* Retrieved on from http://ussen.org/

U.S. Solidarity Economy Network (SEN). (2012b). *What is the solidarity economy?* Retrieved from http://ussen.org/solidarity/what

Van der Veer, G. (2006). Training trainers for counselors and psychosocial workers in areas of armed conflict: Some basic principles. *Intervention: International Journal of Mental Health Psychosocial Work and Counseling in Areas of Conflict, 4*(2), 97–107.

Van Dyke, N., & McCammon, H. J. (2010a). Introduction: Social movement coalition formation. In N. Van Dyke, & H. J. McCammon (Eds.), *Strategic alliances: Coalition building and social movements* (p. 11–27). Minneapolis, MN: University of Minnesota Press.

Van Dyke, N., & McCammon, H. J. (2010b). Applying qualitative comparative analysis to empirical studies of social movement coalition formation. In N. Van Dyke & H. J. McCammon (Eds.), *Strategic alliances: Coalition building and social movements* (pp. 292–315). Minneapolis, MN: University of Minnesota Press.

Van Soest, D. (1994). Strange bedfellows: A call for reordering national priorities from three social justice perspectives. *Social Work, 39(6),* 710–717.

Van Soest, D. (2007). Human Rights and Social and Economic Justice. In D. Lum (Ed.), *Culturally competent practice: A framework for understanding diverse groups* (pp. 83–120). Belmont, CA: Brooks/Cole.

Van Wormer, K. (2010). Economic globalization and transnational migration: An anti-oppressive framework. In N. J. Negi, & R. Furman (Eds.), *Transnational social work practice.* New York: Columbia University Press.

Van Wormer, K., & Besthorn, F. H. (2010). *Human behavior and the social environment: Macro level: groups, communities and organizations.* New York: Oxford University Press.

Volser, N. (1990). Assessing family access to basic resources: An essential component of social work practice. *Social Work, 35*(5), 434–441.

Wagner, D. (1989). Radical movements in social services: A theoretical framework. *Social Services Review, 63*(2), 264–284.

Wakefield, J. C. (1988). Psychotherapy, distributive justice, and social work: Part 1: Distributive justice as a conceptual framework for social work. *The Social Service Review, 62*(2), 187–210.

Wallerstein, N., & Bernstein, E. (1988). Empowerment education: Freire's ideas adapted to health education. *Health Education Quarterly, 15*(4), 379–394.

Wang, C., & Burris, M. A. (1997). Photovoice: Concept, methodology, and use for participatory needs assessment. *Health Education & Behavior, 24*(3), 369–387.

Ward, D., & Mullender, A. (1991). Empowerment and oppression: An indissoluble pairing for contemporary social work. *Critical Social Policy, 32,* 21–30.

Weeks, J. (1990). The value of difference. In J. Rutherford (Ed.), *Identity: Community, culture and difference.* London, UK: Lawrence & Wishart.

Weil, M. (2005a). Introduction: Contexts and challenges for 21st-century communities. In M. Weil (Ed.), *The handbook of community practice* (pp. 3–33). Thousand Oaks, CA: SAGE.

Weil, M. (2005b). Social planning with communities. In M. Weil (Ed.), *The handbook of community practice* (pp. 215–243). Thousand Oaks, CA: SAGE.

Weil, M., & Gamble, D. (2010). *Community practice skills: Local to global perspectives*. New York: Columbia University Press.

Weinberg, M. (2008). Structural social work: A moral compass for ethics in practice. *Critical Social Work, 9*(1).

Weingarten, K. (1995). Radical listening: Challenging cultural beliefs for and about mothers. In K. Weingarten (Ed.), *Cultural resistance: Challenging beliefs about men, women and therapy* (pp.7–23). Binghamton, NY: Harrington Park.

Whitchurch, G., & Constantine, L. (1993). Systems theory. In P. Boss, W. Doherty, R. LaRossa, W. Schumm, & S. Steinmetz (Eds.), *Sourcebook of family theories and methods: A contextual approach*. New York: Plenum Press.

Williams, L., & Sewpaul, V. (2004). Modernism, postmodernism and global standards setting. *Social Work Education, 23*(5), 555–565.

Wilson, A., & Beresford, P. (2000). Anti-oppressive practice: Emancipation or appropriation? *The British Journal of Social Work, 30*(5), 553–573.

Wise, J. B. (2005). *Empowerment practice with families in distress*. New York: Columbia University Press.

Women in Congress. (n.d.). *Jeannette Rankin*. Retrieved from http://womenincongress.house.gov/member-profiles/profile.html?intID=202

Wood, G., & Tully, C. (2006). *The structural approach to direct practice in social work: A social constructionist perspective* (3rd ed.). New York: Columbia University Press.

Yee, J. Y. (2005). Critical anti-racism praxis: The concept of whiteness implicated. In S. Hick, J. Fook, & R. Pozzuto (Eds.), *Social work: A critical turn* (pp. 87–103). Toronto, Canada: Thompson Educational.

Yip, K. (2004). A Chinese cultural critique of the Global Qualifying Standards for social work education. *Social Work Education, 23*(5), 597–612.

Yip, K. S. (2005). A dynamic Asian response to globalization: Its meanings, rationales and implications. *Intercultural Education, 13*(1), 593–607.

Young, I. M. (1990). *Justice and the politics of difference*. Princeton, NJ: Princeton University Press.

Young, I. M. (2010). Five faces of oppression. In I. M. Young (Ed.), *Justice and the politics of difference* (pp. 39–65). Princeton, NJ: Princeton University Press.

Youth on Board (YOB). (n.d. a). *About Youth on Board*. Retrieved from http://www.youthonboard.org/about-youth-board

Youth on Board (YOB). (n.d. b). *Organizational assessment checklist*. Retrieved from http://www.youthonboard.org/assessment-checklist

Zafirovski, M. (2011). *The enlightenment and its effects on modern society*. New York: Springer.

Zald, M. N., & Ash, R. (1966). Social movement organizations: Growth, decay and change. *Social Forces, 44*(3), 327–341.

About the Authors

 **Karen Morgaine (PhD)** is a queer, white academic with a penchant for critical theory and anarchist/Buddhist/feminist/postcolonial perspectives. After working in the domestic violence and community mental health fields for ten years, she completed her PhD in Social Work and Social Research at Portland State University. She fortuitously landed in a sociology department at California State University Northridge, where she teaches a variety of courses related to social welfare and social justice, including courses in community organizing, social movements, and LGBTQQI (Lesbian, Gay, Bisexual, Transgender, Queer, Questioning, and Intersex) communities. Her research leans toward analysis of social movement framing and issues related to power and privilege within social movements and identity groups. When not in the classroom or in front of the computer, she can be found dining all around Los Angeles, biking/doing yoga/lifting weights, and laughing a lot with her partner.

 **Moshoula Capous-Desyllas (PhD, MSW)** is an artist-activist-academic. As an assistant professor of sociology at California State University Northridge, she teaches social work courses in anti-oppressive practice, diversity and social justice, human behavior in the social environment, and social work methods. Her interests include arts-based research approaches, community-based participatory action research, community organizing and advocacy, social work with immigrants, trans-global migration issues, commercial sex work, and intersecting oppressions. She is committed to facilitating community dialogue and a deeper understanding about issues of diversity and social justice through art. Her passion lies in highlighting the voices of marginalized communities through the use of art as a form of activism, empowerment, and social change. When school isn't in session, she can be found kayaking in the Sea of Cortez or the Aegean Sea, or lost in the global South with a backpack in tow.

About the Contributors

 **Gabriel Arkles** is a collective member of the Sylvia Rivera Law Project, a board member of the Lorena Borjas Community Fund, and an acting assistant professor of lawyering at NYU School of Law. He is a transgender, white, U.S. citizen, queer, Muslim, male professional who grew up wealthy and has psychiatric disabilities. Also, he loves science fiction and cats. Gabriel aspires (without ever fully succeeding) to do social justice and anti-oppression work with humility, courage, compassion, accountability, practicality, idealism, and a commitment to community-building and self-care.

Email: gabriel.arkles@nyu.edu

Website: www.srlp.org/

 Deborah Burton is an LA CAN community organizer, a formerly homeless woman who has lived and worked in downtown Los Angeles for the past 10 years, and prior to that lived in South Central LA. Deborah first worked with LA CAN as a resident involved in the 2003 Hunger Action Day and their food access campaigns. She completed LA CAN's community intern program in 2004 and was hired in 2005. Deborah has multiple certifications in community organizing, peer education, and domestic violence intervention. She leads efforts in housing, women's rights, and violence prevention.

Email: DeborahB@cangress.org

 **Charles Ray Cochran** is a gay theater artist professional who changed careers midlife to become a social worker to advocate for his LGBT brothers and sisters. He lives in Silver Lake, California, with his wonderfully supportive partner, two indifferent felines, and a high-strung cattle dog. Currently, he is studying toward a master's in social work degree at UCLA.

Email: raycochran@gmail.com

 **Leslie Colwell** recalls how when she was teaching middle school in Los Angeles, she was struck by how many things affecting her on a daily basis—from the amount of resources she had in her classroom, to her job status when budget cuts came—were conditions set by folks at all levels of government. She became interested in how she could have an impact on education at the macro level, and worked for a while with *Teach for America* alumni who were interested in running for political office or doing policy and

advocacy work focused on education. In her current role as legislative director for a Colorado state senator, most of her work focuses on education issues and ensuring that every student in Colorado (her home state!) has access to a high-quality education.

Email: leslie.colwell@gmail.com

***Juston Cooper* (also known as "JC")** is a co-founder and director of administration of The Youth Connection (TYC) in Denver, Colorado. He has worked on a variety of projects and initiatives with nonprofit agencies and governmental departments, including political engagement strategy with federal, state, and locally elected officials, policy planning and development, organizational development, revenue expansion, collaboration and coalition building, facilitation, and strategic planning and management. Juston's work has been instrumental in ensuring the judicious use of resources in mentoring programs, community services projects, and public and nonprofit agencies committed to urban development and youth intervention initiatives. Juston holds a master's in public administration from the University of Colorado at Denver and a bachelor's of science in business marketing from Metropolitan State University in Denver.

Email: jc@tycdenver.org

Website: www.tycdenver.org/

Minh Dang is a 28-year-old Vietnamese-American woman who identifies as a scholar-activist, artist, lover, dreamer, lifelong learner, and modern-day abolitionist. She is informed by the philosophies of attachment theory, interpersonal neurobiology, liberation psychology, community-based participatory research, and black feminism. She describes her work as "the practice of freedom," working to liberate minds, bodies, and souls from the oppression of slavery. A close friend calls her a "love-warrior."

Email: minhdang8@gmail.com

Owen Daniel-McCarter is an activist for transgender liberation for over a decade. He is one of the founding collective members and attorney for the Transformative Justice Law Project (TJLP) of Illinois, which provides free, zealous, life-affirming, and gender-affirming holistic legal services to poor transgender and gender non-conforming people targeted by the criminal legal system in Chicago, as well as folks in prison throughout Illinois. TJLP provides legal services with a commitment to three core values: the right to gender self-determination, vision toward a long-term goal of prison abolition, and dedication to resisting state-sponsored systems of control through transformative justice and community empowerment models. Owen has also taught at DePaul University since 2008 in the departments of Sociology and Women & Gender Studies, the Peace, Justice & Conflict Studies Program, and at the Law School. Owen is a graduate of the City University of New York School of Law and the University of Vermont where he co-founded the Translating Identity Conference—a national conference on transgender issues now in its eleventh year.

Email: owen@tjlp.org

Website: www.tjlp.org/

 ***Joseph Nicholas DeFilippis*** is a doctoral student at the Portland State University School of Social Work. He received his undergraduate degree at Vassar College and a master's degree in community organizing at the Hunter College School of Social Work. He spent years doing volunteer work as a welfare rights organizer. Then, from 1999 to 2003, he served as the director of SAGE/Queens, an organization for LGBT senior citizens. In 2003, Joseph became the founding director of Queers for Economic Justice (QEJ), an organization working with low-income and homeless LGBT people, and led the organization for six years. He served on (and as a member of the steering committees) for two major activist coalitions in New York State: The Welfare Reform Network (1999–2002) and the NYS LGBT Health and Human Services Network (1995–2005). He is one of the primary authors of the infamous "Beyond Same-Sex Marriage" (which publicly critiqued the direction of the marriage equality movement) and one of the editors of "A New Queer Agenda" published this year by the Barnard Center for Research on Women. Joseph also served as an adjunct faculty member in social work programs at Fordham University, Hunter College, and Portland State University, where he taught various courses in political economy, social justice, social welfare policy, community organizing, and sexuality. He identifies as a biracial gay man, born and raised in New York City, the son of two immigrants. His work has always been informed by Marxism, black feminism, and queer theory.

Email: jndefilippis@gmail.com

Website: www.q4ej.org/

 ***Steve Diaz*** is an LA CAN community organizer who lived in the downtown LA community for over 9 years and in 2002 joined LA CAN's housing preservation campaigns as a teenager who lived in a residential hotel at-risk of conversion. He has completed two organizing certification programs and is in the process of obtaining his AA degree. Steve completed LA CAN's community intern program in 2003, and was hired as a paid organizer in 2004. He provides support to all of their campaigns and is the lead organizer on housing campaigns.

Email: SteveD@cangress.org

 ***Cheryl Distaso*** bases her work on the Freirian model, understanding that lasting change only occurs when leadership comes from within marginalized groups. Working with a feminist lens, she believes that as the rigidity of professional roles gives way to authentic relationships, the beginnings of true community emerge. She is the coordinator of the Fort Collins Community Action Network and is currently working on a master's of social work degree at Colorado State University.

Email: cdistaso@frii.com

***Jean East* (MSW, PhD)** is a professor at the University of Denver, Graduate School of Social Work and co-founder of Project WISE, a Women's Initiative for Service and Empowerment. Identifying as a feminist and lesbian, Jean has dedicated her social work career to giving voice to the struggles of women in poverty, recognizing women's many strengths and courage in an unjust society. Project WISE was founded in 1995 with Susan Kenney, MSW, with the goal of providing an opportunity for women to overcome isolation, mental health, and well-being struggles and to engage women in changing oppressive policies in the community. Jean has a passion for teaching and mentoring women, and sees each relationship as an opportunity to practice humility through connection.

Email: Jean.East@du.edu

Website: www.denverprojectwise.org

Chuck Fraser has been a working-class social activist all his life. His mother raised four children by herself, while working as a practical nurse. He witnessed that life is not fair and that certain citizens were marginalized by mainstream patriarchal powers. Chuck has been active in the nuclear disarmament and trade union movements, antipoverty, and antiracism organizations, and Amnesty International. He came to terms with his white male privilege. Corporate downsizing forced him to find another way to support his family. Chuck identifies as an egalitarian socialist and entered the social work field to obtain a master's and began an anti-oppressive anti-colonial practice, which as a social activist is a 24/7 commitment. Chuck writes liberatory poetry working with the walking wounded of colonization with the intent to inform, thus, getting folks to become allies in the struggle for a just and civil planet for all.

Email: aroha@shaw.ca

***Carly Goldberg* (DSW, LCSW)** is a doctoral trained clinical social worker. By day, she works as a psychotherapist specializing in women's psychological development and traumatic stress and is a lecturer at the University of Pennsylvania's School of Social Policy and Practice. By night (well, by day too) she is a fierce advocate for women's rights. Carly founded Woman Centered—an online platform for progressive, woman-centered thought leadership that cultivates personal development and social action. Carly deeply believes in embracing women's unique intersectional identities, change, education, and community, oh and starting revolutions from the corner of her couch.

Email: carly@drcarlygoldberg.com

Website: www.womancentered.org/

Website: drcarlygoldberg.com

Heather Horizon Greene is a queer, fat, female-bodied, earth-loving weaver of joy, embodiment, justice, and magic. She does her best anti-oppressive work inside the cracks in the concrete and plants seeds of justice by mentoring other justice weavers in radical social work practice.

Email: heather.joyfulawakening@gmail.com

Websites: www.justicecenteredsocialwork.com/ and http://joyfulawakeningpractice.com/

Heidi Grove is a co-founder and director of operations of The Youth Connection (TYC) in Denver, Colorado. She holds a master's degree in counseling from Regis University and a bachelor's degree in psychology with a minor in human services. She is certified in At-Risk Youth Studies from Metropolitan State College of Denver. In 2008, she was nominated and awarded the Father Ignacio Martin-Baro Advocacy and Social Justice Award, the most prestigious social justice award of Regis University in recognition of her work with disengaged youth in the Denver metropolitan area. Heidi brings ten years of experience in research design, program design, implementation, and evaluation, and dissemination of research findings into the private, nonprofit and government sectors. Additionally, she brings ten years of experience working with systems of care, including but not limited to: social services, child welfare (local and state), juvenile justice, probation, public education, law enforcement, and nonprofit service providers. Heidi is the author of an innovative gang intervention curriculum that incorporates grief and loss as a treatment modality.

Email: heidi@tycdenver.org

Website: www.tycdenver.org/

Lorraine Kerwood **(LMSW)** hails originally from Germantown, Philadelphia, one of the most ethnically diverse neighborhoods in the United States. Labeled first retarded, then mentally ill, finally with Asperger's Syndrome, she has experienced homelessness and many of the horrors that happen to young women living on the street. She found the resources she needed to heal, then flourish—and soon thereafter she began to serve children who were experiencing some of the things, and more, that she'd gone through. Founder of NextStep Recycling, winner of several national and local awards for both her environmental work and her service to marginalized communities, Lorraine now focuses her attention on empowering young people who experience what is currently being labeled "first episode psychosis." Lorraine believes she is blessed to join the ranks of the people making the world a more equitable place to live. She dreams of obtaining her doctorate degree some day—because she now knows she can.

Email: lorrainekerwood@gmail.com

Websites: http://www.nextsteprecycling.org and http://easacommunity.org

Jeff Kim is a student of life and a lover of Mother Earth who dreams of different possibilities for the future. He is an antiracist, anti-patriarchal, anti-oppressive and antifascist activist committed to creating a better world in solidarity with all those who struggle around the globe. The foundational tenets of his organizing work are horizontalism, transparency, autonomy, and diversity of tactics.

Email: jeff.kim.84@gmail.com

Stormy Ogden McCloud is a longtime activist and advocate for Native rights and for the rights of prisoners. Stormy has written several articles and given presentations on the PIC (prison industrial complex) and how its roots are part of the violent mechanism of colonization. She is currently involved with "Chumkawiwat ~ Words with Wings" which sends Native language material into the prisons for the Native women and men.

Email: yokutstorm@gmail.com

Daniel Moore is a father, husband, and student. Being a father has expanded his capacity to love and be loved, being a husband has expanded his ability to communicate and to listen, and being a student has expanded his skill set for advocating for social justice. Daniel loves hearing the stories of people's lives and believes that our ability to create sustainable social change relies on our ability and willingness to connect to each other on a deep, personal level. Daniel is a recent graduate of California State University Northridge's bachelor's in sociology program with an emphasis in social welfare and social justice.

Email: daniel.moore.333@my.csun.edu

Anya Mukarji-Connolly is a graduate of the City University of New York School of Law and a former Equal Justice Works fellow. She has been an advocate for low-income and homeless communities in New York City for ten years. Anya is currently an attorney with the Brooklyn Family Defense Project (BFDP) where she represents low-income parents in child welfare proceedings. BFDP works to support families and prevent them from being torn apart while also seeking to change the child welfare policies and practices that disproportionately target low-income communities. Prior to joining BFDP, Anya had been an advocate for homeless lesbian, gay, bisexual, transgender, queer and questioning (LGBTQQ) youth for over eight years at the Peter Cicchino Youth Project (PCYP) of the Urban Justice Center. While at PCYP, Anya represented LGBTQ youth struggling to survive on New York City's streets, and in its foster care, juvenile justice, and shelter systems. In 2002, Anya was awarded an Equal Justice Works fellowship to represent LGBTQ youth who were at risk of entering the foster care system. Anya is currently on the Board of Directors of Streetwise and Safe (SAS), a youth development project for LGBTQ youth of color in New York City. From 2004 until 2006, Anya sat on the Board of Directors of FIERCE!, a community organizing project for Transgender, Lesbian, Gay, Bisexual, Two Spirit, Queer, and Questioning youth of color in New York City (Brooklyn, New York).

Email: amukarjiconnolly@bfdp.ls-nyc.org

Website: www.bfdp.org/

***Jose Miguel Paez* (LCSW)** is a full-time lecturer at CSUN (California State University, Northridge) since fall of 2009. He received his MSW from the University of Southern California in 2001, with an emphasis on families and children. He has many years of experience working with disenfranchised communities and families. He served as a bilingual outpatient clinician for Hathaway-Sycamores Child and Family Services for six years. In 2007, he worked in collaboration with the University of Southern California (USC) School of Social Work, the USC Civic and Community Relations, and the USC Community Education Academy to create and develop an anti-oppressive social work–based services program that served as a free community resource to residents within the area, and also as field education placement for first year social work graduate students at USC. He served as the program director, field instructor, and clinical supervisor. He continues to provide ongoing consultation, mentoring, and socio-educational trainings to families and professionals. His current teaching and research interests focus on critical race theory, trauma informed practice, restorative justice, liberation and transformative-based social work practice, and examining social inequality and pursuing change efforts toward equity and peace. Jose has a background in theatre, improvization, spoken word, and was also a basketball coach at various levels for over ten years.

Email: jose.paez.84@csun.edu

Meg Panichelli is a doctoral student in the Social Work and Social Research Program at Portland State University. Prior to starting school, she taught sexual violence prevention education in Santa Fe, New Mexico, at Solace Crisis Treatment Center and coordinated a harm reduction program for sex workers and drug users in Philadelphia, Pennsylvania. As white, queer, femme, and feminist, she enters this work through her position in multiple identities, work experiences, educational experiences, and life experience, which all weaves together and cannot be separated or unattached to professional and academic work. Her interests in research, activism, teaching, and excitement about life include: antiracist and transnational feminisms, critical pedagogies, intersections of sexuality and drug use, sex work and academia, intimate partner violence in queer and transgender communities, intersections of privilege, and of course, dance parties and talking about consent to hundreds of students at a time.

Email: mpanichelli@gmail.com

Website: http://findsolace.org/

***Lynn Parker* (MSW, PhD)** is a professor of social work at the University of Denver, Graduate School of Social Work (GSSW), a faculty and supervisor with the Denver Family Institute, and a postgraduate of the family therapy training center. Lynn also maintains a small private practice. The term *practitioner-scholar* comes closest to describing her professional identity—since she has enjoyed 40+ years in social work practice. As a former school social worker, she strives to make schools healthier and more inclusive so that referrals to people like her diminish. And as a mental health worker, she works to understand the origins of individual and family suffering along with the mediating social factors. Her passion in both her practice and teaching centers on how to address issues of power, privilege, and oppression in relationships and more broadly in society. At GSSW, she coordinates the family therapy concentration classes which she also teaches. Additionally, Lynn teaches a course, Global Relations and Poverty in Mexico, which is taught in Cuernavaca, Mexico, and is based in Paulo Freire's liberation-based pedagogy. She is currently writing a book that is a collection of stories of liberation and resistance based on interviews with some of her community partners in Mexico. Her other book is *Transformative Family Therapy: Just Families in a Just Society*, coauthored with Rhea Almeida and Ken Dolan-Del Vecchio. It provides tools and case examples for integrating social justice values into practical therapeutic interventions.

Email: lparker@du.edu

Nitika Raj is a queer South Asian upper-class femme. She does social justice work for the same reason she prays—to seek truth and build peace. Born in India and raised in Kuwait and the United States, she has a transnational heart and family. She currently loves and writes from New York City, and is happily employed at Resource Generation.

Email: nitika@resourcegeneration.org

Website: www.resourcegeneration.org/

Choya Renata is a queer white feminist woman with able-body privilege and a range of class experiences. She struggles with internalized classism, sexism, and a sense of entitlement to defining what is real, what is true. Choya strives for humility in her work—whether professional or activist in nature; those lines are often blurred anyway. After several years working to support people who experience marginalization, primarily those surviving domestic/sexual violence and homelessness, her experiences and observations of systemic inequities inspired her interest in community education and systems-level advocacy toward bold goals of social change. In addition to her work with the YWCA of Greater Portland, she currently serves on the Board of Directors for Sisters of the Road, an organization dedicated to building community and creating systemic solutions to homelessness and poverty.

Email: choyarenata@gmail.com

Websites: https://ywcapdx.org/ and www.sistersoftheroad.org

Emmy Ritter is currently the director of programs and services at Raphael House of Portland, a mom, an occasional supervisor to MSWs seeking licensure, and chaser of the ever evading time. As a LCSW, she has worked with Lifeworks NW as the clinical supervisor to the New Options Program, a mental health and addictions program set up to provide treatment and support for women and girls involved in prostitution. Prior to that role, she was the mental health and addictions consultant for the Domestic Violence Collaborative Response project. She has worked with women and children affected and infected by HIV as the family services coordinator and director of Camp Starlight with WIAR (Women's Intercommunity AIDS Resource). She has been involved in violence against women work since 1991.

Email: eritter@raphpaelhouse.com

Website: http://raphaelhouse.com/

 Samantha Rogers is a strong woman of color, mother of four, and grand-mother of seven. She is a survivor of the prison industrial complex (PIC) and the founder of the self-empowerment group at San Francisco County jail called FIRED-UP! She was recently hired as a part-time program assistant at the California Coalition for Women Prisoners (CCWP).

Email: samjr1202@gmail.com

Website: http://womenprisoners.org/

 ***Gabby Santos*** is the director of LGBT Health Services for In Our Own Voices, a culturally specific organization based out of Albany, NY. She has worked with survivors of sexual violence in roles ranging from inmate trauma support group facilitator, to policy work on behalf of LGBT People of Color. Racial justice work, transgender activism, and criminal justice reform are at the heart of her passion. Gabby is committed to promoting the sexual health of LGBT POC and their communities in order to end sexual violence. She provides leadership to various projects, including Unity Through Diversity, a National LGBT POC Health Summit, and the Annual Black & Latino Gay Pride of the Capital District of New York. She is also a member of the Arte Sana board of directors, a national Latina sexual assault organization.

Email: gabvocate@gmail.com.

 ***Allison Sinclair*** is currently a mental health therapist for children, ado-lescents, and families as well as a substance use disorder therapist for children and adolescents. She lives in Eugene, Oregon, with her best friend of 15 years, as well as her cat Ivan, and her two dogs, Simon and Lucha. She is very much a dog lover and treats her animals like children. To her, they are her children. Allison was raised in a very small mountain town, Sonora, California (close to Yosemite National Park) on what is primarily a cattle ranch. At the age of 15, she became a vegetarian because of the inhumane way the cattle were treated. She is an avid swimmer and loves the water more than the land. She is deeply com-mitted to working with children and families, but has a special interest in adolescents. Allison has worked with severely traumatized children and adolescents in residential treatment for several years and was also a treatment foster care provider for 4 children, ages 10 to 14, one

at a time, for close to 4 years. She is truly dedicated to social justice issues and has spent a good portion of her life challenging the status quo, with the aim of breaking down structural oppression and achieving a world where no one from any walk of life is denied equality, freedom, justice, and acceptance. She is also a writer and hopes that her work in this profession helps to break down the walls of structural oppression and reveals the invisible nature of white privilege and how it helps maintain the status quo of inequality. Allison is informed by attachment theory, family systems theory, interpersonal neurobiology, critical race theory, and feminist theory. She recently completed her master's in social work at Portland State University and is currently pursuing her LCSW. Afterwards, she plans to pursue her PhD in social research and social justice.

Email: ale.sin4@yahoo.com

Whitney Stark is a queer feminist into social justice. After a BA in Media Arts from Antioch College, she spent several years pursuing activist and NGO work, producing and teaching socially conscious video, media literacy, and rape culture 101s, and working with homeless teenagers—as well as pouring countless cups of coffee and working on a few terrible reality TV shows. Whitney is committed to principals of anti-oppression and increasingly shifting activism in order to work toward less violent ways of being, and to build beautiful, intentional communities. She is currently working on a master's degree in gender studies through the GEMMA consortium, a joint multinational interdisciplinary program.

Email: stark.whitney@gmail.com

Natasha Surendranath is a gay, biracial woman from an upper-middle-class family. Coming from a shielded, privileged upbringing, her experience in the field has broken down personal assumptions about stigmatized groups. Natasha is a graduate of California State University Northridge with a bachelor's degree in sociology and an emphasis in social welfare and social justice. Natasha plans to continue working in the field as an advocate for social justice.

Email: nasurendranath@gmail.com

Crystal Tenty has been dedicated to the empowerment of women since 2002 when she began working as a student advocate in the Women's Resource Center at Portland Community College as part of the Women's Leadership Program. Since then, she has focused her educational and career goals toward social justice issues, specifically those impacting women, through an anti-oppression, feminist, and empowerment-based lens. She received her master's of arts in conflict resolution from Portland State University with a focus on international and intercultural conflict. Her thesis focused on sex work and moral conflict and the use of the photovoice method as a form of transcendent discourse.

She has spent the past seven years working with survivors of intimate partner violence and recently entered the field of higher education as a student success coach.

Email: crystal.tenty@gmail.com

 ***Jessie Workman*** is a youth worker and writer living in Santa Fe, New Mexico. She is a white butch woman raised in the Midwest, and the landscapes and heart of Southern Ohio are deeply embedded in her approach to the world. She has spent all of her adult life working with youth and most often finds herself engaged within communities of incarcerated youth and young people who are experiencing homelessness. She is deeply committed to liberatory social work practices and believes that knowledge of the interconnectedness of oppressions as well as the intrinsic goodness of all of humanity (no matter what) must be paramount in any approach to social work. That said, she forever will be firmly planted in the corner of under-served youth—striving to support and understand their struggles and dreams and seeking creative ways to facilitate their growth and brilliance. A graduate of Antioch College in Ohio, she currently has little involvement within the academy, but finds herself deeply pulled to the study of law as an avenue for furthering her work, and foresees endless piles of torts and contracts in her near future.

Email: jayceework@gmail.com

Website: http://findsolace.org/

 ***Marcos Zamora-Sánchez*** is a Chican@ from Colima, Mexico, raised in South Central Los Angeles. Zamora-Sánchez began organizing in high school during the war on Iraq. As a trained macro-social worker, most of his work includes building on analysis of gender and sexuality in community, educational, organizational, and work spaces. Marcos currently facilitates and hosts the Queer Healing Oasis, a monthly gathering space for sharing and promoting growth, knowledge, and queer healing at El Hormiguero, a collective home that actively works toward building a safe, sustainable, and community-oriented space.

Email: marcos.zamora-sanchez@hsala.org

Index

⑤SAGE researchmethods

The essential online tool for researchers from the world's leading methods publisher

Find exactly what you are looking for, from basic explanations to advanced discussion

More content and new features added this year!

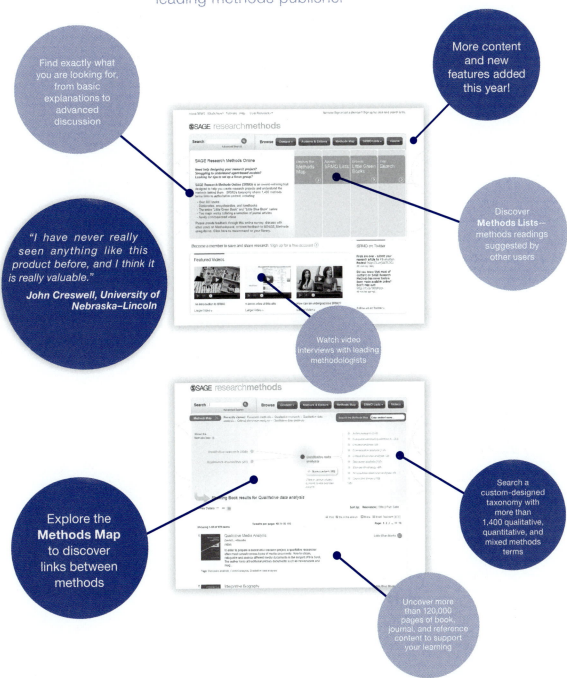

"I have never really seen anything like this product before, and I think it is really valuable."

John Creswell, University of Nebraska–Lincoln

Discover **Methods Lists**-- methods readings suggested by other users

Watch video interviews with leading methodologists

Explore the **Methods Map** to discover links between methods

Search a custom-designed taxonomy with more than 1,400 qualitative, quantitative, and mixed methods terms

Uncover more than 120,000 pages of book, journal, and reference content to support your learning

Find out more at
www.sageresearchmethods.com